Commands

EXPLORATIONS IN LINGUISTIC TYPOLOGY

GENERAL EDITORS: Alexandra Y. Aikhenvald and R. M. W. Dixon
Language and Cultural Research Centre, James Cook University

This series focuses on aspects of language that are of current theoretical interest and for which there has not previously or recently been any full-scale cross-linguistic study. Its books are for typologists, fieldworkers, and theory developers, and designed for use in advanced seminars and courses.

PUBLISHED

1 Adjective Classes
edited by R. M. W. Dixon and Alexandra Y. Aikhenvald

2 Serial Verb Constructions
edited by Alexandra Y. Aikhenvald and R. M. W. Dixon

3 Complementation
edited by R. M. W. Dixon and Alexandra Y. Aikhenvald

4 Grammars in Contact
edited by Alexandra Y. Aikhenvald and R. M. W. Dixon

5 The Semantics of Clause Linking
edited by R. M. W. Dixon and Alexandra Y. Aikhenvald

6 Possession and Ownership
edited by Alexandra Y. Aikhenvald and R. M. W. Dixon

7 The Grammar of Knowledge
edited by Alexandra Y. Aikhenvald and R. M. W. Dixon

8 Commands
edited by Alexandra Y. Aikhenvald and R. M. W. Dixon

PUBLISHED IN ASSOCIATION WITH THE SERIES

Areal Diffusion and Genetic Inheritance
Problems in Comparative Linguistics
edited by Alexandra Y. Aikhenvald and R. M. W. Dixon

Commands

A Cross-Linguistic Typology

Edited by
ALEXANDRA Y. AIKHENVALD and
R. M. W. DIXON

Language and Culture Research Centre
James Cook University

OXFORD
UNIVERSITY PRESS

OXFORD
UNIVERSITY PRESS

Great Clarendon Street, Oxford, OX2 6DP,
United Kingdom

Oxford University Press is a department of the University of Oxford.
It furthers the University's objective of excellence in research, scholarship,
and education by publishing worldwide. Oxford is a registered trade mark of
Oxford University Press in the UK and in certain other countries

First published 2017
First published in paperback 2020

Published in the United States of America by Oxford University Press
198 Madison Avenue, New York, NY 10016, United States of America

British Library Cataloguing in Publication Data
Data available

Library of Congress Cataloging in Publication Data
Data available

ISBN 978-0-19-880322-5 (Hbk.)
ISBN 978-0-19-885250-6 (Pbk.)

Contents

Preface

Every language has numerous means for getting someone to do something. These cover orders, pleas, entreaties, and other directives. They correlate with social conventions, existing hierarchies, and even kinship systems. This volume focuses on the form and the function of commands (or directive speech acts), their interrelationship with cultural stereotypes and practices, and their origins and development, especially in the light of language contact under different circumstances.

The volume starts with a typological introduction outlining the marking, and the meaning, of imperatives and other ways of expressing commands and directives, together with their cultural and social aspects and historical developments. It is followed by revised versions of fourteen presentations from the International Workshop 'Commands', held at the Language and Culture Research Centre, James Cook University, 28 September–3 October 2015. An earlier version of Chapter 1 had been circulated to the contributors, with a list of points to be addressed, so as to ensure that their detailed studies of individual languages were cast in terms of a common set of typological parameters. (This is the eighth monograph in the series *Explorations in Linguistic Typology*, devoted to volumes from International Workshops organized by the co-editors.)

The week of the workshop was intellectually stimulating and exciting, full of discussions and cross-fertilization of ideas. Each author has undertaken intensive fieldwork, in addition to experience of working on linguistic typology, historical comparative issues, and problems of areal diffusion. The analysis is cast in terms of basic linguistic theory—the cumulative typological functional framework in terms of which almost all descriptive grammars are cast—and avoids formalisms (which provide reinterpretations rather than explanations, and come and go with such frequency that any statement made in terms of them is likely soon to become inaccessible).

It is our hope that this volume will provide a consolidated conceptual and analytic framework. We aim at covering the major parameters of variation in the expression of commands and a plethora of directive speech acts in general across languages of the world.

We are grateful to all the participants in the Workshops and colleagues who took part in the discussion and provided feedback on presentations at various stages, particularly Grant Aiton, Yongxian Luo, Cassy Nancarrow, Colleeen Oates, Howard Oates, Ryan Pennington, Nick Piper, and Kasia Wojtylak. We are grateful to the Honourable Jan McLucas, Labor Senator for Queensland, for her official opening of the Workshop and support. We owe a special debt of gratitude to Amanda Parsonage and Brigitta Flick, for helping us organize the Workshop in a most efficient manner. Brigitta Flick's and Jolene Overall's support and editorial assistance were invaluable.

The Workshop was made possible partly through the Australian Research Council Discovery Project 'How languages differ and why'. We gratefully acknowledge financial assistance from the College of Arts, Education and Social Sciences, the Cairns Institute and the Division of Research and Innovation at James Cook University.

Notes on the contributors

WILLEM F. H. ADELAAR is Professor of Amerindian Languages and Cultures at Leiden University. He has conducted extensive field research on different varieties of Quechua and on the minor languages of the Andes. He has also worked on the genetic relations of South American languages of the Andes and the Amazonian region, and of Mesoamerica, on linguistic typology, contact and areal linguistics, and has been involved in international activities addressing the issue of language endangerment. His further areas of expertise cover oral literature and cultural history of Native American peoples, and the interface of linguistic studies with archaeological and historical research. His publications include *Tarma Quechua* (1977) and a comprehensive volume *The languages of the Andes* (2004) of which he is the main author. *Address:* University of Leiden, Vakgroep VTW, Postbus 9515, 2300 RA Leiden, The Netherlands; *e-mail:* W.F.H.Adelaar@hum.leidenuniv.nl

ALEXANDRA Y. AIKHENVALD is Distinguished Professor, Australian Laureate Fellow and Director of the Language and Culture Research Centre at James Cook University. She is a major authority on languages of the Arawak family, from northern Amazonia, and has written grammars of Bare (1995) and Warekena (1998), plus *A grammar of Tariana, from northwest Amazonia* (Cambridge University Press, 2003), in addition to essays on various typological and areal features of South American languages. Her other major publications, with OUP, include *Classifiers: a typology of noun categorization devices* (2000), *Language contact in Amazonia* (2002), *Evidentiality* (2004), *The Manambu language from East Sepik, Papua New Guinea* (2008), *Imperatives and commands* (2010), *Languages of the Amazon* (2012), *The art of grammar* (2015), *How gender shapes the world* (2016), and *Serial verbs* (2018). *Address:* Language and Culture Research Centre, D3, James Cook University, PO Box 6811, Cairns, N Qld 4780, Australia; *e-mail:* Alexandra.Aikhenvald@jcu.edu.au

AZEB AMHA is a researcher at the African Studies Centre in Leiden and associate of the Leiden University Centre for Linguistics. She is interested in linguistic typology and grammatical description, with fieldwork focus on Omotic languages. Her publications include a grammar of Maale (the topic of her PhD, from the University of Leiden), papers on Wolaitta and Zargulla, an overview article on the Omotic language family in a volume on Afroasiatic languages (edited by Zygmunt Frajzyngier and Erin Shay, Cambridge University Press, 2012) and three co-edited volumes. Currently she is investigating the grammar of mood and modality in Omotic languages. *Address:* African Studies Centre Leiden, PO Box 9555, 2300 RB Leiden, The Netherlands; *e-mail:* amhaa@ascleiden.nl

ERIC W. CAMPBELL is Assistant Professor of Linguistics at the University of California, Santa Barbara. He received his PhD from the University of Texas at Austin in 2014, with a dissertation on the phonology and morphology of Zenzontepec Chatino. His other writings have addressed inflectional classes, verbal valency, tone, a Zenzontepec Chatino–Spanish dictionary, and historical linguistics and subgrouping of Chatino and Zapotec languages. He does fieldwork and community linguistics and literacy training with speakers of several language groups in Mexico and California. *Address:* Department of Linguistics, South Hall 3432, University of California, Santa Barbara, CA 93106-3100, USA; *e-mail:* ecampbell@linguistics.ucsb.edu

R. M. W. DIXON is Adjunct Professor and Deputy Director of the Language and Culture Research Centre at James Cook University. He has published grammars of a number of Australian languages (including Dyirbal and Yidiñ), in addition to *Edible gender, mother-in-law style and other grammatical wonders* (Oxford University Press, 2015), *A grammar of Boumaa Fijian* (University of Chicago Press, 1988), *The Jarawara language of southern Amazonia* (Oxford University Press, 2004, paperback 2011), *A semantic approach to English grammar* (Oxford University Press, 2005), and *Making new words: morphological derivation in English* (Oxford University Press, 2014). His works on typological theory include *Where have all the adjectives gone? and other essays in semantics and syntax* (Mouton, 1982) and *Ergativity* (Cambridge University Press, 1994). *The rise and fall of languages* (Cambridge University Press, 1997) expounded a punctuated equilibrium model for language development; this is the basis for his detailed case study *Australian languages: their nature and development* (Cambridge University Press, 2002). He is also the author of the three-volume work *Basic linguistic theory* (Oxford University Press, 2010–12) and of an academic autobiography *I am a linguist* (Brill, 2011). His controversial study *Are some languages better than others?* was published by Oxford University Press in 2016. *Address:* Language and Culture Research Centre, D3, James Cook University, PO Box 6811, Cairns, N Qld 4780, Australia; *e-mail:* robert.dixon@jcu.edu.au

N. J. ENFIELD is Professor of Linguistics at the University of Sydney and Director of the Sydney Centre for Language Research. His research on language, culture, and cognition, from both micro and macro perspectives, is based on extended field work in mainland Southeast Asia, especially Laos. His books include *Mainland Southeast Asian Languages: A Concise Typological Introduction* (Cambridge, 2019), *The Concept of Action* (with Jack Sidnell, Cambridge 2017), *How We Talk* (Basic Books 2017), *The Utility of Meaning* (Oxford, 2015), *Natural Causes of Language* (Language Science Press, 2014), and *A Grammar of Lao* (Mouton, 2007). *Address:* Linguistics, University of Sydney, NSW, 2006, Australia; *e-mail:* nick.enfield@sydney.edu.au

VALÉRIE GUÉRIN obtained a PhD from the University of Hawai'i at Mānoa in 2008 for her work on Maṽea, a moribund language of Vanuatu (grammar published in 2011 by Hawai'i University Press). She has been working on Tayatuk, a language from the Morobe Province of Papua New Guinea, since 2013. She is Adjunct Fellow at the Language and Culture Research Centre, James Cook University. *Address:* LCRC D3, JCU Cairns, PO Box 6811, Cairns, Qld 4780, Australia; *e-mail:* valerie. guerin@gmail.com

ROSITA HENRY is Professor of Anthropology at James Cook University, Australia. She has been employed at James Cook University since 1992, and is currently serving as Head of Social Science (College of Art, Society and Education) at JCU. She conducts research and teaches in the field of social and cultural anthropology. Her research concerns relationships between people and places across Australia and the Pacific as expressed through cultural festivals, the political economy of public performances, cultural heritage, land tenure conflict, and the relationship between indigenous peoples and the state. Her many publications include a monograph, *Performing place, practicing memory: indigenous Australians, hippies and the state* (Oxford and New York: Berghahn, 2012). She is currently working on an ethnographic biography based on the life of a woman of the Western Highlands, Maggie Wilson, who passed away in 2009. *Address:* CASE, JCU Townsville, Douglas Campus, N Qld, 4811 Australia. *e-mail:* Rosita.Henry@jcu.edu.au

NERIDA JARKEY is Senior Lecturer in Japanese Studies at the University of Sydney. She has a particular interest in the semantics of grammar, with a focus on multi-verb constructions and on transitivity in Japanese and White Hmong. She also works on the expression of subjectivity and identity in Japanese. Nerida is the author of *Serial verbs in White Hmong* (Brill's Studies in Language, Cognition and Culture, 2015) and is Editor for Language and Socio-Linguistics for the journal *Japanese Studies. Address:* School of Languages and Cultures (A18), University of Sydney, NSW, 2006, Australia; *e-mail:* nerida.jarkey@sydney.edu.au

ELENA MIHAS is a Visiting Scholar, Center for Latin American and Caribbean Studies, University of Wisconsin, Milwaukee. She earned her doctoral degree in Linguistics from the University of Wisconsin-Milwaukee in 2010. Since 2008, she has been actively engaged in the Alto Perené (Arawak) language documentation project in the Chanchamayo province, Junín Department of Peru. She is the author of two monographs, *Upper Perené narratives of history, landscape and ritual* (Nebraska University Press, 2014) and *A grammar of Alto Perené (Arawak)* (De Gruyter, 2015). *Address:* University of Wisconsin–Milwaukee, Center for Latin American and Caribbean Studies, P.O. Box 413, Milwaukee, WI 53201, USA; *e-mail:* elmihas@uwm.edu

SIMON E. OVERALL is a Postdoctoral Research Fellow at the Language and Culture Research Centre, James Cook University. He has been working on the Aguaruna language and culture since 2004, and his grammar of the language was published in 2017 (Mouton Grammar Library, de Gruyter). His current research project is on Kandozi, an isolate spoken in Peru to the east of the Aguaruna speaking area. More generally, he is interested in the synchronic and diachronic relations between discourse and grammar, and the linguistic situation in the eastern foothills of the Andes, on which he has published numerous papers. *Address:* Language and Culture Research Centre, D3, James Cook University, PO Box 6811, Cairns, N Qld 4780, Australia; *e-mail:* simon.overall@jcu.edu.au

HANNAH S. SARVASY received her PhD in 2015 from James Cook University. She has conducted immersion fieldwork on Nungon (Papuan), Kim and Bom (Atlantic; Sierra Leone), and Tashelhit Berber. Her publications include *A grammar of Nungon* (2017, Brill), an edited journal issue on Finisterre Papuan languages, and articles and book chapters on topics in Nungon grammar, fieldwork methodology, Bantu linguistics, and ethnobiology, as well as Kim and Bom language primers. She has taught at UCLA, served as Research Fellow at the Australian National University, and currently holds an ARC Discovery Early Career Researcher Award at the MARCS Institute for Brain, Behaviour, and Development at Western Sydney University. *Address*: MARCS Institute for Brain, Behaviour, and Development, Western Sydney University, Locked Bag 1797, Penrith, NSW, 2751, Australia, *e-mail*: h.Sarvasy @westernsydney.edu.au

BORUT TELBAN is Professor of Anthropology and Research Advisor at the Research Centre of the Slovenian Academy of Sciences and Arts and Head of the anthropology programme at its postgraduate school. His anthropological research among the Karawari-speaking people of the East Sepik Province, Papua New Guinea, has spanned more than twenty-five years. In his published books, articles, and chapters he has explored in detail Ambonwari cosmology, cultural construction of space and time, kinship and social organization, ritual, death, poetics, and sociocultural change pertaining to the impact of the Catholic charismatic movement. He is the author of three books, including *Dancing through time: a Sepik cosmology* (Clarendon Press, Oxford, 1998), and is currently working on an encyclopaedic and ethnographic dictionary of the Karawari language. *Address:* Institute for Anthropological and Spatial Studies, Research Centre of the Slovenian Academy of Sciences and Arts, Novi trg 2, 1000 Ljubljana, Slovenia; *e-mail:* Borut.Telban@zrc-sazu.si

TIM THORNES is an Associate Professor of Linguistics in the English Department at Boise State University. He received his PhD in 2003 from the University of Oregon, having written a comprehensive grammatical description of Northern Paiute (a Western Numic language within the Uto-Aztecan family). He has conducted documentary fieldwork on five distinct varieties of the language, and his publications include work on stem-formation processes, causatives, and single-word serial verb constructions, as well as relative clauses and the evolution of grammar. *Functional-historical approaches to explanation* (John Benjamins 2013) was co-edited with Erik Andvik, Gwendolyn Hyslop, and Joana Jansen. *Address:* Department of English, Boise State University, 1910 University Ave, Boise, ID, USA; *e-mail:* timthornes@boisestate.edu

LOURENS DE VRIES is Professor of General Linguistics at the Vrije Universiteit, Amsterdam, The Netherlands. The description and typology of Papuan languages is his research focus. He has conducted intensive fieldwork on numerous languages of West Papua, especially Korowai and Kombai. He published books on Wambon (1992, Leiden: KITLV Press), Korowai (1997, Oxford University Press), Kombai (1993, ANU Press, Canberra) and Inanwatan (ANU Press, Canberra). He spent seventeen years in Indonesian West Papua, mostly in the southern lowlands, doing fieldwork on languages of the Greater Awyu family. *Address:* Afd. Taal en Communicatie Letteren, Vrije Universiteit, De Boelelaan 1105, 1081 HV Amsterdam, The Netherlands; *e-mail:* l.j.de.vries@vu.nl

Abbreviations

/	either/or
:	portmanteau
[]	clause boundaries
1	1st person
2	2nd person
3	3rd person
1sg>2sg	1sg subject acts on 2sg object
4	inclusive first person (Chapter 2)
4	obviative; low topicality pronoun (Chapter 7)
I	masculine etc. gender in Dyirbal (Chapter 6)
II	feminine etc. gender in Dyirbal (Chapter 6)
IV	neuter gender in Dyirbal (Chapter 6)
I	nominal group I (Chapter 13)
III	nominal group III (Chapter 13)
IV	nominal group IV (Chapter 13)
V	nominal group V (Chapter 13)
VI	nominal group VI (Chapter 13)
VII	nominal group VII (Chapter 13)
A	transitive subject
ABL	ablative
ABS	absolutive
ACC	accusative
ADD	additive; additive focus (Chapter 4)
ADEM	adverbal demonstrative
ADJ	adjective
ADJZ	adjectivizer
ADV	adverb, adverbial form
AFF	affect
AG	agentive nominalizer
AHON	addressee honorific
ALL	allative case

ALT	alternative
ANA	anaphoric
ANT	anterior
APASS	antipassive
APPLIC	applicative
APPLIC.CAUS.SOC	causative-sociative applicative
APPLIC.GEN	generalized applicative
APPLIC.REAS	applicative of reason
APPR	apprehensive
AQ	Ayacucho Quechua
ART	article
ASSERT	assertive
ATT	attention
AUG	augmentative
BARE	bare (non 'respect/politeness')
BEN	benefactive
C	child
CANINE	dog-directed speech
CAUS	causative
CC	copula complement
CFACT	counterfactual
CHAR	characteristic
CISL	cislocative
CNT.ASSERT	counter-assertive
COLL	collective, collaborative
COMIT	comitative
COMPL	completive
CON	conative
CONC	concessive
COND	conditional
CONJ	conjunction
CONN	connective
CONT	continuous
CONTR	contrastive
CONVB	converb

COORD	coordinator
COP	copula
COUNTR	counterfactual
COURT	courteous
CS	copula subject
CT	class term
DAT	dative
DEC	declarative
DEF	definite article
DEL	delayed
DEM	demonstrative
DEM.NON.PROX	demonstrative nonproximal
DEP	dependent
DESID	desiderative
DIM	diminutive
DIR	directional
DISC.M	discourse marker
DIST	distal
DISTN	distance
DM	discourse marker
DS	different subject
du, DU	dual
DUB	dubitative
DUR	durative
eB	elder brother
EMPH	emphasis
EP	epenthetic
ERG	ergative
EXC, exc	exclusive
EXCL	exclamative
EXH	exhaustive focus
EXIST	existential
EXPL	expletive
EXPLIC	explicating
eZ	elder sister

F, f	feminine, female
FAC	factive
FAM	familiar
FOC	focus
FOC.TERM	focalized terminative aspect
FRML	formal
FUT	future
GEN	genitive
GENL	general
GERUND	gerund
GOAL	goal (no abbreviation)
H	human
HAB	habitual
HESIT	hesitation
HON	honorific prefix
HORT	hortative
HYPOTH	hypothetical
ID	identifier
IDEO	ideophone
IFUT	intentional future
IMM	immediate
IMMED	immediate
IMP	imperative
IMPERV	imperfective
INAN	inanimate
inc, INC	inclusive
INCH	inchoative
INFER	inferring
INFIN	infinitive
INFRML	informal
INST	instrumental
INT	intentional
INTENS	intensifier
INTER	interrogative
INTERJ	interjection

INTS	intensive
INV	inverse
IP	instrumental prefix, short tag
IPART	illocutionary particle
IRR	irrealis
ITER	iterative
JUS	jussive
LDEM	local demonstrative
LOC	locative
LOGO	logophoric reference
M, m	masculine
M	mother (Chapter 11)
MASC	masculine
MC	modifier classifier
MED	medial
MID	middle
Mo	mother
MOD	modal
MOM	momentaneous
MV	medial verb
MVII	medial verb II
NEG	negation
NEG.IMP	negative imperative
NEWS	proposition is news for addressee
NF	near future (Chapter 11)
NF	non-final (Chapter 10)
NJQ	North Junín Quechua
NM	non-masculine
NO.ADO	without any ado, right away
NOM	nominative
NOMZ	nominalizer
NON1	non-first person (or 2nd/3rd person)
NONPROX	demonstrative (non-proximal)
NP	noun phrase
NP	near past (Chapter 11)

NPAST	non-past
NSBJ	non-subject
nsg	non-singular
NSPC	non-specific
NVIS	non-visible demonstrative
O	transitive object
OBJ	object
OBL	oblique
OHON	object honorific
ON.RCD	on record
OPT	optative
Pa	parent
PARTIC	participle
PASS	passive
PAST	past (no abbreviation)
PER	perfect
PERIPH	peripheral
PERV	perfective
pl, PL	plural
PLEAD	pleading
POL	polite
POL.IMP	polite imperative
POSS	possessive
POT	potentiality (Chapter 6); potential (Chapters 5, 10, 13)
PP	positive polarity
PQ	Pacaraos Quechua
PRED	predicative
PREP	preparatory aspect/modality
PRES	present
PRESM	presuming
PRO	pronoun
PROB	probable
PROG	progressive
PROHIB	prohibitive
PROX	proximal

PSSD	possessed
PUNC	punctual
Q	interrogative, question particle
QI	Quechua I
QII	Quechua II
QPLR	polar question marker
QUOT	quotative
REAL	realis
RECIP	reciprocal
REDUP	reduplicated
REFL	reflexive
REL	relative
REM	remote
REQST	requestive
RES	resultative
RESIG	resignation
RESTR	restrictive
RF	remote future
RHET	rhetorical
RNDM	random motion
RP	remote past
RSP	respectful
RSTR	restrictive
RUSH	rushing, hastening
S	subject of intransitive verb
s.o.	someone
SAP	speech act participant
SB	shared benefit
SE	social enabler
SEMB	semblative case, semblance
SEMELF	semelfactive
SEQ	sequential
sg, SG	singular
Sh	short
SHON	subject honorific (shows respect to the subject referent)

SIM	simultaneous
SIMIL	similative
SOFT	softening
SPEC	specifier
SS	same subject
STAT	stative aspect
SU	subject
SUBORD	subordinate
SUBORD:SS	subordinator same subjects
SUGG	suggesting
T.LNK	topic linker
TAG	tag question
TENT	tentative
TERM	terminative
TOP	topic
TOPZ	topicalizer
TQ	Tarma Quechua (phonologically innovative sub-variety of NJQ)
TR	transitional sound (Chapter 12)
TR	transitive (Chapter 7)
TRNSL	translocative
TTL	title
UNIMP	addressee presumed to be unimpeded
V	verb
VAL	validator
VEN	ventive ('hither')
VN	verbal noun
VOC	vocative
VULG	vulgar
WH	interrogative word
yG	younger sibling

1

Imperatives and commands: a cross-linguistic view

ALEXANDRA Y. AIKHENVALD

1 Preamble

Some linguistic categories show more correlations with cultural values, social hierarchies, and their conceptualizations than others. Genders, noun classes, and classifiers tend to mirror social and cultural stereotypes, and patterns of human perception. Meanings encoded within possessive structures often reflect relationships within a society, and change if the society changes.[1]

As Enfield (2004: 3) put it, 'grammar is thick with cultural meaning. Encoded in the semantics of grammar we find cultural values and ideas, we find clues about social structures which speakers maintain, we find evidence, both historically and otherwise, of the social organization of speech communities'. Imperatives, and other ways of framing commands and directives, are particularly instructive: their use is shaped by conventions and norms people are socialized to follow.

In every language one can make a statement, ask a question, or tell someone what to do. The ways in which imperatives and other directives—including wishes, entreaties, invitations, and more—are framed may reflect societal structures, interpersonal relationships, gender roles, existing hierarchies, and kinship systems. The relationship between the speaker and the addressee, their age and social status, the conventions appropriate for a particular genre, and many more features may be at play in the ways people get one another to do things, using directives.

This introductory chapter focuses on the forms and the functions of imperatives and other ways of phrasing commands, their possible relationships with cultural values, practices, and attitudes, and their origin and development. We start with a brief summary of how imperatives interrelate with commands and directives in general.

---

[1] Correlations between possession and cultural parameters are addressed in Aikhenvald and Dixon (2013); see Aikhenvald (2015: Chapter 13) on how cultural parameters are reflected in other categories.

2 Imperatives and commands

There are three major types of speech acts. This is reflected in the category of 'mood'. The form of a statement is declarative, and that of a question is interrogative. A command—that is, an utterance whose function is to get someone to do something—corresponds to the imperative mood. Just as there can be covert questions (not framed as interrogatives), one can express a command without using a dedicated imperative form.[2]

It is not uncommon for a linguistic term to have a counterpart in the real world. The idea of 'time' in the real world translates into 'tense' when expressed in a language. 'Time' is what our watch shows and what often passes too quickly; 'tense' is a grammaticalized set of forms we have to use in a particular language. Not every time distinction acquires grammatical expression in the language: the possibilities for time are unlimited, and for tense they are limited. Along similar lines, 'evidentiality' is a linguistic category whose real-life counterpart is information source. Similarly, an 'imperative' is a category in the language, while a 'command' is a phenomenon of the real world (Figure 1). Languages of the world have limited grammatical means of expressing imperatives. The ways in which commands—or directives—may be phrased are open-ended.

In day-to-day English usage, the adjective and the noun, *imperative*, share a similar meaning to do with 'commanding'. A bossy person talks 'in a quick imperative tone'. It is 'imperative' that scholars 'check their quotations'. Being 'imperative' implies demanding obedience, execution, action, obligation—*The situation makes it imperative that you should return at once* and *The work is quite imperative, and its result will be most beneficial*. Philosophers talk about 'the unconditional imperative of the moral law'.

GRAMMATICAL CATEGORY	COUNTERPART IN THE REAL WORLD
tense	time
gender	sex etc.
evidential	information source
imperative	**command**

FIGURE 1. Grammatical categories and their 'real world' counterparts

---

[2] Aikhenvald (2010) contains details on the typological parameters in imperatives and commands. A collection edited by Xrakovskij (2001) (a somewhat expanded translation of the Russian original, Xrakovskij 1992a) offers a selection of chapters dealing with imperatives in a few languages. These are uneven in quality, with each contribution following a restrictive 'typological questionnaire' (Xrakovskij 1992b). An overview of typological and language-specific work on imperatives is in Aikhenvald (2010: 15–16). A different, formally-oriented approach to imperatives in a narrow sense is in Jary and Kissine (2014). The present chapter takes into account the data on 600 languages (expanded on Aikhenvald 2010). Whenever relevant, we draw on examples from languages discussed in this volume.

The opposite—negative imperative, or 'prohibitive'—implies making someone not do something, having the effect of forbidding, preventing, or restricting. Prices may be *prohibitive*, if they are too high.

Imperatives can be rich in their meanings. They may cover entreaties and requests: *Let me go to the party!* and *Try and behave!* Advice and instructions are often cast in the form of an imperative—*Don't repeat other people's mistakes!* or *Mix two spoonfuls of water with flour.* Imperatives may also express invitations: *Meet the Joneses!* Or principles and life mottoes: *Publish or perish!*

An imperative may have an 'anti-command', or a mock-command meaning. A 'recipe for disaster' may be cast in an imperative. A spoofy passage on how to destroy your festive season contains mock commands—which tell you what not to do unless you want your Christmas time to become a disaster: *Drive to somewhere terrible for a holiday. Stay in three motels with plumbing that gargles and screams all night. Break out in acne. Get food poisoning* (from Börjars and Burridge 2001: 130).

Conditions, threats, and ultimatums may be cast in the form of an imperative: *Buy from that shop and you will regret it* or *Be quiet or I'll send you to bed.* Saying *Take care!* or *Fare thee well!* are not commands; these are conventional speech formulae, part of our linguistic repertoire.

'Imperative' and 'command' do not always refer to the same thing. *Go away!* is a command, and is imperative in form. But I can say the same thing jokingly to someone without meaning to chase them away—this will be reflected in my tone of voice or intonation. *Get out!*, an imperative in form, can be used as an exclamation, to express extreme surprise. And one can command without using an imperative. A question *Why don't you go away?*, or a stern statement *You will go away*, or just one word *Away!* serve the same purpose. *Could you pass the water?* is a conventionalized form for requesting water, and not a question about a person's capabilities.

But such forms will not be used under the same circumstances. Their appropriateness will depend on relationships between the speaker ('commander') and the addressee, in terms of social hierarchy, kinship relations, age, status, social gender, and peer group membership. It will also depend on speaker's and addressee's entitlements in terms of authority and obligations to comply. Directives of any sort are essentially 'social acts': in many societies 'marking and differentiation of the category of directive acts' reflect the ways people 'think about and order their ongoing social bonds and deeds', and 'the "force" of speech acts depends on things participants expect' (using Rosaldo's 1982: 228–9 words).[3]

---

[3] 'Directives', or verbal means of getting people to do things, were identified by the philosopher Searle (1994 [1969]: 21), as one of five types of speech acts, the other four being assertives, commissives, expressives, and declaratives. These speech acts are not mutually exclusive. For instance, as we will see throughout this volume, a statement—cast as an assertive speech act—can be used in lieu of a directive (see Enfield 2013: 89–90 on the nature and permeability of speech acts). In Chapter 15, Rosita Henry offers an

In theory, the set of means for getting others to do things is unlimited. But in the practice of language communities it is far from being the case: different languages, and different societies where they are spoken, use different conventionalized strategies for commands, requests, and other directives (see also Enfield 2014; Clark 1979). A polite request in Kuuk Thayorre, an Australian language from the Cape York peninsula, is usually phrased as a negative statement. So, saying 'You won't work for me' is best translated into English as a polite 'Would you do some work for me?' (Gaby 2007: 494). Commands couched as questions in Ku Waru, a Papuan language of the Western Highlands of Papua New Guinea, may express sarcasm rather than polite or gentle overtones of a wish or an entreaty (see §5 of Chapter 15). What kind of forms are favoured by different languages for getting others to do things, and why? This is what we are out to discover.

A command can be expressed without using language. A glance, a gesture, or a picture can do the job. Pictorial command strategies may contain unequivocal prohibitions (or permissions). For instance, a picture of a mobile phone with a line across is a conventional command not to use the device (the red colour of the line is an additional sign meaning 'don't do it'). The Ambonwari people in the Sepik area of New Guinea use 'visual prohibitives', in the form of leaves tied around the trunk, as a means of protecting their coconut and betel nut palms (see Chapter 13; so do the Tayatuk: Valérie Guérin, p.c.). A comprehensive study of such extralinguistic command techniques would be a fascinating enterprise, which lies beyond our scope here.

In many languages imperatives stand clearly apart from other clause types in their grammatical properties. As Jakobson (1971: 191) put it, 'the lonely imperative' stands apart from declaratives and from interrogatives. Imperative mood is the commonest way of expressing commands, and a multitude of related meanings, in the languages of the world. In some languages, imperatives may give the impression of simplicity in form. In other languages, they can also be dauntingly complex. In §§3–5, we briefly look at some special features of addressee-oriented (or 'canonical') imperatives and imperatives oriented towards other persons (called 'non-canonical'). Negative imperatives, or prohibitives, are the topic of §6. In §7 we turn to grammatical restrictions on forming imperatives, and their interaction with questions. Non-command meanings of imperatives are the topic of §8.

Non-imperative forms—statements, questions, exclamations—are frequently co-opted to express varied overtones of command-like meanings, intruding into the imperative domain. We will be referring to these as command strategies and discuss them in §9. We then turn to the development of imperatives and their spread in language contact, in §10. The ways in which imperatives are used are the topic of §11. The last section focuses on the structure of this volume.

---

outline of speech act theory, and a further division of speech acts into locutionary, illocutionary, and perlocutionary; see the critique by Rosaldo (1982).

3 Canonical and non-canonical imperatives

The most straightforward command is the one directed at the addressee. If a language has a special set of imperative forms, it will have a special form for a command to second person. Such addressee-oriented, or 'canonical', imperatives (in a 'narrow sense') may stand apart from other verbal forms in a language. They are commonly expressed by the bare root, or stem, of the verb, as is the case in Northern Paiute, a Uto-Aztecan language (§6 of Chapter 7) and Tayatuk, a Papuan language from Morobe Province in Papua New Guinea (Chapter 10). Such short and snappy forms may give an impression of superficial simplicity—as if the imperatives were, in some sense, poor relations of their declarative and interrogative counterparts. This simplicity is often a mere illusion, as we will see throughout this chapter, and throughout the volume.

Imperatives may also be oriented towards third person and first person.[4] In agreement with Aikhenvald (2010), we call them 'non-canonical' imperatives. In a number of languages, all imperative forms may form one paradigm—this is what justifies considering them together. The example in Table 1 comes from Yemsa, an Omotic language from Ethiopia (Zaugg-Coretti 2009: 136–7). The second person singular form is the shortest of all and the least formally marked. All plural imperatives (except for first person) bear a plural marker. In Mauwake (a Papuan language of Madang province), canonical and non-canonical imperatives are marked with suffixes and form one paradigm. Berghäll (2010: 132–3) explicitly states that there is

TABLE 1. The imperative paradigm in Yemsa: *kássū* 'bake'

PERSON	SG	PL
1	*kássú-nā*	*kássú-nī*
2	*kássú*	*kássú-sō-tì*
2 Polite	*kássú-nì*	*kássú-sō-nì*
3 feminine	*kássú-n*	*kássú-sō-n*
3 masculine	*kássú-wó*	*kássú-sō-wó*
3 Polite	*kássú-tó*	*kássú-sō-tó*

---

[4] In contrast to declaratives and interrogatives, imperatives do not have any further person distinctions. A number of languages, including the majority of languages from the Arawak language family, have a further term in their person system, with 'impersonal' meaning, roughly corresponding to a generic *you* or *one* in English, *on* in French, and *man* in German. An imperative cannot be formed on an impersonal form in Tariana and other Arawak languages. See Dixon (2010: 204–5) on further person distinctions (including proximal and obviative in Algonquian languages); these are not relevant for imperatives. In §4, we return to the person system in imperatives compared to that of other clause types.

TABLE 2. Imperative markers in Mauwake

PERSON AND NUMBER	SUFFIXES
1 dual	*-u*
1 plural	*-ikua*
2 singular	*-e(-a)*
2 plural	*-eka (aka)*
3 singular	*-inok*
3 plural	*-uk*

'no valid reason to divide them' into different categories based on person. The imperative markers which attach to a verb in Mauwake are in Table 2 (Berghäll 2010: 133).

All the person values of imperative forms constitute one paradigm in Nungon, a Papuan language from Morobe Province (see Table 1 and §2 of Chapter 11), and in Awara, a related language (§3 of Chapter 10). Similarly to many Papuan languages, the distinction between second and third person is neutralized in non-singular numbers in Nungon declarative, interrogative, and also imperative forms. This is an additional piece of evidence in favour of considering all person values of the imperative in Nungon as forming one paradigm. Three persons of imperatives also form one paradigm in Korowai, a Greater Awyu language from West Papua (see (5) in §3.2 in Chapter 12), and also Wolaitta, an Omotic language from Ethiopia (§3.1 in Chapter 14). (Further examples and discussion are in Aikhenvald 2010: 49–51.)

In some languages, imperatives may have gaps in their paradigms. In Quechua, imperatives oriented towards second and third persons, and also 'fourth' person (or 'first person inclusive you and me'), form one paradigm. But unlike declaratives and interrogatives, the imperative does not have a first person singular form (see Tables 1 and 3 in Chapter 2). This is a most common gap, to which we return shortly.

In other languages, non-addressee-oriented imperatives may stand apart from the addressee-oriented ones in their expression (see also Chapter 5, on Zenzontepec Chatino). In Dolakha Newar, a Tibeto-Burman language from Nepal (Genetti 2007: 337–41, 179–86), dedicated imperative forms are restricted to the canonical (addressee-oriented) imperative. They have distinct forms for singular and plural addressees.

(1) jana   mica   ya-ŋ   *Dolakha Newar*
     1sgGENITIVE   daughter   take-IMP.SG:TRANSITIVE
     Take my daughter!

(2) chipe   thau   thau   chē   o-n   *Dolakha Newar*
     2sgGENITIVE   REFL   REFL   house   go-IMP.PL:INTRANSITIVE
     Go each to your own house!

A special construction is used for first person inclusive commands, involving the addressee and the speaker: the marker *-lau* attaches to the infinitive form of the verb, as in (3):

(3) isi   chē=kuu   ū-i-lau   nā   *Dolakha Newar*
     1pl.EXC.GEN   house=LOC go-INFINITIVE-1PL   AGREEMENT.PARTICLE
     Let's go to our house!

Commands oriented towards first person are the only verb forms in the language to have a special form just for inclusive reference. Other verbal forms do not distinguish inclusive and exclusive forms (Genetti 2007: 159); this distinction is reflected in personal pronouns (as we can see from (3)). To issue a command to a third person, the optative form is used, as in (4):

(4) tha-hat   *Dolakha Newar*
     OPTATIVE-speak
     May he speak!

The major meaning of the optative is to express a wish that something should happen.

Heterogenous expression of canonical imperatives, on the one hand, and non-canonical ones, on the other, is a feature of many languages (especially Indo-European and Semitic: see Aikhenvald 2010: 47–66). Within this volume we find a similar principle in Aguaruna (Chapter 3), Ashaninka Satipo (Chapter 4), Zenzontepec Chatino (Chapter 5), Northern Paiute (Chapter 7), and Tayatuk (Chapter 10).

In many traditional linguistic terminologies, different person values of imperative are assigned different terms. The most frequent ones are hortative or cohortative for first person, and jussive for third person, reserving 'imperative' just for second person. We saw, in (1)–(4) from Dolakha Newar, that first and third person imperatives stand apart from second person imperatives in their make-up. This offers a formal reason for assigning different names to different persons in this language.

Different person values of an imperative may differ in their meanings. Second person imperatives are primarily commands. In contrast, first person imperatives may develop overtones of suggestion or permission, and the ones oriented towards third person shade into the expression of indirect, mediated wishes. Incidentally, this is something one finds even in languages where imperatives undoubtedly form one paradigmatic set: first person imperative in Hungarian has permissive overtones (see Kenesei et al. 1998: 21–2, 310–12, for the full imperative paradigm in the language). We find similar meanings in Nungon (see §3.1 of Chapter 11). We return to the special meanings of different person forms of imperatives in §5.1.

This terminological 'splitter'—which ultimately stems from Indo-European and Semitic languages—is at variance with the analysis of other clause types. No grammar would use one label for first person declarative or interrogative, another one for second person, and yet another one for third. Having different terms for different person is hardly appropriate for analysing languages where all person values of an imperative form one paradigm—something we have seen in Table 1, for Yemsa, and also in Chapter 2 for Quechua, and in Chapters 11 and 12, for Nungon and Korowai respectively.

A splitter approach can be justified if different persons of imperative differ in their formal features. This is what we have seen in Dolakha Newar (and a number of other languages, including English: see Aikhenvald 2010: 54–73). Only canonical imperatives in Zenzontepec Chatino are marked with an imperative prefix; non-canonical imperatives employ the potential mood (§§4–5 of Chapter 5).

In Ashaninka Satipo only canonical imperatives can be negated (§8 of Chapter 4). The first person commands contain a special particle *tsame* (originally a suppletive first person command form of the verb *ja* 'go'). The first person plural imperative in Aguaruna is negated with the same suffix as non-imperative (declarative and interrogative forms). Second and third person prohibitives contain an 'apprehensive' marker (§3, §3.5.1 of Chapter 3). In such instances, different terms for different person values are justified by language facts.

4 Non-imperative forms in lieu of imperatives

Imperatives may be heterogenous in further ways. Some languages have a dedicated imperative form just for second person singular. A second person plural imperative will be 'co-opted' from another set of verbal forms. In Supyire, a Gur language from Mali (Carlson 1994: 520–6), the dedicated imperative which consists of the verb root without a subject marker or auxiliary can only be used to command one person, as in (5):

(5) Lwɔhɔ   kan   náhá   *Supyire*
    water   give   here
    Give me some water (lit. Give water here)

The subjunctive form (also used in adverbial and complement clauses) is used to command second person plural addressees in Supyire:

(6) Yìi   à   wá!   *Supyire*
    you.PL   SUBJUNCTIVE.IMPERFECTIVE   go
    Go (you plural)

Members of an imperative paradigm may overlap with other, non-imperative forms in their formal expression. In Italian, the second person singular imperative is segmentally identical to the third person singular present indicative for verbs of the first conjugation, e.g. *canta!* 'sing!', *canta* 'he/she sings', or second person singular present indicative, for verbs of other conjugations, e.g. *dormi!* 'sleep!', *dormi* 'you are sleeping'. First person plural imperative is always identical to the first person plural present indicative, e.g. *cantiamo!* 'let's sing', *cantiamo* 'we are singing'. The second person plural imperative has the same form as the second person plural present indicative, e.g. *cantate!* 'you pl sing!', *cantate* 'you pl are singing'. In contrast, third person imperative (singular and plural) is expressed by using subjunctive form, e.g. *canti!* 'May she sing!' or 'Sing (singular polite)', *cantino!* 'May they sing!' or 'Sing (plural polite)' (Maiden and Robustelli 2007: 247–8). These overlaps have led some scholars to argue that the imperative in Italian has no segmental form of its own—it is parasitic on other forms. There are however extra features that make imperatives stand out: the special intonation and other suprasegmental clues ensure that the addressee will distinguish a command from a statement or a wish.

A language may lack an imperative paradigm altogether. Another verbal category is then 'co-opted' in its stead. A command and a non-command meaning of the same form will be distinguished by context, and by prosodic and other clues (intonation, or an eye-gaze).

In Athabaskan languages, a declarative verb marked for imperfective aspect is a conventional way of expressing commands, in the absence of dedicated command forms. The sentence in (7), from the Hare dialect of Slave, is ambiguous (Rice 1989: 1109). The two meanings can presumably be differentiated by intonation, eye-gaze, and situational clues.[5]

(7) Ɂáradįɬa   *Hare dialect of Slave*
     you.sg.IMPERFECTIVE.go.home
     You (sg) go home!
     You (sg) are going home

This usage reminds us of a cross-linguistic tendency to employ declarative clauses as an option for expressing directives. In many languages, including English, saying *You are going home now* can be understood as a stern command. In English, a language with a specialized imperative, such directive use of a non-directive verb form is part of a plethora of command strategies (we return to these in §9).

A primarily non-directive form can become a conventionalized command; this is a typical path for the development of dedicated imperatives. Canonical and non-canonical imperatives in Ashaninka Satipo are based on irrealis forms. They differ from the declarative irrealis in a number of features, including intonation, the meanings of verbal categories (especially aspect: see §5.3 below), and patterns of

---

[5] In languages lacking a special set of imperative-only forms, commands can also be expressed with present tense forms or forms unmarked for tense; future forms, forms of various modalities, or with irrealis; see Aikhenvald (2010: 38–44).

negation (see Chapter 4). The near future form in Tayatuk commands is a conventional way of expressing a distal command, for an action to be carried out far from the speaker (§5.1 of Chapter 10).

Imperative forms in Northern Paiute and in Japanese developed out of dependent verb forms (Chapters 7 and 8). A close connection between irrealis and imperative in Korowai (and other languages from the Greater Awyu family) points towards a shared origin (§4 in Chapter 12); the same is true of the link between irrealis and delayed imperative in Nungon (Chapter 11). In §10, we will return to the pathways of development of dedicated imperative forms.

But the issue may lie deeper than 'mere' grammaticalization and reinterpretation of non-command forms. Some Australian languages have no dedicated forms for commands. Future forms are a standard way of getting people to do things in Bunuba, Nunggubuyu, and Rembarnga (see Rumsey 2000: 91; see further examples and references in Aikhenvald 2010: 40–1, 81). Other languages employ intentional or potential forms in what can be interpreted as commands and directives. Why so?

A form with a potential or intentional meaning refers to the possibility of something happening. A command or a directive can be viewed as presentation of such a possibility, something as yet unrealized—as suggested by Davies (1986: 57). This link provides an intuitively plausible reason for using the same form to express potentiality, future, and also a command. But the overtones of such forms might reveal clues of their social underpinnings.

As R. M. W. Dixon puts it (§2 of Chapter 6), in the traditional Dyirbal society 'a significant feature was that one person did not order another to do something or forbid them from doing something; there was no verb "order". And there was *no clearly defined speech act of commands*.' The 'potentiality' inflection in Dyirbal is versatile: this form is frequently used with second person subject, and 'then provides a suggestion or advice' (§2 of Chapter 6). But this inflection—which Dixon had called 'imperative' in his earlier work, following 'a temptation to describe languages in terms of conventional categories' (§7 of Chapter 6)—has a number of other meanings, including wishes, possibilities, and (in its negated form) caution and warning. In Dixon's words (§2 of Chapter 6), the most appropriate characterization for such forms is 'a potentiality, which is likely to be realized, but may not be'. Calling such forms 'commands' or 'imperatives' would be at odds with the pragmatic import of their use in the traditional society.

Trying to establish a straightforward connection between the structure of a language and beliefs and attitudes of its speakers is a dangerous venture. And yet the absence of dedicated command forms in some speech communities may be indicative of speech practices deeply embedded in the original ethos and egalitarian social structure. Could it be the case that commands were not appropriate in the essentially egalitarian traditional Australian language communities, and so the dedicated forms were lacking? And could the lack of specialized command forms in Hare, Western Apache, and other Athabaskan languages have been facilitated by 'the Athabaskan attitudes about the autonomy of the person' and the inappropriateness of issuing orders to others (cf. de Reuse 2003: 96 and references therein)? These connections—tempting as they are—remain a conjecture.

5 Imperatives, their grammar, and meanings

Imperatives are often easy to recognize by the way they sound. In Warekena, an Arawak language from north-west Amazonia, a declarative clause has a flat intonation; an imperative clause—which has the same segmental make-up—shows falling intonation on the last word. In Ashaninka Satipo, the intonation contour of a command shows a boost in the pitch range which is higher than the usual pitch register in statements and questions (see §3 of Chapter 4). Commands in Nungon (§1 of Chapter 11) can involve greater pitch ranges than declarative clauses (this applies to both dedicated imperatives and some imperative strategies). Distinctive suprasegmental properties are a frequent, if not a ubiquitous, feature of imperatives and commands.[6]

We now turn to other features of imperatives: person and number (§5.1), grammatical relations and constituent order (§5.2), verbal categories including tense and aspect (§5.3), and imperative-specific categories (§5.4).

5.1 Person and number in imperatives

Canonical imperatives (that is, addressee-oriented imperatives) are pervasive. The most frequently attested non-canonical imperatives are the ones with first person inclusive reference. First person imperatives in general tend to have inclusive (rather than exclusive) reference (see, for instance, (3), from Dolakha Newar). First person inclusive (but not first person singular or exclusive) can be expressed in the imperative forms in Macushi (Abbott 1991: 49) and in Trio (Carlin 2004: 308), two North Carib languages from Brazil and Suriname respectively.

First person inclusive imperatives (but no other first person values) are part of the imperative paradigm in Quechua (Chapter 2). First person commands have only an inclusive meaning in Northern Paiute (Chapter 7) and Zenzontepec Chatino (Chapter 5). The first-person-directed construction in Ashaninka Satipo marked by *tsame* has exclusively inclusive reference (Chapter 4). First person dual and plural imperatives in Manambu, a Papuan language from the Sepik area of New Guinea, are the only grammatical forms in the language which have inclusive-only reference (Aikhenvald 2016). And, as noted by Trubetzkoy in a 1931 letter to Jakobson (1985:

---

[6] Whether or not having a special intonation for imperatives and commands is universal remains a matter for further investigation; see for instance Adelaar (§1 of Chapter 2) on the lack of 'functional space' for intonation in Quechua imperatives due to their explicit and complex morphological marking.

224–5), a first person plural command in Russian has an inclusive overtone (there are no other inclusive distinctions in the language) (see Dobrushina and Goussev 2005 for other examples).

Imperatives with first person exclusive reference appear to be rather rare. Apalaí, a North Carib language from Brazil (Koehn and Koehn 1986: 107), has a full paradigm of imperatives, including first person singular, first person inclusive, and first person exclusive. We hypothesize that if a language has an imperative with first person exclusive reference, it will also have one referring to 'you and me', that is, inclusive (in line with Aikhenvald 2010: 76).

Imperatives may differ from other clause types in terms of their number and person meanings. In Nakkara, an Australian language from Arnhem Land, the canonical imperative takes the pronominal prefix of what would be third person in a declarative clause (Eather 2011: 201; see further examples in Aikhenvald 2010: 102, 116). In his grammar of Mara, another Australian language, Heath (1981: 189) offers a functional explanation for this: the third person is the least marked option in the declarative clauses, and the second person is the least marked option in imperatives. The functionally unmarked third person declarative marker extends to cover another functionally unmarked term—the second person. Similarly, the overt subject of the canonical imperative of suppletive verbs in Western Shoshoni (a Uto-Aztecan language from the Numic branch) takes the third person reflexive form (rather than that of a second person) (see §12 of Chapter 7).

In Mauwake (a Papuan language of Madang province in Papua New Guinea), the imperative has a dual form just in the first person. There is no dual number elsewhere in the language (Berghäll 2010: 133). The imperative paradigm in Korowai has its own set of person-number prefixes and is the only paradigm in the language to distinguish first, second, and third persons (other Korowai verb paradigms distinguish just two grammatical persons: first and non-first) (see §3.1 of Chapter 12).

5.2 Grammatical relations in imperatives

Imperatives may differ from their interrogative and declarative counterparts in the way grammatical relations are expressed, with what Tim Thornes (§12 of Chapter 7) refers to as 'atypical subject coding'. A number of Numic (Uto-Aztecan) languages employ the subject (rather than the object) case form for objects of canonical imperatives (see examples (63)–(64) from Southern Paiute; and similar examples from Northern Paiute in (65)–(66)).[7]

The expression of subject in the imperative is another issue. As Jespersen (1928: 222) points out, 'the express indication of the subject (the second person) is generally

---

[7] Further examples of special marking of grammatical relations in imperatives, from Estonian, Finnish, and a selection of Uto-Aztecan and Australian languages, are in Aikhenvald (2010: 145–7). A summary of imperative and person in English and references are in Aikhenvald (2010: 66–75).

superfluous with an imperative' in English (while it is required in clauses of other types). One usually says just *Take your time!* or *Close the door!* Adding the second person subject has a specific effect: it may have a patronizing effect, as in *You take your time*, or reflect an 'attitude of impatient hearer-directed anger on the part of the addressee', as in *You close the door* (Schmerling 1975: 502). The exact meaning depends on the context and the intonation: it appears, however, that, by using a second person pronoun, in many instances the speaker is 'laying claim to a certain authority over his addressee' (Davies 1986: 147).

Omission of subject pronouns in imperatives is far from universal. In Mauwake subject pronouns are often omitted in declarative and interrogative clauses, but included in imperatives. Berghäll (2010: 82, 104) estimates that 39 per cent of imperative clauses in Mauwake contain an overt personal pronoun (as against 6 per cent in statements).

The constituent order in imperatives may differ from that in other sentence types. In Zenzontepec Chatino (§7 of Chapter 5), the constituent order is fixed in imperatives. Elsewhere, the order is typically discourse-based and fairly flexible.

5.3 Verbal categories and their meanings in imperatives

Imperative forms may stand apart from their declarative and interrogative counterparts in the verbal categories expressed. In some languages, including Tayatuk (Chapter 10), no verbal categories can be marked in imperative forms. Alternatively, markers of aspects, modalities and motion may have special meanings once they appear in imperative forms.

Imperatives appear to be poorer than declaratives and interrogatives in the ways tense is expressed. The most frequently attested tense distinction in imperatives is that of immediate versus delayed, or future (in agreement with the prediction by Lyons 1977: 746–7). This seemingly simple binary opposition contrasts with a wider range of possibilities for future meanings grammaticalized in declarative clauses. Alternatively, different kinds of future can be expressed in imperatives and in declaratives.

Koasati, a Muskogean language (Kimball 1991: 263–72) has two delayed imperatives, one meaning 'do later on' and the other one 'do much later on', illustrated in (9) and (10). A simple 'root' imperative in Koasati has the force of a command to be performed immediately:

(8) lakáwwi-ø-DEL   *Koasati*
     LIFT-2sgIMP-PHRASE.TERMINAL.MARKER
     Lift it!

(9) am-awí:ci-ø-Y̌h   *Koasati*
     1sgDATIVE-HELP-2sgIMP-DELAY
     Help me later!

(10) taɬa-:ý:hah   *Koasati*
      weave(IMP)-LONG.DELAY
      Weave it a lot later!

Declarative clauses in Koasati have only one future form (in contrast to imperatives).

A future versus non-future distinction found in imperatives may be lacking from declarative clauses. Haida, an isolate spoken in British Columbia, distinguishes 'neutral' and 'non-immediate' imperatives. Neutral imperatives order 'a familiar addressee to immediately perform a certain action (or be in a certain state)' (Enrico 2003: 121). Declarative clauses in Haida do not distinguish between immediate and delayed future; there are no grammaticalized future markers in the language.[8]

Imperatives may have aspectual distinctions—typically, fewer than declaratives. The most common aspect is continuous. In Yidiñ, an Australian language, it is marked with the suffix -:ji-n 'continuous action', and involves a command to 'continue an action that is already in progress' (Dixon 1977: 371, 291 and p.c.):

(11) mandi-:   gala-bujun   gali-ŋa-:ji-n   jaba:n-gu   *Yidiñ*
      hand-LOC   spear-STILL go-COMIT-CONT+IMP   eel-PURP
      Keep going, with your spear still in your hand, for eels!

Continuous and continuous habitual are the only aspects marked in imperatives in Nungon (Chapter 11) (see also example (8) in Chapter 13, for an instance of continuous aspect in Karawari imperatives). Perfective and completive aspectual meanings can be expressed in imperatives in Quechua (Chapter 2). Imperatives in Aguaruna (Chapter 3) may take the durative aspect. Northern Paiute imperatives can be marked with the punctual aspect which imparts telic overtones to a command (§6 of Chapter 7).

Semantic overtones of verbal aspects in imperatives may be at variance with their declarative counterparts. For instance, the imperfective aspect in Yemsa has continuous meaning if used with an imperative: the action to be performed is expected to last for a long time. Imperfective forms in main clauses have a habitual meaning (Zaugg-Coretti 2009: 137, 156–7). Progressive aspect marker in Quechua commands implies an invitation to carry on with an action already begun or to start an action before the speaker is able to join it (§8 of Chapter 2).

Imperatives in Ashaninka Satipo are particularly rich in aspectual meanings expressed: each of the progressive, perfective, terminative, imperfective, durative,

---

[8] Further examples of an immediate versus delayed future in North American Indian languages are in Mithun (1999: 153–4); see also Aikhenvald (2014). Having an imperative referring to the past may appear implausible. However, in a few languages a past tense form may be used in a command, with a meaning of 'ought to have done', or a reproach, as in Estonian (Erelt, Metslang, and Pajusalu 2006: 129): *tul-nud poiss koju* (come-PAST.PARTICIPLE boy home) 'The boy ought to have come home!' (further examples and references are in Aikhenvald 2010: 132–3).

and semelfactive aspects can occur in imperative structures (see §7.2 of Chapter 4). But their meanings and pragmatic overtones are not the same as in statements. The progressive suffix *-atiy* is often used in the imperative construction expressing a categorical order. The durative *-vee~-vei* marks a tentative wish in second person imperative forms (example (26) in Chapter 4). And the iterative semelfactive marker *-apaint* makes the imperative sound more tentative.

This semelfactive *-apaint* 'do once' in a command is associated with diminution, implying to do less of X-ing than is normally expected. It is typically used by women, who tend to go for diminutives and attenuating speech registers, partly due to their lower social status in the male-oriented Ashaninka society. Using a semelfactive in a diminutive sense is reminiscent of the common use of attenuative markers in commands in Japanese (*chotto* 'just a little': Chapter 8). Along similar lines, the particle *dèè1* 'Do it, please, it's not a big thing' in Lao softens or plays down the burden of the request (see examples (44)–(46) in §4 of Chapter 9); in declarative clauses *dèè1* serves to attenuate the strength of a proposition, along the lines of 'a little', 'partly' (see examples (47)–(48), in Chapter 9; see also Aikhenvald 2010: 204).

In contrast, the terminative suffix *-aj*, the suffix *-ajant* 'focalized terminative', and perfective *-ak* in Ashaninka make the imperative form sound categorical. These forms tend to be used by speakers commanding a superior social role. Similarly, perfective forms as commands in Ku Waru (§5 of Chapter 15) are stern and peremptory. Along similar lines, in Quechua the presence of a perfective aspect marker *-ru-* may imply rudeness: it incites the addressee to hurry up (§8 of Chapter 2). We hypothesize that, in the context of a command, focus on completion or result implies authority and imposition (similar examples are discussed in Aikhenvald 2010: 104–5, 127).

Modality markers can have command-specific meanings. The dubitative modality in Nungon commands is used as a marker of suggestion (§3.3 of Chapter 11). Markers of motion and direction can also develop imperative-specific overtones. The suffix *-rku-/-rgu-* in North Junín Quechua is a directional indicating 'upward motion'. When used with imperatives, it has a secondary function as a 'social enabler'. By using it the speaker asks for the addressee's permission or consent and, if possible, their active participation (it is translated into Spanish as 'con (su) permiso'). Another directional affix *-y(k)u-* 'inward motion' has acquired an additional function as a plea for attention in requests (§9 of Chapter 2).

In many languages with grammatical evidentials, only the reported specification can occur in commands (see Aikhenvald 2010: 138–41), e.g. (12), from Tariana, a language with five evidentials in declarative clauses.

(12) pi-ñha-pida   *Tariana*
      2sg-eat-REPORTED.IMPERATIVE
      Eat on someone else's order!

The meaning of an evidential morpheme in a command may differ from that in a statement. In Quechua, the direct evidential *-mi* with a future form used in lieu of a command denotes the speaker's 'conviction or certainty' rather than the information source (see §4 of Chapter 2, and example (1)). Other evidentials are not used with imperatives.

Special meanings of verbal categories set imperatives apart from other sentence types. We now turn to special traits which only imperatives have.

5.4 *Imperative-specific categories*

Verbal categories found just in imperatives include distance in space (and also 'extralocality', that is, a command to perform an action in a different location, and motion, as in some Carib languages: Carlin 2004). A simple immediate and formally unmarked imperative in Tariana, an Arawak language from north-west Amazonia, is shown in (13):

(13) pi-ñha   *Tariana*
      2sg-eat
      Eat! (here and now)

Examples (14)–(15) illustrate special marking of distance in space (close to the speaker versus far from the speaker; a semantically similar command in Tayatuk is in §5.1 of Chapter 10).

(14) pi-ñha-si   *Tariana*
      2sg-eat-PROXIMATE.IMPERATIVE
      Eat here (close to the speaker)

(15) pi-ñha-kada   *Tariana*
      2sg-eat-DISTAL.IMPERATIVE
      Eat over there (away from where the speaker is; addressed to people outside the house)

A delayed imperative, 'do later on', is marked in a different way; this is shown in (16):

(16) desu   pi-ñha-wa   *Tariana*
      tomorrow   2sg-go-DELAYED.IMPERATIVE
      Eat tomorrow!

There is also a conative imperative. Note that Tariana does not have a dedicated conative marker for declarative clauses.

(17) pi-ñha-thara   *Tariana*
      2sg-eat-CONATIVE.IMPERATIVE
      Try and eat (please); eat it to try it out

TABLE 3. Number marking in canonical imperatives in Maale

NUMBER OF ADDRESSEE	REGULAR IMPERATIVE	POLITE IMPERATIVE	IMPOLITE IMPERATIVE
singular	Verb-*é*	Verb-*é-tera*	Verb-*ibay*
plural	Verb-*uwáte*	Verb-*uwátera*	

A further salient category imperatives have is 'strength' of command and politeness. Tariana has a special polite imperative shown in (18):

(18) pi-ñha-nha   *Tariana*
      2sg-eat-POLITE.IMPERATIVE
      Would you like to eat; could you please eat?

Maale, an Omotic language from Ethiopia, has three canonical (addressee-oriented) imperatives, which differ in the degree of politeness. The regular imperative and the polite imperative distinguish singular and plural forms—see Table 3 (Amha 2001: 126). The polite imperative is built on the regular one. The impolite imperative does not distinguish number.

Aguaruna (§3.3 of Chapter 3) distinguishes between plain and familiar imperatives: according to the speakers, 'the familiar form is more likely to be used with family members and children', and the plain form in other circumstances.

Overtones of politeness tend to be a prerogative of imperatives (special polite forms for second and third persons in Yemsa were shown in Table 1). Aspectual forms may have overtones of politeness when used with imperatives. We can recall, from §5.3, that perfective forms in commands in Ashaninka and in Ku Waru have peremptory overtones. The imperfective imperatives in Supyire (Carlson 1994: 521) and in Yankunytjatjara (Goddard 1983) have polite overtones.

Politeness interrelates with societal hierarchies and conventions. The ways in which interpersonal relations (to do with the relative status of the speaker and the addressee) are reflected in commands are particularly spectacular in languages with honorific registers. Dolakha Newar (Genetti 2007: 130–1, 180–2) has two honorific registers. Honorific imperatives (and honorific personal pronouns) are used if the speaker is 'considerably younger than the addressee'; they are also used 'to address deities, or others held in reverence'. For Korean, Sohn (1994: 9–11, 41–3) describes six levels of honorification, which display a complex interaction between the speaker's relative age, social status, and relationship to the addressee. In a similar vein, a judicial employment of honorific forms is integral to issuing commands and any kind of directive speech acts in Japanese. Social distance, deference, in-group membership, and social gender each play a role: this is discussed at length in Chapter 8.

Politeness distinctions in Maale (Table 3) do not directly relate to any social hierarchy. The regular, or neutral, imperative can be used for orders and to instruct someone how to perform a certain task—for instance, in describing how to get somewhere. The polite imperative has 'begging' connotations, and does not show strict correlations with age and status of the speaker with respect to the addressee. The impolite imperative does: it is used 'when ordering somebody who is younger or low in status, parents to children when they are angry and most often among children when one of them acts as a boss. The impolite imperative is also used in chasing away pet animals' (Amha 2001: 126).

Imperatives can be looked upon as a means of categorizing the addressee in terms of who they are, and what their status is with respect to the one issuing the directive. A few languages have special command forms for special addressees: Ashaninka Satipo has a set of special commands to pets and domesticated animals (§15 and Table 6 in Chapter 4), Nungon has a set of commands to dogs only (§7 of Chapter 11), while Wolaitta is rich in directives to domestic animals such as oxen and cows (see Table 3 in Chapter 14).

The strength of a command or a request, the speaker's stance, and the addressee's compliance are among special meanings expressed just in imperatives. Quechua has a variety of postverbal clitics that can be used with imperatives, indicating emotional involvement of the speaker, or knowledge shared by speaker and addressee, or reassurance (§12 of Chapter 2).

Imperative-specific particles set statements and questions apart from commands in Lao (Table 1 and §2.1 of Chapter 9). Special meanings expressed in imperative particles cover suggestion (*saa3*), pleading (*duu2* 'do it for me'), and softening or playing down the burden of the request (*dèè1*). A further particle asks the addressee to 'hurry' (*vaj2*), and another one (*mèè4*) is used if 'the addressee is unimpeded', and 'there is nothing stopping the addressee doing the action'.

Not infrequently, imperatives are negated differently from their declarative counterparts. This is what we turn to now.

6 Negating an imperative

How can an imperative be negated, turning a positive command into a prohibition?[9] In many languages, an imperative occurs with a special negative marker used just for this purpose, e.g. the prohibitive particle *me* in Mauwake (Berghäll 2010), or *da-* in Dolakha Newar (Genetti 2007: 338), or the prohibitive marker *ama* in Quechua (§6 of Chapter 2). Or a prohibitive may contain a future or an irrealis form and a special marker. Prohibitives in Nungon (§2.4 of Chapter 11) consist of a future

---

[9] Van der Auwera (2006) summarizes some features of prohibitives across the world. See also an outline of a typology of prohibitives in Aikhenvald (2010: 166–97).

irrealis form marked with the suffix -*a* (we return to its origins in §10). Prohibitives in Korowai are based on the irrealis negative paradigm and the negative imperative adverb (§3.5 of Chapter 12). A prohibitive in Japanese is formed by adding the negative particle *na* to the non-past form of the verb (§3.2 of Chapter 8). Alternatively, prohibitives may be marked by a special verbal affix, as in Wolaitta (§3.5 of Chapter 14) and Yonggom Wambon (§3.7 of Chapter 12).

An imperative can be negated with the same marker as the declarative (as is the case in French and German). Or it can involve a special form of the verb. A negative imperative in Cupeño, a Uto-Aztecan language, contains a negative particle *qay* (which is also used in declarative clauses) and requires an irrealis form of the verb (Hill 2005). A prohibitive in Northern Paiute involves the general negator *kai* at the beginning of a clause, and the prohibitive enclitic =*paana* attached to the verb (§8 of Chapter 7). A further option is a combination of a prohibitive marker and a special verbal inflection. A negative imperative in Karawari (§4.3 of Chapter 13) is formed using the negative particle *wara* and a negative suffix -*a*. The 'caution' form in Dyirbal (§6 of Chapter 6), roughly comparable to a negative command, consists of a combination of a particle *galga* and a dedicated verbal suffix.

Prohibitives may share their forms with non-canonical imperatives. In Zenzontepec Chatino prohibitives consist of one of the standard negation particles followed by the verb inflected for potential mood: this makes them formally similar to non-canonical imperatives which also involve the potential (§5.1 of Chapter 5). The negative imperative in Tayatuk (§4 of Chapter 10) involves the negative particle *ma* used to negate irrealis forms (which are also used for non-canonical imperatives) and the verb marked for second/third plural present tense agreement marker -*kang*.

Negative imperative in Lao is expressed via a dedicated preverbal negative imperative marker *jaa1* (§3 of Chapter 9). The form *jaa1* is also used as a verb meaning 'desist'. A negative imperative in Lao can be interpreted as a serial verb construction with a grammaticalized second component (the form *jaa1*) (we return to the grammaticalization of verbs as markers of prohibitives in §10).

Canonical and non-canonical imperatives may differ in how they are negated. In Aguaruna, only first person commands can include a negative marker, and for other persons the prohibitives are based on the apprehensive forms (§3.5.1 of Chapter 3). In Ashaninka Satipo, non-canonical imperatives cannot be negated at all (Chapter 4). Canonical and non-canonical imperatives are negated in the same way in Nungon (§2.4.2 of Chapter 11)—hardly unexpected, since they form one paradigm in that language.

Categories expressed in positive imperatives tend to be neutralized under negation. That is, one negative imperative form corresponds to several positive imperatives. Negative imperatives in Tariana do not distinguish distance in space and time; nor do they have a special polite form (further examples are in Aikhenvald 2010: 181–6). Imperative particles in Lao are not used with prohibitives (Chapter 9). In Tayatuk, all person and number distinctions expressed in canonical positive imperatives are neutralized in prohibitives (§4 of Chapter 10). Verbal categories used with imperatives do not occur if a command is negated in Aguaruna, Ashaninka Satipo, Korowai, and Karawari (Chapters 3, 4, 12, and 13). The potentiality form in Dyirbal occurs with an antipassive, and also with affixes meaning 'do repeatedly' and 'do a lot'; but the 'caution' form (similar in its use to a negative imperative) appears not to occur (Chapter 6). This is consistent with a general cross-linguistic tendency—that fewer grammatical meanings may be expressed in negative than in positive forms (Aikhenvald and Dixon 1998).

In a number of languages, negative imperatives go against this tendency. Manambu, a Ndu language from the Sepik area of New Guinea, and also Urarina, an isolate from Peru, have more prohibitive than imperative forms (see Aikhenvald 2010: 189–90; Olawsky 2006: 190). More options appear to be available for prohibitives than for positive imperatives in Korowai: a special prohibitive paradigm coexists with negative irrealis forms (§3.5 of Chapter 12). Karawari (§3 of Chapter 13) has a special negative-only command *pasi* 'don't!', with no positive counterpart. Or a prohibitive may have a wider usage than its positive counterpart. As Adelaar (§6 of Chapter 2) puts it, for Quechua, the prohibitive negator *'ama* can be used in any construction that denotes an overtone of suggestion, recommendation, admonition, reproach, etc. In this way, the choice of the prohibitive adverb adds an extra dimension which makes it possible to introduce notions of command in non-imperative contexts.' And there can be restrictions on forming positive commands which do not apply to prohibitions. This is what we turn to now.

7 The limits of imperatives

A prototypical directive speech act involves an action the addressee may be able to control. Many languages have a restriction on using in commands verbs which describe an uncontrolled action or a state. Stative verbs such as 'be cold', 'be sick', 'be afraid' and verbs of physical and mental states cannot form imperatives in Tariana. In Bagvalal, a north-east Caucasian language, verbs which refer to physical states (such as 'tremble', 'die', 'sob'), to emotional and mental states, and uncontrolled perception typically cannot form imperatives (Dobrushina 1999: 321–2). Imperatives cannot be formed on non-volitional verbs in Arapaho (Cowell 2007) and Haida (Enrico 2003). Similarly, non-agentive verbs in Zenzontepec Chatino have no imperative form; these include 'die', 'get old', 'be born', and 'grow' (§4.4 of Chapter 5). In Quechua imperatives are not formed on verbal adjectives and verbs referring to permanent material qualities ('be sour', 'be spicy') (§8 of Chapter 2). Verbs referring to non-controllable states tend not to occur in imperative form in Ashaninka Satipo (§7.3 of Chapter 4); a focus construction with the verb meaning 'be the case' is used instead, as a command strategy (see §9).

Verbs of perception—'see' and 'hear'—typically acquire telic meanings of 'look' and 'listen' when used in an imperative context, as in Tayatuk (§2 of Chapter 10), in agreement with Aikhenvald and Storch (2013).

As Nerida Jarkey puts it in §4.1 of Chapter 8, 'the first key criterion for the use of an imperative form in Japanese is that the action or event can be conceived of as volitional.' As a consequence, there are no imperatives of adjectives, or state verbs.

Even in English—which appears to allow imperative formation on any verb imaginable, if an appropriate context is supplied—an imperative like *Weigh 50 kilos!* may sound strange, unless cast in the context of a weight loss programme, a fairy tale, or a conditional construction (*Weigh 50 kilos, and you won't have to pay for the excess weight on this flight*).

Restrictions on the use of commands may not be more than a tendency. In Lao (§4 of Chapter 9), commands tend only to occur with verbs that are controlled, and 'if they are used with non-controlled verbs, they coerce a controlled reading'. They tend not to occur with stative verbs (but examples (36)–(37) in Chapter 9 show that this rule is not steadfast). Passive forms in Japanese (§4.1 of Chapter 8) can only be used in the imperative if the context is clear enough to indicate the 'situation is subject to the volitional control of the subject' (see example (10) in Chapter 8). In present-day Quechua the imperative can be formed on impersonal verbs, such as those referring to weather conditions (*tamya-* 'to rain', *rašta-*, *rawu-* 'to snow', etc.), but only with a third person subject. Adelaar (§8 of Chapter 2) suggests that this may have been different in pre-Hispanic and pre-Christian times when the forces of nature may have been conceived of as being controllable, so much so that one could address and command them directly (see also Adelaar 1994).

Curiously, none of these restrictions may have to apply to negative imperatives. In Japanese prohibitives can be freely formed on passives, in contrast to positive imperatives (§4.1 of Chapter 8, and Takahashi 2000). Stative verbs and verbs of emotion and cognition tend not to occur in positive commands in Zenzontepec Chatino; there are no such restrictions in negative commands (§5.1 of Chapter 5). In Tayatuk, prohibitives, but not positive imperatives, can be formed on verbs such as 'sense' (§4 of Chapter 10; and similar examples in Aikhenvald 2010: 188–9). As Huddleston (2002: 933) puts it, positive passives with *be* in English 'are not often found with directive force', but 'negatives lend themselves more readily to such an interpretation' (Huddleston 2002: 933). *Don't be intimidated by those cowards!* is perfectly acceptable, and can be interpreted as 'Don't allow yourself to be intimidated'.

Why so? An argument can be made that social constraints and prohibitions are highly important in many cultures, perhaps more so than mere requests and instructions. Or, in Davies's (1986: 15) words, it is 'sometimes easier to conceive of a person's being able to avoid an experience (such as being hurt or being misled) than to imagine his [their] ability to deliberately undergo it'. This is reminiscent of those languages—mentioned under §5.4—which have more options for negative than for positive commands.

Not every language has limits on imperative formation. For instance, in Aguaruna (§4.3 of Chapter 3), Korowai (§3.8 of Chapter 12), and Wolaitta (§3.2 of Chapter 14) an imperative can be formed on any verb. Restrictions on canonical imperatives may not extend to non-canonical imperatives. Non-canonical imperatives in Zenzontepec Chatino—based on potential, or irrealis, verbs—can be formed on any verb (Chapter 5).

Imperatives and prohibitives appear to be fairly uniform in their scope. Serial verb constructions are always within the scope of imperatives: having one mood specification per construction is one of the definitional properties of serial verbs (see Chapter 4, on Ashaninka Satipo; Chapter 6, on Dyirbal; and Chapter 9 on Lao). In clause-chaining languages, the complete chain is within the scope of an imperative. Just the last verb in a clause chain—which expresses a sequence of commands— acquires the imperative marker: see examples (33)–(34) in Aguaruna (Chapter 3), (6)–(7) in Nungon (Chapter 11) and (29) in Karawari (Chapter 13); see also §3.6 of Chapter 12, for a discussion of the scope of imperative over a clause chain in Korowai. The scope effect of an imperative is linked to the fact that in many languages imperatives cannot be formed on non-final verbs and verbs in embedded clauses (see the discussion of Nungon in §2.1 of Chapter 11).

However, this is not universally so (*pace* Whaley 1997: 237). In a few Papuan languages of New Guinea, imperatives can be used in embedded clauses. This was described by Renck (1975: 121) for Yagaria, a Kamano-Yagaria language from the Highlands of Papua (and for the closely related Hua by Haiman 1980: 61–3, 162–3, and unrelated Amele: Roberts 1987: 40). Example (19) shows a medial clause marked for imperative:

(19) eli-ga-ta'a-o   elemi-s-u'-agi   *Yagaria*
      take-DS-1dual-IMP   go.down-1FUT-1dual-EMPH
      Take it, and let us two go down! (lit. After you take! it, let us two go down)

An imperative can appear in a medial clause in Korowai (see example (20d) from §3.6 of Chapter 12). Examples (20)–(21), from Yalaku, a Ndu language of the Sepik region of New Guinea, illustrate a further, rarer, option: depending on the placement of the imperative prefix *me-* the whole clause chain, or just the main final verb, may be within the scope of an imperative (from author's own fieldwork):

(20) mə-[hara-ta   və]   *Yalaku*
      IMP-get-ss   look
      Get (it) and have a look!

(21) [hara-ta]   [mə-və]   *Yalaku*
      get-ss   IMP-look
      Having got it (first), have a look!

There are no similar scope effects in prohibitives.

Imperatives and interrogatives correspond to different speech acts. It is therefore hardly surprising that in many languages of the world imperatives simply cannot be used in questions. And if they are, they have special meanings. Imperatives occur in rhetorical questions in Tatar (Nasilov et al. 2001: 217; Aikhenvald 2010: 251). First person immediate imperatives in Nungon can be used when asking for permission (§3.1 of Chapter 11; similar uses of first person imperatives are found in Manambu, from the Ndu family (Aikhenvald 2010: 74), and in Hungarian (Kenesei et al. 1998: 21–2)). In Nungon two imperative forms can be conjoined as alternatives in alternative questions (example (31) in Chapter 11), and even in polar questions, as in example (33) (Chapter 11) which contains question functioning as a mild command from a mother to a child.

Imperative and interrogative particles cannot be used in one clause in Lao (§2.5 of Chapter 9) since they occupy the same grammatical slot. But it is possible to combine an imperative and an interrogative within one sentence in two separate clauses. An imperative in one clause can be followed by a tag question, as a way of softening a command (something we return to in §9).

Potentiality inflection in Dyirbal can occur in questions of all kinds (examples (17)–(19) of Chapter 6), and even be accompanied by a rise in pitch typical for questions. This, and their semantics of suggestion, advice, statement of potentiality, and intention, highlights the 'inadvisability' of equating them with imperatives—and commands as a special act—in other languages. Cross-linguistically speaking, imperative forms may express meanings other than getting people to do things. This is the topic of the next section.

8 Imperatives which do not 'command'

Imperative forms are semantically pliable and versatile. They can express wishes, suggestions, intentions, permissions, requests, and entreaties. First person imperatives can be a way of asking for permission (rather than commanding oneself to do something) as we saw in the previous section.

Imperative forms in English 'are often used in such a way that no real request is meant: the hearer or reader is only asked to imagine some condition, and then the consequence is stated', as in *Let women into your plans, and you never know where it'll end* (Jespersen 1933: 295). An imperative in the first clause in a complex sentence in English will be commonly interpreted as a conditional. A sentence *Do it again and you will regret it* is commonly interpreted as 'If you do it again you will regret it'—or even as an indirect way of saying 'Don't do it again'.

Some languages have no special causative forms. Then, imperatives within speech reports can be the only way of expressing causation, as in example (11) from Karawari (Chapter 13). A common feature of many Papuan languages is framing speaker's intention as a speech report: this is one occasion when first person directive is very common (as in Korowai, see example (26) in Chapter 12 and the discussion of

Nungon in §3.4 of Chapter 11). This is also a common feature in Quechua (see Adelaar 1990).

Imperatives are used in speech formulae—blessing, curses, greetings, and farewells—in many languages, among them Aguaruna, Tayatuk, Wolaitta, Karawari, Nungon, and Japanese, just as in English *Bless you, Take care*, or *Fare thee well*. Imperative forms often give rise to discourse markers and attention-getting devices, as in Italian *guarda* 'look!', or Portuguese *olha* 'look!' (see Waltereit 2002, for examples from European languages; and §5.1 of Chapter 3, for phatic functions of imperative forms in Aguaruna). The second person imperative 'look here' in Nungon (§3.5 in Chapter 11) is used as an attention-getting device (a similar example is the imperative 'you see' in example (63) in Zenzontepec Chatino in Chapter 5). The imperative in Tayatuk can be addressed to someone who is already doing what they are being told to do. For instance, someone who is rolling a cigarette and is about to smoke may hear an imperative form 'smoke your tobacco!' addressed to them. The pragmatic import of such an imperative is approval of the speaker (§5 of Chapter 10). The first person imperative in Manambu of the verb 'speak' is a way of signalling the speaker's turn in a conversation. Mastering the discourse use of such imperative form is important for communicating properly.

Given the right context, an imperative may imply the opposite of a directive: we can recall, from §1, that imperative forms in English can be used, sarcastically, in a mock-command meaning. 'Mock-up' commands in Ashaninka Satipo (§13, example (46) of Chapter 4) are a way of expressing disagreement with what the addressee is supposed to do (a similar example in Lao is (57) in Chapter 9, where a man is mockingly encouraging a dog to steal sausages). The unmarked verb *faaw4* 'hurry!' has the force of a negative command meaning 'Slow down' (§3 of Chapter 9). A conventionalized command may have an opposite meaning. In Tayatuk classrooms, *kasuk kasuk* 'noise!' is a common request for immediate silence, that is, to stop the noise (§5 of Chapter 10).

The exact meaning of an imperative form depends on the context, and the relations between the speaker and the addressee. Versatile as they are, imperatives may sound too abrupt and embarrassingly imposing, or not as strong as desired. Then other forms are co-opted to express further nuances. This is the essence of command strategies.

9 Command strategies

The expression of imperatives tends to follow the principle of iconic motivation, whereby the meaning of the form is reflected in the form itself. A short command to the addressee expressed with a short canonical imperative is likely to have overtones of immediacy; it may well sound brusque and abrupt. In contrast, a longer form used in a directive speech act will sound milder, politer, and less insistent and face-threatening (see also Brown and Levinson 1987). As Haiman (2003: 59) puts it, 'the greater the politeness, the longer the message'.

That is, if a language has several imperative forms, the shortest one is likely to be an abrupt order, not infrequently perceived as rude, or as having overtones of urgency and immediacy. Conventionalized verbless directives in Nungon demand immediate reaction and compliance (§4.1 of Chapter 11). A bare noun or an adverb in Tayatuk can be used as a directive to be followed immediately (§5 of Chapter 10), e.g. *tap!* 'salt' as a request for salt. Similarly, in Karawari shouting *Kamin!* 'Flies!' is a demand to the addressee to chase the flies away (§3 of Chapter 13). As Nerida Jarkey (§7.1.8 of Chapter 8) puts it, 'Japanese husbands are notorious for using a single noun' when they want their wife to fetch something. Women would almost never use this very direct command strategy, as something incompatible with the stereotypical representation of a Japanese woman as polite, self-effacing, and essentially powerless (§2 of Chapter 8 and Smith 1992).

In contrast, imperatives with further specifications—such as delayed, or future ('do later on'), distal ('do elsewhere'), reported ('do following someone else's order'), and others—will always be segmentally longer and more formally marked, in line with the examples in the preceding sections. The abruptness of a brief imperative form may impose limits on its use (in the contexts of lack of social equality and the desire of being especially nice and mild). And this is where other means of framing commands, requests, and other meanings under the umbrella of directive speech acts come into play.

Command strategies cover a wide variety of forms, many of them language-specific. Command strategies and their choice may reflect what Brown and Levinson (1987: 70) call 'conventionalised indirectness'. So, *Can you pass the salt?* would be read as a request by a native speaker. It will hardly ever be taken to be a question about the addressee's strength or capacity of performing this action. *Why don't you come to the blackboard?* is not a question asking for a reason why the student remains seated—it is a directive to come to the blackboard. Non-native speakers of English may miss out on understanding such 'pseudo-questions' as commands.[10]

Recurrent forms 'co-opted' as command strategies include interrogative forms of all sorts, statements (including those cast in present, or future), free-standing (or de-subordinated) non-main clauses, and nominalized verbal forms (see Aikhenvald 2010: 256–95 for further details).

---

[10] Conventionalized 'command strategies' are called 'non-imperative directives' by Huddleston (2002: 939–42). Another term for these is 'semantic imperative' (Press 1979: 80–1). In contrast to 'syntactic' imperatives which have an imperative form, semantic imperatives have the function, but not the form, of commands. Martin (1975: 965ff) refers to command strategies in Japanese as 'circumlocutions'.

English has a wide variety of interrogative directives. 'Ability questions' typically start with *can you, could you, are you able,* and so on. In Huddleston's words, they 'lend themselves to indirect directions, since a likely reason for me to be interested in your ability to do something is that I want you to do it' (Huddleston 2002: 940). A question (pronounced without question intonation) *Would you open the door* or *Will you pass me the salt* is normally understood as a request, and a special explanation would be required if it were to be understood as a polar question (Comrie 1984: 281). A negative counterpart, *Won't you pass me the salt,* has overtones of being less 'civil' (Jespersen 1928: 481). Negative interrogatives in Japanese 'carry a tone of criticism or scolding' (§7.1.4 of Chapter 8). They have falling rather than rising intonation, unlike information-seeking questions.

Questions in Lao can serve as indirect request strategies, and an ability tag question following an imperative softens the command (§2.5 of Chapter 9). The pragmatic effects of questions as directives can be markedly different. In Ashaninka Satipo (§11.3 of Chapter 4), questions in requests require addressee's immediate reaction. In Zenzontepec Chatino (§6 of Chapter 5, example (61)), a question as a command strategy builds in 'a presupposition that the action will occur, limiting the addressee's freedom'. A short question 'What are you doing?' in Karawari is a negative command, to stop doing it (§3 of Chapter 13). And in Ku Waru, commands phrased as questions express sarcasm (see §5 of Chapter 15). In all likelihood, the reason for overtones of authority in questions as directives lies in their face-threatening nature.

Forms expressing potentiality, intention, and wish soften commands. The desiderative marker in Korowai (§3.9 of Chapter 12) makes a request more elaborate and more polite. The potential mood in Zenzontepec Chatino generally makes a command to a second person sound less forceful than a straightforward imperative (§6 of Chapter 5). However, a priest telling a troublesome youth what to do uses the potential mood in (60) leaving 'no room for dissent'. The context and the relationships between the speaker and the addressee determine the exact overtones of a command strategy.

Future forms as directives vary in their meanings. In English, a present or a future form of a verb can be used as a stern command. *You will go to school tomorrow,* said to a hooky-playing teenager, implies authority. In a similar vein, future forms are used in Nungon (E in §4 of Chapter 11) as stern commands. Not so in Nyangumarta, an Australian language: here an imperative is perceived as 'a very direct way of speaking, and often a more respectful way of issuing a command is to use the future tense' (Sharp 2004: 185).[11] In Arapaho, an Algonquian language, 'the use of the future often makes the utterance not really a command at all, but instead

---

[11] Similar examples come from Marthuthunira, an Australian language (Dench 2009), Nishnaambewin (Algonquian: Valentine 2001: 994), and Modern Hebrew (Malygina 2001).

a recognition of the strong authority of the other person, who cannot be commanded, or prevented from acting, but only deferred to' (Cowell 2007: 57). Future is the mildest and the most indirect way of suggesting to someone what they may wish to do.

Near future forms in Tayatuk (§5.1 of Chapter 10) 'soften a command to a mild request'. They also express a distal command, for an action to be carried out far from the speaker. Future in commands in Huallaga Quechua can indicate that the action has to be performed in the future. Or it may make the command sound more polite (Weber 1989: 103).

Non-main clauses can be used on their own, to issue a command, or a request. An imperative form in Mauwake is the most common way of getting someone to do something. To make an order softer and less direct, one can use a non-final form of a verb with different subject marking (the final clause is left out altogether). This is especially common for commands to children, e.g. *P-ekap-eya* (BRING.PREFIX-come-2/3sgDS) 'Bring it!' (Berghäll 2010: 284). Medial verbs marked for different subject in Nungon (C under §4 in Chapter 11) have gentle overtones when used in commands. A medial verb as a command strategy can be used as an alternative to a dedicated imperative in Nungon: the two forms appear linked by *ha* 'or' (example (40) in Chapter 11).

A directive in Northern Paiute (§7 of Chapter 7) may be softened by adding the suffix *-si* to the bare verbs stem. This suffix is related to the sequential suffix *-si* (which marks the action as preceding that in the main clause). In Tim Thornes' words in §7 of Chapter 7, 'the non-final, incomplete "feel" of a verb in this form may motivate its use in a gentle imperative context'.

Free-standing desubordinated *if*-clauses in Modern English are used more and more frequently as a way of asking people to do something, as in *If Mr and Mrs Smith could make their way to the Qantas desk* and *If you come down and support the film*. Stirling (1998) shows how these—seemingly incomplete—clauses are developing into a separate clause type, with a specific function of mild request. It is perhaps their 'incompleteness' and an overtone of tentativeness that makes them milder than a straightforward *Come down and support the film!*[12]

Desubordinated same subject medial clauses with completive meaning in Manambu are used in an exact opposite way—as stern commands to be obeyed immediately, e.g. *Wapwi kusu-ku!* (clothes put.on-COMPLETIVE.SS) 'Put your clothes on!'. A similar form can be used to address 'us', implying immediacy: *Mel kuse-ku!* (eye close-COMPLETIVE.SS) 'Let's pray' (lit. having closed eye). Dependent non-final verbs in Nungon (A and B under §4 of Chapter 11) function as strong and urgent

---

[12] Contreras (1960) offers examples of independent clauses marked with *si* 'if' in Spanish used as mild commands and suggestions with polite overtones; further uses of desubordinated *si*-clauses in Spanish are discussed in Pérez (1985).

commands, and medial verbs not inflected for different subject have impersonal and stern connotations. Desubordinated medial clauses containing the speech verb 'say' in Tayatuk have a stronger directive force than bare imperatives (§5.2 of Chapter 10). The authoritative and abrupt effect of these desubordinated clauses is akin to the effects of conventionalized ellipsis and abbreviated commands demanding immediate reaction. But in an appropriate context they can also be used as very mild entreaties.

Over time, a non-imperative form in a directive function may come to be used as the only available means for expressing a command: this is what we have seen in languages such as Slave in (7). Free-standing desubordinated clauses may also follow this grammaticalization path. In Iyo, a Papuan language spoken in Madang Province of Papua New Guinea, imperative sentences are marked with a medial verb form inflected with an imperative marker (Minter 2009: 103). The Japanese imperative which ends in -te is a conventionalized form of a gerund, or an erstwhile linking form (§7.1.1 of Chapter 8). We return to the imperative forms originating in command strategies in §10.

Free-standing nominalizations, participles, and other derivations can be used as directives. In many European languages, infinitives (citation forms) are frequent especially in written instructions, as in German *nicht hinauslehnen* '(people must) not lean out (of a train)'; Estonian *mitte suitsetada* 'not to smoke; smoking is forbidden'. A directive cast in the infinitive in Russian 'denotes a peremptory order, a categorical prescription and command', and also 'expresses obligatoriness of an action, its fatal inevitability…' (Vinogradov 1947: 604–5), e.g. *Uvolitj!* 'To dismiss!'. An infinitive in Armenian can be used as a directive only in utterances addressed by a superior to their subordinates (Kozintseva 2001: 265–6). Participle commands in German used with motion and posture verbs are typically used if the person issuing a command is in a position of authority. *Stehengeblieben!* 'Stand still!' can be said by a policeman to an offender; or by annoyed parents or teachers to a child.

Along similar lines, a nominalization in Japanese 'presents an action as a fact, and thus functions as a very firm strategy for issuing a command that will brook no argument' (§7.1.5 of Chapter 8). A future nominalization in Quechua (§15 of Chapter 2) expresses a strong obligation. Only negated deverbal nominalizations are used as command strategies in Nungon (G under §4 of Chapter 11): they have general impersonal overtones, similar to a statement 'X is not done'. In contrast, nominalized clauses in Northern Paiute have a 'flavour of offering advice', as a softer and indirect command strategy (§7 of Chapter 7). Converbal clauses in Siberian Yupik Eskimo when used on their own as commands have overtones of suggestion and polite request (Vaxtin 2001: 140).

Statements can be used as directives, with varying overtones. In Zenzontepec Chatino (§6 of Chapter 5) they are tantamount to strong commands. Non-past declarative forms in Japanese sound quite firm; they are used for assigning tasks in the workplace (§7.1.6 of Chapter 8). To redress aberrant behaviour, speakers of Nungon invoke socially established practices, using statements such as 'they do X' or 'they don't do X'—this is what Sarvasy (F under §4 in Chapter 11) calls 'the reasonable people strategy'. We can recall, from §5.3, that perfective forms—which presuppose completion of an action—impart strong and peremptory overtones to a command. This is the case in Ku Waru (§5 of Chapter 15).

A declarative form marked with *-ta* 'past' in Japanese sounds rough and vulgar when used in commands (§7.1.6 of Chapter 8). And adding a perfective marker to a potential form in Quechua makes the command sound threatening (§15 of Chapter 2). In many languages, presenting a desired way of action as a 'fait accompli' and further marking its accomplishment and endpoint carry with them an element of speaker's imposition on the addressee.

Alternatively, a statement may have the force of an indirect command. Among the Matsigenka (whose language is closely related to Ashaninka Satipo), a married couple would not command one another. If a woman wants her husband to hunt, 'it is enough for her to say quietly, "There is no meat"' (Johnson 2003: 94). This is an instance of an indirect 'requestive hint' (see an overview in Weizman 1993, Enfield 2014, and a survey of request techniques in Drew and Couper-Kuhlen 2014). The effect of indirect ways of asking people to do things depends on the shared back-ground between the speaker and the addressee, and the willingness of addressee in understanding a hidden request (see Slotta 2015: 525–6, for some examples of possible misunderstandings). The 'agentive role' of listeners is instrumental in 'uncovering' the veiled commands (along the lines of §5 of Chapter 15).

In many European languages, just about any form can be understood as an instruction what to do—given the right context. But it is absolutely *not* the case for every language. Amha (2001: 127) remarks that speakers of Maale do not interpret questions as commands (neither do Jarawara: see Dixon 2004, Tariana, or Haya: see Lehman 1977: 148). The degree of conventionalization of each imperative strategy is language-specific, and may correlate with the overtones of each of the grammatical structures concerned. For instance, questions in Tariana are limited in use to seeking information; over-using them creates an impression of being nosy and domineering. This may explain their lack of command function.

Further conventionalized command strategies include self-quotes in Aguaruna, which make a command sound stronger and more abrupt than a straightforward imperative (§5 of Chapter 3). In Ashaninka Satipo, modal verbs, including *ontima-tiye* 'be necessary', are used to express advice to younger people (§11.1 of Chapter 4). The modal word *karka* 'must' can be used to strengthen a command in Karawari (§4.4 of Chapter 13).

Japanese employs a plethora of expressions all of which also have non-command functions. If used by those above the speaker in the vertical dimension of an unwritten social hierarchy (*meue-no hito* 'people above one's eyes') to try and get the addressee to do something, they are interpreted as directives—if the expectation is that the speaker wants the addressee to do something. We find grammaticalized 'giving' verbs, evaluative expressions ('it's best if...'), and object honorific verbs of request. The choice of a strategy depends on the context, and above all the relationship between the speaker and the addressee (§7.1 of Chapter 8).

Other means serve to mitigate the directive force. Honorific address forms in Korowai and Kombai are used in directives and suggestions to people conceived as senior with regard to the speaker (§3.9 in Chapter 12). Vocative forms of nouns referring to close kin and respected persons in Quechua have a similar function (§14 of Chapter 2). Adding an exclamative interjection to a directive in Korowai may enhance the force of a command (§3.9 of Chapter 12).

A combination of a vocative phrase, the desiderative adverb and the pronominal subject in an imperative clause in Korowai make the sentence longer and more elaborate; following the principle of iconicity (Haiman 2003), this 'softens the intrusion on the autonomy of the addressee' (§3.9 of Chapter 12). In Lao commands, social hierarchies are reflected in the judicious use of vocative particles with kin terms (based on sibling seniority, pronouns, and titles); examples (65)–(66) in §6 of Chapter 9 show some expressive possibilities of a combination of command strategies with dedicated imperative particles.

10 Imperatives in language history

Two opposite forces appear to be at work in the history of imperative forms. In quite a few languages, canonical imperatives are archaic in their form and in their behaviour. Archaic features of imperatives in Indo-European languages have been described by Kuryłowicz (1964: 136–7) and Lockwood (1969: 114). The common Australian marker -*ga* for second person imperative recurs in many languages (Dixon 2002: 213–14). Panyjima, an Australian language, is overwhelmingly nominative-accusative. The relics of an original ergative-absolutive pattern survive just in the imperatives (Dench 1991: 138, 173, 204).

A tendency towards enrichment and renewal of imperatives is at work in other languages. An erstwhile command strategy can gradually replace an imperative, if the dedicated imperative form is not quite appropriate. Nerida Jarkey (§8 of Chapter 8) summarizes this process, and its cultural underpinnings, for Japanese:

Issuing commands in a social context that is characterized by constraints on who can command whom, and on how one maintains good relationships, good demeanour, and socially acceptable gender identity, clearly presents a challenge to effectively getting others to do what you want them to do. In such a context it is no surprise that there are numerous strategies to avoid using direct, imperative forms, and also evidence of the loss of the euphemistic qualities of several of these command strategies, as they gradually come to be reinterpreted as imperative forms themselves.

We saw in §9 that forms with overtones of intention, potentiality, and unrealized wish can be used in lieu of imperatives, as command strategies. They may gradually become dedicated commands. A close connection between irrealis and imperative forms in Tayatuk (Chapter 10) and Korowai (alongside other languages of the Greater Awyu family) points towards this possible path of development (§4 of Chapter 12). In Nungon, counterfactual forms are closely related to the immediate imperative (§5 of Chapter 11). Irrealis forms are used for polite and distal commands in many other Papuan languages (Roberts 1990).

Not only do vocatives play a role in nuancing commands. Formal similarities between vocatives and imperatives may suggest a common origin (as hypothesized for Aguaruna in §5.2 of Chapter 3). The delayed imperative in Nungon (§2 and Table 5 in Chapter 11) may have originated through alteration (raising or backing) of the vowel of the final syllable of Future Irrealis forms. This iconic vowel change is frequently employed as a means of expressive marking of long duration, and to carry speech over long distance, calling over to someone. Delayed imperative in Nungon may stem from an erstwhile vocative strategy, iconic in its nature.

Over time, free-standing dependent (or desubordinated) clauses, as a means of expressing directives, become conventionalized as dedicated command forms. The erstwhile converbal marker -si in Northern Paiute has now developed into a marker of mild commands (§7 of Chapter 7). Along similar lines, the converbal form marked by -te in Japanese has acquired the status of a dedicated command (see Table 3 in Chapter 8; also see §7.1.6 of Chapter 8). Prohibitives in Northern Paiute go back to independent concessive adverbial clauses (§9 of Chapter 7).

A common path for the development of a prohibitive involves a form meaning 'stop, abandon, desist', e.g. Welsh *peidio* 'cease, stop' as a prohibitive marker (King 1993: 227; and other examples in Aikhenvald 2010: 358–60). The prohibitive in Lao involves a grammaticalized verb *jaa1* 'desist' (§3 of Chapter 9). The 'caution' marker in Dyirbal is similar in form to the transitive verb *galga-l* 'leave (it)' (Dixon 1972: 112). Prohibitive in Nungon consists of a positive future irrealis form plus a final suffix -a. In all likelihood, this suffix is related to the attention-getting marker -a (the two homonymous markers are in complementary distribution) (§2.4.2 of Chapter 11). This opens up a hitherto barely attested pathway of development of a prohibitive.

The bare form of the verb is a frequent means of expressing a canonical imperative. In a few languages within this volume, the bare form of a verbal root has a range of further meanings. In Korowai and other languages of the Greater Awyu family, the zero-marked paradigm covers imperative, irrealis, optative, and desiderative. The potentiality forms in Dyirbal (whose second person value is the least formally marked in the language) cover most of those same meanings. Immediate imperatives, counterfactuals, and different subject forms in Nungon share a similar set of tenseless forms (§5 of Chapter 11). This is somewhat similar to a multifunctional 'injunctive' form (which takes person and number but not tense or aspect) reconstructed for proto-Indo-European (Kiparsky 2005). Perhaps, the origin of imperatives across languages lies in essentially tenseless forms—a question for future pursuit.

In a situation of intensive language contact, one language may evolve imperative constructions similar to those in the neighbouring languages, through grammaticalizing verbs and reinterpreting existing morphemes. Within the multilingual Vaupés River Basin, one future marker in Tariana has become reinterpreted as delayed imperative (-*wa* in (16)), and the other one as proximal imperative, 'do here' (-*si* in (14)). A secondhand imperative, 'do on someone else's order' (-*pida* in (12)), has been developed out of an erstwhile reported or quotative evidential. As a result, the imperative categories in Tariana parallel those in East Tucanoan languages, in which Tariana speakers are fully proficient. East Tucanoan languages and Tariana are spoken within the same Vaupés River Basin linguistic area. The degree of structural similarities between them is rather striking. And the imperative meanings found in Tariana are absent from closely related Arawak languages (Aikhenvald 2018). This offers further evidence in favour of their contact-induced origin in Tariana (see Aikhenvald 2008). But things are not always that clear-cut. The way desubordinated conditional clauses are used in Zenzontepec Chatino commands is reminiscent of similar expressions in rural Spanish (§6 of Chapter 5, and example (60)). The direction of diffusion here remains an open question.

Imperatives in Nivkh, a highly obsolescent Paleosiberian isolate spoken in a situation of intensive language contact, have adjusted to the dominant Russian patterns (Gruzdeva 2002). In many Aboriginal languages of Australia negative imperatives have become more like English than they were traditionally (Laughren 2002: 116 on Warlpiri; Schmidt 1985 on Young People's Dyirbal). And individual one-word imperative forms are highly borrowable. The Turkish particle *hajde!* 'go, hurry up!' was borrowed into Bulgarian, and also Serbian and Croatian (Borut Telban, p.c.) as an uninflected form. Speakers of Modern Hebrew use Arabic *yalla!* 'let's go, come on'. Speakers of the Young People's Dyirbal used the particle *nomo*, from English *no more*, as a marker of negative imperative (instead of the 'caution' form described in Chapter 6). A few animal commands in Ashaninka Satipo (§15 of Chapter 4) are borrowings from Spanish and from Quechua.

What accounts for the diffusibility of imperative meanings and forms? In the course of intensive language contact, similar situations tend to be conceptualized in similar ways and warrant similar verbal description. A major factor behind the diffusion of patterns in a situation of societal multilingualism is the desire to be able to say what one's neighbour can say—making 'the categories existing in the languages that are in contact mutually compatible and more readily intertranslatable' (Heine and Kuteva 2003: 561). For the coexisting systems to converge, functional, semantic, and formal matching is desirable. Frequency is a major facilitating factor in linguistic diffusion: the more frequent the category in one language, the likelier it is to diffuse into another. In many languages, commands are among the highest frequency forms in conversations and narratives.

Sharing pragmatic patterns and types of context, and subsequent diffusion of organizing discourse structures, results in common genres, idiomatic expressions, and further ways of saying things for languages in contact (see references in Aikhenvald 2006). Commands are highly prominent in greetings and speech formulae throughout the Vaupés area. The Tariana farewell formula *matʃa-pida* (be.good-REPORTED.IMPERATIVE) 'good-bye; best wishes' (lit. let it be good on (our) behalf) is a calque from Tucano *āyu-áto* (good-REPORTED.IMPERATIVE), with the same meaning. The farewell formula was calqued from Tucano into Tariana, creating an anomalous structure: a secondhand—or any other—imperative cannot be formed on stative verbs except in this case.

A further factor that facilitates the diffusion of categories is the impact a category has on cultural norms and behavioural requirements. An obligatory category in a language which correlates with behavioural requirements is more susceptible to diffusion than one which does not. For instance, obligatory evidentials often correlate with a cultural requirement for an explicit statement about how one knows things. Those who are not explicit run the danger of being treated as liars, or as incompetent. This cultural requirement may explain why evidentiality spreads so easily into contact languages, including some varieties of South American Indian English, Latin American Spanish, and Amazonian Portuguese; it also tends to diffuse across linguistic areas (Aikhenvald 2004, 2012). Imperatives are embedded in cultural practices and reflect societal structures—another reason for their easy spread in language contact. This takes us to our next section.

11 Understanding imperatives

What are imperatives good for? Imperative forms in English (and perhaps in many other languages with just one dedicated imperative) are versatile in their meanings (see also Huddleston 2002: 929–31; Davies 1986). As Jespersen (1928: 467) put it, they may 'range from brutal commands through many intermediate steps (demands, injunctions, implorations, invitations) to the most modest and humble prayer (entreaty, supplication)'.

The English-speaking world abounds in imperative forms, used to command, entice, and invite. In *Alice in Wonderland*, the cake instructs Alice: *Eat me!*, and the bottle joins in: *Drink me!* Houses in real estate advertisements beg us *Make me your home!*

A more inventive command to the same effect urges: *Do not drive faster than your guardian angel can fly*. A neon sign projects a mock-command: *Drink and drive—you are a bloody idiot.* Commands and instructions do not have to contain an imperative: *Drowsy drivers die,* or *A power nap will save your life* could well be rephrased as *Break your drive and have a rest!*

Despite an overwhelming frequency of imperatives in many genres of English, imperatives enjoy a bad reputation: over-using them in conversation creates an image of a bossy and unpleasant person. Imperatives are often avoided because they are face-threatening.

In her comparison of what she perceived as gentle and mild Arapesh culture with the harsh and rough Mundugumor, Margaret Mead (1935: 199–200) observed: 'the first lessons that a Mundugumor child learns are a series of prohibitions', and then adds, in a footnote:

The people make an extraordinarily frequent use of the imperative form. When I think of a Mundugumor verb it is always the imperative form that leaps into my mind, in strong contrast to my memory of Arapesh, in which imperatives were very seldom used.

She goes on to describe how the life of a Mundugumor is governed by strict rules, creating an impression of a highly rigid and unfriendly society replete with prohib-itions (in contrast with the mild and undemanding Arapesh, conceivably free of the demanding 'kinship imperative'). This is what over-using imperative forms implies, for Margaret Mead as a Western scholar.

Mildred Larson, in her guide to translators, warns her readers against projecting one's European intuitions onto another language with different communication strategies (Larson 1998: 471):

In Africa, a friend might come and put down a couple of dishes of food on one's doorstep and say, 'Eat!'. To a person of some other culture, such as American, it might sound very harsh, and the person would feel they must obey. But, as a matter of fact, that is not the intent in the African culture. The friend has cooked supper and is simply inviting the other person to share it. That person is free to eat a full meal or just take a few mouthfuls and then say that they are satisfied. If in a text translated from an African language and culture into English, such a situation were a part of the story, the translator would not use the English imperative 'Eat!'. The translator should rather say, 'Would you like some?' or 'Help yourself, if you would like'. The words *would like* give the attitude and cultural information which was communi-cated by the command 'Eat!' in the African story.

Along similar lines, John Saeed, in his grammar of Somali (1993: 83), remarks: 'Note that, possibly as a result of the egalitarian nature of traditional Somali society, imperatives do not have the same associations of power and impoliteness as in English and are consequently much more commonly used.'

Commands and other directives reflect relationships between people—including kinship roles and mutual expectations. As Borut Telban puts it (§2 of Chapter 13), 'commands are pervasive in daily interactions between people...While for a cultur-ally insensitive foreigner these often abrupt and quite loud speech acts may be disconcerting...for the Ambonwari it is just the opposite. For such an egalitarian kinship-based society commands are actually a common way of daily communication reflecting the closeness of living together and directness of expressions clearly showing people's desires and intentions.' Using Telban's words, in a Karawari-speaking society,

Commands correspond to the intrinsic verbal component of sharing, exchange, and cooperation, on which people's lives and society as a whole depend. Moreover, if or when somebody did not use them, or tried to express his or her wishes in a more 'polite' way, people would soon become suspicious, thinking that such a person is insincere and hides his or her intentions.

Judicious use of commands is similar to a social glue within communities—especially those which are 'intensely egalitarian in their political ethos', as are the Korowai of West Papua. As Lourens de Vries puts it (§3.8 of Chapter 12), the absence of any negative politeness strategies 'signals solidarity, harmony, trust, and cooperation' essential for living together.

Commands and directives of all sorts are pervasive in everyday communication among the Ashaninka Satipo. The form of directives depends on people's status within the group. Someone who is inferior would use a canonical imperative attenuated by a modal marker. And someone who feels they have a right to demand compliance will draw on one of the perfective affixes and other means which make their command sound more categorical (§16 of Chapter 4 and Table 7 there).

Japanese social relations are metaphorically conceived of as involving a vertical and a horizontal dimension. In Nerida Jarkey's (§2 of Chapter 8) words,

in the vertical dimension, other people tend to be viewed as *meue-no hito* 'people above one's eyes' and *meshita-no hito* 'people below one's eyes' ... It is not appropriate to issue commands to those above one (*meue-no hito*), nor to equals. Japanese people are also constrained in their use of commands in the 'horizontal' social dimension, where the metaphors *uchi* 'inside' and *soto* 'outside' characterize relationships. One's in-group members are those with whom one identifies most closely in a particular context, such as people in one's family or school, fellow club members, employees, etc. Commands are made only to those within one's in-group and then only to *meshita-no hito* 'people below one's eyes'. It is generally inappropriate to issue commands to out-group members, even to those lower in status. Here social distance rather than deference is the key factor.

The interaction of linguistic and cultural constraints may account for differences in the actual usage of imperatives. In many Australian Aboriginal societies asking information questions is tantamount to showing yourself as nosy and intrusive. Information is volunteered rather than directly requested—this makes communication indirect and minimally face-threatening. The same applies to commands and directive acts of all sorts. A polite request in Kuuk Thayorre is phrased as a negative statement (Gaby 2007). In Yankunytjatjara, another Australian language (Goddard 1983: 306–7), a parent-in-law cannot directly address the son-in-law asking him for food. A request has to be done through an intermediary. This intermediary is also not allowed to use a direct way of commanding—that is, an imperative. Social and kinship relationships within a community restrict the imperative usage.

And if a command, or a prohibition, is to be used, it is often contextualized, and an explanation is offered as to why something is to be done or not. This is a conventionalized technique in Yidiñ (Dixon 1977: 350, p.c.) (see also (59), from Zenzontepec Chatino in Chapter 5, (38) from Dyirbal in Chapter 6, and examples from Northern Paiute in §9 of Chapter 7).

(22) ñundu   giyi   gali-n   wanda:-nji   *Yidiñ*
     2sgNOM   PROHIBITIVE   go-IMP   fall.down-APPREHENSIVE
     Don't you go (there), you might fall down

Understanding and mastering directive speech acts—the ways of commanding, requesting, and so on—in a language is a key to successful interaction (along the lines of Grice's 1989: 26 'cooperative principle'). And using a wrong way of requesting is a sure way towards a breakdown in communication. When children acquire their first language, commands and requests are what they hear most frequently from their care-givers, and what they learn first. Imperatives and command strategies are extensively used in child-directed speech among the Nungon (§6 of Chapter 11) and are acquired at an early age (in line with earlier work on the Ku Waru of the New Guinea Highlands, by Rumsey 2003: 180–3 and Rumsey 2015). The early acquisition of imperatives in many languages (including Hebrew, Japanese, Catalan, and Ku Waru) is related to their frequency in carers' speech, and maybe also to the relative simplicity of their form.

Imperatives can hardly be considered 'poor relatives' of declaratives or interrogatives—we saw in §§5–6 that they have numerous complexities and special traits. We have also seen that in many languages, an imperative form may be too strong, or not strong enough—and other forms may be co-opted to express more fine-tuned overtones of requests, entreaties, and wishes. The meanings of such 'command strategies' are not uniform across languages. Similar grammatical categories have different overtones when used as command strategies in different languages (as we saw in §9). And some non-primarily imperative forms may, over time, acquire unmistakably explicit command meanings. These are a frequent source for imperatives as separate forms, throughout the languages' history.

Imperatives and other command forms are used and manipulated to reflect the conventions and their renegotiation in human communication in different societies across the world, with different roles and hierarchies behind them. The plethora of commanding and requesting techniques in any given language reflect an ongoing struggle, between the desire to save face and striving to reach the required result.

Imperatives and directive speech acts reflect societal relationships and attitudes. In some societies one advises rather than commands. In others, commanding is a normal course of action. Imperatives and the ways of phrasing directives offer a fertile ground for collaborative research for scholars from all walks of linguistics—synchronic language analysts, historical linguists, typologists, sociolinguists, psycholinguists, and anthropological linguists—jointly with anthropologists.

12 About this volume

This volume aims at offering a glimpse into cross-linguistically diverse imperatives, prohibitives, and other means of expressing directives, in terms of the parameters and issues outlined in the present chapter. We focus on an in-depth discussion of fourteen languages from a variety of families and areas, all of different typological make-up. The languages discussed—with the exception of Japanese and Lao—are spoken by minority peoples. Each reflects their own specific culture and social hierarchies, which have not yet been depleted by the sweeping winds of globalization. Each chapter systematically addresses grammatical devices used in expressing commands, requests, and other ways of getting people to do things, their pragmatic and communicative correlates, and also their histories. Besides numerous language-specific features, we find the expression of universal tendencies—including a special status for canonical imperatives, the possibility of all the person values falling into a single paradigm, and the deployment of similar command strategies (including interrogatives, conditionals, and nominalizations).

We start with languages of South America, the locus of substantial linguistic diversity. In Chapter 2, 'Imperatives and commands in Quechua', Willem F. H. Adelaar focuses on the dedicated imperative paradigm and other means of expressing directives across the Quechua language family, of the Andean region in Peru, Bolivia, Ecuador, Argentina, and Colombia. Chapter 3, 'The grammatical representation of commands and prohibitions in Aguaruna', by Simon E. Overall, discusses the imperative mood in this Jivaroan (or Chicham) language, spoken at the foothills of the Andes in Peruvian Amazon. A striking feature of imperatives in Aguaruna is a distinction between plain and familiar forms (absent from the prohibitives). Ashaninka Satipo, a member of the Kampa subgroup of the Arawak language family in Peru, offers a different story. Irrealis forms are co-opted to be used in commands. Canonical imperatives have a distinctive intonation pattern of their own, and non-canonical imperatives stand apart in a number of features. The ways in which people get one another to do things correlate with their status within the Ashaninka community. This is discussed in detail in Chapter 4, 'Imperatives in Ashaninka Satipo (Kampa Arawak) of Peru', by Elena Mihas.

Zenzontepec Chatino, an Otomanguean language from Oaxaca state in Mexico, has a set of special forms for canonical imperatives whose morphological complexity reflects the 'idiosyncratic and prodigiously complex inflectional morphology' of the language. Other imperative forms—including non-canonical imperatives and prohibitives—are marked with potential mood, which also covers potentiality, probability, wishes, and intentions. Its range of meanings is comparable to irrealis in Ashaninka Satipo and other languages. The expression and the marking of commands in their varied uses is the topic of Chapter 5, 'Commands in Zenzontepec Chatino (Otomanguean)', by Eric W. Campbell.

Potentiality inflection on verbs in Dyirbal, from Queensland in Australia, are not dissimilar to potential mood in Zenzontepec Chatino or to irrealis in many languages. At a pinch, some of them can be rendered into English as imperatives. And a combination of particle plus verbal suffix provides 'advice about some negative happening which might eventuate'. This is the closest Dyirbal gets to expressing a negative command. There is indeed 'a temptation' to try and force Dyirbal categories into 'a familiar frame', and to label the potentiality inflection a positive imperative and the caution forms a negative imperative. As R. M. W. Dixon demonstrates in Chapter 6, 'What Dyirbal uses instead of commands', this would not 'fully bring out the genius of the language' and the multitude of uses of the forms themselves. Traditional Dyirbal, spoken in a society where 'life was regulated by common consent', did not have specifically directive speech acts, commands, or prohibitions. The potentiality form—expressed with the bare stem of the verb—expresses 'a potentiality, which is likely to be realized, but may not be', and the 'caution' form is typically an advice and a warning rather than a command not to.

Northern Paiute, a Uto-Aztecan language, spoken in the northern Great Basin region of western North America, has a dedicated canonical imperative which coexists with a variety of forms which can be used for canonical and non-canonical person values. Many of the forms and the strategies can be reconstructed for proto-Numic. The versatility of commands and their marking in Northern Paiute is captured in the title of Chapter 7, by Tim Thornes, 'On the heterogeneity of Northern Paiute directives'.

Imperatives and commands in Japanese, with its rigid and complex set of constraints on social relationships, are also daunting in their heterogeneity, and correlations with honorifics, types of addressee, social gender, and many other subtle parameters. In Chapter 8, 'Imperatives and commands in Japanese', Nerida Jarkey offers a detailed study of directives of various sorts jointly with the social parameters which may warrant their use or constrain it.

Imperatives in Lao, a Tai-Kadai language of Laos, are marked with a set of special particles (as befits an isolating language with no bound morphology). This is what distinguishes them from statements and questions. A range of strategies for mitigating or indirectly conveying the force of a command depend on the addressee and their relationship with the speaker, and the social hierarchy. The intricacies of Lao directives are the topic of Chapter 9, by N. J. Enfield ('Linguistic expression of commands in Lao').

The next four chapters focus on languages from three different areas on the island of New Guinea, a locus of remarkable linguistic diversity rivalling only Amazonia.

Tayatuk, a Finisterre-Huon language spoken in Morobe Province of Papua New Guinea, has dedicated forms for canonical imperatives. Non-canonical imperatives are expressed through irrealis. Negative imperative shares its negator with irrealis. Near future is a way of framing a command to do something far from where the speaker is. In Chapter 10, 'Imperatives and command strategies in Tayatuk (Morobe, PNG)', Valérie Guérin focuses on these and other features of Tayatuk directives.

Nungon and Tayatuk are spoken in adjacent areas; in all likelihood the two languages are genetically related. But their imperatives, and other means of phrasing commands and directives, are quite different. The three person values of imperative in Nungon form one paradigm. There is a special set of forms for distal imperative. This is in addition to numerous strategies mitigating the force of commands, or making them sound more stern. Imperatives show intricate links with irrealis and counterfactual forms. Commands are acquired by children at an early stage—in Chapter 11 ('Imperatives and commands in Nungon'), Hannah S. Sarvasy offers a discussion of directives in mother–child interaction in the language.

Having a full set of person values in the imperative paradigm is a property of Korowai and related languages from the Greater Awyu family, spoken in West Papua. In Chapter 12 ('The imperative paradigm of Korowai, a Greater Awyu language of West Papua'), Lourens de Vries discusses the form and the meanings of the Korowai imperatives and other means of mitigating directives, in the context of an egalitarian society. Imperative and irrealis paradigms are closely related, both synchronically and diachronically. And both are zero-marked—something that alerts us to the basic character of imperative as a 'paradigm case of an unmarked mood form'.

Among the Karawari of the Ambonwari village in the Sepik region of New Guinea, commands 'generate and reflect close relationships and intimacy between people'. The language has dedicated forms for canonical and for non-canonical imperatives, and numerous ways of softening or strengthening a command. Based on several decades of ethnographic and linguistic fieldwork, Borut Telban (Chapter 13, 'Commands as a form of intimacy among the Karawari of Papua New Guinea') combines an in-depth analysis of the form of commands with an exploration of the nature and the usage of directives, as an indispensable part of the Karawari social life and harmonious interaction.

Canonical and non-canonical imperatives form one paradigm in many Omotic languages (as we can recall from the example of Yemsa, in Table 1). Chapter 14, by Azeb Amha, focuses on 'Commands in Wolaitta', the largest Omotic language in Ethiopia, the composition of the imperative paradigm (where first person imperatives have a special status), and constraints on its use. Wolaitta and other related languages have a rich set of directives to domestic animals.

The final chapter, 'Veiled commands: anthropological perspectives on directives', by Rosita Henry, focuses on the cross-cultural and cross-linguistic nature of commands as an integral component of human interaction. Each of Chapters 2–14 addresses the ways in which linguistic form of directives may reflect societal hierarchies and patterns of interaction. The angle in Chapter 15 is somewhat different—this chapter is a reflection on how directives work in an intersubjective world, starting with an example from English and going on to a brief summary of Searle's (1976) theory of speech acts, and subsequent criticisms, especially by Rosaldo (1982). The author then turns to speech acts and 'veiled' commands disguised in other linguistic forms in the context of further indirect ways of talking among the people of the Western Highlands of Papua New Guinea (including the Melpa and related groups). The concepts of personhood, kinship, autonomy, and responsibility, and the awareness of the world of 'intentional others full of hopes, desires, and fears, and the capacity not only for honesty and sincerity but also for deception and trickery' underlie the 'veiling' of commands as part of figurative speech, perhaps, at a more general level.

This volume spans languages with and without dedicated imperative paradigms, focusing on a range of forms employed as directives under various circumstances, their functions and history. We investigate the range of ways in which communicative practices shape the expression of directives of all sorts. This is an integral part of exploring what Ameka (2013: 225) referred to as 'the reflexive relation between language, culture, and modes of thinking, and in particular of the ways in which culture and cognition are encoded in grammar'. Directives and their nearest approximations are particularly sensitive to reflecting all of these. And this makes them a useful case study for a general question—why languages are the way they are.

References

Abbott, M. 1991. 'Macushi', pp. 23–160 of *Handbook of Amazonian languages*, Vol. 1, edited by Desmond C. Derbyshire and Geoffrey K. Pullum. Berlin: Mouton de Gruyter.

Adelaar, Willem F. H. 1990. 'The role of quotations in Andean discourse', pp. 1–12 of *Unity in diversity: Papers presented to Simon C. Dik on his 50th birthday*, edited by Harm Pinkster and Inge Genee. Dordrecht: Foris Publications.

Adelaar, Willem F. H. 1994. 'A grammatical category for manifestations of the supernatural in early colonial Quechua', pp. 116–25 of *Language in the Andes*, edited by Peter Cole, Gabriella Hermon, and Mario Daniel Martín. Newark: University of Delaware Latin American Studies Program.

Aikhenvald, Alexandra Y. 2004. *Evidentiality*. Oxford: Oxford University Press.

Aikhenvald, Alexandra Y. 2006. 'Grammars in contact: A typological perspective', pp. 1–66 of *Grammars in contact: A cross-linguistic typology*, edited by Alexandra Y. Aikhenvald and R. M. W. Dixon. Oxford: Oxford University Press.

Aikhenvald, Alexandra Y. 2008. 'Multilingual imperatives: The elaboration of a category in north-west Amazonia', *International Journal of American Linguistics* 74: 189–225.

Aikhenvald, Alexandra Y. 2010. *Imperatives and commands*. Oxford: Oxford University Press.

Aikhenvald, Alexandra Y. 2012. *The languages of the Amazon*. Oxford: Oxford University Press.

Aikhenvald, Alexandra Y. 2014. 'On future in commands', pp. 205–18 of *Future tenses, future times*, edited by Mikhail Kissine et al. Oxford: Oxford University Press.

Aikhenvald, Alexandra Y. 2015. *The art of grammar: A practical guide*. Oxford: Oxford University Press.

Aikhenvald, Alexandra Y. 2016. 'Imperatives and commands in Manambu', *Oceanic Linguistics* 55: 639–73.

Aikhenvald, Alexandra Y. 2018. ' "Me", "us", and "others": Expressing the self in Arawak languages of South America', pp. 13–39 of *Expressing the self: Cultural diversity and cognitive universals*, edited by M. Huang and K. Jaszczolt. Oxford: Oxford University Press.

Aikhenvald, Alexandra Y. and Dixon, R. M. W. 1998. 'Dependencies between grammatical systems', *Language* 74: 56–80.

Aikhenvald, Alexandra Y. and Dixon, R. M. W. 2013. Editors of *Possession and ownership: A cross-linguistic typology*. Oxford: Oxford University Press.

Aikhenvald, Alexandra Y. and Storch, Anne. 2013. 'Perception and cognition in typological perspective', pp. 1–46 of *Perception and cognition in language and culture*, edited by Alexandra Y. Aikhenvald and Anne Storch. Leiden: Brill.

Ameka, Felix K. 2013. 'Possessive constructions in Likpe (Sɛkpɛlé)', pp. 224–42 of Aikhenvald and Dixon (eds).

Amha, Azeb. 2001. *The Maale language*. Leiden: CNWS.

Berghäll, Liisa. 2010. *Mauwake reference grammar*. University of Helsinki, Faculty of Arts.

Börjars, Kersti and Burridge, Kate. 2001. *Introducing English grammar*. London: Arnold.

Brown, Penelope and Levinson, Stephen C. 1987. *Politeness: Some universals in language usage*. Cambridge: Cambridge University Press.

Carlin, Eithne B. 2004. *A grammar of Trio, a Cariban language of Suriname*. Frankfurt am Main: Peter Lang.

Carlson, Robert. 1994. *A grammar of Supyire*. Berlin: Mouton de Gruyter.

Clark, Herbert, H. 1979. 'Responding to indirect speech acts', *Cognitive Psychology* 11: 430–77.

Comrie, Bernard. 1984. [Plenary session discussion], pp. 255–87 of *Interrogativity: A colloquium on the grammar, typology and pragmatics of questions in seven diverse languages*, edited by William S. Chisholm. Amsterdam: John Benjamins.

Contreras, L. 1960. 'Oraciones independientes introducidas por *si*', *Boletin de Filologia de la Universidad de Chile* 12: 273–90.

Cowell, Andrew. 2007. 'Arapaho imperatives: Indirectness, politeness and communal "face"', *Journal of Linguistic Anthropology* 17: 44–60.

Davies, E. 1986. *The English imperative*. London: Croom Helm.

Dench, Alan. 1991. 'Panyjima', pp. 125–244 of *The handbook of Australian languages*, Vol. 4, edited by R. M. W. Dixon and Barry J. Blake. Oxford: Oxford University Press.

Dench, Alan. 2009. 'The semantics of clause linking in Marthuthunira', pp. 261–84 of *Semantics of clause linking: A cross-linguistic typology*, edited by R. M. W. Dixon and A. Y. Aikhenvald. Oxford: Oxford University Press.

Dixon, R. M. W. 1972. *The Dyirbal language of North Queensland* (Cambridge Studies in Linguistics, 9). Cambridge: Cambridge University Press.

Dixon, R. M. W. 1977. *A grammar of Yidiɲ*. Cambridge: Cambridge University Press.

Dixon, R. M. W. 2002. *Australian languages: Their nature and development*. Cambridge: Cambridge University Press.

Dixon, R. M. W. 2004. *The Jarawara language of southern Amazonia*. Oxford: Oxford University Press.

Dixon, R. M. W. 2010. *Basic linguistic theory*, Vol. 2, *Grammatical topics*. Oxford: Oxford University Press.

Dobrushina, N. R. 1999. 'Forms of irrealis', pp. 262–8; 'Forms of imperative series', pp. 278–85 of *Elements of Tsakhur language in typological perspective*, edited by A. E. Kibrik with Ya. G. Testelec. Moscow: Nasledie.

Dobrushina, Nina and Goussev, Valentin. 2005. 'Inclusive imperative', pp. 179–211 of *Clusivity*, edited by Elena Filimonova. Amsterdam: John Benjamins.

Drew, Paul and Couper-Kuhlen, Elizabeth. 2014. 'Requesting—from speech act to recruitment', pp. 1–34 of *Requesting in social interaction*, edited by Paul Drew and Elizabeth Couper-Kuhlen. Amsterdam: John Benjamins.

Eather, Bronwyn. 2011. *A grammar of Nakkara (Central Arnhem Land coast)*. Munich: Lincom Europa.

Enfield, N. J. 2004. 'Ethnosyntax: introduction', pp. 3–30 of *Ethnosyntax: Explorations in grammar and culture*, edited by N. J. Enfield. Oxford: Oxford University Press.

Enfield, N. J. 2013. *Relationship thinking: Agency, enchrony, and human sociality*. Oxford: Oxford University Press.

Enfield, N. J. 2014. 'Human agency and the infrastructure for requests', pp. 36–53 of *Requesting in social interaction*, edited by Paul Drew and Elizabeth Couper-Kuhlen. Amsterdam: John Benjamins.

Enrico, John. 2003. *Haida Syntax*. 2 vols. Lincoln: University of Nebraska Press.

Erelt, Mati; Metslang, Helle; and Pajusalu, Karl. 2006. 'Tense and evidentiality in Estonian', *Belgian Journal of Linguistics* 20: 126–36.

Gaby, Alice. 2007. A grammar of Kuuk Thaayorre. PhD Thesis. University of Melbourne.

Genetti, Carol. 2007. *A grammar of Dolakha Newar*. Berlin: Mouton de Gruyter.

Goddard, C. 1983. A semantically-oriented grammar of the Yankunytjatjara dialect of the Western Desert language. PhD Dissertation. Australian National University.

Grice, Paul. 1989. *Studies in the way of words*. Cambridge, MA: Harvard University Press.

Gruzdeva, Ekaterina Yu. 2002. 'The linguistic consequences of Nivkh language attrition', *SKY Journal of Linguistics* 15: 85–103.

Haiman, J. 1980. *Hua: A Papuan language of the Eastern Highlands of New Guinea*. Amsterdam: John Benjamins.

Haiman, John. 2003. 'Iconicity', pp. 453–6 of *Encyclopedia of cognitive science*, edited by Lynn Nadel. London, New York, and Tokyo: Nature Publishing Group.

Heath, Jeffrey. 1981. *Basic materials in Mara: Grammar, texts and dictionary*. Canberra: Pacific Linguistics.

Heine, Bernd and Kuteva, Tania. 2003. 'On contact-induced grammaticalization', *Studies in Language* 27: 529–72.

Hill, Jane H. 2005. *A grammar of Cupeño*. Berkeley: University of California Press.

Huddleston, Rodney D. 2002. 'Clause type and illocutionary force', pp. 851–945 of *The Cambridge grammar of the English language*, chief authors Rodney D. Huddleston and Geoffrey K. Pullum. Cambridge: Cambridge University Press.

Jakobson, Roman O. 1971. 'Stroj ukrainskogo imperativa (Organization of the Ukrainian imperative)', pp. 190–7 of Vol. 2 of Jakobson's *Selected writings: Word and language*. The Hague and Paris: Mouton.

Jakobson, R. O. 1985. *N. S. Trubetzkoy's letters and notes*. Prepared for publication by Roman Jakobson. The Hague: Mouton.

Jary, Mark and Kissine, Mikhail. 2014. *Imperatives*. Cambridge: Cambridge University Press.

Jespersen, Otto. 1928. *A modern English grammar on historical principles*, Part III. Copenhagen: E. Munksgaard.

Jespersen, Otto. 1933. *Essentials of English grammar*. London: George Allen and Unwin.

Johnson, Allen. 2003. *Families of the forest: The Matsigenka Indians of the Peruvian Amazon*. Berkeley: University of California Press.

Kenesei, I.; Vago, R. M.; and Fenyvesi, A. 1998. *Hungarian*. London: Routledge.

Kimball, Geoffrey D. 1991. *Koasati grammar*. Lincoln: University of Nebraska Press.

King, Garreth. 1993. *Modern Welsh: A comprehensive grammar*. London: Routledge.

Kiparsky, Paul. 2005. 'The Vedic injunctive: Historical and synchronic implications', pp. 219–35 of *The yearbook of South Asian languages 2005*, edited by Rajendra Singh and Tanmoy Bhattacharya. New Delhi: Sage Publications.

Koehn, E. and Koehn, S. 1986. 'Apalai', pp. 33–127 of *Handbook of Amazonian languages*, Vol. 1, edited by D. C. Derbyshire and G. K. Pullum. Berlin: Mouton de Gruyter.

Kozintseva, N. A. 2001. 'Imperative sentences in Armenian', pp. 245–67 of *Typology of imperative constructions*, edited by V. S. Xrakovskij. Munich: Lincom Europa.

Kuryłowicz, J. 1964. *The inflectional categories of Indo-European*. Heidelberg: Carl Winter Universitätsverlag.

Larson, Mildred L. 1998. *A guide to cross-language equivalence*. Oxford: University Press of America.

Laughren, Mary. 2002. 'Syntactic constraints in a "free word order" language', pp. 83–130 of *Language universals and variation*, edited by Mengistu Amberber and Peter Collins. London: Prager.

Lehman, Christina. 1977. 'Imperatives', pp. 143–8 of *Haya grammatical structure. Southern California Occasional Papers in Linguistics* 6, edited by E. R. Byarushengo, A. Duranti, and L. M. Hyman.

Lockwood, W. B. 1969. *Indo-European philology*. London: Hutchinson University Library.

Lyons, John. 1977. *Semantics*, Vol. 2. Cambridge: Cambridge University Press.

Maiden, Martin and Robustelli, Cecilia. 2007. *A reference grammar of Modern Italian*. 2nd edition. New York: McGraw Hill.

Malygina, L. V. 2001. 'Imperative sentences in Modern Hebrew', pp. 268–86 of *Typology of imperative constructions*, edited by V. S. Xrakovskij. Munich: Lincom Europa.

Martin, Samuel E. 1975. *A reference grammar of Japanese*. Tokyo: Charles E. Tuttle Company.

Mead, M. 1935. *Sex and temperament in three primitive societies*. New York: Morrow.

Minter, P. 2009. *Iyo grammar essentials*. SIL Academic Publications.

Mithun, Marianne. 1999. *The languages of Native North America*. Cambridge: Cambridge University Press.

Nasilov, D. M.; Isxakova, X. F.; and Safarov, Sh. S. 2001. 'Imperative sentences in Turkic languages', pp. 181–220 of *Typology of imperative constructions*, edited by V. S. Xrakovskij. Munich: Lincom Europa.

Olawsky, K. 2006. *A grammar of Urarina*. Berlin: Mouton de Gruyter.

Pérez, R. Almela. 1985. 'El *si* introductor de oraciones independientes en español', *Lingüística Española Actual* 7: 5–13.

Press, Margaret. 1979. *Chemehuevi: A grammar and lexicon*. Berkeley: University of California Press.

Renck, G. L. 1975. *A grammar of Yagaria*. Canberra: Pacific Linguistics.

de Reuse, W. J. 2003. 'Evidentiality in Western Apache', pp. 79–100 of *Studies in evidentiality*, edited by A. Y. Aikhenvald and R. M. W. Dixon. Amsterdam: John Benjamins.

Rice, Keren. 1989. *A grammar of Slave*. Berlin: Mouton de Gruyter.

Roberts, John. 1987. *Amele*. London: Routledge.

Roberts, John. 1990. 'Modality in Amele and other Papuan languages', *Journal of Linguistics* 26: 363–401.

Rosaldo, M. Z. 1982. 'The things we do with words: Ilongot speech acts and speech act theory in philosophy', *Language in Society* 11: 203–37.

Rumsey, Alan. 2000. 'Bunuba', pp. 34–152 of *Handbook of Australian languages*, Vol. 5, edited by R. M. W. Dixon and Barry J. Blake. Melbourne: Oxford University Press.

Rumsey, Alan. 2003. 'Language, desire, and the ontogenesis of intersubjectivity', *Language and Communication* 23: 169–87.

Rumsey, Alan. 2015. 'Language, affect and the inculcation of social norms in the New Guinea Highlands and beyond', *The Australian Journal of Anthropology* 26: 349–65.

Saeed, John I. 1993. *Somali reference grammar*. Kensington: Dunwoody Press.

Schmerling, Susan F. 1975. 'Imperative subject deletion and some related matters', *Linguistic Inquiry* 6: 501–11.

Schmidt, Annette. 1985. *Young People's Dyirbal: An example of language death from Australia*. Cambridge: Cambridge University Press.

Searle, J. R. 1976. 'The classification of illocutionary acts', *Language in Society* 5(1): 1–23.

Searle, J. R. 1994 [1969]. *Speech acts: An essay in the philosophy of language*. Cambridge: Cambridge University Press.

Sharp, Janet K. 2004. *A grammar of Nyangumarta*. Canberra: Pacific Linguistics.

Slotta, James. 2015. 'The perlocutionary is political: Listening as self-determination in a Papua New Guinean polity', *Language in Society* 44: 525–52.

Smith, Janet S. 1992. 'Women in charge: Politeness and directives in the speech of Japanese women', *Language in Society* 21: 59–82.

Sohn, Ho-Min. 1994. *Korean*. London and New York: Routledge.

Stirling, Lesley. 1998. 'Isolated *if*-clauses in Australian English', pp. 273–94 of *The clause in English: In honour of Rodney Huddleston*, edited by P. Collins and D. Lee. Amsterdam: John Benjamins.

Takahashi, Hidemitsu. 2000. 'English imperatives and passives', pp. 239–58 of *Constructions in cognitive linguistics*, edited by Ad Foolen and Frederike van der Leek. Amsterdam: John Benjamins.

Valentine, J. Randolph. 2001. *Nishnaabemwin reference grammar*. Toronto: University of Toronto Press.

van der Auwera, Johan. 2006. 'Why languages prefer prohibitives', *Journal of Foreign Languages* 1: 1–25.

Vaxtin, N. B. 2001. 'Imperative sentences in Asiatic Eskimo', pp. 129–44 of *Typology of imperative constructions*, edited by V. S. Xrakovskij. Munich: Lincom Europa.

Vinogradov, V. V. 1947. *Russkij Jazyk* (The Russian language). Moscow: Uchpedgiz.

Waltereit, Richard. 2002. 'Imperatives, interruption in conversation, and the rise of discourse markers: A study of Italian *guarda*', *Linguistics* 40: 987–1010.

Weber, D. J. 1989. *A grammar of Huallaga (Huánuco) Quechua*. Berkeley: University of California Press.

Weizman, Elda. 1993. 'Interlanguage requestive hints', pp. 123–37 of *Interlanguage pragmatics*, edited by Gabriele Kasper and Shishana Blum-Kulka. New York: Oxford University Press.

Whaley, L. J. 1997. *Introduction to typology: The unity and diversity of language*. London: Sage Publications.

Xrakovskij, Victor S. (ed.) 1992a. *Tipologija imperativnyh konstrukcij* (The typology of imperative constructions). St Petersburg: Nauka.

Xrakovskij, Victor S. 1992b. 'Typological questionnaire for the description of imperative constructions', pp. 50–4 of *Tipologija imperativnyh konstrukcij* (The typology of imperative constructions), edited by V. S. Xrakovskij. St Petersburg: Nauka.

Xrakovskij, Victor S. (ed.) 2001. *Typology of imperative constructions*. Munich: Lincom Europa.

Zaugg-Coretti, Silvia. 2009. The verbal system of Yemsa. PhD Thesis. University of Zürich.

2

Imperatives and commands in Quechua

WILLEM F. H. ADELAAR

1 Preliminary information on Quechua

Quechua is the denomination of a family of closely related linguistic varieties that are distributed over large areas in western South America and which are spoken, in order of numerical importance, in Peru, Bolivia, Ecuador, Argentina, and Colombia. Local varieties of Quechua are traditionally referred to as 'dialects' (Spanish *dialectos*), a term which is inappropriate for several reasons. It denotes an expression of the low prestige generally accorded to Quechua by users of the national language (Spanish), and it underscores the difficulty of subdividing this language group into individual languages due to the diffuseness of the boundaries that obtain between its different varieties. The internal linguistic diversity of Quechua is characterized by a mix of gradual transitions ('dialect chains' following the definition in Kaufman 1990) and more or less abrupt divisions attributable to historical splits. Quechua varieties also differ in the amount of contact they have undergone with non-Quechuan languages. There is no universally recognized Quechua standard language, but at least for one variety, Cuzco Quechua, a status of 'correctness' and 'authenticity' has been claimed that may be motivated on historical, but not on linguistic, grounds. The internal diversity of the Quechua language family holds evidence of an initial binary split that may have occurred before AD 500, the approximate date of formation of the Wari state in south-central Peru, suggesting an even earlier date for the Quechua proto-language (Adelaar 2012a, 2012b). The branches resulting from this bifurcation were denominated Quechua I (located in north-central Peru) and Quechua II (all the remaining varieties) in Torero's classification (1964).[1] All Quechua varieties without

---

[1] In Parker's (1963) classification these groups were denominated Quechua B and Quechua A, respectively. Torero's terminology is more generally used at present.

Commands. First edition. Alexandra Y. Aikhenvald and R. M. W. Dixon (eds)
This chapter © Willem F. H. Adelaar 2017. First published 2017 by Oxford University Press

exception present evidence of a strong Aymaran substrate, which apparently had a formative effect on Proto-Quechua.

(a) General features of Quechua structure and morpho-syntax

The structure of Quechua is predominantly agglutinating and is characterized by extensive suffixation. Prefixes do not occur at all. Reduplication is frequent in expressive language. Every category of expression (including questions, commands, exclamations, etc.) as well as the articulation of discourse in sentences is covered by affixes, leaving practically no functional space for intonation. In addition, there is also a small amount of fusion as portmanteau affixes are frequently used in verbal inflection. Furthermore, rules of vowel modification may affect the shape of affixes when they occur in a sequence. Formal irregularities in the morphology are rare, but semantic idiosyncrasies (that is, unpredictable meanings of derivational affixes used in combination with specific verbal roots) are common.

The preferred constituent order is verb-final AOV/SV. This order is not always respected, but it is required in non-finite clauses. As a rule, modifiers precede their heads. Exceptions to this rule are relative clauses which contain a nominalized predicate. They can be located after their antecedent in many Quechua varieties. Case affixes and clitics that would follow the antecedent if there were no relative clause are then attached to the nominalized predicate instead.

(b) Word classes

Verbs and nominals are characterized by distinct morphologies as well as by the shape of their roots. Verbal roots must end in a vowel and are always followed by at least one affix, or if not, are affected by lengthening of their final vowel (only in Quechua I). For most nominals there are no restrictions of this kind. Nominalization (of verbs) and verbalization (of nouns and adjectives) are frequent and play a central role in Quechua morpho-syntax. In addition, there are also ambivalent roots that can function as free nouns and as verb roots at the same time.

Verbs constitute an open class, but the nominal class can be divided into subclasses which are either open (nouns, adjectives) or closed (numerals, personal pronouns, demonstratives, interrogatives, indefinites, etc.). Adjectives can be analysed as a subclass of the nominals with specific morpho-syntactic properties. As an open subclass they can accommodate borrowings. Some adjective-like expressions are verbal in nature, especially terms referring to taste and other sensory categories. Unlike the more common nominal adjectives, they are not accompanied by the copula *ka-* 'to be' but verbalized by morphological means instead. All Quechua varieties also have a set of adverbs of heterogeneous origin and some grammatical words of limited morphological valency (particles).

In the Quechua personal reference system, verbal subject markers and nominal possessive markers are similar in form, though not entirely identical. The lexically free personal pronouns stand out in that they are not formally related to any of these personal reference markers.

(c) Grammatical categories for open classes

Nouns can be marked for person-of-possessor, number (unmarked or plural), and case. In addition there are affixes referring to ownership ('having/not-having') and, in some varieties, degree (mainly with adjectives).

The inflection of finite verbs is organized in three different moods: Indicative (neutral), Potential (also referred to as the 'Conditional'), and Imperative. There is also a fourth, Subordinative mood which includes non-finite verbs that are subject to switch-reference distinctions (same subject versus different subjects).

Verbs in all moods, as well as nominalized verbs, occur with personal reference markers that identify both the subject and, when relevant, a human or humanized object (either direct or indirect). Object marking is just as obligatory as subject marking in that case. It can be complemented but not replaced with a lexical expression outside the verb form. Non-SAP objects are not expressed morphologically. Conservative Quechua varieties, as the ones illustrated in this chapter, use a four-person system consisting of Speaker (1), Addressee (2), non-SAP (3), and Speaker + Addressee (4). The last category may coincide with first person plural inclusive in a cross-linguistic perspective but is often referred to as the 'fourth person' in the Quechuanist descriptive tradition, so as to highlight its status as a separate, non-derived term of the Quechua personal reference system (cf. Dixon 2012, vol. 2: 203–5, for the polysemy of the term 'fourth person'). This system did not include number in its original form, but most Quechua varieties have developed elaborate number marking which can apply to the subject, as well as to the object. Number marking varies considerably between the Quechua varieties and is evidently of recent origin.

Tense distinctions are semantically well defined and elaborate (between five and eight tenses according to variety). They are limited to the Indicative and, to a lesser extent, the Potential mood, which has only two tenses (Present and Past). Habitual Past, Perfect and Mirative (Sudden Discovery) are treated as Indicative tenses. As we shall see, Imperative tense (Present versus Future) is a matter of debate. Nominalized verbs are subject to a relative tense distinction (Realized versus Prospective).

Aspect is formally and functionally separate from tense and can combine with any tense, mood, or nominalization. Quechua I varieties have developed structured aspect systems including mutually exclusive categories such as Progressive and Perfective. Further non-derivational categories are Speaker-orientation ('Ventive' or 'hither', etc.), Limitative ('Diminutive'), and Beneficiary. Non-derivational verbal morphology is not used for the creation of new lexical items.

Finally, verbal derivation comprises a large amount of affixes with multiple and heterogeneous functions (different types of valency-change, reflexive and reciprocal, state and continuation, assisted action, space and direction, movement back and forth, multiple objects, repetition, conative, inceptive, interrupted action, non-control, different sorts of pragmatic usage, etc.). As indicated before, idiomatic fusion of verbal roots with derivational affixes is frequent and an important source of lexical innovation in Quechua.

(d) Grammatical categories for all classes

All Quechua varieties have a set of sentential or independent affixes, often referred to as 'clitics'. They behave like affixes from a phonological point of view and can be attached to the final element in a sentence constituent regardless of its word-class. They may indicate validation (Evidentials), interrogation, negation, topic, contrast, sequence, inclusion ('also', 'even'), completion ('already'), and anticipation ('still').

There are also some true clitics which play a role in recently identified cases of shared knowledge interaction between speaker and addressee (Hintz and Hintz 2017). Clitics are also used for emphasis, in tag questions, pleas for corroboration, etc.

(e) Transitivity classes of verbs

Quechua has a nominative-accusative structure. It has no ergative features whatsoever. Whereas subjects remain unmarked, direct objects are obligatorily marked for Accusative case, except when immediately preceding a nominalized verb. Quechua verbs appear to be insensitive to the transitive/intransitive distinction, as none of the usual morpho-syntactic criteria necessary for establishing such a distinction seems to work. Many non-derived verbs can have both transitive (S = A) and intransitive (S = O) interpretations without any formal distinction (cf. English 'to break', 'to turn'). In transitive constructions there is no formal difference between verbs with a non-SAP object and verbs with non-identified or irrelevant objects (antipassive interpretation). In line with the limited function of the transitivity parameter, there is no morphological passive, nor any syntactic construction fulfilling that role.[2] Morphological derivations including those that commonly function as transitivizers (Causative, Applicative) can be applied to any verb regardless of its inherent transitivity status.

(f) Marking of grammatical relations

Grammatical relations are marked by nominal Case, attached at the end of a noun phrase. Only subjects, nominal complements of a copula verb, and direct objects or goals that immediately precede a nominalized verb are not marked for Case. The

---

[2] As is the case with most features of Quechua structure, the reduced status of the (in)transitivity distinction is shared with the Aymaran languages (cf. Cerrón-Palomino 2008).

function and semantic interpretation of case markers are straightforward and pre-dictable. Stacking of case markers is common, and several of them appear to have originated from combinations of other case markers.

(g) Clause types

Only main clauses can contain a finite verb. As a rule, copula verbs with a non-SAP subject are omitted unless they contain relevant morphology that cannot be expressed otherwise. When copula verbs are omitted, the predicate consists of the nominal complement alone.

Subordinate clauses are formed on the basis of non-finite verbs in the Subordinative mood and may function as con-verbs, temporal or causal clauses. Clauses constructed with a nominalized verb, followed or not by a case marker, are frequent. Most relative clauses belong to this category.

2 Nature of the sources

The data presented in this chapter were selected from varieties of each of the two main Quechua branches that are spoken in the Andes of Central Peru. North Junín Quechua (or *Yaru*), a Quechua I variety, is taken as the point of departure for the presentation of the data. Most examples are from Tarma Quechua, a sub-variety of North Junín Quechua. When relevant, data from other Central Peruvian varieties (QI Ancash, QI Huancayo, QI Pacaraos, and QII Ayacucho) are included. All these varieties are conservative and exhibit roughly the prototypical structure of the Quechua family by default of relevant innovations. The data are from the author's fieldwork in the 1970s and 1980s on North Junín (Tarma) and Pacaraos Quechua (Adelaar 1977, 1987), and from published literature on other varieties: Cerrón-Palomino (1976) on Huancayo, Parker (1976) on Ancash, and Soto Ruiz (1979) on Ayacucho Quechua.

3 Expression of imperatives

For the expression of commands Quechua has a dedicated Imperative mood with basic forms for 2nd, 3rd, and 4th person subject, as shown in Table 1.

TABLE 1. **Basic forms of the Imperative in Quechua**

1st	——	——	
2nd	-y	*rima-y*	'speak!'
3rd	-čun	*rima-čun*	'let him/her speak!'
4th	-šun	*rima-šun*	'let us speak!'

TABLE 2. Complex pronominal forms of the Imperative in Quechua

2nd > 1st	-ma-y	*maqa-ma-y*	'beat me!'
3rd > 1st	-ma:-čun	*maqa-ma:-čun*	'let him/her beat me!'
3rd > 4th	-ma:-šun	*maqa-ma:-šun*	'let him/her beat us!'
3rd > 2nd	-šu-nki	*maqa-šu-nki*	'let him/her beat you!'

In the early literature on Quechua the non-canonical 3rd person form *-čun* was not immediately recognized as part of the Imperative mood. It contains an element *-n*, which is identical in form to the Present tense ending for 3rd person subject. Parker (1969: 30), for instance, did not incorporate *-čun* in the Imperative paradigm but interpreted the element *-ču-* as an Injunctive suffix with a limited distribution.

The 4th person (first person plural inclusive) Imperative form is identical to the 4th person Future tense form. Its parallel interpretation as an imperative was recognized at a relatively early stage.

The 2nd person form *-y* is identical to the ending of the Infinitive nominalization (as in *rima-y* 'to speak'). Chances of confusion are scarce due to contextual information and the presence of affixes pertaining to nominal morphology, because Infinitives behave like nouns. A historical relation between the Imperative and Infinitive endings cannot be excluded but remains highly speculative as it would take us beyond the stage of Proto-Quechua.

The affix *-y* is also a marker for 1st person subject in the Quechua II dialects. This affix is now restricted to positions in the paradigms in which ambiguity with the Imperative is excluded. In other environments, it has been replaced by a suffix *-ni*.

As shown in Table 2, the Imperative paradigm has further forms that in addition to the subject encode a SAP object. Three of these forms, 2nd > 1st, 3rd > 1st, and 3rd > 4th, contain the element *-ma(:)-* (primary meaning 1st person object). In most dialects there is no dedicated ending for 3rd > 2nd imperative. The ending *-šu-nki* is the same as the one used for Present Tense and Future.[3]

4 Imperative and Future tense

In order to establish the independent character of the Imperative it is necessary to also look at the Future tense paradigm (Table 3). There is a considerable overlap between the two paradigms. The use of Future tense is obligatory for any statement referring to an event expected to occur after the moment of speaking.

---

[3] In Ancash Quechua (QI) the 3rd > 2nd imperative ending has been restructured to *-šu-y* (Parker 1976).

TABLE 3. Quechua Future tense paradigm

	Future tense	Imperative
1st	-šaq	——
2nd	-nki	-y
3rd	-nqa	-čun
4th	-šun	-šun
1st > 2nd	-šay(ki)[a]	——
2nd > 1st	-ma-nki	-ma-y
3rd > 1st	-ma-nqa	-ma:-čun
3rd > 2nd	-šu-nki	-šu-nki
3rd > 4th	-ma:-šun	-ma:-šun

[a] In North Junín Quechua the element -*ki* of the ending -*šay(ki)* is optionally present in word-final position and silent elsewhere. When -*ki* is not pronounced in word-final position the ending is realized as -*šáy* with stress on the final syllable. Normally, stress is located on the penultimate syllable.

Already in early colonial sources (Gonzales Holguín 1607: 85) Future tense was recognized as a delayed alternative for the plain Imperative, a 'Future imperative', and it is still frequently used with that function. Nevertheless, Future tense forms can also occur in questions, and they combine freely with affixes of the Validator or Evidential set -*m(i)* (Assertive), -*š(i)* (Reportative), and -*ĉ(i)* (Conjectural), in particular, with the Assertive marker -*m(i)*, which in this case denotes conviction or certainty rather than any evidential meaning. Imperative forms do not occur in questions and do not take validators. Accordingly, one may assume that the use of Validators/Evidentials would also be blocked with Future tense forms that are used in commands, but that is *not* the case. The Assertive Validator can be used in connection with Future tense forms denoting command, as in (2) and (3).

(1) aywa-mu-nki   čay-ĉu   lapa-nči mika-paku-na-nči-pa   (NJQ)
     go-VEN-2S:FUT that-LOC all-4POSS eat-SB-NOMZ-4S-BEN
     You must come so that we can all have something to eat there!

(2) ama-*m*   maqa-wa-nki-ĉu-qa   tayta   (AQ)
     NEG-VAL beat-1O-2S:FUT-NEG-CONTR sir
     But you are not going to hit me, sir! (Don't you dare!)   (Soto Ruiz 1979: 331)

(3) supay-pa waĉa-sqa-n   ĉutu, ama-*m* nʸuqa-ta-qa (Soto Ruiz 1979: 331)
     devil-GEN give.birth-NOMZ-3POSS EXPL NEG-ASS me-ACC-TOP
     kuti-pa-wa-nki-ĉu
     return-APPLIC-1O-2S:FUT-NEG
     !!!EXPLETIVE!!! born from the Devil! You are not going to talk back to me!

It may be tempting to further assign Imperative status to the 1st person subject Future forms that are missing from the Imperative paradigm, considering the overlap in the rest of the paradigm, but there is no evidence that these 1st person forms occur in the typical Imperative environments in which the use of Validators/Evidentials is excluded. This is a good reason not to consider them as possible Imperatives (although further research is needed).

5 Negative commands

Negation is expressed at the sentence level by the combination of a negative adverb (*mana, ama*) and the sentential affix *-ču*. In negative statements and commands the sentential affix cannot be attached to the negative adverb itself, as its location reflects the scope of the negation. In subordinate clauses, nominalized clauses, and other units below the sentence level the same negative adverbs are used without the affix *-ču*. As a rule, *mana* is found in declarative statements, whereas *ama* is used for negative commands, suggestions, exhortations, admonitions, intentions, etc.

(4) mana-m mayla-ku-nki-ču   (NJQ)
     NEG-VAL wash-REFL-2S:FUT-NEG
     You will not wash yourself.

(5) ama   rima-pa-y-ču   (NJQ)
     PROHIB speak-APPLIC-2S.IMP-NEG
     Do not talk to him!

(6) ama-m   huk-huk-ta-qa   aw ni-nki-ču   (TQ)
     PROHIB-VAL one-one-ACC-TOP yes say-2S:FUT-NEG
     You should not say 'yes' to everyone.

As can be seen in (6), the use of *ama* is *not* incompatible with the Assertive validator *-m(i)*.

6 Prohibitive adverb *ama*

In negative commands constructed with the Imperative the prohibitive adverb *ama* is the only option ((5), (7)); *mana* is excluded.

(7) ama   lagi.ku-čun-ču   (TQ)
     PROHIB worry-3S:IMP-NEG
     He/she should not worry!' (Let him/her not worry!)

Reversely, the difference in use between *ama* and *mana* does not coincide with the boundary between negative commands and statements. *Ama* can be used in any construction that denotes an overtone of suggestion, recommendation, admonition, reproach, etc. In this way, the choice of the prohibitive adverb adds an extra dimension which makes it possible to introduce notions of command in non-imperative contexts. In (8) a prohibition is expressed by means of the Past Potential (irrealis) and in (9) a Future tense is used.

(8) ama wila-nki-man-ču ga-ra   (TQ)
     PROHIB warn-2S-POT-NEG be-PAST:3S
     You should not have warned him.

(9) ama aywa-šaq-ču ni-:-mi   (TQ)
     PROHIB go-1S:FUT-NEG say-1S-VAL
     I think I should rather not go. (I say I would better not go.)

(10) ama kaču-su-na-yki-paq tanta-ta qu-nki alʸqu-man   (AQ)
     PROHIB bite-INV-NOMZ-2S-BEN bread-ACC give-2S:FUT dog-ALL
     You will/must give bread to the dog so that it would not bite you.
                                                        (Soto Ruiz 1979)

The prohibitive adverb *ama* is also found in the expression:

(11) ama čay-nuy-qa ka-la-y-ču   (NJQ)
     PROHIB that-SEMB-TOP be-DIM-2S:IMP-NEG
     Don't be like that! (Don't be so mean!)

The expression in (11) corresponds to Andean Spanish *¡no seas así!* by which an asker seeks to anticipate an expected refusal by his addressee. The parallel expression in Ayacucho Quechua is *ama hina ka-y-ču* 'don't be like that!' It can be transposed into a subordinate clause *ama hina ka-spa* or *ama hina ka-spa-yki* ('(you) not please being so mean'), which has acquired the general meaning of 'please!', 'I beg you'. In this way the prohibitive adverb has come to modify a non-finite subordinate verb. Example (12) shows that *ama* retains its illocutionary effect even in such a reduced syntactic environment.

(12) ama   hina ka-spa   haywa-yka-mu-wa-y   (AQ)
     PROHIB thus be-SUBORD:ss   hand.over-ATT-VEN-1O-2S:IMP
     waqta-yki-pi   ka-q qata-ta
     side-2POSS-LOC be-AG blanket-ACC
     'Please hand me the blanket that is beside you!'   (Soto Ruiz 1979)

7 The copula construction in an imperative environment

Within a copula construction (Nominal complement + *ka-* 'to be'), the Nominal complement comes first and hosts the sentential affixes if any. The Copula verb 'to be', if expressed at all, does not take any sentential affixes. This state of affairs holds for all non-imperative finite environments. However, in Imperative clauses, the Copula verb is always expressed and does receive the sentential affixes if any. As a rule, none of the latter remains on the Nominal complement (for a rare exception see (11)). This divergent behaviour of the copula construction in Imperative utterances suggests that the Imperative endows the verb 'to be' with a more active and more deliberate meaning than it has in non-imperative sentences.

(13) mana-m suwa-ču ka-nki   (NJQ constructed example)
      NEG-VAL thief-NEG be-2S
      You are not a thief.

(14) ama suwa ka-y-ču   (NJQ constructed example)
      NEG thief be-2S:IMP-NEG
      Don't be a thief!

8 Grammatical categories of imperatives

The Imperative mood in Quechua is compatible with categories of Aspect and Number as any other mood. There are no restrictions that are specific for the Imperative. Nevertheless, there may be some semantic effects associated with Aspect. For instance, the presence of a Perfective Aspect marker -*ru*- may imply rudeness because it incites the addressee to hurry up.[4] Also in the imperative context, the presence of a Progressive Aspect marker is an invitation to carry on with an action already begun or to start an action before the speaker is able to join it. Some Quechua dialects (Cajamarca, Huancayo) have different Progressive Aspect markers in order to distinguish between continued action and anticipated action.

As we have seen, the Imperative mood is incompatible with Tense and Evidentiality. The only possible tense distinction is related to the use of Future tense in lieu of Imperative (see §4), in which case the Imperative mood would function as an immediate imperative and Future tense as a delayed imperative. As we have seen, it is not certain that such Future tense forms can be analysed as Imperatives. Evidential markers are typically absent from Imperative clauses but not from Future tense expressions with an imperative connotation. Other sentential affixes combine with the Imperative without any problem.

Quechua has no gender, nor voice distinctions. The interference with Imperative is null. However, one verbal derivational category, Non-control -*ka(:)*-, refers explicitly to actions performed outside one's own will (e.g. *iški-ka(:)*- 'to lose one's balance and fall', from *iški*- 'to fall'). A combination with the Imperative seems unlikely, although specific research is needed to corroborate this.

---

[4] By contrast, Cerrón-Palomino (1976: 180, 205) reports that the presence of a Perfective Aspect marker, *eductivo* ('Outward motion') in the author's terminology, can indicate urgency but also produce an attenuating effect in Huancayo Quechua (QI). Of course, it may be that the secondary effects of the Aspect/Imperative combination differ from region to region. Further research is evidently needed.

In a similar way it is unlikely that the Imperative would be combined with the subclass of verbal adjectives that refer to permanent material qualities (*pučqu-* 'to be sour', *aya-* 'to be spicy', etc.) and other verbs referring to permanent material qualities. A 2s Imperative cannot be combined with impersonal verbs, such as those referring to weather conditions (*tamya-* 'to rain', *rašta-*, *rawu-* 'to snow', etc.), although this may have been different in pre-Hispanic times.

9 Politeness

The impact of an Imperative command in North Junín Quechua can be attenuated by the use of specific verbal derivational affixes. The suffix *-rku-/-rgu-* primarily functions as a Directional affix indicating 'Upward motion'. In addition, it has developed a secondary function as a social enabler. By using it the speaker asks for the addressee's permission or consent and, if possible, his active participation. Hence the Spanish translation 'con (su) permiso'. Another Directional affix *-y(k)u-* 'Inward motion' has acquired a secondary function as a plea for attention in requests. Both are frequently used in Imperatives, but not exclusively.

(15) upya-ku-rgu-šun   (TQ)
      drink-REFL-SE-4S:IMP
      Let us have a drink together! (If you feel like it.)

(16) šayu-yu-y   (TQ)
      stop-ATT-2S:IMP
      Please stop for a moment!

Another derivational affix frequently used in Imperative commands is the Conative *-ĉa:ri-*.

(17) rima-ĉa:ri-y   (NJQ)
      speak-CON-2S:IMP
      Talk to him! (Why don't you try?)

The Conative is frequently used with the pre-imperative element *ma(:)* (see below).

10 Pre-imperatives

The element *ma:* (QI) or *ma* (QII) is probably found in all Quechua varieties. It introduces commands, although not exclusively. It denotes a strong incitation to perform an action, sometimes with the connotation of an experiment (English 'come on!' 'let us see!'), but its use is not necessarily impolite.

(18) ma: šargu-rgu-r kanan wila-ba:-ma-y yaĉa-či-nqa-q-ta   (TQ)
      come.on! stand-SEQ-SUBORD:SS now tell-APPLIC-1O-2S:IMP learn-CAUS-NOMZ-
      1S:2O-ACC
      Come on, stand up and now tell me what I have taught you!

Example (18) also shows how a series of actions in a command is encoded. Only the main verb is in the Imperative form in this case, whereas the subordinate one has the shape of a con-verb.

11 Special imperatives

Another ubiquitous element associated with Imperatives is *aku* (~*akuči, akuču*) (Ayacucho Quechua *haku*). It represents an exhortation to get moving (Spanish *¡vamos!*). *Aku* can be used alone or as a substitute for an Imperative verb of motion in the 4th person (1st person Inclusive), followed by an Agentive (nominalized) verb that indicates the purpose of the motion.

(19) aku   urya-q   (NJQ)
      let.us.go work-AG
      Let us go work!

In Ayacucho Quechua and other southern Peruvian varieties it is also frequently followed by a finite verb in the 4th person Imperative.

(20) haku   ripu-sun   (AQ)
      let.us.go go.away-4S:IMP
      Come on, let us go away (for good)!

12 Postverbal clitics

The effect of an Imperative can be strengthened or attenuated by the addition of clitics at the end of the Imperative form. Such clitics may indicate an emotional involvement of the speaker or refer to interpersonal interaction (shared knowledge). They usually exhibit a divergent stress pattern. It is a domain that has only recently begun to be investigated for the Ancash varieties of Quechua (Hintz and Hintz 2017). Quechua dialects vary widely in the clitics they use, and these are seldom restricted to the Imperative. North Junín Quechua uses a clitic *ar* with Imperatives. It denotes resignation or reassurance.

(21) urya-y=ár   muna-r-q[a]=ár   o sino: ama-si   (TQ)
      work-2S:IMP=RESIG want-SUBORD:SS-TOP=RESIG or otherwise PROHIB-ADD
      Work if you want, or else you don't!

Pacaraos Quechua, an archaic Quechua I dialect, frequently uses an emphatic clitic *a:* attached to the Imperative form. It is not exclusive for imperative commands.

(22) rima-šun=a: yača.ku-y=á: (PQ)
      speak-4S:IMP=EMPH learn-2S:IMP=EMPH
      Let us talk! Learn!

13 Imperative in quotations

Imperatives are frequently used in direct discourse.

(23) kasara:-šun   ni-r   inga:n^{y}u-ta rura-ru-ra   (NJQ)
       marry-4S:IMP say-SUBORD:SS deceit-ACC   do-PERF-PAST:3S
       Saying 'let us get married!' he cheated them.

14 Vocatives

A dedicated Vocative is found with nouns referring to close kin and persons of
respect in southern Peruvian Quechua (including Ayacucho). It consists in the
addition of an affix -*y* with stress assignment to the preceding vowel. If the word
ends in a consonant the vowel preceding that consonant becomes stressed, e.g. in
mamáy 'mother! Madam!' and *sen^{y}ór* 'Sir!'

15 Imperative strategies

Quechua has several strategies to express commands without having recourse to the
dedicated Imperative. We can only cite a few examples. A common strategy is the use
of the Present Potential, usually in combination with a Perfective Aspect marker in
order to enhance the element of threat.

(24) supay=aba-ru-nki-man[5]   (TQ)
       devil=carry-PERF-2S-POT
       May the Devil carry you away! (May you rot in Hell!)

An apprehensive construction in Quechua is expressed by the same technique, except
that the Potential form is followed by a sentential suffix -*taq*, which in other
environments indicates a contrast between parallel sequences (among other things).
Despite the intention of a negative admonition proper to this construction no
grammatical negation is involved at all.

(25) yata-ru-nki-man-taq   (NJQ)
       touch-PERF-2S-POT-CONTR
       Be careful not to touch it!

A deontic construction involving the Future (non-realized) nominalization in -*na*
provides the speaker with still another way to express a command, as can be seen in
the following example from Pacaraos Quechua.

---

[5] The expression *supay=aba-* ('devil-carry') is a rare case of a compound verb. Its common interpretation is 'to be carried away by the Devil', 'to rot in Hell'.

(26) kicwa-kta-m   rima-*na*   (PQ)
     Quechua-ACC-VAL speak-FUT:NOMZ
     One has to speak Quechua!' (Spanish *¡Hay que hablar quechua!*)

16 A final word

The function of command and prohibition in Quechua is covered by a dedicated Imperative mood, which cannot be combined with sentential affixes referring to validation and evidentiality. Competing verbal categories, such as Potential mood and Future tense, can be used in contexts that imply a command but they lack the typical imperative properties that exclude validation and evidentiality. A remarkable role is reserved for the Prohibitive adverb *ama*, which operates as a lexical instrument introducing a connotation of command in syntactic environments that are not otherwise associated with the Imperative.

Acknowledgements

The research leading to this chapter has received funding from the Australian Research Council and from the European Research Council under the European Union's Seventh Framework Programme (FP7/2007–2013) / ERC grant agreement no. 295918.

References

Adelaar, Willem F. H. 1977. *Tarma Quechua: Grammar, texts, dictionary.* Lisse: Peter de Ridder Press.

Adelaar, Willem F. H. 1987. *Morfología del quechua de Pacaraos.* Lima: Universidad Nacional Mayor de San Marcos, Facultad de Letras y Ciencias Humanas.

Adelaar, Willem F. H. 2012a. 'Modeling convergence: Towards a reconstruction of the history of Quechuan–Aymaran interaction' *Lingua*, 122(5): 461–9.

Adelaar, Willem F. H. 2012b. 'Cajamarca Quechua and the expansion of the Huari state', pp. 197–217 of *Archaeology and Language in the Andes: A cross-disciplinary exploration of prehistory*, edited by Paul Heggarty and David Beresford-Jones. *Proceedings of the British Academy*, Vol. 173. Oxford and New York: Oxford University Press.

Cerrón-Palomino, Rodolfo M. 1976. *Gramática Quechua Junín-Huanca.* Lima: Instituto de Estudios Peruanos.

Cerrón-Palomino, Rodolfo M. 2008. *Quechumara: Estructuras paralelas del quechua y del aimara.* La Paz: Universidad Mayor de San Simón, ProeibANDES and Plural editors.

Dixon, R. M. W. 2012. *Basic linguistic theory: Further grammatical topics.* Oxford: Oxford University Press.

Gonzales Holguín, Diego. 1607. *Gramática y arte nueva de la lengua general de todo el Perú llamada lengua qquichua o lengua del Inca.* Lima: Francisco del Canto.

Hintz, Daniel J. and Hintz, Diane M. 2017. 'The evidential category of mutual knowledge in Quechua', *Lingua* 186–7: 88–109.

Kaufman, Terrence S. 1990. 'Language history in South America: What we know and how to know more', pp. 13–73 of *Amazonian Linguistics: Studies in lowland South American languages*. Austin: University of Texas Press.

Parker, Gary J. 1963. 'La clasificación genética de los dialectos quechuas', *Revista del Museo nacional* (Lima) 32: 241–52.

Parker, Gary J. 1969. *Ayacucho Quechua grammar and dictionary*. The Hague and Paris: Mouton.

Parker, Gary J. 1976. *Gramática quechua Ancash-Huailas*. Lima: Ministerio de Educación and Instituto de Estudios Peruanos.

Soto Ruiz, Clodoaldo. 1979. *Quechua, manual de enseñanza*. Lima: Instituto de Estudios Peruanos.

Torero, Alfredo. 1964. 'Los dialectos quechuas', *Anales científicos de la Universidad Agraria de La Molina* (Lima) 6(3–4): 291–316.

3

The grammatical representation of commands and prohibitions in Aguaruna

SIMON E. OVERALL

1 Introduction

This chapter describes the formation of commands and prohibitions in Aguaruna. Aguaruna is a Chicham (formerly known as Jivaroan[1]) language spoken in north Peru; it is known to its speakers as *iiniá chicham*, and the official name of the language in Peru is *awajún*. Ethnic Aguaruna people numbered about 55,000 in the most recent census (INEI 2009); there is no data on speaker numbers, but my informal observation is that there is near complete overlap between ethnic Aguaruna and speakers of the language. The other four recognized Chicham languages are Huambisa or Wampis; Shuar; Shiwiar; and Achuar. All are spoken in the area of the border between Peru and Ecuador, in an area stretching from the eastern foothills of the Andes down to the Amazon lowlands. The languages are very closely related and largely mutually intelligible, and there is no known genetic link between Chicham and any other language family.

Commands and prohibitions fall under a general category of speech acts labelled directives, following Searle (1979), who defines them: '[t]he illocutionary point of these [directives] consists in the fact that they are attempts...by the speaker to get the hearer to do something' (Searle 1979: 13). Searle's characterization of directives is extralinguistic, referring to the dynamics of interpersonal manipulation; the question of how directives are encoded within the grammar of a language is a linguistic one. The formal constructions that are used to command and prohibit form the category

---

[1] The language family has traditionally been called Jivaroan, but the term *jívaro* is an ethnic slur in Ecuador; consequently the name Chicham (meaning 'language' in all members of the family) was proposed by Katan Jua (2011) and has become more widely used among linguists.

Commands. First edition. Alexandra Y. Aikhenvald and R. M. W. Dixon (eds)

of imperative mood (Aikhenvald 2010: 2), and there is a large but by no means complete overlap between directive speech acts and grammatical imperatives.

For Aguaruna, there are clear grammatical properties that identify an imperative mood (see §3), used primarily to encode directive speech acts. Within this formal category are 'canonical' and 'non-canonical' imperatives (Aikhenvald 2010), the latter including hortative, with first person plural subject, and jussive, with third person subject. Canonical imperatives are typically defined in terms of an interaction between speaker and addressee: 'Imperatives are centred on speech-act participants—commander and addressee' (Aikhenvald 2010: 4). There is no difficulty in integrating hortative into this definition, as the addressee is one of the intended actors. Although the forms with third person subject appear on the face of it to 'bypass' the addressee, the examples presented below show that jussive is typically used in contexts where action is required from the addressee (§3.2), like the canonical imperative. The third person forms can also be used with a more speaker-oriented optative sense, and this is explained by their development from a future tense marker.

This chapter is the first detailed discussion of commands in Aguaruna grammar, and is largely descriptive in its scope. The bulk of the data comes from narrative texts collected during fieldwork conducted since 2004, as well as participant observation and elicitation to fill out paradigms. The fieldwork data have been supplemented by data from written sources in various genres: a translation of the New Testament into Aguaruna (YCA 2008); personal correspondence from native speakers in the form of emails and chat; and social media posts by native speakers. As yet there is no existing corpus of recorded natural conversation in Aguaruna, so written interactions remain the best available data source for genres other than narrative monologues.

The chapter is structured as follows. §2 provides a brief overview of Aguaruna grammar, and §3 contains the bulk of the description, covering the formal representation of directives. §4 goes into more detail regarding the grammatical categories associated with imperative marking, and the interaction of imperatives with other aspects of the grammar. §5 describes the use of commands in interaction, as inferred from discourse data. Finally, §6 offers some concluding remarks.

2 Typological profile

This section provides a brief overview of Aguaruna grammar, focusing on the morphology of finite verbs. Major word classes in Aguaruna are verb and noun; adjectives are morphologically noun-like but can be distinguished syntactically. Other word classes are time, location, and manner adverbs; ideophones; and a few particles. Main clauses typically show AOV/SV constituent order, and verb-final order is obligatory in dependent clauses. Arguments need not be represented by overt NPs, if they are recoverable from context. The grammar is both head and dependent marking: subjects and objects are marked with verbal suffixes (third person objects are zero marked) and with case markers on the NP; possession is marked on the possessed noun and on overt possessors. Aguaruna has a strongly nominative-accusative grammatical profile. Nominative case is formally unmarked, while accusative is marked with the NP enclitic =*na*. There is a split in accusative case marking: while SAP object NPs are always marked accusative, third person objects appear in nominative case when the subject is second person singular or plural, or first person plural. With first person singular and third person subjects, all object NPs receive accusative case. Split accusative marking does not affect the points discussed in this chapter. Oblique cases are locative, ablative, comitative, and instrumental.

The morphology is almost entirely suffixing, and agglutinating with some fusion. There is extensive vowel elision—examples are given in the surface forms, but bound morphemes cited in isolation are given the full underlying form. The examples are given in a practical orthography that follows the IPA except that <ch> = /tʃ/, <sh> = /ʃ/ and <y> = /j/. Examples taken from written sources have been adjusted to conform to this system.

2.1 *Finiteness and verbal morphology*

Aguaruna has a set of obligatory verbal grammatical categories, making finite and dependent verbs morphologically distinct. Figure 1 gives an outline of the morphology of a finite verb.[2] The formal expression of directives and other speech acts form a paradigm of mood markers, marked mainly in slot G. Morphology up to slot D can be included in finite, dependent, and nominalized verbs; slots E to G host categories that are unique to finite verbs. Dependent verbs take no tense nor mood marking, but add markers of dependency, a different set of person markers, and switch-reference markers (dependent verb morphology is not relevant to this chapter). It is important to note that while the categories of tense, person, and mood are obligatorily SPECIFIED for finite verbs, the corresponding morphological slots are not obligatorily FILLED: in some cases a grammatical value may be marked elsewhere in the clause. For example, the polar question marker =*ka* appears on the verb in (1), but in (2) it appears on the adjective *piŋkɨha* 'good', as the focus of interrogation. In this case the verb has no marker in slot G.

	A	B	C	D	E	F	G
ROOT	VALENCY CHANGE	OBJECT	ASPECT + PLURAL	NEGATION	TENSE	PERSON	MOOD

FIGURE 1. Verbal morphological slots

---

[2] Figure 1 is an idealized representation—in fact perfective and plural are marked with separate suffixes in slot C, and if there is a negative marker in slot D then the plural marker FOLLOWS this suffix.

(1) wi-a-mɨ=k?
     go-IMPERV-2=Q
     Are you going?

(2) amɨ=sh   piŋkɨha=k   puha-m?
     2sg=Q.TOP   good=Q   live.IMPERV-2
     Are you well?

The following sections briefly review the properties of morphological slots C to G in finite verbs.

2.1.1 *Slot C: Aspect*

Slot C distinguishes four aspect-marked stems: imperfective, perfective, potential, and durative. An unmarked stem, with no morphology in slot C, can also appear in some verb forms. Table 1 summarizes the properties of the five verb stems. The perfective stem takes different forms relating to verbal semantics, as shown in Table 2. Normally a given verb root always takes the same marker, but there is some possibility of alternation to change the meaning (see (3)). In particular, the 'attenuative' marker -*sa* may be substituted in imperative forms to soften them (see §4.2). The perfective markers themselves do not vary for number, but may be accompanied by a plural subject suffix -*aha*. (3a) shows the verb *umut* 'drink' with its default 'pluractional' suffix; in (b) this is replaced with the 'intensive' suffix, changing the meaning of the resulting word.

TABLE 1. **Verb stems**

STEM	MARKER	FUNCTION
Imperfective	Singular subject -*a* Plural subject -*ina*	Marks a temporally unbounded action or situation. Appears in present tense and some nominalizations.
Perfective	Marked with a set of suffixes that also convey limited information on verbal semantics, see Table 2	Marks a temporally bounded action or situation. Appears in most past and future tense forms, as well as imperative.
Potential	-*mai*	Marks possibility or ability. Potential stems of transitive verbs become S=O ambitransitive.
Durative	-*ma*; also triggers lengthening of the preceding vowel	Marks an action to be continued. Compatible only with imperative verb forms.
Unmarked	No marker in slot C	Used with some nominalizers and remote past tense.

TABLE 2. **Perfective suffixes**

SUFFIX	GLOSS	ASSOCIATED MEANING
-ka	intensive	intensive effort by subject (A or S)
-ki(ni)	transferred	associated movement
-sa	attenuative	attenuative or affectionate
-ha	pluractional	plural action (iterative), or involving liquid
-a(w)	high affectedness	change of state of O or location of S
-i(ni)	low affectedness	no change of state for O or location of S

(3) a. uwa-ŋ-ta
      drink-PERV-IMP
      Drink!

   b. uwa-k-ta
      drink-PERV-IMP
      Drink (an unusual amount, e.g. more than one vessel)!

The selection of verb stem is largely morphologically conditioned: most past and future tenses require the perfective stem; remote past can take the unmarked, perfective, or imperfective stem; imperative takes the perfective or durative stem; nominalizers vary in the stems selected. Where more than one stem is possible, the selection changes the meaning, as shown by comparing the (a) and (b) examples in (4).

(4) a. ma-a-ha-i
      bathe-IMPERV-1sg-DEC
      I'm bathing.

   b. ma-i-ha-i
      bathe-PERV-1sg-DEC
      I'm finished bathing.

(5) a. yu-wa-ta!
      eat-PERV-IMP
      Eat!

   b. yuu-ma-ta!
      eat-DUR-IMP
      Keep on eating!

2.1.2 *Slot E: Tense*

Aguaruna has a rich system of tense marking, both synthetic and periphrastic (combining finite auxiliary verbs with non-finite main verbs). Present tense is unmarked, and selects the imperfective stem. There are six synthetic past tense forms, of which one is formed with a nominalized verb. Most select the perfective stem. In addition, a nominalizer -*u* often replaces tense marking in narratives, with a past-tense non-firsthand evidentiality reading (as in example (25); and see Overall 2014). Of the three future forms, one is formed with a nominalization. All three select the perfective stem. As shown in §3 below, the imperative suffix has its origins in a future tense marker, and is marked in slot E, unlike the other mood markers which occupy slot G.

2.1.3 Slots C and F: Person and number

Three persons and singular/plural number are distinguished in verbal morphology and pronouns. There is no number marking on nouns. In finite verbs, person marking in slot F distinguishes singular and plural for first and second persons; there is no distinct third person plural marker for most finite forms.

As noted above, plural subject may also be marked in slot C along with imperfective and perfective aspects. This marking is not obligatory, but it is the only way to mark third person subjects as plural in most contexts. For first and second person, plural marking in slot C can combine with the plural person markers in slot F, in which case it emphasizes a large number of participants, relative to expectations. There is no evidence that the system distinguishes any non-singular number other than plural.[3]

Table 3 shows the suffixes that mark person and number of the subject in finite declarative verbs. There are a few differences in non-declarative forms, including imperatives, as will be shown below.

TABLE 3. **Person markers in finite declarative verbs**

	SG	PL
1	-*ha*	-*hi*
2	-*mi*	-*humi* [a]
3	-*wa* only in present and definite future tense *change of final vowel* in other tenses	-*numi* only in remote past tense

[a] I analyse this as a single suffix for morphological reasons detailed in Overall (2008: 361–2), but it is clearly etymologically composed of a plural marker *-*hu* + second person -*mi*.

[3] Although Regan et al. (1991) and Corbera Mori (1994: 233, 235) have suggested that the first person plural forms without slot C plural marking are dual inclusive, while the plural form includes one or more non-addressee participants, my data do not support this analysis and dual number does not feature elsewhere in the grammar.

TABLE 4. **Formally marked moods/modalities in slot G**

SPEECH ACT	MOOD/MODALITY	MARKER
Statement	Declarative	*-i*
	Counter-expectation	*-hama*
	Narrative	*tuwahamɨ*
	Speculative	*-(tsa)...tai*
Question	Polar interrogative	=*ka* (or -Ø if marked elsewhere in the clause)
	Content interrogative	Suppression of apocope (clause contains interrogative word)
	Tag question	*-api*
Directive	Imperative	(marked in slot E)
	Familiar imperative	(marked in slot E)
	Jussive	(marked in slot E)
	Hortative	(marked in slot E)
	Apprehensive	(marked in slot E)
	Prohibitive	(marked in slot E)
Exclamation	Exclamative	-Ø

2.1.4 Slot G: Mood and modality

The final slot of a finite verb is typically filled by one of a set of markers that form a paradigm of mood and modality. These are shown in Table 4, grouped according to the speech act represented. The markers form a single paradigm, covering traditional mood as well as epistemic modality. The imperative moods involve no formal marking in slot G, but are marked in slot E—for the canonical imperative and jussive forms, this reflects an origin in future tense marking. These markers do impart a mood value to the clause, and form part of the same paradigm as those in slot G: the presence of an imperative marker in slot E blocks any marker from appearing in slot G. In the following section I describe the formal properties of imperative forms.

3 Formal marking of directives

Directives are marked with a single set of imperative markers, shown in Table 5. Within this group, the first distinction that can be made is between commands and prohibitions, which are semantic converses, although formally distinct. As is to be expected, second person singular imperative is the least formally marked of all the forms. Second person imperative shows a further subdivision into etymologically distinct PLAIN and FAMILIAR forms. Plain imperative and jussive forms are based on a future tense marker. Prohibitive forms are based on an apprehensive marker.

TABLE 5. Imperative verb forms

PERSON	POSITIVE/COMMAND		NEGATIVE/PROHIBITION
	PLAIN	FAMILIAR	
2sg	-ta	-kia	-i-pa
2pl	-ta-hum	-khua	-i-hupa
3sg	-ti		-ĩ-ka
3pl	-ti-numĩ		-i-numĩ-ka
1pl	-mi		-cha-mi

Hortative stands out both functionally and formally: rather than a straightforward command, it is a suggestion or invitation; and formally, negative hortative is formed with the same negator as is used in tensed verb forms.

3.1 Intentional future

The etymon underlying the canonical imperative and jussive forms is -ta. This is historically a future tense marker, and still functions as such in some constructions, where I gloss it IFUT 'intentional future'. It appears in declarative clauses only with first person subject, and expresses an intention or desire, as in (6) and (7).

(6) wii   haanchi=n   suma-ŋ-ka-t-hami
     1sg   clothes=ACC   buy-APPLIC-PERV-IFUT-1sg>2sg.DEC
     I will buy you clothes.

The context of (7) is that a woman who has been lost in the forest arrives at an agouti's house, and finds all sorts of good food and drink there. The woman uses the intentional future form twice, expressing a desire with overtones of seeking permission. (Note that speech reports in examples are underlined.)

(7) [[imaŋ=num   puhu-s-ta-ha-i   tus
     INTENS.ADJ=LOC   live-PERV-IFUT-1sg-DEC   say.SUBORD.3.SS
     puha-u=n]NP:O
     live+IMPERV-NOMZ=ACC
     ma?   aha=num   wi-a-ha-i   tu-sã]
     HESIT   garden=LOC   go-IMPERV-1sg-DEC   say-SUBORD.3.SS
     wɨ-taĩ
     go-SUBORD.1/3.DS
     wɨ=sha   mini-t-ha-i   tu-taĩ
     1sg=ADD   come.PERV-IFUT-1sg-DEC   say-SUBORD.1/3.DS
     The woman said 'I'm going to stay in this great place', and the agouti said to her 'well, I'm going to the garden', then the woman said 'I want to come too'…

Intentional future is also used in speech reports where there is no addressee. Example (8) is from reported internal monologue, where a man reflects on his mortality after a serious accident and decides to become Christian.

(8) [dɨkas   apahui=ai   suhuman-ka-t-ha-i
    truly   God=INST   convert-PERV-IFUT-1SG-DEC
    tu-sa-n]   suhuman-ka-bia-ha-i
    say-SUBORD-1sg.SS   convert-PERV-PAST-1sg-DEC
    Saying 'I will certainly convert to God (i.e. Christianity)', I converted.

The same marker appears in (mostly rhetorical) questions, where it has an irrealis sense. In these contexts it is compatible with first (9), second (10) and third person subjects (11).

(9) wi=sha   waã-nu=k   aika-t-hamɨ?
    1sg=Q.TOP   why-1sg.SS=Q.RHET do.PERV-IFUT-1sg>2sg
    Why would I do that to you?

(10) waŋka   ahapa-sh-ta-mɨ?
     why   give.birth.PERV-NEG-IFUT-2sg
     Why won't you give birth?

(11) wãã=ŋ   nĩĩ=sh   puhu-ti?
     why=Q.RHET   3sg=Q.TOP   stay.PERV-IFUT.3
     Why should she stay?

In the following section I describe the use of this marker in imperative clauses.

3.2 *Imperatives formed with* -ta

The marker *-ta* appears with second and third person subjects as imperative and jussive marking, respectively, as shown in Table 6. Unlike the examples in §3.1, these forms do not allow any further mood marking in slot G (or elsewhere). Just as second and third person do not appear in declarative contexts, so first person singular does not appear in the imperative paradigm (first plural does, but not with forms based on *-ta*—see §3.4).

TABLE 6. **Imperatives with etymon *-ta**

	SG	PL
2	-ta	-ta-humɨ
		-IMP-2PL
3	-ti	-ti-numɨ
	-JUS.3	-JUS-3PL

3.2.1 Canonical imperative

Second person singular imperative is unmarked for person (12). Second person plural takes the marker -*humi* seen in other finite verb forms (13).

(12) tsaŋkuŋ-tu-ŋ-ta   inia-s-ta-hami̵,
      forgive-1sg.OBJ-PERV-IMP   ask.question-PERV-IFUT-1sg>2sg.DEC
      ya=ita   apa=sh?
      who=COP.3   father.PSSD.2=Q.TOP
      Excuse me I want to ask you a question, who is your father? (Facebook post)

(13) anu=ĩ   wãỹã-hum   *like* ta-wa=nu
      DEM.MED=LOC   enter.PERV-2PL.SS *like* say.IMPERV-3=ANA
      su-sa-ta-hum
      give-PERV-IMP-2pl
      Enter there (to that Facebook page) and like it! (lit. Give that of which one says 'like') (Facebook post, 27 September 2015)

3.2.2 Jussive

Third person subject is marked with vowel change: -*ta* > -*ti*, and third person plural adds a suffix -*numi̵*, which otherwise only appears with remote past tense and apprehensive/prohibitive forms (§3.5.1).

   In (14), a young man has been told that his sister-in-law should accompany him to fetch water, as there is a jaguar on the prowl. But when he tells the other men this, they mock him and tell him to go alone.

(14) nuwa=k   puhuu-ma-ti,   ami̵=k   ut-i-ta!
      woman=TOP   live-DUR-JUS   2sg=RESTR   fetch-PERV-IMP
      The woman should stay (here), you fetch (the water) by yourself!

The context of (15) is a conflict that forced a family to take refuge in the forest, and village leaders are trying to negotiate the children's return to school.

(15) dita   kaunã   papi   au-sa-t-numi̵!
      3pl   come.PL.PERV.3.SS book.ACC   study-PERV-JUS-3pl
      They (the children) should come and study!

Note that in neither example is the command directed to the intended actor, who need not even be aware of it. Nor is the addressee expected to simply pass on the command to the third person; instead, the addressee is requested to take some action to allow or bring about the action expressed in the jussive form. Note that the third person imperative is combined with a second person imperative in (14). This is a common pattern. In (16), a post on Facebook which the author asks the readers to share, the jussive-marked clause functions like a purpose clause.

(16) uba-ŋ   kai-ŋ
      sibling.opp.sex-PSSD.1sg   sister.same.sex-PSSD.1sg
      a-ina-u   i-wainma-k-ta-hum,   ashi
      COP-PL.IMPERV-NOMZ   CAUS-see-PERV-IMP-2pl   all
      dika-ti-nmɨ
      know.PERV-JUS-3pl
      Brothers and sisters please show [the post to your contacts], everyone should
      know about it. (Facebook post, 25 November 2015)

Similarly, jussive is used in speech reports forming different-subject purpose clauses.
Here it does not have the sense of a command, but an optative, as there is no
addressee.

(17) iwi-ya-hi   [tɨpɨ-s-ti!   tu-sa]
      raise.hand-REM.PAST-1pl.DEC lie.down-PERV-JUS   say-SUBORD.1pl.ss
      We raised our hands to stop the truck. (lit. We raised our hands, saying 'the
      truck should stop!')

(18) [*Cultura Awajun*   ashi   aɨnts   dika-mu
      P.N.   all   person   know.IMPERV-NON.SU.NOMZ
      a-ti   tu-sa]   taka-ku
      COP-JUS say-SUBORD.1pl.ss   work.IMPERV-SIM.1pl.ss
      puha-hi
      live.IMPERV-1pl.DEC
      We are working so that *Cultura Awajun* will be known by everybody. (lit. We
      are working, saying 'Cultura Awajun should be known by everybody!') (Face-
      book post, 30 September 2015)

This optative sense is also present in the conversational formula in (19), where the
addressee cannot be expected to take any relevant action.

(19) apahui   yaim-pa-k-ti!
      God   help-2.OBJ-PERV-JUS
      God bless you!

TABLE 7. **Distribution of marker *-ta* across clause types**

PERSON	DECLARATIVE	IMPERATIVE	INTERROGATIVE
1sg	Yes	–	Yes
2	–	Yes	Yes
3	–	Yes	Yes

In sum, the marker -*ta* has a split distribution across clause types, shown in Table 7: in declarative clauses it may only appear with 1sg subject, and conversely it appears only with non-1sg subject in imperative clauses.

3.3 *Familiar imperative* -(k)ia, -khua

Canonical imperative distinguishes the plain form marked with -*ta* and a familiar form, with different contexts of use. The singular familiar imperative is -*kia* (examples (20a, b), except following the 'attenuative' perfective aspect suffix -*sa* when the latter is in a position to have its vowel elided—then the combination surfaces as /sia/ (example (20c)). The plural form is -*khua* (example (20d)).[4]

(20) a. ta-a-kia!
         come-PERV-IMP.FAM
         Come here!

      b. yu-sa-kia!
         eat-PERV-IMP.FAM
         Eat!

      c. dii-s-ia!
         look-PERV-IMP.FAM
         Look!

      d. yu-wa-khua!
         eat-PERV-IMP.FAM.PL
         Eat!

Speakers characterize the distinction between plain and familiar imperatives as relating to formality: the familiar form is more likely to be used with family members and children. Familiar imperative may also convey exasperation, as in (21) from a story about a woman who gets lost in the forest and ends up at the home of a group of cannibals. When her child dies she tries to bury it but they keep telling her that the grave sites she selects are unsuitable, until she says:

(21) untsu   ta-ku-ŋmɨ=k,   yu-wa-khua!
      well.then say.IMPERV-SIM-2pl.SS=COND   eat-PERV-IMP.FAM.PL
      Well then if you say so, just eat it!

With very few examples in my corpus, more data is needed before I can give a fuller account of the distribution of familiar imperative. There is no obvious etymological source for the familiar imperative suffixes.

---

[4] This suggests a morphologically complex construction: singular -*ki-a*, with plural marker *-*hu* inserted to give *-k(i)-hu-a*.

3.4 Hortative -mi

First person plural subject commands/suggestions are marked with hortative *-mi*. Plural marking can be included in the stem—compare (22a and b). The plural form is used as elsewhere in the grammar, to emphasize that a large number of people (relative to expectations) are included.

(22)   a.   yu-wa-mi!
          eat-PERV-HORT
          Let's eat!

       b.   yu-waw-aŋ-mi!
          eat-PERV-PL-HORT
          Let's all eat!

In (23) the plural form is explicitly accompanied by the word *ashi* 'all'.

(23)   ashi   wɨ-aŋ-mi,   [*Lima*   batsat-u-ti=k]$_{NP:S}$
       all   go.PERV-PL-HORT   Lima   live.PL.IMPERV-NOMZ-SAP.1pl=TOP
       Let's all go, those of us who live in Lima! (Facebook post)

Hortative is the only imperative form that can be negated (§3.5.2).

3.5 Negation of directives

3.5.1 Apprehensive and prohibitive

Only hortative can include a negative marker. For other imperative forms, the semantically converse prohibitive form is built upon an apprehensive form that is marked with a dedicated suffix *-i* in a paradigm shown in Table 8. Note that third person plural takes the suffix *-numɨ*, as with jussive forms. The apprehensive suffix takes slot E, preceded by perfective markers and followed by person markers. It is not compatible with negation or slot C plural marking. Like the other command type forms, apprehensive blocks any further mood marking in slot G. The syntactic status of apprehensive verbs is ambiguous: subject is marked as for finite verbs, and there is

TABLE 8. Apprehensive marking

PERSON	SINGULAR	PLURAL
1	*-i-ha* -APPR-1sg	*-i-hi* -APPR-1pl
2	*-i-mɨ* -APPR-2	*-i-humɨ* -APPR-2pl
3	*-ĩ* -APPR+3sg	*-i-numɨ* -APPR-3pl

no switch-reference morphology, but semantically they appear dependent. Apprehensive is most commonly used in speech report constructions, forming a negative counterpart of purpose clauses ((24), (25))—but the form in (26) also has the feel of a dependent clause, despite being morphologically independent.

(24) aima-k   imamkɨma-s
      fill.IMPERV-SIM.3.SS   be.careful-SUBORD.3.SS
      [inta-ha-i-ŋ   tus]
      break-PERV-APPR-1sg   say.SUBORD.3.SS
      Filling it carefully, lest he should break it…(lit. saying 'lest I break it').

(25) takimpa-ŋ   kuitam-ka-u=ai   shiiŋ
      hatch-PERV.3.SS   care.for-PERV-NOMZ=COP.3.DEC   well
      [ha-ka-ɨ̄   tus]
      die-PERV-APPR.3sg   say.SUBORD.3.SS
      Having hatched it, she cared for it well, lest it should die. (lit.…saying 'lest it die')

(26) wakɨt-ki-ta   amɨ=k,   man-tam-aw-ai-num!
      go.back-PERV-IMP   2sg=TOP   kill-2.OBJ-PERV-APPR-3pl
      You go back, lest they kill you!

Prohibitive forms retain the apprehensive suffix -*i*, but involve some morphological changes, shown in Table 9. Second person is marked with (sg) -*pa* (27a), (pl) -*hupa* (27b) or -*pa-humɨ* (28) (there does not appear to be any semantic distinction between the two forms for second person plural). The same suffixes mark second person in some interrogative contexts (see §5.2). Third person forms take an overt suffix -*ka* 'prohibitive' that does not appear elsewhere in the grammar.

(27) a. achi-ka-i-pa!
         touch-PERV-APPR-2
         Don't touch (it)!

      b. achi-ka-i-ŋpa!
         touch-PERV-APPR-2PL
         Don't touch (it)!

TABLE 9. **Prohibitive marking**

PERSON	SINGULAR	PLURAL
2	-*i-pa* -APPR-2	-*i-hupa* or -*i-pa-humɨ* -APPR-2pl or -APPR-2-2PL
3	-*ɨ̄-ka* -APPR+3sg-PROHIB	-*ɨ̄-numɨ-ka* -APPR-3pl-PROHIB

(28) wainka-m   ihu-i-pa-hum!
      in.vain-2   stab-APPR-2-2PL
      Don't stab it in vain!

Prohibitive is the negative counterpart of canonical imperative, and like imperative expects action from the addressee. Also like imperative, there are third person forms (but no first person).

The semantic distinction between apprehensive and prohibitive is clear with second person subject: the former expresses a desire and the latter demands some (in)action from the addressee. With a third person subject the distinction between apprehensive and prohibitive is more subtle. In (29), third person prohibitive clearly has the force of an instruction to the addressee, as we saw with jussive.

(29) uchi   [hu=na   saip-chi-hĩ=n
      child   DEM.PROX=ACC   rind-DIM-3=ACC
      iya-u=na=kɨ=sh]$_{NP:O}$ yu-waw-aĩ-ka!
      fall.IMPERV-NOMZ=ACC=RESTR=ADD   eat-PERV-APPR.3sg-PROHIB
      Don't let the child eat this rind that is falling!

And in (30), from the Bible, an instruction is being given to some potential subset of the addressees. As in the English translation, the prohibitive form is third person but it is the addressees who are expected to carry out the instruction.

(30) tuhã   nuwa   apahui nɨma-h-in,   [aishĩ
      but   woman   God   follow-APPLIC-NOMZ husband.PSSD.3
      apahui   nɨma-ŋ-chau=waita-k]
      God   follow-APPLIC-NEG.NOMZ=COP.3-SIM.3.SS
      [nĩĩ=hãĩ=ŋ   puhu-s-tatus
      3sg=COMIT=TOP   live-PERV-INT.3.SS
      wakɨɨ-tai=k]   uku-k-i-nmɨ-ka
      want-SUBORD.3.DS=COND leave-PERV-APPR-3pl-PROHIB
      If any woman has a husband who is an unbeliever, and he consents to live with her, she should not divorce him. (YCA 2008: 308; 1 Corinthians 7: 13)

3.5.2 Negative hortative

In contrast to the other imperative types, hortative can simply be combined with the same negative marking as declarative verbs ((31), (32)).

(31) dii-s-cha-mi!
      look-PERV-NEG-HORT
      Let's not look!

(32) wakit-ki-bia-ha-i   [hu-ni   wɨkaɨ-cha-mi!
      return-PERV-PAST-1sg-DEC   DEM.PROX-ALL   walk.PERV-NEG-HORT
      tu-sa-n]
      say-SUBORD-1sg.SS
      I went back, saying 'let's not walk this way!'

To summarize, we see that purpose clauses have a negative counterpart in apprehensive clauses, that may or may not be couched in a speech report; imperative and jussive have their negative counterpart in prohibitive clauses; and hortative clauses are negated by the same means as declarative verbs. Note that 'intentional future' -*ta* is also negated in the usual way in non-imperative clauses, even with second person subject (see example (10)).

4 Commands in grammar

Having described the morphology of imperative forms, I now consider the wider relationships these forms have within the grammar. I describe the syntactic possibilities of imperative (§4.1), combinations of imperative forms with verbal aspect (§4.2), and compatibility of imperative with verbal semantics (§4.3). Imperatives in clause chaining are addressed in §4.1.

4.1 Syntax of imperative clauses

The syntax of imperative clauses is not appreciably different from that of declarative clauses. Subject, object, and oblique arguments may be overt, or omitted if recoverable from context. The presence of pronominal second person subjects is rare, and it is not clear precisely what they add semantically to the clause when present. Note in (14) that the second person pronoun hosts the restrictive enclitic, giving the sense 'only you'; and in (26) the pronoun hosts the topic enclitic, marking it as contrastive ('YOU go back!'). Time adverbials can be included to indicate that an action is to be performed later, as in (33). There is no special delayed imperative form.

Imperatives, like other finite verb forms, can be preceded by one or more subordinate clauses. Imperative mood has scope over same-subject subordinate clauses, and a chain of such clauses is preferred to using two or more imperatives in succession. In (33) a single subordinate clause precedes the imperative-marked final verb, and in (34) three subordinate clauses are associated with the hortative-marked final verb.

(33) [hu=ɨ̄   kana-ha-m]   kashin   wɨ-ta!
      DEM.PROX=LOC   sleep-PERV-2.SS   tomorrow   go.PERV-IMP
      Sleep here and go tomorrow! (lit. You having slept here, go tomorrow!)

(34) [atushat   yuha-u-ti]_{NP:S}

far.away   go.PL.IMPERV-NOMZ-SAP.1pl

[iba-chi=k   dii-sa]

INTENS-DIM=RESTR   look-SUBORD.1pl.SS

[ii=na   nuŋkɨ   ibau   piŋkɨ-hama-pɨ

1pl=ACC   land.PSSD.1pl   INTENS.LOC   good-ASSERT-Q.TAG

tu-sa]   [wakɨt-hu-k-tasa]

say-SUBORD.1pl.SS   go.back-APPLIC-PERV-INTENT.1pl.SS

anɨntaim-ha-mi!

think-PERV-HORT

Those of us who have migrated far away, just looking a bit and saying 'our distant land is great', let's think about going back there! (Facebook post, 23 September 2015)

4.2 Verb stems

Imperatives share the grammatical category of aspect with other verb forms. Imperative, jussive, and hortative forms typically select the perfective verb stem, but imperative and jussive are also compatible with the durative stem marked with *-ma* (examples (35) and (14)). The durative has the sense of 'keep on doing [verb]', and implies that the speaker will not be present. Example (35) (repeated from (5b)) would be appropriately uttered if a host is called away during a meal, and wants to encourage the guest to feel at home.

(35) yuu-ma-ta!

eat-DUR-IMP

Keep on eating!

And in example (14), the implication is that the woman should stay when the addressee leaves (also compare the leave-taking formula 'keep on living!' in (46)). As far as I am aware, the durative stem cannot take any morphology other than imperative or jussive marking (no examples with hortative are attested). The durative stem is only appropriate when the action is already under way, and conversely imperatives with the perfective stem are used for actions that are not yet begun. Prohibitive, however, can be used in both circumstances: 'don't do X' or 'stop doing X'.

For those imperatives that are formed on the perfective stem, almost all morphology available to perfective stems is available, including valency change and object marking (as in (36)). But imperatives other than hortative cannot be negated, instead using prohibitive forms (§3.5).

(36) su-hu-s-ta!

give-1sg.OBJ-PERV-IMP

Give it to me!

As noted in §2.1, every verb root has a default perfective form. Those verbs that do not select the attenuative suffix *-sa* by default have the option of substituting this suffix to soften an imperative, as in (37b).

(37) a. uwa-ŋ-ta!
          drink-PERV-IMP
          Drink!

      b. uwa-s-ta!
          drink-PERV-IMP
          Please drink!

Periphrastic aspectual constructions are also available to imperative forms. In (38), a construction using a subordinate simultaneous verb form and the copula as auxiliary marks progressive aspect.

(38) diiya-ku-m   a-ta!
      look.IMPERV-SIM-2.SS   COP-IMP
      Be watching!

4.3 Compatibility with verbal semantics

There appear to be no lexical restrictions on the formation of imperatives. Positive imperative (39), prohibitive (40), and hortative are all compatible with the copula (also compare the use of imperative marking on copula functioning as auxiliary in (38)).

(39) aishmaŋ a-ta!
      man   COP-IMP
      Be a man!

(40) kasa   a-i-pa!
      thief COP-APPR-2
      Don't be a thief!

Although prohibitive forms a direct command, it is compatible with non-agentive verbs, as in (41).

(41) tuha=sh   [sinchi   anintaim-ku-m]   wait-tsa-i-pa
      but=CONC   strongly   think.IMPERV-SIM-2   suffer-PERV-APPR-2
      But don't suffer because of worrying a lot. (personal correspondence)

There are two 'defective verbs', that have the semantics and the formal appearance of imperatives but never appear in any other form ((42), (43)).

(42) haasta!
      Wait!

(43) iista!
      Go on!

Example (42) can be parsed as **haa-s-ta* '*wait-PERV-IMP'; and it has a familiar imperative variant *haasia*. But there is no independently attested verb root *haa-* 'wait'. The word in (43) is used to encourage people or hunting dogs. This form suggests a verb root **ii-* 'go ahead', but, again, such a root is not otherwise attested. There is, however, a verb *iima-* 'go ahead', and also a reduced form *iis!* used to shoo dogs away.

5 Commands in interaction

Imperatives are not common in narrative texts, nor in procedural discourse, which makes use of a special 'normative' verb form to express 'the way we do things'. They are, however, frequent in conversation, and there are no conventionalized imperative avoidance strategies for politeness or face-saving. Although there exists the distinction between plain and familiar imperative, the plain form does not equate to a more formal register. There is a construction translating as 'please' (44), and, as noted above, the attenuative perfective marker *-sa* may replace the usual perfective suffix for a verb to soften an imperative.

(44) wait   ania-sa-m
      pity   feel-SUBORD-2.SS
      Please (lit. feeling pity)

Conversely, an imperative may be made more abrupt by a self-quoting strategy, as in (45).

(45) maʔ   antu-k-ta!   ta-ha!
      hey   listen-PERV-IMP   say.IMPERV-1sg.EXCL
      waŋka   anta-s-mi?
      why   listen.IMPERV-NEG-2
      waamak   wi-ta-ha-i   ta-ha!
      quickly   go.PERV-IFUT-1sg-DEC   say.IMPERV-1sg.EXCL
      Hey, 'listen!' I say! Why don't you listen? 'I'm in a hurry' I say!

The appropriate response to a command is *ayu* 'OK' (or *atsa* 'no'; the latter is also an appropriate response to polar questions, where a positive response is *hiʔa* 'yes').

5.1 Phatic functions

Some conversational formulae make use of imperatives (others consist of question and answer pairs, Overall 2008). (46) is the standard leave-taking formula. (47) is used by Christians (reformulated as *ahutap yaimpakti* 'may the *ahutap* spirit bless you' among non-Christians). (48) is commonly used at the end of conversations

involving planning or negotiation; the anaphoric pronoun *nu* refers back to the plans
that have been agreed upon. Hortative is used as in (49).

(46) puhuu-ma-ta!
      live-DUR-IMP
      Keep on living!

(47) apahui   yaĩ-pa-k-ti!
      God   help-2.OBJ-PERV-JUS
      God bless you!

(48) nu   a-ti!
      ANA   exist-JUS
      Let it be so!

(49) ahum   wai-ni-a-mi!
      later   see-RECIP-PERV-HORT
      See you later!

Example (50), from a text chat conversation, shows how leave-taking formulae may
be combined.

(50) a. yatsu-ta   wi-sha   taka-ku-n
         brother-VOC   1sg-FOC   work.IMPERV-SIM-1sg.SS
         wi-ɰa-ha-i
         go-IMPERV-1sg-DEC

      b. kashin   chicha-s-mi
         tomorrow   speak-PERV-HORT

      c. kuitama-m-sa-m   puhu-s-ta
         care.for-REFL-SUBORD-2.SS live-PERV-IMP

      d. atus   a-ti
         thus   COP-JUS

      e. ahutap   yaĩ-pa-k-ti!
         ajutap   help-2.OBJ-PERV-JUS
         [a] Brother, I'm going to work; [b] let's talk tomorrow; [c] look after yourself; [d] let
         it be thus; [e] may the *ajutap* spirit help you!

And imperatives may form a response to expressed intention, as in the brief exchange
in (51).

(51) A: kana-ŋ-ta-ha-i
         sleep-PERV-IFUT-1sg-DEC
         I'm going to sleep.

B: ayu   kana-ŋ-ta!
ok   sleep-PERV-IMP
OK, sleep!

5.2 *Formal overlap with vocative and interrogative*

Three 'addressee-oriented' forms show some formal overlap that is probably not coincidental: vocative, interrogative, and imperative. Example (45) illustrated a self-quoting use of the speech verb *tuta* 'say'. There is also an unproductive vocative suffix -*ta* for some kinship nouns that may be a reduced form of the speech verb (the default pattern for vocative is suppression of the usual apocope rule and accent shift to the final vowel); and note that this suffix is homophonous with imperative.

(52)   a. yatsu-ta!
          brother.of.m-VOC
          Hey brother!

       b. uchi-ta!
          child-VOC
          Hey kid!

I showed in §3.5.1 that prohibitive differs from apprehensive in that it uses the second person marker -*pa*, which is otherwise only found in questions.

Finally, there is a very informal and non-systematic process of vowel raising that can affect vocatives, imperatives, and interrogatives ((53)–(56)).

(53)   puhuu-ma-ta!   >   [puhuumatɨ]
       live-DUR-IMP
       Keep on living! (i.e. goodbye!)

(54)   mama!   >   [mamau]
       mum.VOC

(55)   simoŋka!   >   [simoŋku]
       Simon.VOC

(56)   ya=it-pa?   >   [yaitpu]
       who=COP-2
       Who are you? (on hearing a visitor approaching the house, whom speaker assumes to be her mother)

These three types of utterance have in common the expectation of a response from the addressee, and the formal similarities are presumably not coincidental, although more research is required to move beyond simple observation.

6 Final comments

The previous description shows that there is a formally distinct set of imperative mood markers in Aguaruna, covering both canonical and non-canonical imperatives, the latter including jussive and hortative. Discourse data show that the imperatives all have in common the function of eliciting action from the addressee, conforming to Searle's (1979: 14) characterization: 'The propositional content is always that the hearer *H* does some future action *A*.'

There is no first person singular form in the imperative mood paradigm, although the same form that marks imperative can be used with first person singular subject in declarative and interrogative clauses.

With respect to overlap with other parts of the grammar, the third person forms get extended to the formation of different-subject purpose clauses, and all imperative forms have some phatic functions. There appear to be no conventionalized strategies for avoiding imperative use.

Finally, some formal properties are shared among imperatives, vocatives, and questions. This is suggestive of a wider category of 'addressee-oriented' forms, and would be a worthwhile topic of further study.

References

Aikhenvald, Alexandra Y. 2010. *Imperatives and commands*. Oxford: Oxford University Press.

Corbera Mori, Angel. 1994. *Fonologia e gramática do Aguaruna (Jívaro)*. PhD Dissertation, University of Campinas, Brazil.

INEI [Instituto Nacional de Estadística e Informática]. 2009. *Resumen Ejecutivo: Resultados definitivos de las comunidades indígenas*. http://www1.inei.gob.pe/biblioineipub/bancopub/Est/Lib0789/Libro.pdf

Katan Jua, Tuntiak. 2011. 'Ii chichame unuimiamu / Investigando nuestra lengua / Investigating our language: Shuar Chicham', pp. 103–5 of *Endangered languages: Voices and images*. Proceedings of the FEL XV conference, edited by Marleen Haboud and Nicholas Ostler. Bath, UK: Foundation for Endangered Languages.

Overall, Simon E. 2008. *A grammar of Aguaruna*. PhD Dissertation, La Trobe University.

Overall, Simon E. 2014. 'Nominalization, knowledge, and information source in Aguaruna (Jivaroan)', pp. 227–44 of *The Grammar of Knowledge*, edited by Alexandra Y. Aikhenvald and R. M. W. Dixon. Oxford: Oxford University Press.

Regan, Jaime; Paz Agkuash, Anfiloquio; Uwarai Yagkug, Abel; and Paz Suikai, Isaac. 1991. *Chichasajmi: Hablemos Aguaruna 1*. Lima: Centro Amazónico de Antropología y Aplicación Práctica.

Searle, John R. 1979. *Expression and meaning: Studies in the theory of speech acts*. Cambridge: Cambridge University Press.

YCA 2008. *Yyamajam [sic] Chicham Apajuinu*. [New Testament in Aguaruna] 5th edition. La Liga Bíblica.

4

Imperatives in Ashaninka Satipo (Kampa Arawak) of Peru

ELENA MIHAS

1 Community background

The Ashaninka language (Kampa, Arawak) is spoken in the Satipo province, which has about 23,000 ethnic Ashaninkas (Datos generales 2015). Ashaninka has at least three dialects. One is spoken in the lower Perené area and the basins of the Satipo and Mazamari rivers. The speakers inhabiting the valleys of the rivers Tambo and Ene (with the tributaries Anapati and Mantaro) are reported to speak separate dialects (Dirks 1953: 302; Pike and Kindberg 1956: 415).

The Satipo Ashaninkas are located in the Districts of Mazamari, Rio Negro, Satipo, Perené, and Llaylla of the Satipo Province. They are organized into over 50 communities with the total population of about 8,700 people (Ñaco 2010: 18). Native communities are governed by elected chiefs. The chiefs regularly report to the heads of the overseeing indigenous political organizations. Among the political institutions, the CECONSEC 'The headquarters of native communities of the Central Rainforest' is the most influential. Many Ashaninka households cultivate and sell agricultural goods such as manioc, sesame and cacao seeds, as well as coffee beans, peanuts, and rice. Commercial endeavours are combined with subsistence activities (gardening, fishing, gathering, and to a lesser extent hunting).

Social interaction norms are based on a social membership system, constructed along the dimensions of kinship, *ayompari* and *compadrazgo* fellowships, age, and gender among interlocutors. Although Kampa societies are usually described as egalitarian (e.g. Descola 1992; Veber 2009), recent sweeping socio-political changes have contributed to the formation of an institutionally based hierarchical system of social relations. This process is facilitated by the nucleation of the residence pattern and rigid centralization of indigenous governance.

Commands. First edition. Alexandra Y. Aikhenvald and R. M. W. Dixon (eds)
This chapter © Elena Mihas 2017. First published 2017 by Oxford University Press

The social institutions of *ayompari* 'trading partner-fellowman' and *compadre* 'godparent' (usually from mestizo settlers) create horizontally built social networks of male Ashaninkas extending beyond the wife's kinfolk. The networks are constitutive of long-term interpersonal relations between males of a comparatively similar status. Gender relations among Kampas are usually characterized by 'male domination' (Veber 1997: 132), evidenced in the past in the practice of polygyny. In modern times, the gender imbalance is observed in a small proportion of females in the positions of power (Vilchez Jiménez 2002: 11–12).

2 The language

The language is highly synthetic, incorporating, agglutinating, primarily suffixing, with rich and complex verbal and nominal morphology.[1] The sound system includes sixteen consonants: voiceless stops p, t, t̪ʲ, k and affricates tsʰ and tʃ, two sibilant fricatives s and ʃ; one glottal fricative h; one liquid with a flap articulation ɾ; two glides, the bilabial approximant w <b> and the palatal glide j. It has three nasal stops m, n, and ɲ, which contrast with the underspecified nasal N. The vowels i, e, a, o have long counterparts. In orthography, the alveolo-palatal stop is <ty>, nasal palatal stop is <ñ>, glottal fricative is <j>, bilabial approximant is <b>; the vowel length is indicated by doubling the grapheme.

There are three open classes: verbs, nouns, and ideophones; the closed classes are adjectives, pronouns, interrogative words, and interjections; there is a semi-closed class of adverbs. Verb roots are bound and minimally require a person prefix and a reality status suffix (or a stative aspect formative). Verbs comprise two classes on the basis of the reality status inflection they take, namely conjugation classes I and A, as summarized in Table 1. The majority of verbs appear to be ambitransitive. Intransitive clauses can show a fluid intransitive marking pattern (see Mihas 2017 for

---

[1] The data come from three field trips to Chanchamayo and Satipo Provinces in 2011, 2014–16, spanning a period of seven months. The research methods included the production of a documentary corpus of audio and video recordings of naturally occurring discourse, observation of speakers' communicative practices, and elicitation of the speakers' judgements on some aspects of Satipo Ashaninka grammar. During fieldwork, the 12-hour corpus of audio and video recordings of 16 speakers was collected. The transcripts of the recorded texts cover approximately 4 hours of recording time. The multi-genre texts (myths, personal narratives, folk stories, procedural texts, conversation, and classroom interaction) were recorded in the villages of Impitato Cascada, Pucharini, Teoria, Rio Negro, Shaanki, and Milagro of the Satipo Province. Additional recordings of speakers from Puerto Ocopa, Pitokuna, and Impitato Cascada were made in the town of Satipo. Some examples of talk are cited from the author's fieldnotes taken in 2015. The study also relies on the collection of 30 stories published by the Satipo-based Asociación de Maestros Bilingües Intercultural de la Selva Central (Cochachi et al. 2009) and eleven stories produced by the Asociación para el Desarrollo y la Cultura (Vargas and Candiotti 2004) with the assistance of the intercultural bilingual education specialists from the Education Department (UGEL) of the Satipo Province. Some examples are also reproduced from the Summer Institute of Linguistics storybook (Icantacota peeraniniri 1985); their relevance to the communicative practices of native speakers residing in the fieldwork area was confirmed by the Satipo Ashaninka language consultants.

TABLE 1. Conjugation classes of verbs

REALITY STATUS	I-CONJUGATION	A-CONJUGATION
Realis	-i~; -e (after -*ak* 'PERV' or *aj*)	-a
Irrealis	-e	-ea

TABLE 2. Argument index-sets

PERSON/NUMBER/ GENDER	A/S	O
1sg	n(o)-	-na
1pl	a-~Ø	-ai
2	p(i)-	-mpi~-mi (in free variation)
3m	i-~y-~Ø (REAL); N-~R- ~Ø- (IRR)	-ri
3nm	o-~Ø	-ro

details). Argument indexation in transitive clauses exhibits nominative-accusative alignment. Core grammatical relations are not coded on nouns. The A and S arguments are marked on the verb by the prefixal index-set; O is expressed by the suffixal index-set, as summarized in Table 2.

Plurality of participants is expressed on the verb by the plural marker *-jei~jee* (in free variation). The suffix's function is restricted to intransitive subjects or transitive objects.

Tense is a minor category. There is a distinction between distal past, coded by the suffix *-ni*, and non-past, which is coded by zero. Aspectual morphology is elaborate, which is a common trait of Kampa (see Mihas 2017). Aspect marking makes two primary distinctions between perfective and imperfective, and anteriority. The inventory of modal formatives covers possibility, contingency, intentional/desiderative, and attitudinal modalities. There are no grammaticalized evidential markers.

The category of reality status is expressed morphologically by two sets of suffixes (see Table 1). Irrealis is expressed by the discontinuous morpheme N-~R-~Ø-...-e (the allomorphy of the prefixal elements is motivated by the phonological environment). The scope of the irrealis suffixes *-e* and *-ea* covers the entire notional range of what is defined as irrealis (unrealized) events, such as future events, imperatives, intentional/desiderative/optative, negated realis clauses, prospective events, habitual events which took place in the past, possible condition, counterfactual condition, purpose, and converbal clauses, and want-complements. Converbal clauses carrying irrealis inflection specify the ongoing nature of the supporting event.

TABLE 3. Standard negation strategy

Reality status	Realis	Irrealis
Construction	*te* v-IRR(*je*)	*eiro* v-REAL(*tsi*)

The standard negation strategy is coded by the negative particles *te* (realis) and *eiro* (irrealis) which precede the verb (Table 3). Under negation, the coding of aspectual values is typically limited to the perfective *-ak* or terminative *-aj*. The verb in negated clauses optionally takes the negative intensifier *-je* in the realis negative clause or the generic intensifier *-tsi* in the irrealis negative clause.

The basic constituent order is VO and VS, with A either preceding the verb or following O. The basic constituent order is strongly pragmatically motivated, as schematically shown in (1).

(1)   Topic and focus slots in the affirmative declarative clause

Left-Dislocated topic	EX SITU Focus	**VERB PREDICATE**	Topic	IN SITU Focus

There are five sets of personal pronouns, with the root morphemes being *na* 'I', *abi* 'you', *iri* 'he', *iro* 'she/it', *a-* 'we.INCL'). Each set has a particular discourse-pragmatic function and is marked by a dedicated suffix: continuous topic *-ro* (excepting third person topic pronouns which do not take it), counter-assertive topic *-inti*, additive focus *-ri*, exhaustive focus *-take*, and 'reflexive'-intensifying *-sati*. The sets of additive focus and counter-assertive topic pronouns are frequently used in second person commands, explicitly marking the addressee for contrastive purposes.

Neither declarative nor interrogative clauses receive special morphology. The prosodies of the declaratives and content interrogatives exhibit differing patterns. The intonational contour of the declarative clause in line 3, example (2), *pishinkita-najea meeka* 'you will get drunk', is shown in Figure 1. The study's figures are produced with the Praat software, www.praat.org. The figures consist of four segments, showing the waveform, pitch tracks, parsed syllabic structure, and values of fundamental frequency (which is an acoustic correlate of pitch). The phonetic transcription adopted is broad: for example, it does not show intervocalic voicing of stops. The figures illustrate the prosodies of three females who have relatively high-pitched voices. Example (2) is cited from a conversation between the fellow villagers Juan and Victoria who discuss their home-made manioc beer.

(2)   1   J   katsija-i-t-ak-e-Ø
             ferment-ICPL-EP-PFV-REAL-3S.SET2
             It (the beer) is being fermented.

2   V   pi-tseiy-ashi-t-a   meeka   abirori
        2S-lie-APL.INT-EP-REAL   now   2FOC.ADD
        You are lying.

3   →   **pi-shinki-t-an-aj-ea**   **meeka**
        2S-get.drunk-EP-DIR-TERM-IRR   now
        You will get drunk.

4   J   ja ja ja
        (laughing)

The assertion formulated as a declarative clause in line 3 is articulated at the mid level of the speaker's pitch range. The values of fundamental frequency remain in the range of 218Hz–223Hz, relatively flat throughout, dropping to 75Hz on the terminal syllable [ka] of the framing device *meeka* 'now'. In contrast, the content question in (3) is produced at the high level of the speaker's pitch range (326Hz–328Hz), with a steep drop of fundamental frequency from 326Hz to 93Hz at the end of the clause.

(3)   paita   pi-mishi-t-ant-a-ri?
      WH   2S-dream-EP-APPLIC.REAS-REAL-NOMZ
      Why did you talk in your dreams?

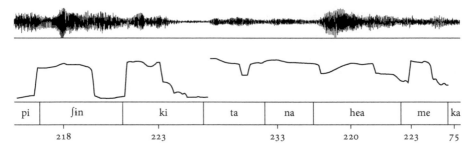

FIGURE 1. Intonational contour of the declarative clause in line 3, example (2)

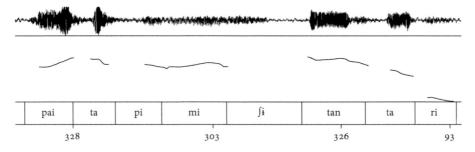

FIGURE 2. Intonational contour of the interrogative clause in (3)

3 The canonical imperative construction

Canonical second-person-directed imperatives are sheer prescriptions which command a speech act participant (the hearer) to perform an action. The hearer is either second person singular or plural.

Minimally, the basic form of the canonical second-person-directed imperative takes the second person marker + root + irrealis suffix, e.g. *p-ir-e* (2s-drink-IRR) 'drink!'. It could have additional morphology, as summarized in (4).

(4) The structural template of the verb used in the canonical imperative construction

second person index A/S	causative prefix	irrealis prefix	ROOT	suffixes			pragmatic and modal enclitics
				degree aspect modality	irrealis	person index O	

The imperative construction preserves the basic constituent order of the declarative clause VO, as illustrated in (5).

(5)   V   O
ani   p-a-an-ak-e=ya   paamari
brother-in-law   2s-take-DIR-PERV-IRR=AFF   fire
Brother-in-law, take a torch. (Cochachi et al. 2009: 65)

The scope of an imperative is limited to a clause. The corpus does not contain examples of an imperative clause being modified by a converbal clause, but complement clauses with reported speech sometimes follow the imperative clause. In (6), the command to tell is cast in irrealis, whereas the first verb in the dependent clause is inflected for realis.

(6) [pi-n-kant-e-ri]   [i-tiyank-ak-e-na   paba
2A-IRR-say-IRR-3M.O   3M.A-send-PERV-REAL-1SG.O   deity
aka   kipatsi-ki]
DEM.ADV   earth-LOC
Tell them that Paba sent me here to the earth. (Cochachi et al. 2009: 29)

The clausal scope of an imperative is illustrated in (7) by the monopredicative serial verb construction, comprising the motion verb *ja* 'go'+ action verb *aa* 'take'. Each verb in the command takes the irrealis marking. The distance suffix *-ai* occurs on the second verb in the serialized sequence, but it could also mark each verb.

(7) pi-ja-t-e   p-ai-t-e   saimpiki
2s-go-EP-IRR   2s-take.DISTN-EP-IRR   dry.twigs
Go and get some twigs.

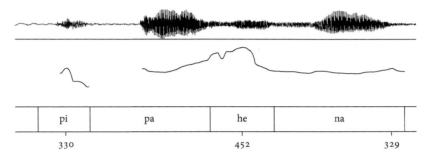

FIGURE 3. Intonational contour of the command in (8)

The defining formal characteristic of the canonical imperative construction is the intonational contour of commands. Figure 3 is an illustration of the contour of the command cited in (8).

(8) pi-m-p-aj-e-na
2A-IRR-give-TERM-IRR-1SG.O
Give it back to me!

The prosody of a command *pimpajena* 'give it back to me!' in (8) is different from the prosodies of the declarative and interrogative clause types, illustrated in Figures 1 and 2, respectively. The command is realized at the high level of the speaker's pitch range, with the Fo values measured at 330Hz at the start and 329Hz at the end of the clause. The strongest intonational prominence carried by the syllable [he] in *pimpajena* 'give it back to me!' has the Fo value of 452Hz. Crucially, the global downtrend is completely suspended.

4 First person cohortative construction

The first person cohortative construction is used to express mutual encouragement of both the speaker and addressee to engage in a proposed activity. There are no first person singular commands. The first-person-plural-directed cohortative construction is formed with the help of the special imperative particle *tsame* 'come on', of unclear origin, followed by any fully inflected action or motion verb. The verb is inflected for irrealis and is either indexed by the 1S/A.PL marker *a-* or by zero on the vowel-initial verb.

(9) [p-am-ak-e   tsitsi]   [tsame   oish-e-ro
2S-bring-PERV-IRR   firewood   come.on   1PL.A.start.fire-IRR-3NM.O
paamari]
fire
Bring firewood, let's make a fire. (Icantacota peeraniniri 1985: 102)

The imperative particle *tsame* takes limited inflectional (the progressive aspect *-atiy* and irrealis suffix *-e*) and derivational (e.g. distance *-ai*) verbal morphology, and the modal formative *=keti* 'urgent'. In a sequence, the function of the imperative particle *tsame* is that of invitation in first position slots in conversation. It conveys acceptance in the second position slot in (10).

(10) 'tsam-**atiy**-**e**-ri   a-ja-t-aj-e'   'tsame'
     come.on-PROG-IRR-NOMZ   1PL.S-go-EP-TERM-IRR   OK
     'Let's go back.' 'OK.'

When used on its own, the particle functions as an alternative cohortative form of the imperative paradigm of the motion verb *ja* 'go', e.g. ***tsame** obanko notsiro* (come.on 3NM.POSS.house 1SG.POSS.sister) 'let's go to my sister's house'. With motion verbs, it is optional.

The cohortative imperative disallows negation. When the standard negation strategy is used to negate first person plural verb forms, the negated verb form lacks a cohortative sense.

5 Third person jussive construction

The jussive construction, directed at third persons (either singular or non-singular), is formed on irrealis stems of verbs with the help of the intentional enclitic*=ta*. The jussive construction has a permissive modal sense, and is interpreted as a mild command. It lacks a negative counterpart. The jussive construction specifies the performer's gender, as illustrated in (11).

(11) o-m-p-e-mpi=**ta**   ora   obame-t-i-mpi-ri
     3NM.A-IRR-give-IRR-2O=INT   DEM.NOM   teach-EP-REAL-2O-NOMZ
     i-sankena-ri   pi-tomi
     3M.POSS-write-NOMZ   2POSS-son
     Let that female teacher (lit. the one who teaches you) provide your son with his books.

Alternatively, the jussive construction is formed with the clause-initial copula verb *kant* 'be this way' which functions as an auxiliary word with a modal sense of possibility in this environment. Both the copula (which receives the intentional marking by *=ta*) and the lexical verb are inflected for irrealis in (12).

(12) i-**kant**-ak-ea=**ta**   ir-o-ya   apaniro
     3M.S-be.this.way-PERV-IRR=INT   3M.IRR-eat-IRR   on.one's.own
     Let him eat on his own.

6 Summary of the imperative paradigm

Depending on the person category, the constructions in Table 4 are formed either synthetically or analytically, as exemplified by canonical second-person-directed imperative and by the first person plural and third person imperatives, respectively. Each imperative construction type has a special grammatical feature. The cohortative construction is marked by a dedicated imperative particle *tsame* 'come on'. The canonical imperative construction is differentiated from other clause types by its special prosody. The jussive construction is formed with the intentional =*ta* which in this context has a permissive meaning. An alternative way of forming a third person imperative is via the copula *kant* 'be this way' followed by a lexical verb. The copula is used as an auxiliary word, with this function being found only in the third person imperative construction. The irrealis marking of the lexical verb is the recurring element in the composition of the imperative paradigm. Another overlapping feature is the full indexation of the subject argument on the verb.

The canonical imperative has a negative counterpart; the first and third persons imperative forms do not have them. An important property of the imperative paradigm is that there is only a first person plural imperative; no singular counterpart exists. The second and third person imperatives are usually unspecified for number. The number of participants is understood from the context. However, if the speaker feels the need to disambiguate, the plural number suffix -*jei* is used (see example (15)).

7 Restrictions on the formation of imperative

7.1 Expression of the category of person

In commands, indexation of the A/S argument on the verb is performed in a regular way. However, there are two 'imperative-only' forms which occur without an A/S person marker. The forms have the semantics of motion and waiting, namely *kaate*

TABLE 4. The imperative paradigm

PERSON	SEMANTICS	MORPHOSYNTAX	SPECIAL FEATURE
1PL	cohortative	*tsame* 'come on'+ 1PL.A/S-verb-IRR	*tsame* 'come on'
2	prescriptive	2A/S-verb-IRR	special intonational contour
3	jussive	3M/NM.A/S-verb-IRR=*ta* 'intentional'	=*ta* has permissive meaning
		3M/NM.S-*kant*-IRR=*ta* + 3M/NM.A/S-verb-IRR	copula *kant* 'be this way'

'come!' and *(a)paata* 'wait!' The roots of these commands are semantically obscure; other elements constitute verbal formatives.

(13)   Composition of the 'imperative-only' verbs

FORM	GLOSS	FUNCTION
kaa-t-e	root-EP-IRR	command to move toward the origo (2p)
apaa=ta	stem=INT	command to wait (2p)

The imperative-only verbs often take the modal clitics *=ta~=tsita* 'intentional', *=ya* 'affect', or *=be* 'exclamative'. Their polarity cannot be changed, i.e. they cannot be negated. These verbs occur in the imperative form only, i.e. there are no corresponding verbs used in other persons. They are pervasive in discourse, being used by the speaker irrespective of their status.

The imperative form *kaate* 'come!' sometimes takes the directional *-an* 'directional source' and aspect markers, perfective *-ak* or progressive *-atiy*. The verb's valency is increased in applicative derivations, as exemplified by (14). The intentional applicative *-ashi* derives a two-place verb, with the goal participant indexed by the person index *-ri* '3M.O'.

(14)   kaa-t-**ashi**-t-e-ri=ta=be!
       move-EP-APPLIC.INT-EP-IRR-3M.O=INT=EXCL
       Move towards him! (Cochachi et al. 2009: 22)

The forms of the verb of waiting *apaata~paata* 'wait!' occur in free variation. They are used in a situation when the speaker commands the addressee to delay their departure or the start of an action. These imperative forms are often used with the modal enclitics *=ya* 'affect' and *=ta~=tsita* 'intentional'.

The 'imperative-only' suppletive verb forms are incorporated into the paradigms of the regular verbs with similar meanings. The regular verbs do not show person suppletion. The imperative form *kaate* 'come!' is associated with the paradigm of the regular motion verb *pok* 'come' (example (15)). The form *apaata~paata* 'wait!' is an alternative form of the regular verb *oyaa* 'wait' (example (32)).

7.2 Expression of plural number and aspects in imperatives

The category of plural number is marked on the verb no matter what person value is selected in the imperative. As illustrated in (15), the plural number suffix *-jei* marks the verb in an invitation issued by the host to a group of visitors.

(15)   pi-m-pok-a-**jei**-t-e
       2S-IRR-come-EP-PL-EP-IRR
       Come you all.

Among the imperfectives, the progressive suffix *-atiy* is often used in the imperative construction expressing a categorical order. The construction serves to emphasize the insistence of the command. When an adult person is the command's recipient, the construction with the irrealis verb inflected for the progressive aspect *-atiy* 'PROGR' and marked by the nominalizer *-ri* 'NMZ' is used. For example, when the host invites a visitor to enter the house, and he is hesitating, the host will enact an insistent commanding action, cited in (16).

(16) pi-n-ke-**atiy**-e-**ri**!
　　 2S-IRR-enter-PROG-IRR-NOMZ
　　 Enter already!

As illustrated in (17), the 'insistent' construction V-*atiy* 'PROG'...*-ri* 'NOMZ' is frequently employed by chiefs, when they instruct fellow villagers at the beginning of collective work, conducted on the premises of the native community (for example, cutting tall grass, repairing the gravel road, or planting flowers and bushes in the common area).

(17) [tsame　　 int-ea-ro]　　　　　 [shintsiji
　　 come.on　 1PL.A.begin-IRR-3NM.O　 quickly
　　 a-tsonk-**atiy**-e-ro-**ri**!]
　　 1PL.A-finish-PROG-IRR-3NM.O-NOMZ
　　 Let's begin it, we'll finish it quickly!

Other imperfectives are used in requests. The durative *-vee~-vei* marks a tentative wish in second person imperative forms (see §9, example (26)). In the same vein, when the iterative semelfactive marker *-apaint* is recruited, it makes the imperative sound more tentative. In (18), the semelfactive *-apaint* 'once' describes a single occurrence of a cycle. The semelfactive in a command is associated with a diminutive sense, implying to do less of X-ing than is normally expected. The imperative in (18) is directed at a child who is hesitant to grab a pen, which is offered by a visitor.

(18) p-a-**apaint**-e-ro
　　 2A-take-SEMEL.F-IRR-3NM.O
　　 Take it.

The imperative in (18) could also be used by a wife who is asking her husband to bring her a tool, or dry twigs, or a container filled with water.

The terminative suffix *-aj* and *-ajant* 'focalized terminative' and perfective *-ak* make the imperative form sound more categorical. In particular, in (19), when the male speaker invites his brother-in-law to check the contents of the fish trap, the focalized terminative *-ajant* highlights the endpoint of the event and its finality.

(19) tsame   a-ja-t-**ajant**-e=ta   shimperi
      come.on   1PL.S-go-EP-FOC.TERM-IRR=INT   fish.trap
      Let's go to the fish trap (to see if there is anything there). (Cochachi et al. 2009: 65)

In (20), the schoolteacher commands the students to listen to her explanation. The verb is marked by the perfective -*ak*.

(20) pi-kem-ab-**ak**-e   abirori
      2s-listen-DIR-PERV-IRR   2ADD.FOC
      You, too, will listen.

Considering other categories, gender (in third persons) and tense (distal past tense) are manifest in declarative and interrogative clause types. In commands, the coding of gender distinctions is limited to the jussive construction. The category of distal tense is not found in imperatives. The formal marking of passive voice is absent in the language, and is accordingly left unexpresssed in commands. Neither is the evidential category present (see §2).

7.3 Formation of imperatives with various types of verbs

Commands are typically formed with action and motion verbs. However, some stative verbs, which are viewed as referring to controllable states, allow the formation of first, second, and third person imperatives. The canonical imperative is illustrated in (21).

(21) pi-**yo**-t-atiy-e   abirori
      2s-know-EP-PROG-IRR   2ADD.FOC
      You, too, will learn!

A special command strategy is employed with verbs which speakers conceive to be referring to uncontrollable states. These include the copula *kant* 'be this way', and state verbs *kenkishire* 'remember', *ñashi* 'suffer', and *joki* 'be sick', the latter exemplified in (22). The strategy is realized via the polar focus construction with the verb *ari~aitake* 'be the case'. Depending on the context, (22) will be interpreted either as a warning or a promise.

(22) **ari** pi-**joki**-t-ak-ea
      PP   2s-be.sick-EP-PERV-IRR
      It is the case that you will get sick.

8 Prohibitives and preventives

As mentioned previously, the non-canonical imperatives do not have negated counterparts. In canonical imperative constructions, the standard negation strategy is used, namely the irrealis particle *eiro* + realis verb (Table 3).

(23) **eiro**   pi-pera-t-**ant**-a-tsi
      NEG.IRR   2s-be.lazy-EP-CHAR-REAL-NEG
      Don't be lazy.

In (23), the suffix -*ant* 'characteristic' marks imperfective aspect (the suffix's semantics has to do with the dispositions of a given entity, expressing an aspectual sense of regular or repeated actions and states; see Mihas 2015b). Overall, in comparison with positive imperatives, negative canonical imperatives exhibit limited morphology. Aspectual and modal suffixes are normally absent.

The apprehensive construction has a special grammatical feature distinguishing it from other imperative constructions formed with lexical verbs. The verb is inflected for realis, and is marked by the dedicated apprehensive enclitic =*kari*, as seen in (24).

(24) p-ob-ak-a-ro=**kari**
      2A-eat-PERV-REAL-3NM.O=APPR
      Beware of eating it.

The apprehensive statement is interpreted as a warning not to do something which could have undesirable consequences for the addressee. The consequences are deemed to be beyond the control of the addressee unless he or she desists from performing the perilous action.

9 Specification of the action's temporal, spatial, and phasal parameters

The default irrealis marking of commands is atemporal, but the language provides resources for specifying the timing of an action in a command. To express the temporal immediacy of the action commanded the modal clitic =*keti* 'urgent' is used, as illustrated in (25).

(25) pi-m-p-aj-e-na=**keti**!
      2A-IRR-give-TERM-IRR-1SG.O=URGENT
      Give it to me right now!

The action is expected to be completed without delay, but in some contexts, the endpoint of the urgent activity spans a period from the speaking moment to a day. The clitic =*keti* exhibits a special intonational contour in commands. It is produced as a separate intonation unit with a rising pitch. In contrast, in declarative clauses, it has a terminal falling pitch. In a declarative statement, it signals that the action is carried out without delay.

The spatial parameter of the action, which is expected to be accomplished far from the origo or the current speaker, is formally expressed by the distance suffix -*ai*, as illustrated in (26). The distance suffix -*ai* could also occur in declarative and interrogative clauses.

(26) pi-n-ken-a-**bee**-t-**ai**-t-e   poshiniri
      2S-IRR-go-EP-DUR-EP-DISTN-EP-IRR   game
      Go hunting for game. (Icantacota peeraniniri 1985: 45)

The wife's weak command in (26) is a statement made in response to the husband's announcement about his forthcoming hunting trip. The durative aspect *-bee~-bei* in (26) describes a temporally extended activity which lasts for a while. However, its use in the command seems to signal the speaker's tentativeness. In contrast, the speaker's insistence is coded via the terminative aspect markers which rigidly set the end point of an activity and convey an expectation of its successful completion (see §7.2).

The construction with the phasal verb *int* 'begin' + lexical verb is often used in instructive environments. In this imperative construction, both verbs are under irrealis and are marked by the second person subject index *pi-*. In (27), a teacher instructs her students to begin writing.

(27) p-**int**-ea-ro   pi-sankena-t-e
      2A-begin-IRR-3NM.O   2S-write-EP-IRR
      Begin writing (in your notebooks).

The aspectual adverb *aikero* 'still' plus a lexical verb form an imperative construction which urges the recipient to go on with their activity. For example, in (28) the mother instructs her son to keep walking behind his grandfather.

(28) **aikero** p-oija-t-e-ri   chaine
      still   2A-follow-EP-IRR-3M.O   grandfather
      Keep following your grandfather.

The negative polarity verb *aitapake~aitapaje* 'it is enough' is used in a command prohibiting the continuation of an action in progress. The construction is composed of the clause-initial *aitapake~aitapaje* followed by a lexical verb. The command in (29) is cited from a story about a young hunter who was warned by the shaman to stop hunting a particular species of monkey, called *osheto* 'maquisapa', 'spider monkey'. The meat of this monkey species is believed to be inedible; it is normally captured to be kept as a pet.

(29) **ai-t-ap-aj-i=be**   pi-mana-t-ak-e-ri   osheto
      PP-EP-DIR-TERM-REAL=EXCL   2A-shoot-EP-PERV-IRR-3M.O   monkey.sp
      Stop shooting spider monkeys! (lit. It is enough that you shoot spider monkeys) (Icantacota peeraniniri 1985: 67)

10 Adjusting the force of commands

10.1 Attenuating modal enclitics

Subordinated interactants usually resort to aspectual markers to attenuate the force of commands (see §7.2, example (18) and §9, example (26)). Modal enclitics are also recruited to manipulate the force of commands. In particular, to mitigate an order given, either =*mpa* 'doubt', or =*te*~=*teeme* 'negative affectivity', or the possible condition =*rika* is attached to the commanding verb. To cast a communicative move as a request, speakers often employ the dubitative =*mpa*. The dubitative clitic =*mpa* in (30) conveys a sense of possibility. The line is cited from a story about Aroshi who tried to attract the Moon man by offering him plantains, the Moon man's favourite food. Aroshi's plan was to hack off a piece of the Moon man's resplendent robe while he was busy consuming the plantains.

Request
(30) pi-b-ap-e=**mpa**   parenti?
      2S-eat-DIR-IRR=DUB   plantain
      Will you eat the plantains, ah? (Vargas and Candiotti 2004: 28)

The enclitic =*te*~=*teeme* 'negative affectivity' softens the force of the command. The enclitic in declarative statements indexes some sort of distress or anxiety, whereas in the imperative construction it indicates a persistent request. In (31), an adult son asks his mother to bring him cooked manioc.

Persistent request
(31) p-am-ak-e=**te**   kaniri
      2S-bring-PERV-IRR=NEG.AFF   manioc
      Bring (me) the manioc, please.

10.2 Intensifying modal enclitics

Strong commands include the basic canonical imperative form, marked by the irrealis suffix on the verb. In addition, emphatic forms are produced by the cliticizing modal formatives, such as =*be* 'exclamative', =*ya* 'affect', or =*ta* 'intentional'. The intensifying modal enclitics make commands sound compulsory and categorical. In (32), the grandmother orders the child to wait at the table before she serves the food, instead of him fetching the food himself. Her command is marked by =*ta* 'intentional', which has an urgent sense in this pragmatic context.

(32) p-oya-ab-ak-e=**ta**
      2S-wait-DIR-PERV-IRR=INT
      Wait for it.

In (33), the father prohibits his children from taking any food from strangers because it could be contaminated with a harmful substance used by sorcerers. His demand not to partake of the food is marked by the affect enclitic =*ya*.

(33) eiro=**ya**   p-a-i-ro-tsi
      NEG.IRR=AFF   2A-take-REAL-3NM.O-NEG
      Don't you ever take it.

11 Command strategies

11.1 *Modal and evaluative verb*

The obligative modal verb *ontimatiye* 'be necessary' occurs in command strategies either to convey a sense of compulsion due to an established rule, or due to the transformative entity's whim. The construction in (34) is often recruited by older adults to advise younger kinfolk.

Advice

(34) **ontimatiye** p-ob-ak-ea ora   kipatsi
  be.necessary 2S-eat-PERV-IRR DEM.NOM dirt
  You should eat that dirt.

The negative polarity evaluative verb *te onkametsate* + irrealis verb is used to give a warning.

Warning

(35) **te**   **o-n-kametsa-t-e**
  NEG.REAL 3NM.S-IRR-be.good-EP-IRR
  pi-kaa-t-ako-t-e-ro   p-iraaja
  2A-bathe-EP-APPLIC.GEN-EP-IRR-3NM.O 2POSS-blood
  It is not good to bathe in the river during your period.

Between male kinsmen and friends of the same sex, the first person cohortative construction or the 'I-want' + complement clause, exemplified in (36), are drawn upon by the initiating interlocutor.

Invitation

(36) **no-kob-ak-e**   y-oija-t-e-na
  1SG.S-want-PERV-REAL 3M.A-follow-EP-IRR-1SG.O
  aparoni ashaninka
  one   fellowman
  I want a fellowman to follow me. (Cochachi et al. 2009: 21)

The response could be articulated as the 'if-you-wish' counter-offer. The counter-offer contains the clause-initial verb form *pikoirika* 'if you wish' + the irrealis verb + counter-assertive topic pronoun *abinti* 'but you', as exemplified in (37). The enclitic *=rika* 'possible condition' makes the counter-offer sound less categorical.

Counter-offer

(37) **pi-ko-i=rika** pi-jiba-t-an-aj-e   **abinti**
  2S-want-IRR=COND 2S-lead-EP-DIR-TERM-IRR 2CNT.ASSERT
  If you wish, you go ahead. (Cochachi et al. 2009: 65)

11.2 Verbless commands

Verbless commands are produced in a situation when the speaker intends to urge the hearer to begin an action at once. Manner adverbs, demonstrative identifiers, ideophones, discourse markers, negative particle *eiro*, and gestures have been found to occur in this function.

The construction with a demonstrative identifier, *jeri* (masc) or *jero* (nmasc) 'here you are' in (38), serves to command the recipient to take hold of something proffered.

(38) 'no-ko-i   n-a-ye   pi-shima-ne'
    1SG.S-want-REAL   1SG.S-take-IRR   2POSS-fish-POSS
    ['jerira]   [p-a-ye']
    DEM.ID   2S-take-IRR
    'I want to take your fish.' 'Here you are, take it.' (Cochachi et al. 2009: 93)

Demonstrative identifiers are used either on their own or in combination with the lexical verb marked by the second person A/S index. The demonstrative enclitics =*ka* 'proximal', =*ra* 'medial', or =*nta* 'distal' are sometimes attached to the demonstrative identifiers.

Some verbless commands are based on the discourse particle *intsi~jentsite*, translated into Spanish *a ver* 'let's see'. The discourse particle functions as a command to begin a new cycle of an activity. In imperative constructions, it can be used on its own or in combination with the inflected lexical verb, indexed by the second person subject marker. The line in (39) is cited from a folk story about a foolish Jaguar man, *maniti*, who is deceived by the Brazilian Cottontail man (forest rabbit species also known as tapeti, *Sylvilagus brasiliensis*), *kiima*. In the preceding dialogue, the Rabbit man offers the Jaguar man help during a windstorm. He wants to tie the Jaguar man to a post. The Jaguar man agrees by giving an order.

(39) [intsi=keti]   [p-oiso-t-ako-t-e-na]
    DISC.M=URGENT   2A-tie.up-EP-APPLIC.GEN-EP-IRR-1SG.O
    Go ahead, tie me up. (Icantacota peeraniniri 1985: 64)

11.3 Questions

Questions could be considered to have a commanding force in certain contexts. In (40), at the meal time, when the father poses a polar question, it functions as a request, because the man's child immediately fetches a spoon for him (see also example (30), §10.1).

(40) timatsi=mpa   pashini   kuchara?
    EXIST=DUB   other   spoon
    Is there a spoon, ah?

Or when a teacher in (41) introduces a newcomer to the class, her question *(paita) ojitari?* (the question word *paita* 'what' is often omitted in casual speech) 'what is it that she is called?' is understood by the children as a command to recite the newcomer's name in chorus.

(41) ['no-n-kinkitsa-t-aka-i-ro   Elena]
       1SG.A-IRR-tell-EP-APPLIC.CAUS.SOC-IRR-3NM.O   NAME
       [o-ji-t-a-ri?']   'Elena'
       3NM.S-be.called-EP-REAL-NOMZ   NAME
       'I will tell (a story) with Elena. What is it that she is called?' 'Elena.'

A special 'wishful thinking' construction is used when the speaker does not envision the present situation to change for the better any time soon. The construction in (42) is cast as a rhetorical question, and is formed with the special invariant optative particle *kantenane* 'powerless wish' plus an irrealis lexical verb.

(42) **kantenane** i-m-pe-ak-ea   maneo?
       OPT   3M.S-IRR-disappear-PFV-IRR   mosquito
       Why don't mosquitoes go away?

12 Responses to commands

12.1 *Agreements*

Commands are usually met with agreement, expressed verbally or non-verbally. The stand-alone forms of the verb *ari* 'it is the case', *aribe* 'it is very much the case', and *aritya* 'gosh, it is the case', the acknowledgement tokens *ja* or *aja* (its approximate equivalent is the English *yeah*) and agreement token *je* 'yes' are often employed. In (43), the first speaker asks his conversationalist to pay him, to which the recipient responds with the acknowledgement token *ja*.

(43) 'intsi=keti   pi-m-p-e-na-ri   no-ireki-te'
       DISC.M=URGENT   2A-IRR-give-IRR-1SG.O-3M.O   1SG.POSS-money-POSS
       'ja   jeri   yoka   kireki'
       INTJ   DEM.ID   DEM.NOM   money
       'Go ahead, give me my money right now.' 'Yeah, here it is, the money.'

Verbal agreement is typically co-expressed by the addressee's brief direct eye contact with the commanding person.

12.2 *Disagreements*

When produced in response to a command, disagreements are usually coded by the disagreement token *te* 'no', without any further elaboration. To intensify the dis-affiliative force of the disagreeing action, the exclamative clitic *=be* is added. In (44), the shaman demands from the child an admission of guilt. The child responds with the short *te, teve* 'no, absolutely no'.

(44) 'abiro   matsi   pi-n-tsabe-t-e'   'te   te=be'
     2TOP   sorcerer   2S-IRR-confess-EP-IRR   no   no=EXCL
     'You are a witch. Confess.' 'No, absolutely no.'

The disagreeing action can be expressed in a more elaborate way, when a reason for the rejection is provided. In rejections, the counter-assertive pronouns are usually used, as illustrated in (45). The pronouns serve the task of countering the prior speaker's presupposition about the addressee's involvement in a given activity. The speaker's intent is to preserve an affiliative bond with the co-conversationalist, while offering an alternative course of action.

(45) 'tsame   amen-ai-t-e   shima'
     come.on   1PL.S.look-DISTN-EP-IRR   fish
     ['te   no-n-ko-ye-ji]   [pi-ja-t-e   **abinti'**]
     NEG.REAL   1SG.S-IRR-want-IRR-NEG   2S-go-EP-IRR   2CNT.ASSERT
     'Let's go fishing.' 'I don't want to. But you go.'

13 Mock-up commands

Interlocutors with superior epistemic access to the relevant knowledge domain use mock-up commands as a subtle way of expressing marked disagreement. In a story about two brothers-in-law, *Tibiito* 'Dung Beetle' and *Pironi* 'Lightning Bug', the Dung Beetle man behaves uncooperatively during the fishing outing. In (46), he rejects his relative's advice to take a torch to illuminate the trail on the way home in the darkness, because he thinks that he is capable of emitting light. The Lightning Bug man responds with what looks like a prohibitive verb form, *eiro paitsi paamari* 'you won't take a torch', but is in fact a veiled negative assessment of the interlocutor's previous statement.

(46) Mock-up command
1 Pi p-a-an-ak-e=ya   paamari
     2S-take-DIR-PERV-IRR=AFF   fire
     a-piy-ant-aj-ea-ri   tsiteni-ri-ki
     1PL.S-return-APPLIC.REAS-TERM-IRR-NOMZ   be.dark-NOMZ-LOC
     Take a torch in order for us to return home in the darkness.

2 Ti [eiro   n-a-i-tsi   paamari]   [ari
     NEG.IRR   1SG.S-take-REAL-NEG   fire   PP
     no-tsiyo-t-an-aj-ea   nainti]
     1SG.S-emit.light-EP-DIR-TERM-IRR   1SG.CNT.ASSERT
     I won't take a torch, but it is the case that I will emit light myself.

3 Pi aritake=te   **eiro**   **p-a-i-tsi**   paamari
     PP=NEG.AFF   NEG.IRR   2S-take-REAL-NEG   fire
     All right then, you won't take a torch. (Cochachi et al. 2009: 65)

TABLE 5. **Calls to spiritual entities**

FORM	FUNCTION	ORIGIN	SPIRITUAL ENTITY INVOKED
kaape kaape!	to call back a sick baby's soul, believed to be taken by a demonic entity	from *kaate* 'come!'	human soul
kemari kemari!	to make manioc grow well	from *kemari* 'tapir'	master-owner of manioc
mashero mashero!	to make manioc beer more potent	from *mashero* 'cane toad'	master-owner of toads

14 Calling people and other spiritual entities

People are usually called by the kin term or name. Sometimes, the interjection *jei*, usually in combination with *kaate(be)* 'come!' is used. A distinctive prosodic property of such calls concerns the articulation of the word-final vowel. When a call is produced, the last vowel of the kin term or proper name is elongated. There are no special vocative forms of personal pronouns.

Calling spiritual entities for help is part of native speakers' ritual behaviour. The calls are recited as ritual formulae. Table 5 summarizes the calls directed at spiritual entities. In particular, when a baby is sick, his or her soul is believed to be snatched by a demonic spiritual being. The baby's mother begins to call out to the baby's soul, *kaape kaape* 'come, come'. The goal is to bring the soul back, which will make the baby recover. Native speakers point out that *kaape* is a version of *kaate* 'come!'

Another ritual call, *kemari kemari*, is addressed to the female master-owner of manioc, asking her to make manioc grow as big as a tapir (*Tapirus terrestris*), called *kemari* in the native language.

A call for help can be directed at the spirit of an amphibian. When manioc beer is made, manioc mass is mashed and left for some time to ferment. To induce stronger fermentation, the call *mashero mashero* is made by the woman pounding the mass in the tub. The reason for asking help from the master-owner of all toad species called *mashero* 'cane toad' (*Bufo marinus*) is that this toad has glands which secrete bitter white milky liquid resembling manioc beer. If consumed in small doses, the effects are similar to the intoxication caused by vegetable drugs. It is believed that invoking the toad's name will make the beer more potent.

15 Commands given to pets and domesticated animals

The range of commands given to pets and domesticated animals is limited. They are either called for feeding or chased away. Overall, when calling pets and domesticated

TABLE 6. **Commands given to pets and domesticated animals**

NAME	CALLING	CHASING AWAY
otsiti 'dog' (often given names)	*shishi~shisho*	*sa sa, shi shi*
michi 'cat'	*mishi mishi*	*sa sa*
ashino 'donkey' (often given names)	calling by name, e.g. *Chokempo* 'brownish'	*vete* 'go away' (Sp.)
obisha 'sheep'	*pachito pachito* (from Sp. *pacho* 'chubby) or *obisha obisha* (from Sp. *oveja* 'sheep')	*vete* 'go away' (Sp.) chasing away with a stick
chancho 'pig' (often given names)	*kuch kuch*	none attested
teapa 'chicken'	*ko ko ko, to to to*, clicks, (or shaking the plate with dry maize)	*shisha shisha*, with shooing gestures
pato 'duck'	*pati pati*	chasing away with a stick
pavo 'turkey'	none attested	chasing away with a stick

animals, speakers either use Spanish or interact non-verbally. Some animals, such as donkeys, sheep, pigs, cats, and turkeys, are infrequently encountered in the households, and there is no long-standing tradition of verbally interacting with them.

As Table 6 illustrates, some calls imitate the sounds the species produce, for example *ko ko ko* or *to to to* are calls directed at chickens. Others use a diminutive form of the species, exemplified by *mishi mishi* (from *michi* 'cat'), *obisha obisha* (from Spanish *oveja* 'sheep'), and *pati pati* (from Spanish *pato* 'duck'). The call directed at pigs, *kuch kuch*, is borrowed from Quechua-speaking settlers. The Quechua word for pig is *kuchi* (Soto Ruiz 1976: 77).

16 Conclusions

In Ashaninka Satipo everyday talk, commanding communicative moves are 'a normal course of action', using the characterization from Aikhenvald's survey of cross-linguistic and cross-cultural patterns of imperatives (p.c.). In positive commands, the verbs are inflected for irrealis. Imperatives form a paradigm consisting of the first person cohortative construction with the discourse particle *tsame* 'come on', second person canonical imperative construction characterized by a special intonation, and the third person jussive construction formed with the intentional =*ta* either on the lexical verb or on the copula *kant* 'be this way' (Table 4). The canonical imperative has a negative counterpart, whereas the cohortative and jussive verb forms lack them. There is no special marker of the 'polite' imperative.

TABLE 7. **Linguistic resources used by co-conversationalists in commands**

SOCIAL ROLE	Basic 2p V-IRR	Attenuating enclitics	Intensifying enclitics	Perfective aspects	Imperfective aspects	-atiy...-ri	Constructions I-want +VIRR and if-you-wish
Superior	✓		✓	✓		✓	
Equal	✓		✓	✓		✓	✓
Inferior	✓	✓			✓		

While commanding, conversationalists tend to select specific linguistic resources which reflect their group membership status. Table 7 is a provisional summary of the interactants' linguistic choices. A subordinated interactant will employ a weak command, with the canonical imperative being coded by an attenuating modal formative, such as =mpa 'dubitative' or =te~=teeme 'negative affect', all of which have a requesting connotation. The semelfactive aspect marker -apaint and the durative -bee~-bei are used to soften the force of the command. In contrast, interactants inhabiting a superior social role usually draw on the perfective aspectual suffixes -ak 'perfective', -aj 'terminative', and -ajant 'focalized terminative', the 'insistent' construction formed with -atiy...-ri, and the modal formatives =ya 'affect' and =ta 'intentional', which make the commands sound more categorical and urgent. Social equals have recourse to the same linguistic means as conversationalists in superior roles, but they also use the 'want' and 'wish' constructions and counter-assertive pronouns. The basic second person imperative forms are employed irrespective of the social status.

The grammatical practices of Ashaninka Satipo commanding actions and command strategies show similitude to those of some other Northern Kampa languages such as Alto Perené. Although the Satipo and Perené Kampa varieties have non-overlapping systems of aspect and modal formatives, the patterns of command formation and their functions are essentially the same (e.g. for Perené, see Mihas 2015a).

Acknowledgements

I acknowledge with gratitude the Satipo Ashaninka language consultants Betsa Nelly Tomás Enrique (Impitato Cascada), Rosalia Huayoki Ernesto (Pitocuna), Seferino Marcial Ruiz (Puerto Ocopa/Tincareni), Emilia Chiri Chiricente (Teoria), Rinel Ruben López (Satipo), Irma Marcelino (Pitocuna), Victoria Iñori Piyabanti (Impitato Cascada), and Juan Maria Mayor (Impitato Cascada) for their contribution to this research. I thank Sasha Aikhenvald for the thought-provoking feedback on the draft of the paper. Fieldwork was funded by the James Cook University Faculty Grant and JCU Language and Culture Research Centre, which I acknowledge with gratitude.

References

Cochachi Vasquez, David Teobaldo (Chiroti), Cirilo Domingo Prado (Sampakiti), Rosa Maria Paulino Romero (Iroshita), and Jhon Edgard Cochachi Vasquez (Kobintsari). 2009. Editors of *Opempe, Oshintsinka noñane. El poder de mi lengua*. Satipo: Amabisec, Andes Books.

Datos generales: Población. 2015. Municipalidad Provincial de Satipo. http://www.munisatipo.gob.pe. Accessed 5 September 2015.

Descola, Philippe. 1992. 'Societies of nature and the nature of society', pp. 107–26 of *Conceptualizing society*, edited by Adam Kuper. London: Routledge.

Dirks, Sylvester. 1953. 'Campa (Arawak) phonemes', *International Journal of American Linguistics* 19(4): 302–4.

Icantacota peeraniniri. Cuentos de los antepasados. 1985. *Colección Literaria y Cultural* 3, *ashaninca*. Yarinacocha: Ministerio de Educación y Instituto Lingüístico de Verano. http://www.sil.org/americas/peru/show_work.asp?id=23313. Accessed 6 September 2015.

Mihas, Elena. 2015a. *A grammar of Alto Perené (Arawak)*. Berlin: Mouton.

Mihas, Elena. 2015b. Non-spatial setting in Ashaninka Satipo (Arawak). Talk given at the Round Table Meeting, Language and Culture Research Centre, James Cook University, 2 September 2015. www.researchgate.net/publication/281507805_Non-spatial_setting_in_Ashaninka_Satipo. DOI: 10.13140/RG.2.1.1124.7840.

Mihas, Elena. 2017. 'The Kampa subgroup of the Arawak language family', pp. 782–813 of *The Cambridge handbook of linguistic typology*, edited by Alexandra Y. Aikhenvald and R. M. W. Dixon. Cambridge: Cambridge University Press.

Ñaco, Guillermo Rosas. 2010. *Mesozonificación ecológica y económica para el desarrollo sostenible de la Provincia de Satipo. Caracterización social y antropológica, informe temático*. Iquitos, Perú: Instituto de Investigaciones de la Amazonía Peruana.

Pike, Kenneth and Kindberg, Willard. 1956. 'A problem in multiple stresses'. *Word* 12: 415–28.

Soto Ruiz, Clodoaldo. 1976. *Diccionario Quechua: Ayacucho-Chanca. Diccionarios de consulta de la lengua Quechua*. Lima: Ministerio de Educación, Insitituto de Estudios Peruanos.

Vargas, Lita and Candiotti, Aída. 2004. Editors of *Historias Ashaninkas para estar despiertos*. Lima: Ministerio de Educación.

Veber, Hanne. 1997. 'Pájaros pintados: Complementariedad entre hombres y mujeres en la visión de los Ashéninka del Gran Pajonal', pp. 125–40 of *Complementariedad entre hombre y mujer: Relaciones de género desde la perspectiva amerindia*, edited by Michel Perrin and Marie Perruchon. Quito: Abya-Yala.

Veber, Hanne. 2009. *Historias para nuestro futuro. Yotantsi ashi otsipaniki. Narraciones autobiográficas de líderes Ashánínka y Ashéninka de la Selva Central del Perú*. Copenhague: Grupo Internacional de Trabajo sobre Asuntos Indígenas.

Vilchez Jiménez, Elsa. 2002. 'El rol de la mujer en algunas comunidades amazónicas', *Escritura y Pensamiento* 5(9): 9–13.

Weiss, Gerald. 1975. 'The world of a forest tribe in South America', *Anthropological Papers of the American Museum of Natural History* 52(5): 219–588.

5

Commands in Zenzontepec Chatino (Otomanguean)

ERIC W. CAMPBELL

1 Introduction

This chapter is a description of commands in Zenzontepec Chatino: their grammar and the ways that speakers use them to get others to do things. The language has a formally complex, but robust, inflectional category of Imperative Mood, which is used strictly for canonical (addressee-directed) imperatives (Aikhenvald 2010: Chapter 1). Depending on the particular verb, Imperative Mood is expressed by one of three imperative prefixes (*kw(i)-*, *ku-*, *k-*) or by co-opting the Perfective Aspect. Second person singular pronominal inflection, marked by tone change, is omitted on verbs with imperative prefixes but retained on those that co-opt the Perfective Aspect and which would otherwise be homophonous with 3rd person declarative verb forms with omitted subjects. The Imperative Mood is a previously undescribed part of the complex inflectional class system of the language (Campbell 2011, 2019), and this chapter sheds light on other parts of the inflectional system, and their historical development.

All commands that are not canonical imperatives are expressed with Potential Mood inflection. This includes 1st and 3rd person directives, alternative strategies for addressee-directed commands, and the negative forms of all directives. The Potential Mood has many grammatical and communicative functions besides the range of nuanced command types, and ultimately the appropriate meaning is determined by the context of the interaction and pragmatic factors. The morphological complexity of canonical imperatives (many forms for one category) contrasted with the morphological uniformity of non-canonical directives (one category for many functions) reflects the grammar of Zenzontepec Chatino more broadly: it has idiosyncratic and prodigiously complex inflectional morphology, and formally simple but fluid syntax in discourse.

Commands. First edition. Alexandra Y. Aikhenvald and R. M. W. Dixon (eds)

Some basic information about Zenzontepec Chatino and the data used for this study is provided in §2. A grammatical sketch is given in §3, highlighting aspects of the language most relevant for understanding commands. Canonical imperatives are presented in §4, and non-canonical directives in §5. Some alternative strategies for expressing commands and the sociocultural and communicative motivations for using them are discussed in §6. Finally, general discussion and conclusions are given in §7.

2 Basic information about Zenzontepec Chatino and the data in this study

Zenzontepec Chatino (ISO 639-3: czn) is an indigenous language spoken by about 8,000 people in the municipalities of Santa Cruz Zenzontepec and San Jacinto Tlacotepec in rural south-western Oaxaca State, Mexico. It is the most divergent variety of Chatino, which is a cluster of at least three languages (Boas 1913; Campbell 2013a): Zenzontepec Chatino, Tataltepec Chatino, and Eastern Chatino, a group of about 15 varieties with varying degrees of inter-intelligibility (Cruz and Woodbury 2014). The map in Figure 1 shows the location and subgrouping of Chatino languages. Chatino and Zapotec together make up the Zapotecan family of the Otomanguean stock.

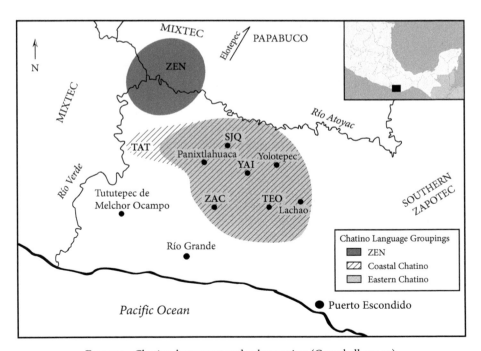

FIGURE 1. Chatino languages and subgrouping (Campbell 2013a)

The data presented in this chapter are from a corpus of about 18 hours of transcribed and translated texts of varied genres created by the author and Zenzontepec community members since 2009. Some examples are true commands from documented interaction, while others are embedded in narratives or description. None are elicited. Each example includes a reference with the name of the text and time within it, and these are accessible in the Endangered Languages Archive (ELAR) (Campbell 2013b).

3 Grammatical sketch

Zenzontepec Chatino is a head-initial language. Predicates by default precede their arguments: (1) shows an existential predicate and (2) an adjectival predicate.[1]

(1) **tāká**   **tyākwę́**
     exist   path
     There was a path. [historia2 16:06]

(2) **ti-katzǭ**   **choō? kę**
     ADJZ-warm.up   aloe
     Aloe is warm(ing). [historia.medicina 3:56]

Verbs obligatorily inflect for aspect/mood, which sets them apart as a lexical class. The intransitive verb in (3) is inflected for Perfective Aspect. Basic constituent order is VS.

(3) lē?   **nku-tiyaa**   tzaka   kwijnya?
     then   PERV-arrive.there   one   mouse
     Then a mouse arrived there. [dos.cuentos.raton 0:37]

Basic constituent order in transitive clauses is VAO. In (4) the verb is initial and the agent *nkwítzą* 'child' follows the definite article and precedes a demonstrative =V?. The patient *jii* 'ash' occurs last. It is introduced into the narrative here; it is non-specific and non-topical.

(4)   V   A   O
     lē?   **nkay-ukwą̄=kā?á**   na   **nkwítzą=V?**   jii
     then   PERV-grab=also   DEF   child=NVIS   ash
     Then the child also grabbed some ash. [nkwitzan.ti7i 4:19]

Constituent order is flexible and determined by pragmatic factors. In (5), which immediately follows (4) in the story, the narrator highlights the word *jii* 'ash', focusing it in initial position with OVA order.

---

[1] The orthography used here differs from the IPA as follows: *kw* = [kʷ], *tz* = [ts], *r* = [ɾ], *ty* = [tʲ], *ly* = [lʲ], *ny* = [nʲ], *ch* = [tʃ], *x* = [ʃ], y = [j], j = [h], Ɏ = nasal vowel, VV = long vowel, Ṽ = mid tone, V́ = high tone, '+' = compound boundary.

(5) **jii**   nti-kwi?   tī   naa
    ash   HAB-speak   TOPZ   1pl.inc
    jii ('ash') we call it.

The same narrative continues in (6), which illustrates two important points about Zenzontepec Chatino discourse and syntax. First, the agent (the child) is pronominal and highly topical, so it is omitted (represented as [.3] in the gloss). Second, the patient (the ash), now referenced with the 'non-visible' demonstrative pronoun *nuwę?*, is preceded by the particle *ji?į*, contracted here to *j-^{M}*, which flags it as a secondary topic (Dalrymple and Nikolaeva 2011).

(6) lē?   nka-tūkwá   **j-nuwę?**   nanē?   kweję
    then   PERV-put.in[.3]   NSBJ-3.NVIS   stomach   bag
    Then he put it in a bag.

Thus, the language has a rich system for encoding information structure, with articles, demonstratives, strategies for indicating topicality, and flexible constituent order, which may all co-occur.

Pronominal arguments of intransitive verbs also immediately follow their predicates. Each pronoun has an independent form and an enclitic form. Both forms of the first person plural exclusive pronoun are shown in S function in (7).

(7) n-tya?ą   **kwaa**   yākwá   n-chóte?ę=ya   tzajlyā
    HAB-go.around   1pl.exc   there   HAB-meet=1pl.exc   graveyard
    We go around there and we meet in the graveyard. [bruja.barbona 1:06]

Unlike 3rd person pronouns, which are often omitted if pronominal and highly topical, 1st and 2nd person pronouns are obligatory. In (8) the A argument is 1sg and the O is 2pl.

(8) k-etzā?=ą́?   ji?į=wą   tzo?ō   tzé?ā
    POT-inform=1sg   NSBJ=2pl   good   precise
    I'll advise you (pl.) very well. [historia.maguey 5:00]

The example in (9) shows the same two pronouns, but with grammatical relations reversed.

(9) nkwi-tyā?ná=wą   jy-ą́?
    PERV-pity=2pl   NSBJ-1sg
    You (pl.) had pity on me. [kwitijyuu 4:07]

Examples (7), (8), and (9) show that Zenzontepec Chatino has nominative-accusative alignment: if all arguments are overtly realized, only S or A may immediately follow the predicate. Only O may be flagged by the particle *ji?į*. In ditransitive constructions, the recipient (R) is always preceded by *ji?į*, and the theme (T) patterns like the

O in monotransitives: it is flagged by *ji ʔį* if topical (10). Thus, Zenzontepec Chatino has indirective alignment in ditransitives (Malchukov et al. 2010).

(10) lē ʔ   nu   nka-tāá   j-nuwę̄ ʔ   j-yū
      then   NOMZ   PERV-give[.3]   NSBJ-3.NVIS   NSBJ-3sg.M
      Then he gave that to him. [santa.maria2 12:08]

The particle *ji ʔį* not only flags objects but may also flag locative (11), beneficiary (12), or maleficiary participants, if topical.

(11) nt-utzę   kwaa   maxi   nu   tz-aa=ya   **ji ʔį**
      HAB-fear   1pl.exc   even.if   NOMZ   POT-go=1pl.exc   NSBJ[.3]
      We would be afraid to even go by **there**. [no.hay.brujos 1:10]

(12) liwrū   k-ujnyā=yu   **ji ʔį**   kitzę
      book   POT-make=3sg.M   NSBJ   village
      He is going to make a book **for** the village. [historia1 30:22]

The particle *ji ʔį* also flags the possessor in alienable possession:

(13)   Possessum   Possessor
      tzo ʔō   nti-ka+kiyā ʔ   na   lúkwī=V ʔ   **ji ʔį̄=ya**   wi ʔ
      good   HAB-be+market   DEF mezcal=NVIS   NSBJ=1pl.exc   there
      Our mezcal sells well there. [lukwi.historia 2:58]

Inalienable possession, in contrast, is expressed by encliticizing (14) or juxtaposing the possessor after the possessum.

(14)   Possessum=Possessor
      tāká=ū ʔ   ló ʔō   **nyá ʔa=ū ʔ**
      exist=3pl   with   mother=3pl
      They lived with their mother. [sol.y.luna 0:51]

Number is not grammatically marked on nouns:

(15) lē ʔ   nti-ji   tī   na   **wātá=V ʔ**   lē ʔ   nti-ji   **jni ʔ=V ʔ**
      then   HAB-die   TOPZ   DEF   cow=NVIS   then   HAB-die   offspring[.3]=NVIS
      Then the cows were dying and their offspring were dying. [vaquero 3:36]

Zenzontepec Chatino is a head-marking language. Most of the morphology occurs on the verb, which may be quite complex and made up of multiple prosodic words (ω). Figure 2 shows the Verbal Template (Campbell 2015). A verb minimally consists of a root plus aspect/mood inflection. There is no morphological tense. Verbs may occur with prefixes and/or enclitics, and may involve compounding. Subject enclitics, if present, occur in final position of the verb. The full set of pronominal enclitics is shown in Table 1, and this single set serves all grammatical functions.

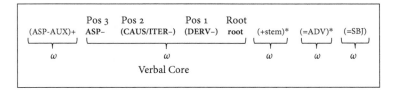

FIGURE 2. Zenzontepec Chatino Verbal Template

TABLE 1. **Zenzontepec Chatino dependent pronouns (Campbell 2016)**

		singular	plural
1st	EXC	=ą̄ʔ	=ya
	INC	—	=na / =ą
2nd		**TONE**	=wą
3rd	(any)	Ø	Ø / =ū̃ʔ ~ =jų̃ʔ
	NSPC	=ū̃ʔ	
	M	=yu	
	F	=chū̃ʔ	
	RSP	=nĩʔ	

Particularly crucial for commands is 2sg pronominal inflection, whose sole exponent is tone change (Campbell 2016). If the final prosodic word of the uninflected stem bears only a single M tone on its final mora, then the 2sg form has that M tone replaced by H tone (16).

(16) (Ø)(Ø)M   →   (Ø)(Ø)H

    a. jlyū   'is big'   →   jlyú   'you're big'

       nt-u-saā̃ʔ   'tears (tr.)'   →   nt-u-saá̃ʔ   'you tear (tr.)'

    b. jne jlyū   'thumb of'   →   jne jlyú   'your thumb'

       ch-uʔu=tzoʔō 'will live well' →   ch-uʔu=tzoʔó   'you will live well'

If the stem has any other tonal melody, then the 2sg form's final prosodic word has M tone on each mora (17).

(17) Any other tone pattern   →   (M)(M)M

    a. jne   'finger of'   Ø   →   M   jnē   'your finger'

       tyuuʔ   'will cough' ØØ   →   MM   tyūūʔ   'you'll cough'

       k-ōó   'will grind' MH   →   MM   k-ōō   'you'll grind'

       nk-y-ánō   'stayed'   HM   →   MM   nk-y-ānō   'you stayed'

       ntē-tákwi   'is flying'   (M)HØ →   MMM   ntē-tākwī   'you're flying'

b. nyá? kula   'grandma of'   →   nyá? kūlā   'your grandma'
   ?ne+tii=rīké   'can guess'   →   ?ne+tii=rīkē   'you can guess'
   y-akwi?+kí?yū   'bragged'   →   y-akwi?+kī?yū   'you bragged'

TABLE 2. Aspect/mood prefix classes (Campbell 2011)

	POT	HAB	PROG	PERV
A-c/A-2	ki-	nti-	nte-	nka-
A-2	ki-	nti-	nte-	nkwi-
B-c	ki-	nti-	nte-	nku-
B-t	(t → ty)	n- (t → ty)	nte-	nku-
B-y	(y → ch)	n- (y → ch)	nte-	nk-
C-a	k-	nti-	nch-	nku-
C-2	k-	nti-	nch- ~ ntey-	y- ~ nkay-

Otomanguean languages are known for having complex inflectional classes (de Angulo 1933; Smith Stark 2002; Wichmann 2006; Palancar 2011). In Zenzontepec Chatino, verbs fall into one of seven classes according to which allomorphs of the aspect/mood prefixes they take. Though the various prefix classes have general semantic and phonological bases (Campbell 2011), a verb's class membership is ultimately unpredictable. Table 2 presents the allomorphs that define the prefix classes.

A verb's tonal melody may change depending on which aspect/mood category it is inflected for, and there are nine such tonal alternation patterns. One cannot predict the tones in all of a verb's forms from any single form. The nine tonal alternation patterns are thus another layer of inflectional classes that cross-cuts, and compounds, the prefix classes, yielding some 39 attested prefix-tone classes, some of which have only one or two members and thus stand little apart from otherwise inflectionally irregular verbs (Campbell 2019).

4 Canonical imperatives: the Imperative Mood

Like other aspect/mood categories, the Imperative Mood in Zenzontepec Chatino has significant allomorphy, but a verb's imperative form is largely predictable from its prefix class. Imperative Mood is marked either by one of the prefixes kw(i)-, ku-, or k-, or by co-opting the Perfective Aspect. It is only used for canonical imperatives (Aikhenvald 2010), that is, pragmatically basic addressee-directed imperatives. In the following discussion, canonical imperatives with singular addressees are discussed first (§4.1), followed by those with plural addressees (§4.2). One irregular imperative exists in the language (§4.3), and some verbs appear to lack imperatives (§4.4). A summary and discussion of canonical imperatives conclude the section (§4.5).

4.1 Singular canonical imperatives

Canonical imperatives are formed by various strategies: the prefix *kw(i)-* (§4.1.1), the prefix *ku-* (§4.1.2), the prefix *k-* (§4.1.3), or by co-opting the Perfective Aspect (§4.1.4).

4.1.1 The Imperative Mood prefix kw(i)-

Verbs that belong to aspect/mood prefix-class A-2 take the special imperative prefix *kw(i)-* in the Imperative Mood (18).

(18) wa?ā   na   kí?yū nu   nch-ātí?   ji?í?   nakwę
     where.is DEF   man   REL   PROG-love[.3] NSBJ.2sg   say[.3]
     Where is the man that is in love with you?, he said,

     kw-etzā?   ji?ī!
     IMP-inform   NSBJ[.3]
     Tell him about it! [novio 1:26]

Prefix class A-2 has relatively few roots, but several of them are productive in forming compounds, which then populate the class with lexemes (Campbell 2011). Verbs with the iterative prefix *i-* fall into this class (19).

(19) **kw-i-tyu?u**   s-ātē?   jā   tz-aa=ą!
     IMP-ITER-be.in   POSS-clothes.2sg   CONJ   POT-go=1pl.inc
     Put your clothes on because we're going! [cotita 8:51]

Tonal 2sg pronominal inflection is absent in these imperatives (20), which is cross-linguistically common, since 2nd person is the default addressee of commands (Sadock and Zwicky 1985: 173; Aikhenvald 2010: 19).

(20) a. **kw-ise+toǫ**   ji?í̜   nī!
        IMP-turn+be.standing   NSBJ.2sg   now
        Stand yours (penis) up now! [cotita 11:07]

     b. #**kw-ise+tōǭ**   ji?í̜   nī!
        IMP-turn+be.standing.2sg NSBJ.2sg   now
        sought meaning: Stand yours (penis) up now!

For verbs with aspect/mood tonal alternations, the imperative stem's tone (21) matches that of the Perfective Aspect (22).

(21) **kw-ī?yá**   tzaka   júų̄   retā   nu   n-tzu?u   tí?no   tzúna   jata!
     IMP-transport   one   rope   load   REL   STAT-be   fifteen   three   armful
     Haul a load of eighteen armfuls (of pine)! [nikolasa 2:11]

(22) Aspect/mood forms of the verb -ĩʔyá 'to transport', organized by tone melody

	MH		ØM
IMP	kw-ĩʔyá!	POT	k-iʔyā
PERV	nkw-ĩʔyá	HAB	nt-iʔyā
STAT	l-ĩʔyá	PROG	nte-k-iʔyā

Some verbs that take the *kwi-* imperative prefix had previously not been classifiable into any one of the prefix classes. Their imperative forms suggest that they belong to prefix-class A-2:

(23) kwi-naʔa   nāá?   lóʔō   nkwítzą   jy=ą́ʔ!   ná
     IMP-see   1sg   and   child   NSBJ=1sg   NEG

     n-tyeję̄   tī   nūwá
     HAB-have.diarrhoea   TOPZ   3.DIST

     Look at me and my kids! They don't get diarrhoea. [historia1 16:10]

4.1.2 The Imperative Mood prefix ku-

Most verbs of motion and posture begin with /t/, and a few with /s/. They belong to aspect/mood prefix class B-t and take the Imperative Mood prefix *ku-*. Like imperatives with the prefix *kw(i)-*, they bear no 2sg tonal inflection:

(24) ku-taʔą!   ku-taʔą   jā   tzoʔō   k-īī!
     IMP-walk   IMP-walk   CONJ   well   POT-feel.2sg

     Walk around! Walk around so that you feel well! [historia.medicina2 6:22]

(25) ku-teję̄+tákwī   jā   yākwá   titzę   l-aa!
     IMP-pass+be.suspended   CONJ   there   frightening   STAT-be[.3]

     Pass across because it's frightening there! [derrumbe 0:19]

The imperative in (26) contains the vocative *jute?* 'ma'am', which also means 'aunt', and is a respectful way to address a woman. Its use serves to soften the force of the command.

(26) nteē   ku-tyukwā   jute?
     here   IMP-sit.relaxed   VOC.aunt

     Sit here ma'am! [lengua.tlaco 48:42]

The word *nkwítzą* 'child' is also used vocatively, to a younger addressee, and carries an endearing tone in imperatives.

A couple of verbs that belong to aspect/mood prefix class C-2 exceptionally take the *ku-* imperative prefix, instead of the Perfective Aspect as expected (§4.1.4):

(27) ku-la?   nyā?ā   kwātī?   tukwi   nya?ne   wá!
     IMP-touch   POT.see.2sg   POT.know.2sg   which   animal   DIST

     Touch (it) and you'll see and know what animal it is! [mujer.gana.diablo 6:55]

(28) ku-ta!
IMP-bathe
Take a bath!

4.1.3 *The Imperative Mood prefix* k-

Verbs of aspect/mood prefix class B-y inflect for Imperative Mood with the prefix *k-*, and 2sg tonal inflection is again omitted:

(29) k-yaą   k-ākū   chaja!
IMP-come   POT-eat.2sg   tortilla
Come and eat tortillas! [el.brujo 0:40]

(30) i   tī   nu   chāā   nyā?ā
and   COND   NOMZ   POT.go.back.2sg   see.2sg
And if you're going back, you see,

k-yaa!
IMP-go.back
go back! [nkwitzan.ti7i 6:05]

The imperative in (31) has a non-volitional addressee: corn plants. Though this might seem unusual, corn is such a central part of Mesoamerican life and subsistence that it is not surprising to see it anthropomorphized.

(31) k-ya+toǫ   nī   kela
IMP-go+be.standing   VOC   corn.plant
Stand up corn plants! [choo.kwe7en 4:29]

4.1.4 *Imperatives formed with Perfective Aspect*

Verbs that belong to prefix class A-c/A-u co-opt the Perfective Aspect to express Imperative Mood (32).

(32) nkā-?nē   tzá?.tzo?ō   ?nē   kwítī   jy-ą́?!   nteē
PERV-do.2sg   favour   POT.do.2sg   medicine   NSBJ-1sg   here
yánā   jy-ą́?
incense   NSBJ-1sg
Do me the favour of curing me! Here is my incense. [medicina1 12:54]

Unlike verbs with the special imperative prefixes, singular imperatives with Perfective Aspect always bear 2sg tonal inflection (33).

(33) a. nkā-tūkwā!   nkā-?nē   tī   jnyá!
PERV-put.in.2sg   PERV-do.2sg   TOPZ   work
Plant (corn)! And do (your) work! [kuna?a.kusu? 6:40]

b. #nka-tūkwá!   nka-ʔne   tī   jnyá!
   PERV-put.in   PERV-do   TOPZ   work
   sought meaning: Plant (corn)! And do (your) work!

Verbs of aspect/mood prefix class C-2 also co-opt the Perfective Aspect for imperatives, marked by the prefix *y-* ~ *nkay-*, and, again, 2sg tonal inflection is obligatory:

(34) y-a+k-īʔyā   ítā   tixi   yākwá   k-ōʔó
      PERV-go+POT-transport.2sg   water   sweet   there   POT-drink
      ų́ʔ   ntē!
      3pl   PROX
      Go get some sodas from there for these guys to drink! [historia1 5:18]

(35) nkay-oʔó   jiʔį̄!   nteē   chiī?   aja̧   nkay-oʔó
      PERV-drink.2sg   NSBJ[.3]   here   young.one   uh-huh   PERV-drink.2sg
      jiʔį̄!
      NSBJ[.3]
      Drink it! Here, young one. Drink it! [historia1 24:37]

4.2 Plural canonical imperatives

Plural canonical imperatives are formed using the same prefixes as their singular counterparts, according to aspect/mood prefix class. For example, class A-u imperatives, with co-opted Perfective Aspect, are shown in (36) and (37).

(36) nka-lōó=wa̧   jy=ą́ʔ?   jā   k-aja=ą̄ʔ!
      PERV-take.out=2pl   NSBJ=1sg   CONJ   POT-die=1sg
      Take me out of here because I'm going to die! [ni7.rosa 3:43]

(37) nka-suʔū=wa̧   jnē?   jiʔį̄   tī   laa?   nu
      PERV-show=2pl   dog   NSBJ[.3]   COND   like.so   NOMZ
      nku-tiyaa̧=kāʔá!
      PERV-arrive.here=again[.3]
      Show them the dogs if they arrive here again like that! [cuento.DSF 5:12]

Unlike singular canonical imperatives, which omit person inflection if they have a prefix unique to Imperative Mood, plural canonical imperatives always occur with the 2pl enclitic =*wa̧*:

(38) k-ya+tūʔú=wa̧!   lyakwā   n-kwanā=wa̧   s-ūʔwá=ą̄??
      IMP-go+be.in=2pl   why   PERV-steal=2pl   POSS-cargo=1sg
      Get up! Why did you steal my bag? [tres.hombres 2:29]

(39) kwī-nána=wa̧   tukwi   k-aku=wa̧   nt-ii=wa̧!
      IMP-ask.for=2pl   what   POT-eat=2pl   HAB-want=2pl
      Ask for what you (pl.) want to eat! [kwini7.laja 14:51]

4.3 Irregular canonical imperative

The verb *-aku* 'to eat' has an irregular imperative form. It is perhaps prefixless, with glottal stop epenthesis to avoid an onsetless syllable.

(40) ʔaku   tī   lākwĩʔ!   nakwę   ná   k-aku   tī   nãáʔ
     IMP.eat   COND   self.2sg   say[.3]   NEG   POT-eat   TOPZ   1sg
     You yourself, eat!, he said. I'm not going to eat. [cuento.DSF 9:47]

4.4 Verbs with (apparently) no imperative form

Aspect/mood prefix-classes B-c (41) and C-a (42) verbs are mostly intransitive and non-agentive. They tend to not occur in Imperative Mood, probably because the addressee has no control over the action.

(41)   Prefix class B-c
        -kiʔi   'get toasted'
        -kūnáʔ   'get thrown away'
        -jnii   'grow'

(42)   Prefix class C-a
        -aja   'die'
        -āsúʔ   'get old'
        -ala   'be born'

4.5 Summary and discussion of canonical imperatives

Canonical imperatives are formed with one of the three Imperative Mood prefixes or by co-opting the Perfective Aspect. Imperative formation is mostly predictable from prefix class. If an imperative verb has a prefix unique to Imperative Mood, 2sg tonal inflection is omitted. If the imperative co-opts the Perfective Aspect, then 2sg tone is required. The use of 2sg tonal inflection disambiguates these imperatives from 3rd person Perfective verb forms with zero anaphora. Plural canonical imperatives always bear 2pl inflection.

As Table 3 shows, the prefixes unique to Imperative Mood (*kw(i)-, ku-, k-*) differ from their corresponding Perfective Aspect prefixes (*nkw(i)-, nku-, nk-*) by lacking the initial nasal. This suggests a morphological or historical connection between the two categories. It is possible that, historically, imperatives were simply formed by co-opting the Perfective Aspect, as is done for verbs of prefix-classes A-u/A-c and C-2. This is in fact the case for 'strong imperatives' in Lachixío Zapotec (Sicoli 2010: 532), a language in the Zapotec group that is sister to Chatino. In Zenzontepec Chatino, all Habitual Aspect and Progressive Aspect prefixes, and most Perfective Aspect prefixes, have a preposed nasal. The Potential Mood prefixes and Imperative Mood prefixes do not. It seems that this nasal was perhaps a realis prefix at an earlier stage.

TABLE 3. Canonical imperative formation, compared with Perfective Aspect

Aspect/mood prefix class	Imperative Mood	2sg tonal inflection in imperative?	Perfective Aspect
A-2	kw(i)-	—	nkw(i)-
B-t	ku-	—	nku-
B-y	k-	—	nk-
A-c/A-u	nka-	✓	nka-
C-2	y- ~ nkay-	✓	y- ~ nkay-
B-c	—	—	nku-
C-a	—	—	nku-

The Perfective Aspect prefix *y-* is an exception, having no nasal, but it was a relatively recent Chatino innovation that has no Zapotec cognates with that function (Campbell 2011). The *nka-* Perfective Aspect prefix, which is co-opted for Imperative Mood, would be expected to have no initial nasal in that function. However, it is another Chatino innovation with no Zapotec cognates.

Coateco Zapotec (Beam de Azcona 2004) is like Zenzontepec Chatino in that Imperative Mood prefixes are nasal-less versions of the various Perfective Aspect prefixes. This shared pattern is either archaic, dating back to proto-Zapotecan, or it is due to language contact between Chatino and Coatecan languages.

5 Prohibitives and non-canonical imperatives

This section describes several types of non-canonical imperatives: addressee-directed prohibitives (§5.1), 1st person directives and prohibitives (§5.2), and 3rd person directives and prohibitives (§5.3). What all of these types of directives share is that they are expressed with Potential Mood inflection and their directive nature is interpreted from context.

5.1 Prohibitives

Prohibitives are directives that command what not to do. Addressee-directed prohibitives in Zenzontepec Chatino are formed with one of the standard negation particles preceding the verb, which is inflected for Potential Mood and 2nd person. For singular addressees, 2sg tonal inflection occurs:

(43) naʔā   ʔnē   jnyá!
      not.any.more   POT.do.2sg   work
      Don't work any more! [nkwitzan.tiʔi 15:28]

(44) ná   nīkwę̄   tu   nāá̰? n-tákwī=ā̰?   kya?a!
      NEG   POT.say.2sg HYPOTH   1sg   STAT-be.hanging=1sg   guilt
      Don't say that it is my fault! [nikolasa 3:16]

In 2nd person plural prohibitives, a negator precedes a verb with Potential Mood and
2pl inflection:

(45) ná   k-u-lā+tḗ?é=wą̄   lyo?o=wą̄!
      NEG   POT-CAUS-let.go+be.located=2pl   spouse=2pl
      Don't abandon your wives!,

      ná   ta+sā?ą́=wą̄   lyo?o   nyatḗ!
      NEG   POT.become+attached=2pl   spouse   person
      Don't hook up with (other) people's wives! [lo7o.suku7we 5:04]

The example in (46) shows a reflexive plural prohibitive.

(46) ná   k-u-nu?u=wą̄   j-wą̄!
      NEG   POT-CAUS-destroy=2pl   NSBJ-2pl
      Don't destroy yourselves! [lo7o.suku7we 4:35]

Huddleston (2002) points out that non-agentive verbs that tend to not occur in
imperatives, such as Zenzontepec Chatino prefix class B-c and C-a verbs (§4.4), may
more likely occur in prohibitives. The verb in (47), -*aka* 'be', is a class C-a verb as a
prohibitive.

(47) ná   k-aka   kwa?ą̄ tzaka chu   to   kiī   chu   kixę̄?!
      NEG POT-be   2pl   one   NOMZ.H at   grass NOMZ.H wild
      Don't be men of the grass or men of the wild! [lo7o.suku7we 4:36]

Verbs of emotion and cognition tend to not occur in canonical imperatives in
Zenzontepec Chatino but regularly occur in prohibitives:

(48) ná   k-uwe=tī?=wą̄!
      NEG POT-get.ground=living.core=2pl
      Don't be sad! [ntelinto.itza? 2:08]

(49) ná   k-īī   tula   k-īī!   nkā-?nē!
      NEG POT-feel.2sg what   POT-feel.2sg   PERV-do=2sg
      'Don't think what you'd think! Do it!' [kuna7a.kusu7 7:19]

The verb -*aku* 'eat', which has an irregular imperative form (§4.3), has irregular
prohibitive forms fused with negators:

(50) na?ā-kū   sukā!   na?ā-kū   jnyá?!
      not.any.more-eat.2sg   sugar   not.any.more-eat.2sg   chilli.pepper
      Don't eat sugar any more! Don't eat chillies any more!,

na?ā-kū   kuwe?!   ná   tukwi k-ākū!
not.any.more-eat.2sg pork   NEG   what   POT-eat.2sg
Don't eat pork any more! Don't eat anything! [historia.medicina1 22:44]

5.2 First person directives

First person directives are commands in which the speaker includes him/herself with the addressee as the target of the command. In Zenzontepec Chatino, these are expressed by inflecting the verb with Potential Mood and 1st person plural inclusive pronouns:

(51) k-ō?ó   naa   nii!
      POT-drink   1pl.inc   now
      Let's drink now! [amigo.borracho 3:25]

(52) tyatīkwá=ą   ji?ī=yu   jā   tyā?ná=yu!
      POT.help=1pl.inc   NSBJ=3sg.M   CONJ   unfortunate=3sg.M
      Let's help him because he's unfortunate! [matrimonio.escarabajo 2:07]

Prohibitive 1st person directives are preceded by a negator particle, but are otherwise the same:

(53) ná   k-ii   naa   laa?
      NEG   POT-feel   1pl.inc   like.so
      Let's not think that way! [familia 21:59]

These directives and prohibitives are homophonous with other 1pl inclusive Potential Mood forms, but context determines the specific communicative function. The verb 'go' is unique in that it has an irregular, even suppletive, hortative form: *kyá?ą* 'let's go!':

(54) kyá?ą   nya?a=na   tī   tza.jnyā?á
      HORT.go.1pl.inc   POT.see=1pl.inc   COND   true
      Let's go see if it's true! [sol.y.luna 6:35]

5.3 Third person directives

Formally, 3rd person commands are like other non-canonical imperatives. They use Potential Mood and person inflection (55), which, being 3rd person, may be omitted if the referent is highly topical:

(55) chaą=jū?   lō nu   k-a+tāká   jūntá!
      POT.come=3pl   when   POT-be+exist   meeting
      That they come when there is a meeting! [lo7o.suku7we 7:12]

The following passage is an elder from Santa María Tlapanalquiahuitl enacting how elders advise incoming authorities about how village people should behave under their watch. It is full of 3rd person prohibitives:

(56) ná   k-ūrá+tyáʔā=jǭʔ!,
NEG   POT-hit+companion=3pl
That they don't fight each other!

ná   tukwi=rūʔ la kosā nu   ki-kwiʔ
NEG what=even be thing NOMZ POT-speak
nyatē̠ nk-ā+kūʔwí=jǭʔ!
person PERV-be+drunk=3pl
That the people don't say things because they're drunk!,

lóʔō ná   tyejē̠+leta=jǭʔ   tzáʔ   kūʔwí!
and NEG POT.pass+path=3pl thing drunk
and that they don't get too drunk!

wisāʔ laaʔ tz-aa tī   kwaʔą̄!
for that like.so POT-go TOPZ 2pl
For that, you (pl.) will go! [lo7o.suku7we 6:52]

The final directive of the passage is addressed to the new authorities using the 2nd person plural. It is cast in Potential Mood because it is not a typical canonical directive with an expected immediate response.

6 Other addressee-directed command strategies

While there is a delimitable morphological category of Imperative Mood for canonical (2nd person) imperatives, there are other strategies available for directing addressees. Like other non-canonical directives (§5), they use the Potential Mood, but with 2nd person inflection. Pragmatic and sociocultural factors play roles in their use, and they display a range of illocutionary force and interactional nuance, from soft commands to stern demands, even threats, manipulations, humble pleas, or idealistic decrees about how people should act. For example, the directive in (57) is a command that is made less direct by packaging it as a statement.

(57) tz-a=lūū   pantiyō̠   jā   k-u-to+kāchíʔ=ą
POT-go=dig.2sg graveyard CONJ POT-CAUS-be.in+hidden=1pl.inc
tzaka jnēʔ!
one   dog
You'll go dig in the graveyard, because we're going to bury a dog! [novio 2:15]

The example in (58) is a plea for forgiveness. It conveys deference and no response is necessarily expected.

(58) ʔne+jlyū=tīʔ   jy-ą́ʔ!
POT.do+big=living.core.2sg NSBJ-1sg
Forgive me! [cuento.DSF 9:50]

A directive can be presented as an offer, but a forceful one with an expectation of acceptance, which is a hallmark of food and drink sharing practices in Mesoamerica (see e.g. Kearney 1972).

(59) k-ākū   chojo perū   wá   níjīkwá?   létā   tzoʔō   nt-aku!
     POT-eat.2sg   watermelon   DIST extremely   very   good   HAB-eat[.3]
     Eat that watermelon! It is extremely good to eat! [niʔ.mateya 5:29]

A directive can also be formulated as a question, as in the first line of (60), which is a desubordinated conditional clause. This strategy of desubordinated clauses as questions and then as commands is common in rural Oaxacan Spanish: *¿Si va a comer?!* 'If you're going to eat?!', or *¿Que no va a comer?!* 'That you're not going to eat?!'. It is not clear yet if this Chatino strategy is due to Spanish influence or vice versa.

(60) tī   nt-īī   tz-āā   la   nto   kyā?   jōʔó=V́?!
     COND   HAB-want.2sg   POT-go.2sg   to   face   slope   sacred=DIST
     Do you want to go to the top of the mountain?!,

     yākwá   tz-āā   tínií!   nakwę
     there   POT-go.2sg   now   say[.3]
     You'll go there now!, he said,

     jā   tz-a+kyāʔā   tzaka   kwénā   jy-ą́?!
     CONJ   POT-go+transport.2sg   one   snake   NSBJ-1sg
     because you'll bring me a snake! [juan.oso 3:49]

The desubordinated clause as question and directive in (60) is followed by two non-imperative addressee-directed commands in the Potential Mood. The scene is a priest commanding a troublesome youth what to do. The two final commands in the passage are pragmatically strong with no room for dissent. Potential Mood thus does not always attenuate the force of commands.

Another command strategy is to drop a question on someone out of nowhere, building in a presupposition that the action will occur, limiting the addressee's freedom (61).

(61) lakwa   k-iso=ą̄?   jį́   nu   k-ūjwī   j-nā
     how.much   POT-pay=1sg NSBJ.2sg   NOMZ   POT-kill   NSBJ-DEF
     torō   mpayū=V?ʔ!
     bull   beige=NVIS
     How much am I gonna pay you to kill the beige bull?! [vaquero 6:41]

Threats may be strong, non-imperative directives. The sequence in (62) begins with a question that is formally a statement, which is followed by further statements, altogether yielding a strong command and threat.

(62) ʔne+k-ākā   ná   ʔne+k-ākā   l-aa   tzáʔ
      POT.do+POT-be.2sg NEG   POT.do+POT-be.2sg STAT-be   word
      nti-kwiʔ   nāáʔʔ!
      HAB-speak   1sg
      Are you going to carry out or not carry out what I am saying?!

      jā   nāáʔ   ki-jnā=ą́ʔ   laʔā   tī   laaʔ   nu
      CONJ   1sg   POT-flee=1sg   well   COND   like.so NOMZ
      ná   ná   ʔne+k-ākā
      1sg   neg   POT.do+POT-be.2sg
      Because, me, I'm going to leave, well, if it's the case that…, that you do not
      succeed

      tz-āā   tz-a+lōʔō   jį̄   jūtī   tz-a+kūnáʔ!
      POT-go.2sg POT-go+with.2sg   NSBJ   father.2sg   POT-go+get.thrown.out[.3]
      in taking your father so that he get tossed away! [santa.maria2 4:18]

One can use 1st person reference to espouse what a collective and inclusive 'we'
should do, and how 'we' should live, in order to politely direct someone in how they
should act. In (63), a man respectfully advises a woman of similar age how to get
through some problems she is facing.

(63) nu jā   chukwi   laaʔ=kāʔá   tāá=na   xile   ji-nā!
      but   entirely like.so=also   POT.give=1pl.inc   strength   NSBJ-1pl.inc
      But just like that too we need to give our efforts!

      k-unána   naa   j-nā   tza tzáą̄   tza tzáą̄
      POT-ask.for   1pl.inc NSBJ-1pl.inc   one day   one day
      We're going to ask ourselves each day for…

      l-aa   k-aku   naa   l-aa   k-ōʔó=na!
      STAT-be   POT-eat 1pl.inc STAT-be   POT-drink=1pl.inc
      what we're going to eat and what we're going to drink!

      tukwi=rúʔ   ītzáʔ   nu   nte-tiyaą   sę ntoǫ   nyāʔā
      what=more   issue   REL PROG-arrive.here base face.1pl.inc POT.see.2sg
      Whatever other problem confronts us, you see,

      wiʔ   ntii   nāáʔ   ji̧ʔį̧   nti-kwiʔ=ą́ʔ   lō   nyāʔā
      NVIS   HAB-want   1sg   NSBJ.2sg   HAB-speak=1sg   like.so   POT.see.2sg
      that is what I want to tell you, you see.

      nkā-ʔnē   nu   tzaka   tīké=rī   tzaka!
      PERV-do.2sg   NOMZ   one   heart=only   one
      Do it with all your heart! [ntetakan7.jute7 6:31]

The last line of the preceding discourse is a canonical 2sg imperative, wrapping up
the whole advice sequence as a set of directives.

7 Conclusion

Though constituent order is typically discourse-based and fairly flexible in Zenzontepec Chatino (§3), it is firmly fixed in imperatives at VS/VAO, the basic constituent order of the language. Almost all canonical imperatives have the verb in absolute initial position, with a preceding adverb in only a couple of examples. Even in non-canonical directives there is a strong preference for verb-initial syntax.

In Zenzontepec Chatino, canonical imperatives form a discrete morphological category, the Imperative Mood, which is realized by one of three imperative prefix allomorphs or by co-opting the Perfective Aspect. Singular person tone occurs only when Perfective Aspect is co-opted. The selection of imperative prefix or Perfective Aspect is purely morphological, not pragmatic; it is based on inflectional class membership of the verb. In contrast, in Lachixío Zapotec (Sicoli 2010) commands are made stronger by perfectivity, and this is also the case in Ashaninka (Mihas, Chapter 4).

For all other commands, the polyfunctional Potential Mood category is employed. These include non-addressee-oriented directives, non-imperative 2nd person commands, and prohibitives of all types, the last being parallel to the use of irrealis in prohibitives in Korowai (de Vries, Chapter 12). All commands that are not canonical imperatives have obligatory person marking. No 1sg directives have been documented. This summary of the formal realization of commands is represented in Figure 3.

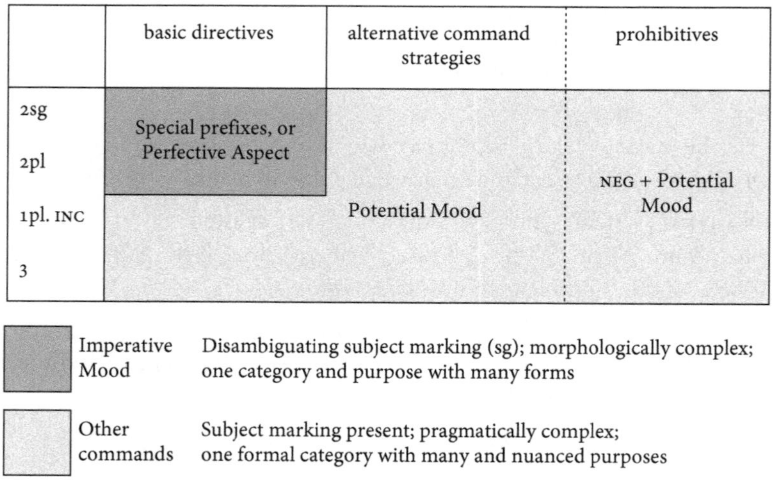

	basic directives	alternative command strategies	prohibitives
2sg 2pl 1pl. INC 3	Special prefixes, or Perfective Aspect	Potential Mood	NEG + Potential Mood

▉	Imperative Mood	Disambiguating subject marking (sg); morphologically complex; one category and purpose with many forms
□	Other commands	Subject marking present; pragmatically complex; one formal category with many and nuanced purposes

FIGURE 3. Zenzontepec Chatino Command structures

Of particular note is where the complexity lies. Canonical imperatives have complex and even idiosyncratic morphology, with rigid syntax, while the wide range of other types of commands are morphologically uniform but pragmatically complex. This is a microcosm of broader Zenzontepec Chatino grammar and discourse: it has prodigious morphological complexity and fluid, highly context-determined syntax and discourse. The two domains are very different, but both are where the action is.

Acknowledgements

Special thanks to Tranquilino Cavero Ramírez and Flor Cruz Ortiz for their collaboration in documenting their Zenzontepec Chatino language. Thanks to Sasha and Bob for the invitation to the conference and volume, and thanks to the other Workshop participants for helpful feedback. Parts of this paper were presented at the Mini-posium on the Chatino languages of Oaxaca, Mexico, at the University of Texas at Austin, 23 April 2015, and at CILLA VII, also at UT Austin, 31 October 2015, where additional helpful feedback was received. All remaining errors are mine alone. This work was supported in part by grants MDP0153 and IGS0080 from the Hans Rausing Endangered Language Programme (ELDP).

References

Aikhenvald, Alexandra Y. 2010. *Imperatives and commands*. Oxford: Oxford University Press.

Angulo, Jaime de. 1933. 'The Chichimeco language (Central Mexico)', *International Journal of American Linguistics* 7: 152–94.

Beam de Azcona. 2004. 'A Coatlán-Loxicha Zapotec grammar (Mexico)', PhD Dissertation, University of California, Berkeley.

Boas, Franz. 1913. 'Notes on the Chatino language of Mexico', *American Anthropologist, New Series* 15: 78–86.

Campbell, Eric. 2011. 'Zenzontepec Chatino aspect morphology and Zapotecan verb classes', *International Journal of American Linguistics* 77: 219–46.

Campbell, Eric. 2013a. 'The internal diversification and subgrouping of Chatino', *International Journal of American Linguistics* 79: 395–420.

Campbell, Eric. 2013b. 'Documentation of Zenzontepec Chatino language and culture', *The Endangered Languages Archive*. London: SOAS, http://elar.soas.ac.uk/deposit/0185.

Campbell, Eric. 2015. 'Valency classes in Zenzontepec Chatino', pp. 1371–406 of *Valency classes in the world's languages*, Vol. 2, *Case studies from Austronesia, the Pacific, the Americas, and theoretical outlook*, edited by Andrej Malchukov and Bernard Comrie. Berlin: De Gruyter Mouton.

Campbell, Eric. 2016. 'Tone and inflection in Zenzontepec Chatino', in *Tone and inflection: New facts under new perspectives*, edited by Enrique L. Palancar and Jean Léo Léonard, 141–62. Berlin: De Gruyter Mouton.

Campbell, Eric W. 2019. 'Layered complexity in Zenzontepec Chatino verbal inflectional Classes'. *Amerindia* 41: 39–74.

Cruz, Emiliana and Woodbury, Anthony C. 2014. 'Finding a way into a family of tone languages: The story and methods of the Chatino Language Documentation Project', *Language Documentation & Conservation* 8: 490–524.

Dalrymple, Mary and Nikolaeva, Irina. 2011. *Objects and information structure*. Cambridge: Cambridge University Press.

Huddleston, Rodney. D. 2002. 'Clause type and illocutionary force', pp. 851–945 of *The Cambridge grammar of the English language*, edited by Rodney D. Huddleston and Geoffrey K. Pullum. Cambridge: Cambridge University Press.

Kearney, Michael. 1972. *The winds of Ixtepeji: World view and society in a Zapotec town*. New York: Holt, Reinhart and Winston.

Malchukov, Andrej; Haspelmath, Martin; and Comrie, Bernard. 2010. 'Ditransitive constructions: A typological overview', pp. 1–64 of *Studies in ditransitive constructions: A comparative handbook*, edited by Andrej Malchukov, Martin Haspelmath, and Bernard Comrie. Berlin: De Gruyter Mouton.

Palancar, Enrique L. 2011. 'Revisiting the conjugation classes of Eastern Highlands Otomi', *Language Typology and Universals* 64: 213–36.

Sadock, J. and Zwicky, Arnold. 1985. 'Speech act distinctions in syntax', pp. 155–96 of *Language typology and syntactic description*, Vol. 1, edited by Timothy Shopen. Cambridge: Cambridge University Press.

Sicoli, Mark A. 2010. 'Shifting voices with participant roles: Voice qualities and speech registers in Mesoamerica', *Language in Society* 39: 521–53.

Smith Stark, Thomas C. 2002. 'Las clases verbales del zapoteco de Chichicapan', pp. 165–212 of *Memorias del VI Encuentro Internacional de Lingüística en el Noroeste*, Vol. 2, edited by Zarina Estrada Fernández and Rosa María Ortiz Ciscomani. Hermosillo: Editorial UniSon.

Wichmann, Søren. 2006. 'Sandhi tonal interno en la morfología verbal tlapaneca', pp. 337–55 of *Memorias del VIII Encuentro Internacional de Lingüística en el Noroeste*, Vol. 2, edited by Rosa María Ortiz Ciscomani. Hermosillo: Editorial UniSon.

6

What Dyirbal uses instead
of commands

R. M. W. DIXON

1 Preface

On beginning fieldwork in Dyirbal in 1963 I was determined to describe the language in its own terms, and not be prejudiced by preconceived ideas. However, I was naive in consideration of some verbal inflections. The bare form of a verbal stem—root, plus optional derivational suffixes—appeared to be used to tell someone to do something and I called this 'positive imperative'. When -m is added to a verbal stem and particle *galga* preposed to it (with dialect variations) this appeared to be 'negative imperative' (Dixon 1972: 110–13). However, these 'traditional grammar' labels are not fully appropriate; they tell only a part of the story. Now, fifty-two years into my study of this wonderful language, I can attempt redress.

2 Introduction

Before their traditional lands were inundated by European invaders (from the 1860s on), speakers of Dyirbal had a rich lifestyle. There was a profusion of food plants in the rain forest and to refer to these they had a fourth gender 'edible fruit and vegetables'. There were legends relating to what actually happened thousands of years in the past (such as the sea level rising). The systems of kinship and allied social organization were intricate, carrying with them specific communal responsibilities. A special language style had to be employed in the presence of taboo relatives such as mother-in-law and son-in-law. Young men underwent an initiation ceremony, and continued to absorb traditional lore and precepts for many decades. Conventions concerning behaving and speaking were followed as a matter of course; to overlook one would be a shameful thing.

Commands. First edition. Alexandra Y. Aikhenvald and R. M. W. Dixon (eds)

Life was regulated by common consent. A significant feature was that one person did not order another to do something or forbid them from doing something; there was no verb 'order'. And there was *no clearly defined speech act of commands*.

It is true that what I had called the 'positive imperative' verb form (glossed IMP) is frequently used with 2nd person subject and then provides a suggestion or advice. Sometimes the 2sg pronoun is stated, as in:

(1) ŋinda$_A$ yugu$_O$ maŋga
     2sg:NOM   stick:ABS   pick.up:IMP
     Why don't you pick up a stick (to kill the snake)?

However, the 2nd person pronoun may simply be understood:

(2) ŋuma!   yala-y   bungi
     father   HERE-LOC   lie.down:IMP
     Father! (You) can lie down (and sleep) here.

Each of these could, alternatively, be rendered by an imperative: 'You pick up the stick!' and 'Father! (You) lie down here!' However, this would not properly convey the pragmatic import of the sentences.

This 'imperative' inflection can be used with all three persons in all numbers (singular, dual, and plural). When the subject is not 2nd person, a translation involving the imperative in English is not possible. Consider, for example, 1du subject in:

(3) ŋa,   ŋali$_A$ munda   jabu$_O$
     yes   1du:NOM   follow:IMP   fish:ABS
     Yes, let us two follow the fish (as it swims upstream).

There are examples with 1sg subject, such as:

(4) jañja   wurrmin-ja   [ŋaja   bulŋgay-bi-ŋu]$_S$
     now   doze-A.LOT:IMP   1sg:NOM   tired-BECOME-REL:ABS
     Having become tired (from walking through the water), I'd like to doze off for a good while.

(The subject pronoun can be included or omitted, whatever its person and number. I have not been able to discern any principle determining when it is included, and when omitted.)

The subject can also be 3rd person. In the early years of the twentieth century, a white man called Dallachy used to terrorize the Dyirbal people, raping and murdering. He was referred to as *Gubarrngubarr* 'scrub itch', a parasitic red mite that causes severe skin itching. Chloe Grant recorded a story about how two Dyirbal men were chained up by Dallachy for purportedly stealing his sweet potatoes and melons. They called upon the spirits of their father and uncle for aid, and the chains fell away. They then burned down the huts in which Dallachy and his workers were sleeping. Early in the narrative, one of the Dyirbal men is quoted as remarking:

(5) [bayi-n-jana   giyi   Gubarrngubarr]$_S$ janja
     THERE:ABS:I-LINK-EMPHASIS   THIS:ABS:I   Dallachy:ABS   now
     jamu   buga-bi,   yimba-ban   bayi
     JUST   dead-BECOME:IMP   no-EMPHASIS   THERE:ABS:I
     gagal
     strong:ABS
     This Dallachy, I wish he was just becoming dead now, but no, he's (too) strong.

Considering these and other instances (a selection of which are given throughout the chapter), it seems that the most appropriate characterization for the bare stem form of the verb (previously called 'positive imperative') is: 'a potentiality, which is likely to be realized, but may not be'.

In (1), the verb form (hereafter glossed POT, in place of the original IMP) indicates that the addressee has the potentiality to pick up a stick in order to kill the snake. (In fact she does pick up the stick but before she can bring it down on the snake's head, it swallows her.) It can be translated by 'You could pick up the stick', or 'Why don't you pick up the stick?' In (2), a cosy sleeping place for father has been prepared by his two daughters, and they invite him to realize the potentiality of sleeping there: 'You can lie down here'.

In (3), two women suggest taking up the possibility of following the fish. The speaker of (4) is tired and decides to realize the potentiality of having a doze. The Dyirbal man uttering (5) muses on the desirable potentiality for Dallachy to die, but adds that it cannot be realized since he is too strong.

What had been called 'negative imperative' (NEG.IMP) involves verbal suffix -*m* and preverbal particle *galga*. A typical example is (with 2sg as the understood O argument of the first and S argument of the second clause):

(6) [ba-ŋgu-l   buŋu-ru]$_A$ bajal-bila,
     THERE-ERG-I   march.fly-ERG   bite-LEST
     galga   buŋa-m   yuramu-gu
     DON'T   go.down-NEG.IMP   river-ALLATIVE

There is a temptation to translate this as 'Don't go down to the river, lest march flies there bite you'. However, the second clause is not a prohibition, but rather a piece of advice, a warning, a caution. A more felicitous rendering is: 'Be cautious about going down to the river, since march flies there might bite you.' This combination of preverbal particle and verbal suffix (previously 'negative imperative') can be labelled 'caution' (and henceforth glossed CAUTION in place of NEG.IMP).

The focus of this chapter is on describing the morphological, syntactic, and semantic possibilities for the caution and potentiality verb forms. We shall need to distinguish the latter from other irrealis specifications: future tense, the purposive suffix which carries a consequential meaning, and the 'lest' form. But first, background information needs to be provided on the language and its grammatical profile.

3 Background

Dyirbal was originally spoken by perhaps 5,000 people, across a dozen or so tribes (situated part-way between Cairns and Townsville, North Queensland), each with its own dialect. When I commenced fieldwork there were several score fluent speakers; the last of them died in March 2011. Data for this chapter is taken from information provided for a comprehensive dictionary/thesaurus, and from recorded narratives and conversations in three dialects. These are, from north to south:

M   Mamu: on the tableland by the South Johnstone River
J   Jirrbal: at the base of the mountains, north of the Murray River
G   Girramay: just inland from the coast, south of the Murray River

There is a smallish phonemic inventory, with three vowels (*i, a, u*) and thirteen consonants. These comprise four stop/nasal pairs (bilabial *b, m*; apico-alveolar *d, n*; lamino-palatal *j, ñ*; and dorso-velar *g, ŋ*), two rhotics (apico-alveolar trill or tap *rr*, and apico-postalveolar continuant *r*), an apico-alveolar lateral, *l*, and two semi-vowels (lamino-palatal *y* and velar/labial *w*).

3.1 Grammatical profile

The language is basically agglutinative, using only suffixes. It is highly elliptical; any kind of constituent may be omitted if it is inferable from co-text and/or context. A full account of the grammar is in Dixon (1972, 2015).

There are four main open word classes:

$$\left.\begin{array}{l}\text{noun}\\\text{adjective}\end{array}\right\}\ \text{nominal}$$
$$\left.\begin{array}{l}\text{verb}\\\text{adverbal}\end{array}\right\}\ \text{verbal}$$

Nouns and adjectives take the same set of cases and share other morphological properties. A main criterion for distinguishing them is that generally a noun can occur with the marker of only one gender, while an adjective may be associated with several genders. Verbs and adverbals also show the same morphological possibilities. Just as an adjective typically modifies a noun, so an adverbal typically modifies a verb.

TABLE 1. **Marking of core syntactic functions in Dyirbal (J and M dialects)**

	1st and 2nd person pronouns e.g. 1 singular	e.g. 1 dual	nominals e.g. 'man'
transitive subject (A)	ŋaja (NOM)	ŋali (NOM)	yara-ŋgu (ERG)
intransitive subject (S)			yara (ABS)
transitive object (O)	ŋaygu-na (ACC)	ŋali-na (ACC)	

Adverbals include *ŋuyma-l* 'do properly', used in (21), and *gudi-l* 'do too much' in (37) and (38a). (The final -*l* indicates the conjugation class of the verbal; see §4.)

As in many Australian languages, 1st and 2nd person pronouns have one form (nominative) for transitive subject (A) and intransitive subject (S) functions, and a second form (accusative) for transitive object (O). In contrast, nominals use ergative case for A, and absolutive for S and O functions. This is illustrated in Table 1 (forms given for the J and M dialects). The major allomorph of ergative case is -*ŋgu*, as used here; there are several phonologically conditioned variants. Absolutive has zero realization. The G dialect differs in that just 1sg and 2sg pronouns have different forms for the three core functions, A, S, and O.

There are no 3sg pronouns. However, there is a set of 'noun markers' which fulfil some of the functions of pronouns in other languages. They commence with *ba(la)*- 'there (and unmarked)', *ya(la)*- 'here' or *ŋa(la)*- 'not visible', followed by a case marker, and finally a gender suffix. There are four genders: I, shown by suffix -*l*, is basically used for human males and all animals; gender II, shown by -*n*, covers human females, fire, drinkable liquids, and fighting; III, with -*m*, is for edible vegetables; and the residue gender, IV, takes no suffix. (There is a full account in Dixon 2015: 21–43.) The one irregularity is that the gender I absolutive 'there' form is *bayi*; this can often be glossed 'he'.

The noun markers, and also demonstratives and 3du, 3pl pronouns, inflect on an absolutive-ergative pattern, like nominals. There is an array of non-core cases, including dative, allative, locative, ablative, and aversive. This last indicates that the referent of the noun to which it is added should be avoided; it is used in (11), (28), and (41).

There are mild preferences for ordering: nominative before accusative pronoun, and absolutive before ergative nominal. However, the corpus demonstrates extensive variations from this pattern. In essence, phrases may occur in almost any order within a clause (their functions being shown by case), and words may occur in almost any order within a phrase, and also within a clause (their constituency being shown by shared case). Indeed, clauses can occur in varied order. For example, a 'lest' clause may be placed before a 'caution' clause, as in (6) and (40), or the other way round, as in (10) and (11).

Although the morphology is split between a linking of A plus S (versus O) for pronouns and a linking of S plus O (versus A) for nominals, there is a single principle for clause linking:

(7) Two clauses can only be linked, to constitute one sentence, if they share an argument which is in S (intransitive subject) or O (transitive object) function in each.

This is known as an 'S/O pivot' (often referred to as 'ergative syntax'). The four possibilities can now be illustrated (at the same time showing various combinations of potentiality, caution, purposive, and lest).

I.   S – S. Common argument is in S function in the first clause (here with potentiality marking) and also in S function in the second (here with purposive marking).
     When I was recording a group of people speaking Dyirbal, Jimmy Murray said to Rosie Runaway (his classificatory mother):

(8) mirra$_S$ ya-lu-bi   yabu$_S$
     front:ABS   HERE-TO.PLACE-BECOME:POT   mother:ABS
     wurrba-wurrbay-gu
     REDUP-talk-PURPOSIVE
     Let your front be in this direction mother, in order to talk a lot (into the microphone).

Here the S argument consists of the 2sg pronoun (not stated) plus *yabu* 'mother', extended in the first clause by *mirra* 'front'. In the first clause the locational adverb *yalu* 'to a place here' takes inchoative suffix *-bi-l* 'become' and the resulting derived intransitive verb is in potentiality form (using just the bare stem). A further example of S – S is in (24).

II. O – O. Common argument, *buni* 'fire', is in O function in the first clause (here with potentiality marking) and also in O function in the second (here with 'lest' marking):

(9) muymba   buni$_O$,   bural-bila   Dambun-du$_A$
     extinguish:POT fire:ABS   see-LEST   Dambun-ERG
     The fire should be extinguished, in case the Dambun spirit see it.

Chloe Grant told how, when she was a child and sitting round the camp fire at night, a noise was heard in the bush. The old people identified it as the Dambun spirit and hurried to extinguish the fire since, if Dambun saw it, she could come and torment the people. A further example of O – O coordination is in (12).

III. O – S. Common argument, *ba-n Dambun*, is in O function in the first clause (here with caution marking) and in S function in the second (here with 'lest' marking):

(10) galga   [ba-n   Dambun]_O   ginda-m
      CAUTION   THERE:ABS-II   Dambun:ABS   shine.light.on-CAUTION
      banim-bila
      come-LEST
      Be cautious about going out with a light (after dark) looking for the Dambun
      spirit, or she might come (and torment you).

Chloe took up a burning torch and set out looking for Dambun, ignoring the old people's warning in (10). Further instances of O – S coordination are in (6), (23), and (40).

IV. S – O. Common argument—which is unstated 2sg—is in S function in the first clause (here with caution marking) and in O function in the second (here with 'lest' marking):

(11) nangalnanga-ra   galga   bala-y   ñina-m,
      black.ant-AVERSIVE   CAUTION   THERE-LOC   sit-CAUTION
      bajal-bila
      bite-LEST
      Be cautious about sitting there because of the adverse effect of the black-ants;
      you might get bitten.

Note that the 2sg argument is omitted from (9), (10), and (11). The common argument—*buni* in (9) and *Dambun* in (10)—is included in the first clause of the coordination but omitted from the second. The argument in S or O function is the syntactic pivot, and in a transitive clause the A argument may not be considered necessary. Thus, the first clause of (9) is best rendered 'The fire should be extinguished' (rather than 'We/you should extinguish the fire'). And the second clause of (11) as 'You might get bitten' (rather than 'The blacks ants might bite you'), even though the identity of the potential biters is clear from the co-text.

4 Verbal structure

With just half-a-dozen exceptions, each verb and adverbal is either strictly intransitive—taking a single core argument, in S function—or strictly transitive—taking two core arguments, in A and O functions. Each verb belongs to one of two conjugation classes, which I show by writing -*y* or -*l* on the stem. There is a correlation, but no coincidence, between the two parameters: about 90% of transitive verbs belong to the -*l* conjugation, and about 80% of intransitives to the -*y* class. Where suffixes have varying forms, they are quoted as -*y* conjugation / -*l* conjugation.

Each verbal word commences with a root, then an optional array of derivational suffixes, and finally a choice from the inflectional system. There are two types of derivational suffix.

(a) Those that affect transitivity

- *-na-y/-ŋa-y*, applies to a transitive and derives an intransitive stem with anti-passive effect. Illustrated in (24).
- *-marri-y/-(yi)rri-y*, also applies to a transitive stem, deriving an intransitive one. Primarily reflexive, but can also be a general intransitivizer. See (17) and (37).
- *-barri-y*, plus reduplication of the first two syllables of the stem. Applies to a transitive stem with non-singular subject, and derives an intransitive stem with reciprocal meaning; see (27).
- *-m(ba)-l*, with applicative effect. Can apply to an intransitive stem, deriving a transitive (with comitative meaning, or as a general transitivizer), or to a transitive stem deriving an extended transitive (with instrumental meaning). See (20).

We can mention here suffixes which derive a verbal from a nominal (nouns or adjective) stem. Causative *-ma-l* forms a transitive verb; for example, *janu-ma* ('piece-CAUSATIVE:POT') 'let it be in many pieces'. And inchoative *-bi-l* creates an intransitive verbal stem with the meaning 'become'; this occurs with potentiality inflection in (5), (8), and (22).

(b) Those which do not affect transitivity and have purely semantic effect

Two of these have been encountered on potentiality forms:

- *-gani-y* 'do repeatedly', illustrated in (13b).
- *-ja-y* 'do a lot, etc.', illustrated in (4).

The other two are *-yarra-y* 'start/continue to do' (this occurs with purposive inflection in (32)), and *-gali-y/-nba-l* 'do quickly'. They have not been encountered on verbs marked for potentiality, but may well so occur within a larger corpus.

Reduplication of the first two syllables of a stem indicates an action being performed to excess, as in (8). This is attested with both potentiality and caution inflections; see (26) and (39).

4.1 Verbal inflections

Each verb and adverbal must make one choice from the following system:

(a) Suffix *-y/-l* or *-muŋa* or *-ginay* forms an agentive participle, e.g. *guñjal-muŋa* 'someone who drinks a lot'.

(b) Suffix *-ŋu* marks the verb in a relative clause. This takes the same case as that of the head noun it is modifying. It is illustrated in (4).

(c) Suffix *-ŋurra* shows that the S or O (pivot) argument of this clause is identical with the A argument of the preceding clause; and also that the activity described by the *-ŋurra* clause takes place immediately after that of the preceding clause; see Dixon (1972: 77–9).

(d) Suffix *-bila* has an apprehensive or 'lest' meaning, indicating something which may happen and would be unwelcome. This is typically accompanied by a potentiality or caution clause, as in (6), (9)–(11), and (40). Or it can be used alone. One day I was in the forest with some Dyirbal friends when we saw a large black goanna (lace monitor, *Varanus varius*) run up a tree. My suggestion that we might catch and eat it met with a single word response: *bajal-bila* 'bite-LEST'; that is, 'it might bite us (which would be unwelcome)'.

(e) Suffix *-gu/-li*, glossed 'purposive', most often occurs on the second clause of a coordination, where the first clause is marked for past, present, potentiality, or caution. Its basic meaning is '(intended or unintended) consequence'. We can have:

- The action of the first clause is performed so that the activity of the purposive clause should be possible (as a deliberate consequence). For example, 'Let your front be in this direction *in order to* talk (into the microphone)' in (8); see also (32).
- The second clause describes something which is a natural (but unintended) consequence of the action of the first clause. For example 'I made-PAST a noise, and as a result they hear-PURPOSIVE me (although I was sneaking around trying not to be noticed)'.

As mentioned before, the order of words in a sentence can be quite free. Consider

(12) giña$_O$ mada-li   budi
      THIS:ABS:IV   throw-PURPOSIVE   take:POT
      This (rotten food) should be taken, to be thrown away.

The rotten food obviously has to be picked up and taken out before it can be thrown away. The two verbs occur in the opposite order to their temporal realizations, but inflections make the sentence unambiguous. (Note that no argument in A function is stated here; it could be 'you' or 'we'.)

Purposive inflection is sometimes used in an initial clause, then referring to something which *has to be* done as a consequence of a need or obligation. For example, when Paddy Biran recorded a story about the origin of the cassowary, he began (addressing his friend Jack Murray, who was sitting alongside):

(13) a. ŋaja$_A$ ŋina$_O$ buway-gu   ñalŋga-ñalŋga-gu   jamu
          1sg:NOM   2sg:ACC   tell-PURPOSIVE   REDUP-child-DAT   JUST
          I have to tell you, just for the sake of the children.

      b. ŋaña$_O$ ŋinda$_A$ ŋaril-gani
          1sg:ACC   2sg:NOM   answer-REPEATEDLY:POT
          You should keep on answering me.

Paddy felt an obligation to record the story so that it would be available for his children, when he was gone, and so used purposive in (13a). Then in (13b) he employed a potentiality form in suggesting to Jack that he help him out by responding, saying 'yes' or repeating key phrases. (The purposive inflection could not have been used in (13b).)

(f) Suffix *-ñu/-n* indicates past tense in all dialects.

(g) Suffix *-njay/-ljay* in the G dialect, *-ñ/-ñ* in J and M, indicates future tense.

In M (and other northern dialects), the future suffix also covers present time, effectively making it a past/non-past system. In J and G (and other southern dialects), the past suffix also covers present, giving a future/non-future system.

Past tense is by far the commonest verbal inflection. Future most often refers to something that is intended or predicted to happen. For instance, Paddy Biran decided to illustrate an episode in a narrative with a related song, and said:

(14) ŋaja$_A$ ŋiña$_O$ baya-ljay
     1sg:NOM   2sg:ACC   sing-FUTURE
     I'll sing (it) to you.

Purposive was used in (13a) to indicate that Paddy felt an obligation to tell the story. The future suffix in (14) expresses an intention.

Future tense is often used with a time adverb, as when two men had been wondering about the weather and one predicted:

(15) gilu   mañji-ñ   garrii-ŋgu$_A$
     later.on.today   shine.on-FUTURE   sun-ERG
     The sun will shine on (us) later on today.

The future suffix has a second meaning, being used in general statements. For example:

(16) [bala   muŋan]$_S$ jana-ñ
     THERE:ABS:IV   mountain:ABS   stand-FUTURE
     The mountain is standing there.

(h) The plain stem, with no suffix, marks potentiality (previously called 'positive imperative'). This is discussed in §5.

(i) Marking of caution (previously called 'negative imperative') involves a preverbal particle and a verbal suffix. There is variation between dialects:

DIALECT	PARTICLE	SUFFIX
G	ŋarru	-mu/-lmu
J	galga	-m/-m
M	ŋarru	-m/-m

This is discussed in §6.

The most frequently occurring verb is the only irregular one. *Yanu(-l)* 'go' has past form *yanu* (where **yanun* would be expected) and potentiality form *yana*.

The potentiality and caution inflections occur on the verb of a main clause. There is no special intonation tune associated with them. (A verb with potentiality inflection in a question, as illustrated in (17)–(19), may show the final rise typical of a question.) It appears that these two inflections may be used with verbs of all semantic types, and with verbalizations of nouns, adjectives, and locational adverbs. (Dyirbal has no copula.)

5 Potentiality inflection

The potentiality form of the verb occurs both in polar questions—illustrated in (17), with 2sg subject—and in content questions—in (18), with 3sg subject, and (19), with 2du subject.

(17) ŋinda$_S$=ma   yala-y   ŋaygun-gu
      2sg:NOM=QUESTION   HERE-LOC   1sg-DAT
      miju-yirri
      take.no.notice.of-REFL:POT
      Will you wait for me here?

Question clitic *=ma* goes onto the first word of the sentence. When transitive verb *miju-l* 'take no notice of' is used with the reflexive suffix *-yirri-y* it means 'wait' (lit. 'take no notice of oneself').

(18) [baybu   wuñja-n   ŋaygu]$_S$ yana
      pipe:ABS   WHERE:ABS-II   1sg:POSS:ABS   go:POT
      Where could my pipe have gone?

The verb here refers to the potentiality of the pipe going somewhere (that is, getting lost) and interrogative word *wuñja-n* 'where (gender II, since this is the gender of the pipe)' enquires where it has gone.

In one legend a man, Mubunginmi, has two sons and two daughters. The sons cheat the daughters over food division and the women kill them. Mubunginmi follows their path and finds the hair, an eye, the skin, a foot of his sons. He uses the transitive interrogative verb *wiyama-l* 'do what to', in potentiality form, when challenging his two daughters:

(19) wiyama   ñubala$_A$
      do.what.to:POT   2du:NOM
      What could you two have done to (them)?

Note that while the verb in (17) is referring to future time, those in (18) and (19) relate to the past.

Since a verb in potentiality form can occur in an interrogative clause, this supports the inadvisability of calling it 'imperative'. The normal use of imperative is to label a mood, complementary to interrogative mood.

A serial verb construction (SVC) involves a predicate which describes a single event but consists of two (or more) verbals; these are underlined in the examples. In Dyirbal the verbals within an SVC must agree in surface transitivity and in inflection. For example:

(20) ninda_A mada   mandalay-mba   birrbubirrbu$_O$
     2sg:NOM   throw:POT   play-APPLIC:POT   cross.boomerang:ABS
     You have a go at playfully throwing the cross-boomerang.

A *birrbubirrbu* consists of two pieces of wood tied in the form of a cross. It can fly like a boomerang and children play with it before graduating to the real thing. The SVC here involves two verbs, transitive *mada-l* 'throw' and intransitive *mandala-y* 'play'. The latter has to be made transitive with applicative derivational suffix -*m(b)a-l*. Both are in potentiality form.

The SVC in (21) involves transitive verb *jurrga-y* 'spear' and transitive adverbal *ŋuyma-l* 'do properly', again both in potentiality form:

(21) dingal_O jurrga ninda_A ŋuyma
     head:ABS   spear:POT   2sg:NOM   do.properly:POT
     You should spear the head (of the eel) properly.

Note that, in keeping with the general freedom of word order, verbs in an SVC do not need to be contiguous.

In (22), noun *wawan* refers to the noise made by someone walking over dry twigs or leaves; an intransitive verb is derived from it by adding inchoative suffix -*bi-l* 'become'.

(22) ninda_S wawan-bi   bani
     2sg:NOM   noise-BECOME:POT   come:POT
     You should make a noise as you come (so as not to surprise people).

As illustrated in §3.1, two clauses can be coordinated to form one sentence if they have a common argument which is in O or S function in each. Sentence (23), which is highly elliptical, illustrates this where both clauses bear potentiality inflection; it comes from the same recording as (8). In 1963, a tape recorder was seen for the first time. Jimmy Murray explains to Rosie Runaway how it could play back the recording just made of her voice:

(23) gilu   ŋamba   wurrba
     later.on   listen.to:POT   speak:POT
     Later on, (you, A) can listen to (the recorder, O) and (the recorder, S) will speak.

In (24) the two clauses, again both in potentiality form, share an argument which is in S function in each:

(24) ŋinda_S   ba-li-dawu   bani,
      2sg:NOM   THERE-TO.DIRECTION-LONG.WAY.UPRIVER   come:POT
      jambun-gu   bañil-ŋa
      grub-DAT   chop-ANTIPASSIVE:POT
      You should come in that direction a long way upriver, and you can chop grubs
      (from a rotten log there).

In underlying structure 'you' would be A argument for the transitive verb *bañi-l* 'chop'. It is placed in surface S function (to meet the pivot condition) by applying antipassive derivation, shown by suffix *-ŋa*. (The underlying O argument, *jambun* 'grub', now takes dative case.)

In fact, the potentiality inflection is only rarely found on an antipassive. When (24) was played back to the narrator, he suggested that, as an alternative, he could have used purposive instead of potentiality; that is, replacing *bañil-ŋa* by *bañil-ŋay-gu* 'in order to chop grubs'.

Exhortative particle *gaji* 'try (to do it)' may be used with a verb with potentiality inflection, as in:

(25) gaji-jan   ŋinda_S   wayñji
      TRY.TO.DO-EMPHATIC   2sg:NOM   move.up:POT
      Go on, see if you can go up (to snatch the only fire in the world from the
      clutches of the rainbow serpent).

5.1 Types of subject

The subject (argument in S or A function) of a verb in potentiality form can be of any person or number. Its statement is always optional.

(a) 2nd person. 2sg is the most common subject for a verb in potentiality inflection, and we have already seen a dozen examples of this. An instance with a reduplicated verb is:

(26) jañja   buni_O   budi-budi
      now   firewood:ABS   REDUP-take:POT
      Now (you) should take lots of firewood (for a giant fire to smoke out the
      murdering grandfather).

A 2du subject is used in (19) and in the reciprocal construction:

(27) ñubala_S   wugal-wugaln-barri
      2du:NOM   REDUP-give-RECIPROCAL:POT
      You two should share things (lit. give them to each other).

(b) 1st person. There are a number of instances of 1st person dual and plural (which, when they have an inclusive sense, include reference to 2sg). For example:

(28) bayi-ñaŋga   yuray   ŋali_S   ñina
      THERE:ABS:I-AVERSIVE   quiet:ABS   1du:NOM   sit:POT
      We must sit quiet for fear of him (if we make a noise he will find us).

Many potentiality sentences with 1du subject may be translated by 'let us'. For instance, (3) 'Let us two follow the fish' and:

(29) ŋali_S   añja   ŋurba
      1du:NOM   NEW.ACTIVITY   return:POT
      Let us two go home (now that we've smoked out grandfather).

In the same way that 1du with potentiality inflection can often be rendered by 'let us', so some instances of 1sg may be appropriately translated by 'let me'. In one of several tellings of the origin of fire legend, a parrot offers to try to snatch the fire from the rainbow serpent, saying:

(30) yugu-gu   yana
      fire-DATIVE   go:POT
      Let (me) go for the fire.

Sometimes there are consecutive sentences, the first with 2sg plus a verb with potentiality inflection and the second an apparent echo of this with 1sg and the same verb with the same inflection. For example:

(31) a. yala-y   ŋinda_S   ñina
         HERE-LOC   2sg:NOM   sit:POT
         (Two sisters suggest to their grandfather:) You can sit here.

      b. ŋa,   yala-y   ñina
         yes   HERE-LOC   sit:POT
         (The grandfather replies:) Yes, I'll sit here.

There is another example of 1sg subject in (4), 'I'd like to doze off for a good while'.

(c) 3rd person. 3sg was exemplified in (5) '(I wish) he was just becoming dead'. A rather different sort of meaning is shown in (32). This is from an origin legend, describing how a boil formed on the thigh of the first man. He had to squeeze it (potentiality inflection) and as a consequence the first child emerged (purposive inflection) from the boil.

(32) añja   ba-ŋgu-l_A   burrubay_O   julma,
      NEW.ACTIVITY   THERE-ERG-I   boil:ABS   squeeze:POT
      [bayi   ñalŋga]_S   mayi-yarray-gu
      THERE:ABS:I   child:ABS   come.out-START-PURPOSIVE
      He needed to squeeze the boil, so that a boy child began to emerge.

One day, Rosie Runaway was sitting outside the local store after doing her fortnightly shopping and had forgotten to pick up her change. Someone brought it out and she exclaimed:

(33) jañja   [*change* ŋaygu]ₛ   banaga   giyiₛ
now   change 1sg:POSS:ABS come.back:POT THIS:ABS:I
Now this (gender I since this is the gender of money) change of mine had to come back (to me).

The change had the potentiality to return to her, and this had been realized. A similar meaning is exhibited in (18), 'Where could my pipe have gone?'

An example of 3du subject in a potentiality clause concerns two boys who, after having broken a strict taboo, had no option but to return to the camp in a state of abject shame:

(34) añja   [balagarra giyan]ₛ   ŋurba
NEW.ACTIVITY 3du:ABS   ashamed:ABS return:POT
The two of them had to return shamefaced.

5.2 Meanings

Some of the translations given here for sentences with potentiality inflection were as provided by bilingual consultants: 'why don't you' in (1), 'have a go' in (20), and 'see if you can' in (25); all these are for 2sg.

In essence, this inflection covers a ranges of meanings from the modality system in English:

- 'should' in (13b), (21), (22), (24), and (26) for 2sg; in (27) for 2du; and in (9) and (12) for 3sg in O function
- 'can' in (2), (23), (24), and (31a) for 2sg
- 'must' in (28) for 1du; 'need to' in (32) for 3sg; 'had to' in (33) for 3sg, and in (34) for 3du
- 'will' in (23) for 3sg; in (31b) for 1sg; in the polar question at (17) for 2sg.

Similar meanings are

- 'let us' in (3) and (29) for 1du; 'let me' in (30) for 1sg; 'let your front be' in (8) for 2sg
- 'would like to' in (4) for 1sg
- 'wish he was' in (5) for 3sg.

In content questions we also get: 'where could it have gone?' in (18) for 3sg, and 'what could you two have done?', referring to the past, in (19) for 2du.

The meaning of potentiality contrasts with future tense, which describes a prediction or definite intention, illustrated in (14)–(15), and also has a generic sense, as in (16). It also contrasts with the purposive inflection which indicates something that happens as a consequence, either of what has just been described or of an unstated need or desire; this was illustrated in (8), (32), and (13a).

These three inflections can be contrasted with 1sg subject *ŋaja* and the verb *yanu(-l)* 'go':

(35)   a. future   ŋaja yanu-ñ   'I will go' (definite intention)
       b. purposive   ŋaja yanu-li 'I need to go' (for some reason)
       c. potentiality ŋaja yana   'Let me go' (the potentiality is open to me, as
                                      in (30))

If one wished to employ traditional grammatical terminology, it would be possible (but not felicitous) to use an English imperative in place of the translations provided above for most of the examples with 2nd person subject—those with 'should', 'can', 'why don't you', 'have a go', and 'see if you can'. This accounts for less than half of the examples given here.

That is, imperative-type meanings (relating to 'directive speech acts') are a sub-part of the wide semantic range of the potentiality inflection in Dyirbal. And if the label 'imperative' were to be used, it should be emphasized that these are not what would be regarded as commands in other societies. They delineate suggestions and advice, needs and wishes. (I am not aware of any other verbal techniques which might correspond to commands in other languages.)

6 Caution inflection

The combination of particle plus verbal suffix essentially provides advice about some negative happening which might eventuate. For example:

(36)   [bayi-m-bayi   murrñu]$_O$
       REDUP-LINKER-THERE:ABS:I   full.of.energy:ABS
       galga   banja-m
       CAUTION   follow-CAUTION
       He's full of energy, it's not a good idea to follow him (you won't be able to keep up).

One of the few ordering constraints in Dyirbal is that the caution particle *galga* (in J) or *ŋarru* (in M and G) must precede the verb (as must general negator *gulu* 'not'). However, it does not have to immediately precede it. In (10) the O NP *ban Dambun* intervenes, and in (11) adverb *balay* 'there' does so; see also (39) and (42).

Like potentiality, caution marking may apply to a serial verb construction where the predicate consists of two verbals referring to a single activity. Particle *galga* or *ŋarru* only occurs once, anywhere before the two verbs, each taking the caution inflection. Note that although the verbs in (37) are contiguous, they do not have to be.

(37) bayi$_S$ galga   waymba-m
     THERE:ABS:I   CAUTION   walkabout-CAUTION
     gudi-yirri-m   Jigubina-gu
     do.too.much-REFL-CAUTION   Jigubina-DAT
     A man (lit. he) should be cautious about walking about too much (at night) for
     Jigubina (the shooting star, an evil spirit, who attacks people wandering about
     alone at night).

This involves intransitive verb *waymba-y* 'go walkabout' and transitive adverbal
gudi-l 'do too much'. The latter is placed in intransitive form by derivational suffix
-yirri-y, to satisfy the transitivity agreement condition on an SVC.

   We occasionally encounter the combination of a potentiality clause, advising what
should be done, and a caution clause, warning about what is inadvisable (these can
occur in either order). For instance, 'You should speak (POT) Dyirbal rather than
speaking (CAUTION) English', and:

(38) a.   ŋarriñji$_O$ galga   gudi-m   janga-m,
          orange:ABS   CAUTION   do.too.much-CAUTION   eat-CAUTION
          (You) shouldn't eat too many oranges,
     b.   yuŋgul$_O$ janga
          one:ABS   eat:POT
          (you) should (just) eat one.

There is another SVC in (38a), with transitive verb *janja-y* 'eat' and transitive
adverbal *gudi-l* 'do too much'.

   A caution clause may occur on its own. For example, a legendary character didn't
want it to be generally known where he was, and warned:

(39) galga   ŋayguna$_O$ mañja-mañja-m
     CAUTION   1sg:ACC   REDUP-draw.attention.to-CAUTION
     Be very careful not to draw attention to me.

However, there is often a reason given for the warning. This may be in the form of a
'lest' clause, as in (6), (10), and

(40) ŋuñiñ-ju$_A$ marbam-bila,   galga   mayi-m
     ghost-ERG   frighten-LEST   CAUTION   go.out-CAUTION
     Be cautious about going out (of the camp after dark) because you might be
     frightened by a ghost (which roam about at night).

Or there can be an NP in aversive case, referring to something best avoided, as in

(41) murju-ŋga   galga   yanu-m   wabu-ŋga-rru
     leech-AVERSIVE   CAUTION   go-CAUTION   scrub-LOC-THROUGH
     Be cautious about walking though the scrub for fear of leeches.

Or there may be an aversive NP plus a 'lest' cause, as in (11), 'Be cautious about sitting there because of the adverse effect of the black-ants; you might get bitten'.

The caution inflection is much less common than potentiality, and morphologic-ally less complex. Whereas the corpus includes the potentiality inflection following half-a-dozen derivational suffixes, with verbs in caution marking we find just the general intransitivizer -*yirri-y*, as in (37), and applicative -*ma-l*; plus reduplication—as in (39)—which indicates 'do to excess'.

The great majority of clauses in caution inflection have stated or implicit 2nd person subject. However, not all do; there is a 3sg subject in (37). The Dallachy narrative, from which example (5) was taken, includes the following, with the 1du pronoun in O function. (An A argument is not stated, but is inferred to be Dallachy, 3sg.)

(42) galga   ŋali-na$_O$ milma-m
      CAUTION   1du-ACC   tie.up-CAUTION
      We two shouldn't have let ourselves get tied up.

There is no formal similarity between potentiality and caution inflections, and their meanings also differ. Whereas only a minority of potentiality clauses could, at a pinch, be rendered by positive imperatives in English, most caution clauses could be paraphrased (albeit infelicitously) with *don't*. For instance, 'Don't draw attention to me!' in (39) and 'Don't walk through the scrub...!' in (41). However, this would not be possible for (37), with 3sg subject, or (42), which is focused on 1du in O function.

In English (and other languages), a negative imperative can be used (a) to forbid someone from doing something they haven't yet started, or (b) to tell them to stop doing something they are in the middle of. The caution inflection in Dyirbal appears only to be used for (a), not for (b). Transitive verb *jabi-l* 'stop someone doing something (physically, or verbally, or by eye gesture), refuse to allow' may be used in reflexive form for meaning (b), literally 'stop yourself (from doing something)'.

7 Conclusion

A clause bearing an inflection other than potentiality or caution can be negated by placing particle *gulu* 'not' anywhere before the verb. *Gulu* may not be used with a verb in potentiality form; the appropriate particle here is *galga/ŋarru* which requires caution inflection. This provides a clear link between potentiality and caution clauses (as was implicit in the erstwhile labels 'positive imperative' and 'negative imperative').

As in most languages, there are formulaic expressions for leave-taking, and these involve potentiality forms. If person X is leaving person Y, then Y may say:

(43) (ŋinda$_A$)   ŋayguna$_O$ galga
      2sg:NOM   1sg:ACC   leave:POT

And X may reply:

(44) (ŋinda_S)   ñina
     2sg:NOM   stay:POT

These are not commands (or directive speech acts) '(You) leave me!' and '(You) stay!' respectively. They are simply statements of what is happening: 'You are leaving me', and 'You are staying'—speech formulae to acknowledge the event.

There is always a temptation to describe languages in terms of conventional categories—to fit (or force) them into a familiar frame. This chapter has attempted to show that using the labels 'positive imperative' and 'negative imperative' (albeit in a wide interpretation) for Dyirbal would not fully bring out the genius of the language. No doubt the same applies for these and further categories in other languages.

References

Dixon, R. M. W. 1972. *The Dyirbal language of North Queensland.* Cambridge: Cambridge University Press.

Dixon, R. M. W. 2015. *Edible gender, mother-in-law style and other grammatical wonders: Studies in Dyirbal, Yidiñ and Warrgamay.* Oxford: Oxford University Press.

7

On the heterogeneity of Northern Paiute directives

TIM THORNES

1 Introduction

In this chapter, I explore a variety of grammatical constructions involved in expressing or asserting a desired action or outcome—what properly (and traditionally) fall
under the functional domain of commands (or directives)—in Northern Paiute
(Western Numic; Uto-Aztecan). I also describe the various situational contexts
appropriate to their use and make a preliminary assessment of their historical
developments, as both grammatical and sociocultural phenomena. This study is
intended to contribute to the typological literature on commands and on non-
declarative speech acts more generally (see, especially, König and Siemund 2007
and Aikhenvald 2010, inter alia).

2 Exploring directive speech

Directive speech has been widely observed to iconically relate form with function in
its grammar (Brown and Levinson 1987; Givón 1990; Haiman 2003). Illocutionary
effort is directly proportional to perceived or presumed social distance between
interlocutors. There is ample literature on the topic of defining what constitutes
social distance, while illocutionary effort, in its particulars, varies from language to
language. Seeking the relevant parameters of variation is, of course, one of the goals
of the typological approach.

　　Another goal of such a study is to seek a connection between grammatical variation
and the functional domain reflected in it. If we consider the simple speech act known
as the greeting, we see differences in the degree of effort coincident with the social
relationship (more elaborate=more formal/distant) or upon broader cultural concerns such as social hierarchy (more elaborate=more hierarchically attenuated).

Commands. First edition. Alexandra Y. Aikhenvald and R. M. W. Dixon (eds)
This chapter © Tim Thornes 2017. First published 2017 by Oxford University Press

Directive speech (including commands proper) may also be approached from this perspective. One approach is to simply elicit command forms from native speakers, arriving at translational equivalents of simple commands in a contact language. Such an approach reveals little of the richness of directive speech, however, which may involve a great deal more subtlety, and involve several grammatical subsystems in the language under study.

A usage-based approach to directive speech allows us to consider a range of so-called command strategies, and in so doing develop hypotheses about the origins and development of dedicated directive speech acts. For this exploration, spontaneously produced speech has been key to discovering and analysing the heterogeneous structures that comprise Northern Paiute directive speech. I invoke the work of others on closely related or neighbouring languages where possible, although the available material relevant to this domain is limited. Since no in-depth exploration of directive speech exists for any Numic language, I will focus my attention on the Northern Paiute materials at my disposal as a starting point. I will supplement my analysis with cognate structures from its nearest relatives to further our understanding of historical developments within Numic and general Uto-Aztecan. Hypotheses regarding these developments are necessarily preliminary until a more thorough comparative study of directive speech across the family can be undertaken.

Following a brief introduction to the language and its grammatical profile, I describe the canonical imperative along with several distinct command strategies, the prohibitive, and non-canonical directives in Northern Paiute. Later sections will take up historical considerations and general implications for a typology of directive speech acts.

3 The language and its speakers

Northern Paiute represents the north-westernmost extent of the Uto-Aztecan language family, consisting of around thirty distinct languages spoken from the northern Great Basin region of the western United States through portions of the American South-West, and across central Mexico as far south as El Salvador. It is one of two members (the other being Mono) of the Western Numic branch of the Numic subfamily. Numic languages have historically occupied most of the Great Basin, with the exception of Washo, a language isolate.

The area of Northern Paiute speech includes much of south-east Oregon, northern Nevada, southern Idaho, and California east of the Sierra Nevada mountain range. A major north–south dialect division is made on phonological grounds, but there are differences internal to this division as well as at all levels of grammar. The information presented here stems from work in the northern area and centres upon the dialect still spoken by members of the Burns Paiute Tribe of eastern Oregon, as well as archival materials.

There are probably no more than 400 speakers of Northern Paiute. In most communities, there reside just a handful of elderly fluent speakers. The vast majority of speakers are over 50 years old.

4 Preliminaries: Northern Paiute grammatical properties

4.1 Morphological and syntactic type

Northern Paiute is structurally agglutinating and highly synthetic, with verbs being the most morphologically complex word class. The language carries most of the features that typify an SV/AOV language, including postpositions and pre-head modifiers, although there is significant pragmatically determined flexibility and extensive ellipsis of arguments in context.

4.2 Word classes and grammatical categories

Nouns and verbs comprise the two large, open word classes of Northern Paiute.

For nouns, number is irregularly marked morphologically only on human nouns. There is no grammatical gender in Northern Paiute, although the language does carry the typical Uto-Aztecan feature of so-called 'absolutive'[1] suffixes—suffixes that appear with certain noun roots in their citation form, but not in other morpho-syntactic contexts. Northern Paiute also has denominalizing morphology indicating verbal notions like HAVE, MAKE, and WEAR.

The most morphologically complex word class, verbs have the general structure formulated in (1).

(1) Object= [Phasal [[Valence [IP/[Root]] Valence] DIR/ASP] SUB/NMLZ]
     PRO=   AUX   THEME   STEM   THEME PREFINAL FINAL

Verbs in Northern Paiute, by and large, fall into fairly strict transitivity classes. These include (1) zero-transitive (mainly weather and other natural phenomena), (2) intransitives that can be classified covertly into two classes, depending upon the semantic outcome of the causative-applicative construction (Thornes 2003, 2013), (3) transitive (generally requiring the addition of the antipassive prefix for object suppression), (4) ambitransitive of the S = O variety (semantically transitive but not requiring the antipassive prefix for object suppression) and (5) ditransitive (in a symmetrical, double-object construction).

A number of high-frequency verbs exhibit the strong stem suppletion common in Native North American languages. The pattern appears mainly sensitive to

---

[1] The use of this label for this particular morphological phenomenon has been widely attributed to Sapir (1930).

participant[2] number (singular versus plural) with an absolutive pivot, either the S of an intransitive verb or the O of a transitive verb. For the three basic posture verbs 'sit', 'stand', and 'lie', we find distinct forms for singular, dual, and plural.[3]

Verbs are rich in morphological markers of aspect and direction, although Northern Paiute is, arguably, tenseless, carrying only what could be considered a relative future tense marker. The historical development of many of these affixes via the language's specialized serial verb construction has been explored in detail in Thornes (2011). Irrealis marking that characterizes some forms of directive speech will be discussed below, as will the nominalizing and subordinating morphology. Northern Paiute verbs also carry several devices for altering, increasing, or decreasing the inherent valence. These may serve, in part, to identify the transitivity class of verbs.

A closed set of basic adjectives that code value, age, and dimension, as well as the lower numerals, share certain morpho-syntactic properties. Chief among these properties is the marking of nominative versus oblique (non-nominative) case. Basic adjectives may also be compounded with noun stems when coding an inherent property or otherwise serving a more restrictive, naming function, and are stripped of case in this context. Colour terms form obligatory compounds with the nouns they modify.

Adverbs and particles form a highly heterogeneous class, morpho-syntactically. Northern Paiute has a wide range of clitic types, which fall mainly into three categories. The first are proclitics functioning as definite determiners and non-subject pronouns, exemplified throughout the chapter. There are also several second position clitics that carry modal-evidential and some pronominal functions. They participate in several varieties of directive speech, along with irrealis marking. Finally, there are a small set of enclitics of narrow scope, indicating polarity, emphasis, and other focus-type functions.

4.3 Verbs and verb structure

Complex verb structures are exemplified below and may consist of stem compounding[4] (example (2)), lexical prefixation of the means and manner (i.e. 'instrumental') type (example (3b)), single word, asymmetrical serial verb constructions (à la Aikhenvald and Dixon 2006) (example (4)), and incorporated phasal auxiliaries (example (5)).

---

[2] Event number, a verbal aspectual category (cf. Corbett 2000), is also at play.

[3] It is my impression as well that this development is peculiar to Numic languages and is not found elsewhere in Uto-Aztecan.

[4] Several factors distinguish stem compounding from single word verb serialization in Northern Paiute. Formally, the applicative suffix will always follow a stem compound, but attach only to the first (main) verb in a serial construction. See Thornes (2011) for a more detailed list of properties.

(2) ɨɨ=sakwa   ka=toissapui   **i=sami-tɨki-kɨ**
     you=MOD   OBL=chokecherry   me=soak-put.SG-APPLIC
     You should put the chokecherries in to soak for me.   (NK[5]: Chokecherries)

(3a) su=tokano   nɨ   tsipugi-si   (3b) **i=tsa-tsipuki**
     NOM=night   I   emerge-SEQ   me=IP/GRASP-emerge
     Once I come out in the night...   Pull me out!

(4) oono   tɨwau   umɨ   na-**tɨničui-pokwa-'yakwi**
     at.that.time also   3.pl MID-tell.stories-lie.PL-HAB
     And then, too, they would lie around telling stories.

                                                (NK: Root-digging Time)

(5) nɨ   mɨ=**misu**-makwɨ-u-kwɨ
     I   PL=can/easily-defeat/finish-PUNC-FUT
     I will easily defeat you all.   (IW: Flying Contest)

Although, synchronically speaking, noun incorporation is not a productive process
in the language, several lexical prefixes have nominal origins, typically from body
part terms, with stem-compounding as their source construction (cf. Thornes 2003,
2009, 2011).

4.4 Grammatical relations

There is no argument agreement in the Northern Paiute verb, although unstressed,
object pronominal forms are bound to the overall verb structure as proclitics, as in
example (5). A formal syncretism exists between object pronominal proclitics on
verbs and the possessor proclitics that attach to nouns, a point related to the
language's extensive use of both lexical and clausal nominalization.

   Northern Paiute exhibits two core cases, which I label nominative (NOM) and
oblique (OBL). These are overtly specified in the form of pronouns and on noun
phrase dependents (modifiers and determiner proclitics).

(6) su=udɨ-ʔyu   naatsi kima-u-gi-na
     NOM=tall-NOM   boy   come-PUNC-CISL-PARTIC
     The tall boy is coming this way.

(7) nɨ   u=punni,   ka=udɨ-u   naatsi
     I   3=see   OBL=tall-OBL boy
     I see him, the tall boy.

---

[5] Examples drawn from texts include the initials of the speaker. Texts from the archived materials of
others include information about the collection in a footnote.

Case marking on head nouns appears to have been lost in Northern Paiute, while persisting, marginally, in the other two branches of Numic (Central and Southern).

4.5 *Clause types*

Northern Paiute basic clauses are fairly straightforward. Coordination at the clausal level is accomplished mainly through simple juxtaposition, although converbal marking is a common clause-chaining device. Interrogatives are also straightforward, with clause-initial question words, and the narrow-scope question enclitic *=ha* for polar questions.

Nominalization is the main strategy in forming a range of subordinate clause types. As a point of empirical fact, it is very rare to find either embedded complement clauses or headed relative clauses in natural discourse (cf. Thornes 2003: 441–7 and Thornes 2012). Nominalized subordinate clauses across the family have no doubt given rise to some of the peculiarities we occasionally find in the case marking of core arguments in directive speech in Numic languages. Diachronic issues will be taken up in §12.

5 Note on sources

Targeted grammatical elicitation and meta-discussion surrounding usage patterns and points of contrast are included and incorporated with caution, in particular since the bilingualism of the most elderly speakers is by no means perfect.

The majority of the data used in this paper are drawn from texts of various genre, both monologic and, to a more limited extent, conversation. Participant observation plays an occasional role in the data gathered here, but challenges are posed by the simple fact that the language is moribund and all modern-day speakers are bilingual in English. As such, the development of a text corpus has played the most significant role in supporting my understanding of the language's rich structure. Text resources also include archived material. All examples drawn from texts or participant observation are cited by the initials of the speaker and include a short title. Archived resources are cited as such.

6 Commands in Northern Paiute

The basic, canonical imperative construction—defined here as the morphologically simplest second person directive as well as the one speakers identify as the most commonly used and direct command form—involves a bare verb stem.

(8)	yadua!	(9)	tinikwihi!	(10)	ti-punni!
	talk.SG		sing.SG		APASS-see
	Speak!		Sing!		Look!

Stress in Northern Paiute is highly regular, falling on the second mora of the phonological word. In the simple commands above, the primary stressed syllable is perceived as more pronounced (usually uttered at a higher pitch) than in citation.

Occasionally, the verb expressing an event in the imperative is accompanied by the punctual aspect suffix *-(h)u*. In these cases, there is a sharp, falling intonation over the suffix.

(11)	kadɨ-u!	(12)	winnɨ-u!	(13)	a=su'a-u!
	sit.SG-PUNC		stand.SG-PUNC		4[6]=consume-PUNC
	Sit down!		Stand up!		Eat it all up!

Thornes (2003: 322) offers a semantic explanation for the appearance of this suffix based upon the inherent aspect of the verb in question. However it is more likely that the main feature determining the presence versus absence of the punctual suffix is whether or not the event encoded is bounded by an endpoint. Verbal predicates encoding telic (bounded) events take the punctual suffix in the imperative, while those encoding atelic (unbounded) events do not, appearing instead as bare verb stems.

One way to test this hypothesis is by altering the inherent aspect of the base predicate. Compare the following examples, both with the verb *habi*, the singular form of the posture verb meaning 'lie'.

(14)	habi-u!	(15)	habi-dabi(*-u)!
	lie.SG-PUNC		lie.SG-KEEP.ON(*-PUNC)
	Lie down!		Stay/Keep lying down!

In (15), an aspectual suffix implicating sustained effort and duration is deemed semantically (and grammatically) incompatible with the punctual suffix in the imperative.

The punctual suffix is compatible with the irrealis subjunctive suffix *-tua*, as we see in the warning in (16).

(16)	ɨɨ=sa'a	wɨ'I-u-dua	
	you=MOD	descend-PUNC-SUBJ	
	You might fall off!		(NK: Porcupine and Coyote)

The punctual suffix merely identifies the encoded event as bounded.

Some sources (Snapp and Anderson 1982; Norris 1986) have suggested that the punctual suffix serves as the primary means for marking an imperative in Northern Paiute. As demonstrated here, such is not the case. I treat the unmarked form of the

---

[6] What I refer to as fourth person represents an object or possessor that is 'very low in topicality' (Thornes 2003: 160), in keeping with the Americanist tradition of obviative.

verb as the basic imperative construction in the language, with the punctual suffix serving to indicate completion of the directed action.

Suppletive verb forms may indicate non-singular addressees, as with the formal three-way verb suppletion of 'sit' in (17)–(19).

(17) namasoa kati-u!
quickly sit.SG-PUNC
Sit down quickly!

(18) mau čigwi-u!
DEM sit.DU-PUNC
Sit down there (you two)!

(19) ma'aatui aata-u!
anywhere sit.PL-PUNC
Sit down anywhere (you all)!

Pluractional CV' reduplication may function like verb suppletion in indicating a non-singular addressee.

(20) u=pu-punni!
3=REDUP-see
Look at him (y'all)!

In other cases where no such alternations are available for dual or plural addressees, an overt second person plural pronoun may be used to disambiguate. Interestingly, I have found no examples in my corpus of overt expression of a singular addressee in the canonical (bare stem) context. The addition of the punctual suffix, although common in commands involving telic event types, may best be described as a frequent command strategy in the language, since its use is not limited to imperatives.

I turn now to several other command strategies used in Northern Paiute.

7 Command strategies

Directive speech acts in Northern Paiute exhibit several features of formal variation that colour the force of the imperative along dimensions like politeness, urgency, entreaty, and realis expectation, among others. In order to get a fuller sense of the development of directive speech in Northern Paiute, it is important to explore these command strategies, defined as 'non-imperative forms used to express imperative-like meanings' (Aikhenvald 2010: 398).

Command strategies that employ the simple addition of an irrealis marker, either the future suffix *-kwi* or the subjunctive *-tua*, are common. Overt expression of the addressee in these cases is optional.

(21) pa-noo-tua   tammi   u=hibi-kwɨ!
      IP/WATER-carry-SUBJ   1.pl.inc   3=drink-FUT
      Go and get water so we can drink [it]!'   (Liljeblad 1966: 10)

The co-presence of the punctual and subjunctive markers provides further evidence that the former is just another command strategy, and not a marker of the imperative, as argued above.

(22) maa-tɨ   sawabi   iwa   hani-u-tua!   yabia-ppɨ!
      DEF.PRO-LOC   sagebrush   much   do-PUNC-SUBJ   hurry-PERF
      Right there put lots of sagebrush. Hurry!   (Liljeblad n.d.: 23)

The following includes overt expression of the addressee, which in this case happens to be a dog, as well as both punctual and irrealis marking.

(23) ɨɨ   kɨ-kwɨ(h)ɨ-u-tua
      you   IP/BITE-get-PUNC-SUBJ
      You fetch!

The following, without any aspectual marking, includes overt reference to the addressee.

(24) 'idza-pɨi   maiku   ta=ma'wi!'   mii=ka.
      coyote-MYTH   DEM   1.du.inc=start.fire   QUOT=so
      'Coyote, make a fire for us!' he said.   (PS: tale 2, page 18, line 145, SLC[7])

In variance with what we have assumed to be the default, direct-force command— one that appears only as a bare verb stem or verb phrase without indication of tense, aspect, or mood—we also find second person singular directives like the following (cf. example (2)):

(25) 'ɨɨ=sakwa   ka=i=mia-si   i=puh-nagi,'   mii.
      you=MOD   OBL=1=go-SEQ   1=IP/EYE-chase   QUOT
      'You should keep watching me where I go,' saying.
                                          (ML: The Five Men Story, MNC[8])

Here the speaker makes overt use of the second person pronoun in addition to the deontic modal enclitic to soften the command issued by the character in this story. It is perhaps the case that the narrator herself is hedging, for the sake of the listener, on whether the command will be followed. Note, too, that in most cases

---

[7] Sven Liljeblad Collection: 86-14 Box 25 'Mss Copy of Texts in Northern Paiute', 216 pp. Pete Snapp (PS), speaker, recorded in 1961, Special Collections, University of Nevada-Reno.

[8] From the Michael Nichols Collection of Northern Paiute sound recordings, Marian Louie (ML), speaker, recorded in 1969, California Language Archive, University of California-Berkeley: http://cla.berkeley.edu/

where a modal is included as part of a command strategy, an overt pronoun serves as its host.

In this and countless other Northern Paiute tales, events pivot on the consequences of not following advice or of violating an interdiction (see §8).

Another variant of the canonical imperative involves the simple addition of the intensifying particle *ini* to indicate a kind of emphatic permissive command that lends an immediacy to the expected action, as in the following:

(26) 'ini   mia! ni mai yongo-kwi,'   miu   su=simi-'yu   ini-na
     INTENS go   I   DEM evening-FUT QUOT NOM=one-NOM   say-PARTIC
     'Go ahead and go! I'll stay here for the night,' the one said...
                                                            (ML: The Five Men Story, MNC)

In the next example from the same text, one man is refusing to violate a food taboo, while at the same time refusing to bar another from doing so:

(27) (u)su='kai   ni! ini   a=tika!,'   mii   u=nimai.
     (3)NOM=NEG   I   INTENS 4=eat   QUOT   3=say
     He_i, 'Not I! Go ahead and eat it,' saying to him_j.

In one case found among the archived materials of Sven Liljeblad, the combination is translated as 'please', which seems to contrast, functionally, with the permissive function just described.

(28) ini   i=tsa-ha'ni-ki!
     INTENS 1.sg.OBJ=IP/GRASP-do/prepare-APPLIC
     Please, turn me loose!   (PS: tale 7, page 124, line 462, SLC)

The context for the utterance is one where a ghost's skeleton is begging a tree it is snagged on to set it free. Interestingly, the intensive particle *ini* alone is often used when bidding farewell to someone, with a meaning like 'Go ahead!' or 'Take care!'

Nominalized clauses pervade Northern Paiute grammar as a means of packaging information in running discourse and may also be used to formulate directives. These have the flavour of offering advice.

(29) pisa-ku   i=tikapi   a=gi'wa'ya-nna,   a=yikwi-u-yai
     good-OBL 2.sg=food 4=chew-PARTIC   4=swallow-PUNC-HAB
     Chew your food well before you swallow it!   (Liljeblad, n.d.: 20)

(30) taibo'o   iai-na!
     white.person caution-PARTIC
     Watch out for white people!   (Liljeblad 1966: 16)

In (31), overt expression of the addressee is in the form of the second person pronominal proclitic, and the verb form again includes the participial (nominalizing) suffix -*na*.

(31) i=ti-buni-nna!
2.sg=APASS-see-PARTIC
Wake up! (lit. your seeing)   (Liljeblad, n.d.: 23)

As with other command strategies, overt expression of the addressee is optional
(compare (29)–(30)). Morpho-syntactically this is a possessor-plus-nominalized
clause construction functioning as a softer, indirect command strategy.

A directive may also be softened by adding the suffix *-si* to the bare verb stem. The
following examples contrast this strategy with the more direct, punctual forms.

(32) (a) kima-u!   (b) kima-si!   kima-si   mu'a!
         come-PUNC   come-SEQ   come-SEQ   grandchild
         Come!   Come (dear)! Come, grandchild!

(33) (a) ka=paa   hibi-u!   (b) ka=paa   hibi-si
         OBL=water   drink-PUNC   OBL=water   drink-SEQ
         Drink the water!   Drink the water, OK?

The (a) examples above always bear falling intonation over the punctual suffix,
whereas the softened command maintains high, level intonation throughout. My
youngest language consultant, a woman in her late fifties, reports using this strategy
when speaking gently to children or the infirm.

The most obvious affinity of the form is to the sequential converbal suffix *-si*. As a
counterpart to *-na*, *-si* marks the situation expressed by one clause as preceding
another, while *-na* generally implies temporal simultaneity. Verbs so marked carry a
connotation of non-finality that one could attribute to the gentle imperative above.
English imperatives that imply encouragement or an entreaty, rather than direct
action, are often followed by a tag expression, as in 'Go to the store, won't you?' or
'Come along with us, OK?' It is as though one expects verbal agreement after
resistance or difficulty in carrying out the directive.

Elsewhere, clauses marked with *-si* in Northern Paiute are used strategically in
cooperative discourse as a back-channelling device to encourage a narrator to
continue. Interactional doublets like the following are common:

(34a) oo=ka   nabiwo'ya-kwinai-u-si?
      thus=KA   MID.drag.lengthwise-throw.SG-PUNC-SEQ
      Listener: Was that when he was dragged out?

(34b) oo=ka   nabiwo'ya-kwinai-u-si, yaisi...
      thus=KA   MID.drag.lengthwise-throw.SG-PUNC-SEQ
      Narrator: That's when he was dragged out, and...(he was crying)
                                  (PS: tale 9, page 183, lines 27–9, SLC)

The non-final, incomplete 'feel' of a verb in this form may motivate its use in a gentle
imperative context.

There are, of course, some contexts where a command, even an indirect one, is simply dis-preferred. When discussing gambling, an extremely popular traditional activity, I attempted to elicit the command to 'Place your bet!' and was instead offered the following, a question whose force amounts to that of a 'veiled' command:

(35) haa=nooko   ɨɨ   tigi-kɨ-kwi
     Q=amount/all you   put.SG-APPLIC-FUT
     How much will you bet?

Games of chance move very quickly, and any delay in playing one's turn is considered tantamount to cheating. This is the only instance I have found so far where an information question was offered as an optional command strategy, but there are no doubt other contexts where the use of interrogatives as veiled commands is appropriate.

8 The prohibitive construction

Prohibitives (negative commands) in Northern Paiute are formed by placing the negative particle *kai* (NEG) at the beginning of the clause and the prohibitive enclitic =*paana* (PROHIB) immediately after the verb, clause-finally.

(36) kai   ɨ=mubi-kwai-tu   tsama=paana!
     NEG   2=nose-LOC-ALL   touch=PROHIB
     Don't pick your nose!

(37) kai   u=tsitsuga=paana!
     NEG   3=point=PROHIB
     Don't point at it! (of a rainbow)

Prohibitive strategies may deviate from the {kai V=paana} prototype. Although such variation typically includes the use of second position modal clitics and/or the overt use of second person pronouns, they do not involve the use of irrealis markers, for historical reasons I explore in §9. The addition of a second position modal enclitic can alter the force of the prohibition to a stern deontic interdiction:

(38) kai=sa'a   inata   naanitama=paana,
     NEG=MOD   hereabout   mock=PROHIB
     yau-tɨ   yaisi   iwa-u   muhu-ga-'yu
     here-LOC   then   many-OBL   owl-HAVE-PRED
     (You) mustn't mock around, as there are lots of owls around here.
                                          (ML: The Five Men Story, MNC)

In (38), the modal second position enclitic =*sa'a* 'softens' the interdiction and the partitive demonstrative *inata* also makes the prohibited activity appear non-specific or undirected.

Prohibitives are extremely common in traditional folktales, which centre on the violation of an interdiction and its consequences. Folktales themselves are the vehicles for instructing others on proper action, with Coyote serving as the quintessential example for wrong action.[9]

9 Development of the prohibitive construction

Prohibitive clauses are frequently, in the appropriate context, followed by a simple-direct (39) or polite-indirect (40) command.

(39) kai   tɨ-tamihoi=paana;   yabi-su   pitɨ-u!
      NEG   APASS-late=PROHIB   quick-ADV   arrive.SG-PUNC
      Don't be late; arrive on time!

(40) kai   yotsi=paana;   mau=sapa   habi-dabi!
      NEG   arise=PROHIB   DEM=MOD   lie.SG-KEEP.ON
      Don't get up; keep lying there (where you are)!

In fact, the negative particle in combination with the prohibitive enclitic serves this particular function only when directed to a second person subject. In non-prohibitive contexts with first or third person subjects, the prohibitive enclitic functions as a kind of disjunctive, counterfactual particle meaning 'but; however' as in the following pair of examples with a first person singular subject.

(41) nɨ   kai   su-kima=paana   kimma
      I   NEG   DESID-come=PROHIB   come.DUR
      I don't want to come, but (I am) coming.

(42) nɨ   su-kima=paana   kai
      I   DESID-come=PROHIB   NEG
      I want(ed) to come, but no.

Likewise, with a first person plural subject:

(43) nɨmmi   ka=kai   taibo   naka=paana
      1.pl.exc   OBL=NEG   white.person   hear=PROHIB
      nɨmmi   u-no   tɨbimua-yakwi
      1.pl.exc   3-COMIT   play-HAB
      We couldn't understand English, but we used to play with him anyway.
                                      (MS: Autobiography)

---

[9] Indeed, the Northern Paiute verb *tinɨčui* means either 'to teach' or 'to tell stories'.

Its role in conjoined clauses with a third person subject also finds it functioning as a disjunctive particle, as in (44):

(44) obi   tia'a   nɨmmi-nɨmi-'yakwi=paana   kai   mɨ=punni
      DEM   thusly   wander-RNDM.SG-HAB=PROHIB   NEG   PL=see.DUR
      ...so (he) would wander around, but didn't see them...

                                                    (NK: Boarding School Days)

Based upon examples such as those of (39)–(44), I would argue that the origin of the prohibitive construction is fundamentally biclausal. A concessive adverbial clause type, with either the declaration or concession marked by negation, sets the stage for the prohibitive construction with an unstated addressee as subject.

As further support for this proposal, the *-na* portion of the enclitic is clearly related to the pan-Uto-Aztecan participial/nominalizing suffix **-na*, a marker of a variety of dependent clause types (Langacker 1977). The core semantic feature of *-na* is event simultaneity, a point that would not contradict the contexts above.

The remainder of the enclitic is likely cognate with the Ute (Southern Numic) 'irrealis' suffix (with allomorphs *-vaa/-paa*). According to Givón (2011), this suffix serves to 'mark more polite or less direct manipulative speech-acts, those of lower deontic force' (306). These include hortatives in Ute.

As pointed out in §8, the prohibitive construction never co-occurs with the markers of irrealis found associated with the command strategies described earlier. This restriction on co-occurrence lends support to a relatively recent grammaticalization of the form. The presence of an older marker of irrealis that forms part of the prohibitive enclitic precludes other irrealis morphology, despite the fact that it is no longer productive in present-day Northern Paiute. The **{-paa-na}* combination is frozen, now carrying this more specialized, disjunctive/prohibitive function.

10 Non-canonical directive: first person (ex)hortative

Northern Paiute carries second position enclitics that express a wide range of modal and evidential functions as in (45)–(46).

(45) mɨ=naana=**sakwa**   mɨ=timadzai
      PL=men=**MOD**   1.pl.exc=help.TR
      The men should help us.

(46) oo=**kaina**   mɨ=tɨya'i-pɨ   miu   ta   na-ni-naka-kɨ-ti
      so=**MOD**   PL=die-PERV   QUOT   1.du   MID-IP/SPEECH-hear-APPLIC-GENL
      Perhaps those who have passed on want us to hear them.   (NK: Old Voices)

As far as directive speech is concerned, first person directed speech, encoded as hortative constructions, utilizes one or another second position modal enclitic.

The second position, deontic modal =*sakwa* in conjunction with either the first person plural or dual inclusive pronoun, comprises the most common form of the Northern Paiute hortative construction:

(47) tammi=sakwa   wɨnai-ga-kwɨ
      1.pl.inc=MOD   throw.SG-TRNSL-FUT
      Let's (three or more) go fishing!

(48) ka=múa   awamoa=sakwa   ta   una   owi-tiu   tɨhona-ga
      OBL=tomorrow   morning=MOD   1.du   DEM   DEM-LOC   dig-TRNSL
      Tomorrow morning, let's (2) go out there to dig roots.   (NK: Bear and Deer)

With first person singular subjects, there is an optative sense to the construction:

(49) 'nɨ=sakwa   u=ma-mua-ga,'   mii   sunami
      I=MOD   3.sg=IP/hand-play-TRNSL   QUOT   think.SG
      'I oughta play a trick on him,' so thinking.   (ML: Wildcat and Skunk, MNC)

Although =*sakwa* is the most common, others, especially =*sapa* and =*sa'a*, may also appear with first person directives:

(50) yau=sapa   ta   tɨ-yoŋo
      here=MOD   1.du   APASS-evening
      Let us camp here.   (NK: Bear and Deer)

Since the inclusive plural and dual forms include a second person referent, they are the ones that appear in Northern Paiute hortatives.

There are occasions where the illocutionary force of a hortative requires only the use of a first person inclusive pronoun. Example (51) was an uttered response to (50):

(51) 'Aha,   uu   ta!'   mii   ɨnakwi
      yes   thusly   1.du.inc   QUOT   reply
      'Yes, let's do that!' she replied.   (NK: Bear and Deer)

Variations on the primary hortative strategy include the use of irrealis (future or subjunctive) marking on the verb, as with Northern Paiute's canonical imperative.

(52) oo'no   tɨka-kwɨ
      at.that.time   eat-FUT
      Then (we) shall eat...   (Liljeblad 1966: 38)

(53) u=kwɨ(h)ɨ-tua-si   tammi   yau   (u=)massɨa   mii=tia'a.
      3=grab-SUBJ-SEQ   1.sg.inc here   (3=)plant   QUOT=thusly
      'We will get it and plant it here,' they said.   (PS: tale 4, page 67, line 30, SLC)

A suggestion to engage in a joint action can also be formulated by means of a clitic/
particle sequence that includes a combination of negative particle, question enclitic,
second position modal enclitic, and inclusive pronoun.

(54) 'kai=ha=sakwa=ta   na-piti-ki-u,'   mii=tia'a
      NEG=Q=MOD=1.du.inc   MID-arrive.SG-APPLIC-PUNC   QUOT=thusly
      'Why don't we have a contest?' so saying.   (NK: Porcupine and Coyote)

Note that both the suggestion (54) and the reply (55) include the punctual aspect
suffix, compatible with modal enclitics.

(55) 'aha   ni=sa'a   mohi-mia-u,'   mii=tia'a
      yes   I=MOD   lead-go-PUNC   QUOT=thusly
      'All right, I shall go first,' so saying.   (NK: Porcupine and Coyote)

The variety one finds in first-person-centred directive speech acts once again points
to the lack of a single paradigm of grammatical imperative in Northern Paiute. That
said, there are familiar elements that come into play—irrealis and/or punctual
marking on the verb and the use of second position modals. I now turn to the
non-canonical third person directive.

11 Non-canonical directive: third person optative

At first blush, the notion of a third person imperative would seem contradictory—
how does one offer or assert a directive to someone outside the message world of the
speech act? Nevertheless, one often directs one's desires toward the actions performed or states entered into by others through optative-type constructions.[10] These
may be expressed via modals or conditional constructions, as in English 'May she do
well!' or 'If only he would pay attention during lecture!'

I have found it difficult to identify examples of such a construction in my corpus of
Northern Paiute recorded discourse. Nonetheless, one finds functionally optative
constructions that utilize the future tense suffix in non-future contexts, as with the
second line of (56):

(56) su=nimi   yaisi   pino'o u=hitta-ki-si   pino'o
      NOM=person   then   also   3=lift-APPLIC-SEQ   also

      kosso-wai-tu   u=tu'i-tsa-winai-hu-kwi-si
      fire-LOC-ALL   3=try-IP/GRASP-throw-PUNC-FUT-SEQ
      The man, too, lifted that (skeleton) in turn, that (he) would try and throw it
      into the fire, and...   (ML: Five Men Story, MNC)

---

[10] As pointed out by an anonymous reviewer, optative constructions are not the only alternative to
directing an imperative to a third person, and indeed, as described in the introduction to the present
volume, such may exist in paradigmatic relationship to canonical addressee-directed commands.

In Northern Paiute, one directs one's thoughts, or well wishes, toward a generic third party with the general expression, *pisa = tia'a* (good/well = thusly) 'may it be/as it is good'.

Further examples come from prayer. What is interesting is that the lines of the prayer are not in the form of direct entreaties or commands, but rather are statements regarding the favoured patterns of thought on the part of the participants and the expected outcomes of the actions taken up.

(57) pisa-u   puni-no'o-kwɨ
      good-OBL   see-GO.ALONG-FUT

      ni=tuamɨ   pisa   maiku   sutɨhai-no'o.   mau!
      1.pl=children good   DEM   bless-GO.ALONG   in.that.way
      ...(what we) look toward is good, that our children may be blessed along the
      way. So be it!   (MP: Prayer 1)

Here we see a combination of future tense marking or irrealis potential and the directional suffix *-no'o*.

We now turn briefly to some points of comparison across the Numic subfamily in order to note some possible reconstructions, both morphologic and syntactic, of directive speech strategies, as well as some interesting points of variation. With these points, we hope to shed light both on earlier stages in the development of Northern Paiute and on features of typological interest. From these, I conclude with some general hypotheses on the development of directive speech acts.

12 Historical considerations

The bulk of the available material on other Numic languages describes imperatives as simply consisting of a bare verb stem and an unexpressed second person addressee, as with the canonical imperative in Northern Paiute. The basic imperative in Western Shoshoni (Central Numic), according to Crum and Dayley (1993: 9ff), is no exception, as seen in examples (58)–(59). The emphatic particle in (59)[11] serves to strengthen the command.

(58) ukka   tempitta   tsahittsaa!   (59) tsu   mi'aku!
      that-OBJ   rock-OBJ   lift   EMPH   go.away
      Lift up that rock!   Leave!

Interestingly, the two examples included by the authors of this latter strategy also end with the 'past, momentaneous completive' suffix *-kkun*,[12] a likely cognate of the Northern Paiute *-(h)u* punctual suffix.

---

[11] The graph {e}, according to the source, stands for the back unrounded vowel [ɯ], corresponding to Northern Paiute's high central unrounded vowel [ɨ].

[12] Orthographic morpheme-final consonants only surface in lexically specified contexts, affecting a following consonant, when present.

Kawaiisu (Southern Numic), a language described in Zigmund, Booth, and Munro (1991), also carries a marker for bounded events in imperative constructions. The authors describe the use of the suffix -nu in commands and state that the '[d]ifferences in meaning between imperatives with and without -nu can be attributed to the momentaneous meaning of this morpheme' (34). By way of example, an unbounded, atelic event expressed with the bare verb nukwi 'Run!' is set in contrast with the bounded, telic event expressed with the bare verb-plus-momentaneous suffix nooki-nu 'Bring it!

Indeed, the same verb root can be the core of the imperative expression, with or without the suffix, with the expected difference in meaning:

(60) (a) ka'a-nu!   (b) ka-ga'a!
          eat-MOM   REDUP-eat
          Eat it!   Eat!

With a specific object implied, -nu appears, but is absent without one. Based on these preliminary observations, it appears likely that this function of the punctual suffix in commands can be reconstructed for proto-Numic.

Atypical subject coding in imperatives may arise, as we have seen, in cases of clausal nominalization (see example (31)). Two additional instances of atypical imperative subject marking may be found elsewhere in Numic. Suppletive verb stems in Western Shoshoni typically appear without an overt subject in the imperative, but when it is expressed, it is in the third person reflexive[13] pronominal form rather than the second person dual or plural subject form (Crum and Dayley 1993: 10).

(61) aikkih   peweh   ne   kemahka   tsatsakki!
     here   3.du.REFL me   next.to   stand.DU
     Stand here beside me you two!

(62) aikkih   pemme   ne   kemahka   topo'i!
     here   3.pl.REFL me   next.to   stand.PL
     Stand here beside me you all!

Overt pronominal forms mainly appear in cases of dual or plural addressees.

In Southern Paiute, a Southern Numic language described in detail in Sapir (1930), but critically evaluated in Bunte (1979), imperative structures exhibit what some Uto-Aztecan language descriptions refer to as **case switch**, whereby theme or patient objects of transitive predicates appear in the nominative case. Consider the following:

(63) timp-ar   mar   yaŋwi-mi-ak
     rock.NOM-ART   that.NOM   carry-CONT-3.VISIBLE
     Take that rock along!

---

[13] These pronominal forms are only used for emphasis in Northern Paiute. The source indicated here does not include a description of that function for Western Shoshoni.

(64) pɨsaxai-ŋu-ŋw   aipač-uŋ
      look.for-MOM-3SG.INVISIBLE   boy.NOM-ART
      Look for the boy!

Note that the rock in (63) and the boy in (64) are notional objects of the imperative utterances. Bunte (1979: 91–6) treats the imperative as a voice construction on structural grounds, thusly aligning it with the more familiar, passive voice construction. As Bunte notes, however, 'the actual explanation has to do with topicality. The theme in imperative sentences is always topical' (1979: 94).

Historical connections between topicality and nominative case are not unusual, cross-linguistically, and can be found in Northern Paiute itself, which has innovated a nominative determiner proclitic *su=* from the emphatic enclitic *=su*. The most likely bridge along this developmental pathway is the third person demonstrative *usu*, consisting of a deictic base and the erstwhile enclitic, marking the form as nominative. Bunte ascribes, on independent grounds, a topicality function to nominative case in Southern Paiute, also accounting for why examples like (63) and (64) are treated as a variety of voice construction.

Although I have not found straightforward examples in Northern Paiute of nominative-marked objects in commands such as those above, the following pair of examples could be so interpreted:

(65) 'yaa i=pabi'i   su=pisa   kama-dɨ   yabi   a=tɨka-hu,'
      here 1.sg=eld.bro NOM=good   taste-NOMZ   hurry   4=eat-PUNC
      'Here, my brother! That which tastes good, hurry and eat it!' (so he said)...
                                              (PS: tale 11, page 197, line 54, SLC)

(66) tai'na=yaisi   paa-wa'ni   na-paa   su=tɨba
      thin=then   water-SIMIL   MID-make.soup   NOM=pinenut
      Make the pinenuts into a soup as thin as water.
                                              (PS: tale 4, page 66, line 18, SLC)

With example (65), nominative case marking appears on a headless subject relative clause meaning 'that which tastes good', regardless of its role in the main imperative clause. Likewise, with (66), the imperative clause is cast in the passive, and so could be interpreted as, 'Thin like water, the pinenuts are made (into) soup', independently motivating the nominative case form here.

As we have already seen, overt expression of the addressee may appear as formally non-subjects, morpho-syntactically. Notional objects appearing in the nominative case, on the other hand, cannot simply be explained by appealing to nominalization as we saw with examples (29)–(31). Rather, I would argue that by considering the biclausal origins of many constructions associated with directive speech acts, we come closer to a unified explanation of the grammar of directives. As we have seen above, this grammar bears a great deal of resemblance to the subordinate half of a biclausal construction elsewhere in the language, and so we need not be too surprised that grammatical relations may be differentially encoded.

A more detailed discussion and analysis of directive speech, especially command strategies, throughout the subfamily is needed, since at present only minimal attention has been given to these construction types in the published literature on these languages.

The Northern Paiute {kai V=paana} prohibitive construction, whose historical development was detailed in §9, is mirrored most closely in Kawaiisu (Southern Numic). The formal pattern for Kawaiisu includes the negative particle *kedu* followed by the bare verb stem-plus-prohibitive enclitic =*vine'e*.

Northern Paiute's nearest relative in Western Numic, Mono, is described in Lamb (1958) as having a prohibitive construction consisting of a special negative form *mino'o* at the beginning of the clause and a clause-final verb marked with either -*tyh* or -*neh*. Both suffixes have clear cognates throughout Numic as general tense markers or nominalizers. The Central Numic languages, Comanche (Charney 1993) and Western Shoshoni (Crum and Dayley 1993), form the prohibitive construction with a cognate of the Uto-Aztecan negative particle *ke and the final suffix -*te(n)*, a pan-Numic nominalizer.

Looking across the Numic subfamily, therefore, we find evidence for a proto-Numic prohibitive construction consisting of a negative particle and a subordinate verb form.

To conclude this preliminary exploration of directives among Northern Paiute's nearest relatives, we see very little information to draw on regarding non-canonical directives, such as hortative constructions, elsewhere in Numic. Givón (2011) describes the hortative in Ute as involving the suffixation of the 'appropriate 2nd [*sic*] person inclusive subject pronoun to the verb or to the first word in the clause' (306). Although it is clear by the examples provided it is the first person dual and plural inclusive forms that are used, the second position enclitic status of the pronoun is less clear. Also, as discussed above, the irrealis suffix -*vaa/-paa* is utilized to mark 'lower epistemic certainty' in this construction in Ute.

13 Summary and conclusion

Northern Paiute exhibits a fair amount of formal and pragmatic variety in directive speech, but no dedicated paradigmatic structure supporting it. In looking at a range of command strategies, whether canonical or non-canonical, one finds many familiar elements—irrealis marking, overlap with deontic modality, nominalized (desubordinated) clauses, etc. Many of the constructions, if not the forms themselves, can be reconstructed for Numic. Future research will be necessary to expand developmental pathways to Uto-Aztecan as a whole, but it is clear that there are cycles of renewal at work here, whereby functionally, if not always formally, related elements enter into the grammar of directive speech across the family.

Considering the history, and heterogeneity, of Northern Paiute directive speech acts has also proven productive in unveiling their origins as parts of biclausal constructions. These dependent, often nominalized, constructions qua directive speech acts make for an intriguing counterpoint to a substantial literature regarding the development of syntactic complexity (Karlsson and Miestamo 2008; Givón and Shibatani 2009; inter alia). Commands and command strategies, I would argue, make interesting fodder for studying the development of syntactic *simplicity* from familiar complex syntactic pathways. A thorough study of directive speech across the Uto-Aztecan family can only be undertaken once detailed analyses of canonical and non-canonical commands and command strategies are described, formally and functionally, in the individual languages.

Acknowledgements

Institutional support for this work has been provided by National Science Foundation grant #0418453 and by the Sven and Astrid Liljeblad foundation for Great Basin studies.

With humility, I express gratitude to my language teachers, including Rena Adams Beers, Ruth Hoodie Lewis, Patricia Teeman Miller, Shirley Tufti, Phyllis Harrington Miller, and Yolanda Manning. I remain deeply grateful to have had the occasion to learn from the late Irwin Weiser (1909–96), Maude Washington Stanley (1913–2000), Myrtle Louie Peck (1934–2006), Nepa Kennedy (1918–2010), Justine Louie Brown (1918–2011), and Lloyd Louie (1936–2013).

Many thanks to Sasha Aikhenvald and Bob Dixon for their insights and encouragement and to all the participants in the International 'Commands' Workshop in Cairns, Australia. Thanks also to an anonymous reviewer for their helpful comments. I bear sole responsibility for any errors of analysis and interpretation.

References

Aikhenvald, Alexandra Y. 2010. *Imperatives and commands.* Oxford: Oxford University Press.
Aikhenvald, Alexandra Y. and Dixon, R. M. W. 2006. Editors of *Serial verb constructions: A cross-linguistic typology.* Oxford: Oxford University Press.
Brown, Penelope and Levinson, Stephen C. 1987. *Politeness: Some universals in language usage.* Cambridge: Cambridge University Press.
Bunte, Pamela. 1979. *Problems in Southern Paiute syntax and semantics.* PhD Dissertation, Indiana University.
Charney, Jean Ormsbee. 1993. *A Grammar of Comanche.* Lincoln: University of Nebraska Press.

Corbett, Greville G. 2000. *Number.* Cambridge University Press.

Crum, Beverly and Dayley, Jon. 1993. *Western Shoshoni grammar.* Boise State University.

Givón, T. 1990. *Syntax: A functional-typological introduction.* Vol. 2. Amsterdam: John Benjamins.

Givón, T. 2011. *Ute reference grammar.* Amsterdam: John Benjamins.

Givón, T. and Shibatani, Masayoshi. 2009. Editors of *Syntactic complexity: Diachrony, acquisition, neuro-cognition, evolution.* Amsterdam: John Benjamins.

Haiman, John. 2003. 'Iconicity', pp. 453–6 of *Encyclopedia of cognitive science*, edited by Lynn Nadel. London, New York, and Tokyo: Nature Publishing Group.

Karlsson, Fred and Miestamo, Matti. 2008. Editors of *Language complexity: Typology, contact, change.* Amsterdam: John Benjamins.

König, Ekkehard and Siemund, Peter. 2007. 'Speech act distinctions in grammar', pp. 276–324 of *Language typology and syntactic description*, Vol. 1, *Clause structure*, 2nd edition, edited by Timothy Shopen. Cambridge: Cambridge University Press.

Lamb, Sidney M. 1958. *Mono grammar.* PhD Dissertation, Berkeley: University of California.

Langacker, R. W. 1977. *Studies in Uto-Aztecan grammar*, Vol. 1, *An overview of Uto-Aztecan grammar.* Arlington, TX: SIL Publications.

Liljeblad, Sven. no date. 'Grammatical notes.' University of Nevada at Reno: Archives. Manuscript.

Liljeblad, Sven. 1966. *Northern Paiute manual: Grammatical sketch of the northern dialects.* Manuscript.

Norris, Evan J. 1986. *A grammar sketch and comparative study of Eastern Mono.* PhD Dissertation. San Diego: University of California.

Sapir, Edward. 1930. 'Southern Paiute: A Shoshonean language', *American Academy of Arts and Sciences* 65: 1–296. Reprinted in *The collected works of Edward Sapir X: Southern Paiute and Ute linguistics and ethnography*, edited by William Bright. New York: Mouton de Gruyter.

Snapp, A. and Anderson, J. 1982. 'Northern Paiute', pp. 1–92 of *Studies in Uto-Aztecan grammar*, Vol. 3, *Uto-Aztecan grammatical sketches*, edited by R. W. Langacker. Dallas: SIL Publications.

Thornes, Tim. 2003. *A grammar of Northern Paiute with texts.* PhD Dissertation, University of Oregon, Eugene.

Thornes, Tim. 2009. 'Historical pathways in Northern Paiute verb formation', pp. 295–320 of *New challenges in typology: Transcending the borders and refining the distinctions*, edited by Patience Epps and Alexandre Arkipov. Berlin and New York: Mouton de Gruyter.

Thornes, Tim. 2011. 'Dimensions of Northern Paiute multi-verb constructions', pp. 27–61 of *Multi-verb constructions: A view from the Americas*, edited by Alexandra Y. Aikhenvald and Pieter Muysken. Leiden and Boston: Brill Publishing.

Thornes, Tim. 2012. 'Functional underpinnings of diachrony in relative clause formation: The nominalization-relativization connection in Northern Paiute', pp. 147–70 of *Relative clauses in languages of the Americas: A typological overview*, edited by Bernard Comrie and Zarina Estrada Fernández. Amsterdam: John Benjamins.

Thornes, Tim. 2013. 'Causation as "functional sink" in Northern Paiute', pp. 237–57 of *Functional-historical approaches to explanation: In honor of Scott DeLancey*, edited by

Tim Thornes, Erik Andvik, Gwendolyn Hyslop, and Joana Jansen. Amsterdam: John Benjamins.

Zigmund, Maurice L.; Booth, Curtis G.; and Munro, Pamela. 1990. *Kawaiisu: A grammar and dictionary with texts. University of California Publications in Linguistics*, Vol. 119. Berkeley: University of California Press.

8

Imperatives and commands in Japanese

NERIDA JARKEY

1 Preliminary information

There are numerous Japanese dialects spoken throughout the Japanese archipelago, as well as the distinct but closely related Ryukyuan languages in the southern islands. This chapter discusses only the standard language (*hyoojungo*), the de facto national language of the 127 million citizens of Japan.

Japanese is a synthetic, agglutinating language. It is predominantly dependent marking and alignment is nominative-accusative. The basic order of constituents in an intransitive clause is SV, and in a transitive clause, AOV. The most common sentence structure is topic-comment, with subject-predicate structure used when the subject is new information. Core arguments, especially subjects, are often omitted if they are clear from the context. Copula clauses have the structure CS-*wa* CC *da* (CS-TOP CC COP).

Constituent order in Japanese is head final. The language is strongly verb final, with only some modals and illocutionary particles following the verb. Because the grammatical functions of nouns are marked by postpositional particles, the constituent order of non-topical arguments is somewhat free and afterthoughts often occur in casual speech (an exception to the verb-final rule).

Nouns and the sub-types of verbal nouns, adjectival nouns, and personal pronouns are all open word classes, while demonstrative pronouns constitute a small, closed class. Verbal nouns are mostly borrowed from Chinese and English; they describe actions and can be used as predicates in combination with the light verb *su-ru* 'do'. Adjectival nouns are primarily Chinese borrowings. They are like adjectives in function but similar to nouns in form, differing only in that they are followed by a distinct modifying form of the copula, -*na* rather than the genitive -*no*, when used attributively. Personal pronouns are also a sub-type of noun; they can be modified by

Commands. First edition. Alexandra Y. Aikhenvald and R. M. W. Dixon (eds)
This chapter © Nerida Jarkey 2017. First published 2017 by Oxford University Press

a relative clause and new members can be created, generally drawn from the broader class of nouns and from demonstrative pronouns.

Verbs and adjectives (a sub-type of verbs) are both large but basically closed classes. New verbs are mostly created by borrowing words into the language as verbal nouns. Adjectives can be used as predicates without a copula. Other closed word classes are quantifiers, numbers, numeral classifiers, postpositional particles, adverbs, onomatopoetic words, conjunctions, illocutionary particles, and interjections.

Nouns are not marked for gender or number. Some nouns can be preceded by the honorific prefix, which generally takes the form *o-* with nouns from the native Japanese lexicon and *go-* with those from Sino-Japanese. In some cases this element has been integrated into the word (e.g. <u>o</u>*cha* 'tea', <u>go</u>*han* 'rice, food'). In others the *o-* prefix tends to be used as an index of the refinement associated with femininity.

Japanese verbs fall into two main conjugation groups: those with a root ending in a vowel (either *-i* or *-e*, e.g. *oki-ru* 'get up', *tabe-ru* 'eat') and those with a root ending in a consonant (e.g. *kak-u* 'write', *nom-u* 'drink'). There are only a small number of irregular verbs: two that are irregular in most forms (*su-ru* 'do' and *ku-ru* 'come') and a few that are just partially irregular (see Table 2 for examples).

Verbs are conjugated for aspect, modality, tense (past and non-past), polarity, voice, and some mood categories, but have no cross-referencing for person. Adjectives are conjugated for tense, polarity, and some mood categories. The negative form of a verb, marked with the suffix *-(a)na-i*, is grammatically an adjective.

Although there is no person marking on verbs, the referent honorific system often serves to convey information about person referents. Subject honorifics show the speaker's respect towards the subject referent. When the subject is omitted, their use usually implies that the interlocutor (or someone closely associated with the interlocutor) is subject. Object honorifics show the speaker's humility towards a non-subject referent. In this case an omitted subject is understood as the speaker (or someone closely associated) and an omitted direct or indirect object, as the interlocutor. Verbs can also take the explicit Addressee Honorific suffix *-mas-u*, which expresses politeness to the interlocutor, regardless of whether respect is directed towards any referent.

With few exceptions, Japanese verbs are clearly either intransitive or transitive (mono-transitive or ditransitive). There are many related transitive/intransitive verb pairs that describe events involving a change in the undergoer. See Table 1 for examples. These verb pairs share the same *kanji* character and are like S=O ambi-transitive verbs. However, they actually have different roots, the forms of which are not predictably related to their transitivity. The intransitive verbs in these pairs are referred to as 'spontaneous intransitives' (Jacobsen 1992).

TABLE 1. **Transitive/intransitive verb pairs**

Transitive			Intransitive		
沸かす	wakas-u	boil	沸く	wak-u	boil
決める	kime-ru	decide	決まる	kimar-u	be decided
割る	war-u	split, divide	割れる	ware-ru	split, divide

2 Cultural parameters, commands, and discourse

The topic of imperatives and commands in Japanese is a fascinating one. In spite of the significant cultural constraints on issuing commands in many contexts in Japanese society, there are a number of well-established imperative forms (§3), along with an array of command strategies employed precisely to avoid using these explicit imperatives (§7). Furthermore, some forms that began as command strategies are now on the pathway to reinterpretation as imperatives (§7.1.1). This phenomenon— of multiple forms with similar functions, along with the loss of the euphemistic qualities in strategies initially introduced to avoid using the most explicit forms—is typical in a language function characterized by taboo. Although commands are highly face-threatening acts in any language, speakers of Japanese encounter particular challenges in using them in socially acceptable ways.

Japanese social relations are thought of metaphorically as involving two 'dimensions': vertical and horizontal. In the vertical dimension, other people tend to be viewed as *meue-no hito* 'people above one's eyes' and *meshita-no hito* 'people below one's eyes'. There is no single term to refer to one's equals; context-specific terms include *dooryoo* 'colleague', *dookyuusei* 'classmate', and *nakama* 'group member'. It is not appropriate to issue commands to those above one (*meue-no hito*), nor to equals.

Japanese people are also constrained in their use of commands in the 'horizontal' social dimension, where the metaphors *uchi* 'inside' and *soto* 'outside' characterize relationships. One's in-group members are those with whom one identifies most closely in a particular context, such as people in one's family or school, fellow club members, employees, etc. Commands are made only to those within one's in-group and then only to *meshita-no hito* 'people below one's eyes'. It is generally inappropriate to issue commands to out-group members, even to those lower in status. Here social distance rather than deference is the key factor.

Typical targets of commands are thus children (in the family or in school), those in the military or in training in sports and martial arts, and juniors in the workplace. All these groups are perceived as 'vertically' beneath others in a tightly knit social context. Even in these cases, however, issuing a command may not always be straightforward. In addition to the nature of the interlocutor, two relevant factors are the identity the speaker wishes to convey and the relationship he or she wants to cultivate with the interlocutor.

Perhaps no group in Japanese society faces greater challenges in issuing commands than women in positions of authority in the workplace. As Smith (1992: 59–63, 79) explains, the stereotype of Japanese women as polite, self-effacing, and powerless sits uncomfortably with the need to get things done at work. She suggests that, rather than 'defeminizing' their speech, women may be developing two command strategies new to the workplace: that of speaking with the forms a mother would use to command her children (the 'Motherese Strategy') and that of asserting the desired action as if it were a *fait accompli* (the 'Passive Power Strategy'). On the other hand, Takano (2005) shows the importance of discourse-level rather than sentence-level strategies, such as the indirect framing of directives and rapport building, in the way female bosses achieve their goals. Furthermore, a study by Saito (2011) found that male bosses also use a range of non-directive, contextual strategies to elicit cooperation, rather than simply issuing commands.

The value of looking beyond forms and considering the broader context of both directive and non-directive discourse strategies is beyond doubt. However, this chapter focuses in more depth than other recent literature on the forms of imperatives and command strategies, as well as on the usage and changes in the usage of these forms in contemporary Japanese. Furthermore, it concentrates particularly on commands rather than on directives more generally. Here a 'command' is understood to be a speech act used when a speaker wants a particular interlocutor to do something for him or her on a specific occasion, and expects that the interlocutor will do it as a result. An appropriate response in Japanese would be to simply affirm one's understanding, as in (1), not to suggest one has the choice to comply, as in (2) (Miyazaki 2002: 44).

(1)   wakar-i-mashi-ta
      understand-INFIN-AHON-PAST
      (I) understand.

(2)   [#]i-i   des-u   yo[1]
      good-NPAST   COP.AHON-NPAST   IPART
      (That's) fine/OK.

The analysis presented in this chapter is based on participant-observation and on texts with corroborative elicitation. Reference to secondary sources has supported

---

[1] The hash (#) sign indicates that the utterance is pragmatically inappropriate, rather than ungrammatical (signalled elsewhere with an asterisk (*)).

and extended the analysis. One primary source text found to be particularly valuable was a set of recordings of Japanese spoken in the workplace (Gendai Nihongo Kenkyuukai 1999, 2002). Both female and male volunteers recorded natural conversations in their diverse workplaces, in both formal and casual situations (including breaks).

This authentic data indicates that imperative forms are rarely used in the workplace; from a total of 16,921 utterances examined, only two imperative forms appeared. However, these forms do frequently occur in *manga* (comics), *anime* (animation), and TV dramas, whether set in the workplace or elsewhere. Here they are used as a strategy for portraying highly stereotyped characters, such as the cranky male boss or the tough career woman.

In the real world, one very noticeable feature of imperatives and commands is the frequency of accompanying strategies to soften the face threat. These include:

- frequent inclusion of explanation/reason;
- softening illocutionary particles;
- frequent pauses and repetitions;
- markers of hesitancy (e.g. *chotto* 'just a little', *ano* 'um', creaky voice, etc.);
- lengthened final vowels and geminate consonants;
- extremely frequent use of the object honorific expressions of request (see §7.2.2), and of honorifics in general. Of all the utterances functioning as commands in the workplace data examined for this study, 70 per cent had one or more honorific components.

3 Expression of imperatives and prohibitives

Table 2 shows the plain imperative, the prohibitive, the polite imperative, and its reduced form. All imperative forms (positive and negative, plain and polite) are characterized by falling intonation, with the exception of the polite imperative reduced form (see §3.4), which is articulated with higher intonation on the final -*na*.

3.1 *Plain imperative*

The shortest and most abrupt imperative forms—the plain imperative forms—are thought of as used exclusively by men (although see §4.2 for examples showing their use by women). As shown in Table 2, vowel-root verbs take the suffix -*ro* and consonant-root verbs, the suffix -*e*.[2] Most of the suppletive subject honorific verbs,

---

[2] Martin (1975) indicates that -*yo* is an optional component of the imperative after the -*e* of consonant-root verbs and -*ro* of vowel-root verbs (Martin 1975: 959). It is possible that this -*yo* came from the Classical Japanese imperative suffix for vowel-root verbs, now heard only in set expressions, proverbs, and

TABLE 2. Imperative and prohibitive forms

	Vowel-root verbs	Consonant-root verbs	Irregular verbs
1. Plain	Root-*ro*	Root-*e*	Strongly irregular
	oki-ro 'Get up!' *tabe-ro* 'Eat!'	*kak-e* 'Write!' *nom-e* 'Drink!'	*shi-ro* 'Do (it)!' *ko-i* 'Come!'
			Partially irregular
			(o)kure 'Give me.'
			Suppletive SHON: *kudasa-i* 'Give me.' *ossha-i* 'Say.' *irrassha-i* 'Go/Come/Be' *nasa-i* 'Do.'
2. Prohibitive	Non-past predicative form *na*		
	oki-ru na 'Don't get up!' *tabe-ru na* 'Don't eat!'	*kak-u na* 'Don't write!' *nom-u na* 'Don't drink!'	*su-ru na* 'Don't do (it)!' *ku-ru na* 'Don't come!'
3. Polite	(o)-Infinitive form-*nasai*		
	(o-)oki-nasai 'Get up.' *(o-)tabe-nasai* 'Eat.'	*(o-)kak-i-nasai* 'Write.' *(o-)nom-i-nasai* 'Drink.'	*(*o-)shi-nasai* 'Do (it).' *(*o-)ki-nasai* 'Come.'
4. Polite reduced	Infinitive form-*na*		
	oki-na 'Get up.' *tabe-na* 'Eat.'	*kak-i-na* 'Write.' *nom-i-na* 'Drink.'	*shi-na* 'Do (it).' *ki-na* 'Come.'

such as *kudasar-u* 'give me', *osshar-u* 'say', are partially irregular, with imperative forms sharing the form of the irregular infinitive (e.g. *kudasa-i, ossha-i*).[3]

period dramas. However, Martin's suggestion does not seem an appropriate analysis for contemporary Japanese, in which *yo* after an imperative is likely to be simply an illocutionary particle functioning to soften the force of the imperative. There are two reasons for this analysis. First, in this position after the imperative, other illocutionary particles can occur in place of *yo*. Secondly, this *yo* never appears in an indirect quotation, but only when the imperative is sentence final:

(i) imooto-ni　　　　　ki.o.tsuke-ro (*yo)　to　　　it-ta
　　　younger.sister-DAT　be.careful-IMP　　QUOT　say-PAST
　　　(I) told my little sister to be careful.

　　[3] An exception is *meshiagar-u* 'eat, drink [respectful]', which has a regular imperative form: *meshiagar-e*.

A possible explanation for this use of the infinitive for the plain imperative of these suppletive subject honorific verbs is that it originated as a command strategy to avoid the incompatibility of an overt command with a verb that shows respect to the interlocutor as subject (see §4.2). This hypothesis is in accord with the fact that the infinitive form is grammatically a noun, and that nominalization can be used as a command strategy (see §7.1.5). Notice, however, that this usage may have spread, with the non-honorific donatory verb *kure-ru* 'give me' also using the infinitive form as the imperative (*kure*), presumably by analogy with its subject honorific counterpart *kudasar-u*.[4]

3.2 Prohibitive

Like the plain imperative, the prohibitive is stereotypically masculine. Because the negative suffix *-(a)na-i* is an adjective in form, negative verbs cannot take an imperative suffix. Instead the prohibitive is formed by appending the particle *na* to the non-past form of the verb. This particle is a reduced form of the Classical Japanese *na-kar-e*, itself a reduction from *na-ku ar-e* (neg-INFIN be-IMP) 'let there not be' (Martin 1975: 966; Miyazaki 2002: 42). The prohibitive is very similar to the plain imperative in intonation (falling), usage, and grammatical categories (see §5).

3.3 Polite imperative

The polite imperative suffix *-nasai* is typically used by a mother to her child or a teacher to a student. It is grammaticalized from the suppletive subject honorific form of *su-ru* (do-NPAST)—*nasar-u* (do(SHON)-NPAST)—in its imperative form: *nasa-i*. The form as a whole—(*o-*)*V-INFIN-nasai* (illustrated in (3a))—seems to be modelled on the productive subject honorific pattern—*o-V-INFIN-ni.nar-u* (HON-V-INFIN-SHON-NPAST) (shown in (3b))—which has a variant form that utilizes the subject honorific verb *nasar-u* 'do' when it occurs with verbal nouns of Sino-Japanese origin: *go-VN-nasar-u* (HON-VN-do(SHON)-NPAST) (as in (3c) with the Sino-Japanese verbal noun *shinpai* 'worry').

(3) a. (o-)kak-i-nasai!
      HON-write-INFIN-POL.IMP
      Write (it)!

  b. sensei-wa   o-kak-i-ni.nar-u
      teacher-TOP   HON-write-INFIN-SHON-NPAST
      The teacher will write (it) [respectful].

---

[4] The Classical Japanese imperatives of these speaker-centred deictic verbs were regular: *kure-ro*, *kudasar-e*. The archaic verb *tama-u*, a subject honorific speaker-centred deictic similar in meaning to *kudasar-u* 'give me', was also regular in the imperative: *tama-e*. This suggests that the use of the infinitive for the imperative of these verbs is an innovation in Modern Japanese.

   c. sensei-wa   go-shinpai-nasar-u
      teacher-TOP   HON-worry-do(SHON)-NPAST
      The teacher is worried [respectful].

The polite imperative suffix *-nasai* has no negative counterpart. The nearest equivalent is *-nai-de kudasai*, the polite negative request form (§7.1.1).

3.4 Reduced polite imperative

The reduced polite suffix *-na* is an abbreviation of the polite imperative suffix *-nasai*. It is attached to the infinitive, without the option of the honorific prefix *o-*. It is distinguished from plain prohibitive particle *na* (§3.2) by its occurrence after the infinitive rather than the final verb form, and by rising instead of falling intonation.

Unlike the unreduced *-nasai* form, the reduced polite imperative *-na* can be used not only to children, students, etc. but also to 'equals', for example to show concern for a friend.

4 Semantics of imperatives

4.1 Volitional control over the action or event

The first key criterion for the use of an imperative form in Japanese is that the action or event can be conceived of as volitional. For this reason, adjectives simply do not have any imperative form. Members of the (extremely small) subclass of state verbs in Japanese do have an imperative form but, as they describe non-volitional situations, these forms are not used: #*dekir-e* 'be able (to do something)!', #*ir-e* 'need (it)!', #*kikoe-ro* 'hear (it)!'

The copula is very rarely used in the imperative. The informal style of the copula (*da*) has no verbal ending, and thus has no imperative form. The formal style of the copula (*de.ar-u*), however, does have the form of a verb and so has an imperative form (*de.ar-e*). Adjectival nouns can, therefore, be used with an imperative copula, provided they can be thought of as under the volitional control of the subject:

(4) tanin-ni   shinsetsu de.ar-e!
     other.people-DAT kind   COP.FRML-IMP
     Be kind to others!

However, the form *de.ar-e* sounds rather archaic, and more like general advice rather than a command. To ensure an interpretation of a command directed to a particular interlocutor on a specific occasion, an alternative with a non-state verb is preferred:

(5) shinsetsu-ni   shi-nasai!
     kind-ADV   do-POL.IMP
     Do (it) kindly!

This suggests that a preference not to use the imperative with states, even those that can be thought of as involving volition, may be increasing in contemporary Japanese.

Spontaneous intransitives (see §1) can be used in the imperative but, again, only if the subject can be thought of as able to influence the occurrence of the change, as in (6a). However, the spontaneous intransitive in (6b), which expresses a change that cannot be controlled by the subject, is not acceptable in the imperative:

(6) a. motto   yase-ro!
         more   get.thin-IMP
         Lose more weight!

     b. *tasukar-e!
         get.saved-IMP
         Get saved!

Predicates of emotion and thought can also occur in the imperative form if they can be thought of as controllable, as shown in (7) and (8):

(7) watashi-no   i-u   koto-o   shinji-ro!
     1-GEN   say-NPAST   thing-ACC   believe-IMP
     Believe what I say!

(8) suki   de.i-ro!
     like   COP.DUR-IMP
     Keep on liking (it)!

Example (8) shows that even an expression of emotion in the form of a state (here an adjectival noun, *suki da* 'like COP') can occur in the imperative when understood to be exhorting the subject to make an effort to maintain that state.

Takahashi (2000: 254) notes that the passive suffix *-(r)are* is 'extremely restricted, if not totally ungrammatical' with an imperative form (although it is sometimes acceptable with the prohibitive):

(9) ?kanojo-ni   suk-are-nasai!
     her-DAT   like-PASS-POL.IMP
     Be liked by her!

However, passives can occur quite naturally in the imperative, as long as the context shows how the situation is subject to the volitional control of the subject:

(10) i-i   shigoto-o   shi-te   mawari-ni
      good-NPAST   work-ACC   do-GERUND   people.around-DAT
      mitome-rare-ro!
      recognize-PASS-IMP
      Do good work and be recognized by those around (you)!

4.2 *The relationship between the speaker and the subject*

While the first key criterion for the use of an imperative form relates to the volitional control of the subject, the second relates to the relationship between the speaker and the subject referent. Because subject honorific verbs express the speaker's respect towards this referent, and thus imply that the referent is *meue* (above one's eyes), their use in the imperative form is generally pragmatically inappropriate in contemporary speech. Example (11) sounds distinctly archaic:

(11)   #o-yom-i-ni.nar-e
        HON-read-INFIN-SHON-IMP
        Peruse (it)! (lit. Read [respectful]!)

However, even today, a woman might use a suppletive subject honorific verb when speaking to children in her role as mother or teacher, or possibly even to her husband in her role as wife.

(12)   a. meshiagar-e!
           eat(SHON)-IMP
           Eat (up) [respectful]!

       b. shoojiki-ni   ossha-i
           honest-ADV   say(SHON)-IMP
           Tell (me) [respectful] honestly!

This combination of the plain imperative with the ostensibly respectful verb sounds firm but feminine, and particularly well bred. (See also §6.1.) This helps explain the motherly overtones of the polite command form *-nasai*, grammaticalized from the plain imperative of the subject honorific verb *nasar-u* 'do(SHON)' (§3.3).

Imperative forms are natural with object honorific verbs, when used to command one's juniors to do something in a humble way:

(13)   sensei-ni   tetsudat-te   itadak-e!
       teacher-DAT   help-GERUND   receive(OHON)-IMP
       lit. [Humbly] receive (the favour of) (your) teacher helping (you)!
       Get (your) teacher to help (you)!

5 Grammatical categories of imperatives

When suffixes (e.g. *-(s)ase-* CAUS, *-mas-* AHON) are added to a verb, the suffix behaves like a verb root and takes further suffixation appropriate to its form (vowel root or consonant root). Thus the causative form *-(s)ase-* in (14) takes the imperative form that occurs with vowel-root verbs, *-ro*, while the addressee honorific suffix *-mas-* in (15) takes the imperative form that occurs with consonant-root verbs, *-e*.

(14)   yom-ase-ro!
       read-CAUS-IMP
       Make (him/her/them) read!'

(15) irassha-i-mas-e!
      come(SHON)-INFIN-AHON-IMP
      Come in [respectful]!

Any grammatical categories can occur with the imperative, provided they do not
violate the semantic conditions explained in §4. For example, aspectual auxiliary
verbs readily co-occur with the imperative (as in (16)), unless they produce a
meaning that cannot be interpreted as involving the volitional control of the subject
(as in (17)):

(16) kai-te   mi-nasai!
      write-GERUND   TENT.INFIN-POL.IMP
      Try writing (it) (and) see!

(17) *kai-te   ar-i-nasai!
      write-GERUND   RES-INFIN-POL.IMP
      lit. Have it been written!

Progressive aspect frequently occurs, with the same meaning as in the declarative—
'be doing V':

(18) ryoori-o   tsukut-te   i-ru   aida
      cooking-ACC   make-GERUND   PROG-NPAST   while
      benkyoo-shi-te   i-nasai!
      homework-do-GERUND   PROG.INFIN-POL.IMP
      While (I'm) making dinner, (you) be doing (your) homework!

6 Non-command meanings of imperatives

In Japanese, as in many other languages, imperative forms can be used in a considerable variety of functions other than to express commands. Greetings, farewells,
wishes, curses, warnings, proverbs, and generic advice can all be conveyed with the
imperative form.

6.1 Greetings and farewells

Both the plain and polite imperative forms occur quite commonly in everyday
greetings and farewells.

(19) it-te   'rassha-i!
      go-GERUND   come(SHON)-IMP
      lit. Go and come!
      Off you go then!

(20) o-kaer-i-nasai!
      HON-return.home-INFIN-POL.IMP
      lit. Come home!
      Welcome home.

In formal expressions of greeting and farewell, the Addressee Honorific suffix -*mas-u* can be used in its plain imperative form:

(21) irassha-i-mas-e!
      come(SHON)-INFIN-AHON-IMP
      Come (in) [respectful]!

6.2 *Wishes*

Although normally only used with a volitional action when expressing a command (see §4.1), imperatives can occur with non-volitional events if they can be interpreted as wishes.

(22) ame   ame,   fur-e   fur-e!
      rain   rain   fall-IMP fall-IMP
      Fall rain, fall!

6.3 *Curses*

The brusque, masculine effect of the plain imperative form lends itself to use in curses:

(23) shin-jima-e!
      die-GERUND.COMPL-IMP
      Drop dead!

(24) kuso   kura-e!
      faeces eat.VULG-IMP
      Eat shit!

A woman wishing to conform to a normative gender role would avoid these forms, preferring an alternative command strategy for uttering a curse, such as:

(25) shin-eba   i-i   no.ni
      die-CFACT   be.good-NPAST   but
      (It'd be) better if (you) (just) died but...

6.4 *Warnings*

Plain imperatives are used to give warnings, especially when there is a sense of urgency. The brusqueness of the form is likely to be interpreted in this context as consideration for the safety of the interlocutor, rather than bossiness or rudeness.

(26) nige-ro!
      flee-IMP
      Run!

(27) sawar-u   na!
     touch-NPAST PROHIB
     Don't touch!

Even in an emergency situation or when consideration for safety is involved, a woman is likely to choose a polite imperative or a command strategy such as a reduced request form (see Table 3 #3), rather than a plain imperative.

(28) a. nige-te
        flee-GERUND
        Run.

     b. sawar-anai-de
        touch-NEG-GERUND
        Don't touch.

6.5 Proverbs and generic advice

Some proverbs that function to give general advice utilize the plain imperative and prohibitive forms.

(29) goo-ni   it-te-wa   goo-ni   shitaga-e!
     village-DAT go-GERUND-TOP   village-DAT obey-IMP
     lit. Entering (a) village, obey (the rules of) the village!
     When in Rome, do as the Romans do!

(30) aki-nasu-wa   yome-ni   kuwas-u-na!
     autumn-eggplants-TOP   daughter.in.law-DAT feed-NPAST-PROHIB
     lit. Don't let (your) daughter-in-law eat (your) autumn eggplants!
     Don't allow yourself to be taken advantage of!

In some proverbs and sayings, a non-canonical imperative with a third person subject functions to express a wish, as in example (31) from Martin (1975: 963):

(31) zen-wa   isog-e!
     goodness-TOP   hurry-IMP
     lit. May the good hasten!
     Strike while the iron is hot!

These third person imperatives differ from canonical second person instances only in that the subject appears overtly as topic. They have a distinctly archaic flavour.

7 Command strategies

The strategies described below are all formally distinct from imperatives and all have alternative, non-command functions. However, when used by *meue-no hito* 'people above one's eyes' in a context in which the expectation is clearly that they want the interlocutor to do something, the forms described below are all interpreted as commands. By providing an alternative to the imperative form, these strategies all reduce the face threat to varying extents.

In most command strategies in Japanese, as in the imperative form itself, the interlocutor is the subject of the verb (§7.1). However, an alternative strategy involves the speaker as subject of the main verb, with the interlocutor as subject of a subordinate verb (§7.2). In his analysis of directives in general, Takano (2005: 659–62) identifies even more directive strategies, including those in which the speaker and interlocutor are presented as joint subjects.

7.1 Interlocutor is subject

7.1.1 Strategies with grammaticalized giving verbs (s.o. gives to me)

One of the most common command strategies is to make a request, using an auxiliary derived from the imperative form of a donatory verb. These auxiliaries are grammaticalized from the speaker-centred deictic verbs meaning 'give (me)': *kure-ru* (Table 3 #1) and its subject honorific counterpart, *kudasar-u* (#2). (See §3.1 regarding imperative forms of these verbs.) The archaic subject honorific *tama-u* (#7) also belongs to this group (see n. 4). It is now almost never used, but when it is, it is often thought of as an imperative rather than a request, characteristic of highly authoritative, elderly males. Another form that is now widely considered an imperative is the reduced request form ending in the gerund *-te* (#3), with no explicit auxiliary following.

While auxiliary verbs follow the gerund of the main verb, the subject honorific auxiliary *kudasai* (grammaticalized from *kudasa-i* (give.me(SHON)-IMP)) can also be used as a suffix (*-kudasai*) following the infinitive of the main verb (Table 3 #6), to form a respectful request. The infinitive is the only form that the archaic suffix *-tamae* (grammaticalized from *tama-e* (give.me(SHON.ARCH)-IMP)) follows (#7). This is apparently a variant of the productive subject honorific *o-VINFIN-ni.nar-u* pattern (see §3.3).

Notice that the non-honorific auxiliary *(o-)kure* (give.me.IMP) (Table 3 #1) can optionally co-occur with the honorific prefix *o-*. Like the use of the infinitive form for the imperative of this verb (see §3.1), this option is presumably also due to analogy with the respectful request form of its subject honorific equivalent *kudasai*.

7.1.2 Evaluative expressions

Other common command strategies employ evaluative expressions—such as *i-i* ('good') and *ikena-i* ('(it) won't do')—following conditionals, comparatives, gerunds, and the like. These patterns function elsewhere to express suggestion, advice, proscription, etc.

TABLE 3. 'Give me (the favour of) V-ing'

	Vowel-root verbs	Consonant-root verbs	Irregular verbs
1. Plain request	Gerund (*o-*)*kure*		
	oki-te (o-)kure 'Get up (for me).' *tabe-te (o-)kure* 'Eat (for me).'	*kai-te (o-)kure* 'Write (for me).' *non-de (o-)kure* 'Drink (for me).'	*shi-te (o-)kure* 'Do (it for me).' *ki-te (o-)kure* 'Come (for me).'
2. Polite request	Gerund *kudasai*		
	oki-te kudasai '(Please) get up.' *tabe-te kudasai* '(Please) eat.'	*kai-te kudasai* '(Please) write.' *non-de kudasai* '(Please) drink.'	*shi-te kudasai* '(Please) do (it).' *ki-te kudasai* '(Please) come.'
3. Reduced request	Gerund		
	oki-te 'Get up.' *tabe-te* 'Eat.'	*kai-te* 'Write.' *non-de* 'Drink.'	*shi-te* 'Do (it).' *ki-te* 'Come.'
4. Polite negative request	Negative gerund *kudasai*		
	oki-nai-de kudasai '(Please) don't get up.' *tabe-nai-de kudasai* 'Please don't eat.'	*kak-anai-de kudasai* '(Please) don't write!' *nom-anai-de kudasai* '(Please) don't drink!'	*shi-nai-de kudasai* '(Please) don't do (it)!' *ko-nai-de kudasai* '(Please) don't come!'
5. Reduced negative request	Negative gerund		
	oki-nai-de 'Don't get up.' *tabe-nai-de* 'Don't eat.'	*kak-anai-de* 'Don't write!' *nom-anai-de* 'Don't drink!'	*shi-nai-de* 'Don't do (it)!' *ko-nai-de* 'Don't come!'
6. Respectful request	*o*-Infinitive form-*kudasai*		
	o-oki-kudasai '(Please) get up.' *o-tabe-kudasai* '(Please) eat.'	*o-kak-i-kudasai* '(Please) write.' *o-nom-i-kudasai* '(Please) drink.'	**o-shi-kudasai* '(Please) do (it).' **o-ki-kudasai* '(Please) come.'
7. Archaic masculine request	Infinitive form-*tamae*		
	oki-tamae 'Get up (for me)' *tabe-tamae* 'Eat (for me).'	*kak-i-tamae* 'Write (for me).' *nom-i-tamae* 'Drink (for me).'	*shi-tamae* 'Do (it for me).' *ki-tamae* 'Come (for me).'

(32) ki.o.tsuke-reba   i-i   des-u
     take.care-COND   good-NPAST   COP.AHON-NPAST
     It's best if (you) take care.

(33) kii-te   oi-ta   hoo-ga   i-i   yo
     ask-GERUND   PREP-PAST   side-NOM   good-NPAST   IPART
     You'd better ask (beforehand).

(34) urusa-ku   shabe-te-wa-ikena-i
     noisy-INFIN   chat-GERUND-TOP-won't.do-NPAST
     Chatting noisily (just) won't do.

7.1.3 Expressions of impossibility

These are used as indirect prohibitions, in a similar way to expressions involving negative evaluation (as in (34)).

(35) o-nori-ni.nar-e-mas-en
     HON-get.on.board-SHON-POT-AHON-NEG
     (You) cannot get on board [respectful] (here).

7.1.4 Negative interrogatives

This form tends to carry a tone of criticism or scolding, and has falling rather than the rising intonation normally characteristic of questions.

(36) haya-ku   mochiba-ni   modor-ana-i   ka?
     fast-INFIN   post-DAT   return-NEG-NPAST   INTER
     Can't (lit. won't) you (just) quickly get back to your post?

7.1.5 Nominalization

The strategy of nominalization presents an action as a fact, and thus functions as a very firm strategy for issuing a command that will brook no argument.[5]

(37) tadachi.ni   kimi-wa   shigoto-kara   hanarer-u
     at.once   2FAM-TOP   work-ABL   separate-NPAST
     n-da
     NOMZ-COP.INFRML.NPAST
     (It is the case that) you (will) get away from work at once.

---

[5] An alternative nominalizer, *koto*, gives a sense of an official instruction or regulation addressed to a non-specific audience (see Morrow 2005: 82), and so is not included in this analysis, which is restricted to commands (see §2).

7.1.6 Declaratives

The non-past declarative form used as a command strategy sounds quite firm, and is employed, for example, in assigning tasks in the workplace.

(38) Suzuki-san,   denwa-sur-u,   Tanaka-san,   memo-su-ru.
     NAME-TTL   phone-do-NPAST   NAME-TTL   memo-do-NPAST
     watashi-ga   matome-mas-u.   ijoo   des-u
     1-NOM   conclude.INFIN-AHON-NPAST   above   COP.AHON-NPAST
     Mr Suzuki, (you) will make the calls, Ms Tanaka, (you) will take the memos.
     I will pull it all together. That's it.

In Japanese, it is not appropriate from an epistemic perspective to assert the intentions of another person, so the first two non-past forms in example (38) are easily interpreted as commands, without the need for any special intonation. The non-past verb *matomemasu* with the first person subject, on the other hand, is understood as a statement of intention: 'I will pull it all together'.

Another declarative form utilizes the suffix *-ta*, now the past form but originating as an abbreviation of the perfect *-tari* form. This form sounds very direct and vulgar, so is rarely used except in rough contexts such as outdoor markets. It is often repeated for emphasis.

(39) doi-ta   doi-ta
     make.way-PAST   make.way-PAST
     Make way, make way.

(40) mat-ta   mat-ta
     wait-PAST   wait-PAST
     Wait, wait.

Yoshida (1971; cited in Martin 1975: 966) mentions that *-tari* was commonly used as a command in the pre-modern Edo period (1603–1868). It was itself a reduced version of the infinitive of the perfect/resultative *-te aru*, with an alternative imperative form *-tar-e!* The meaning was roughly equivalent to the modern *V-te shima-e!* (V-GERUND COMPL-IMP) 'Do it completely!' (Mayuzumi 2014).

7.1.7 Adverbials

An adverbial alone, without any verb, avoids the use of the imperative form. It may sound abrupt or gentle, depending on the intonation, the use of softeners, etc.

(41) shizuka-ni   ne?
     quiet-ADV   IPART
     Quietly, OK?

7.1.8 Nouns

Japanese husbands are notorious for using a single noun as a command strategy when they want their wife to do something for them, e.g. *meshi!* 'Food!', *furo!* '(Get my) bath (ready)!'

7.2 Speaker is subject

7.2.1 Strategies with grammaticalized receiving verbs (I receive from you)

The auxiliary verb *mora-u* (Table 4 #1) and its object honorific equivalent *itadak-u* (#2) are grammaticalized from verbs meaning '(I) receive (from you)'. Many forms of these auxiliaries are used as command strategies, particularly potential questions, potential negative questions, and desideratives. For example:

- itadak-e-mas-en ka (receive(OHON)-POT-AHON-NEG INTER) 'Can't (I) get you to...?'
- itadak-i-ta-i des-u (receive(OHON)-INFIN-DESID-NPAST COP.AHON-NPAST) '(I) want to get you to...'

TABLE 4. 'I will receive (the favour of) you V-ing'

	Vowel-root verbs	Consonant-root verbs	Irregular verbs
1. Plain favour	Gerund *mora-u*		
	oki-te mora-u '(I'll) have (you) get up.' *tabe-te mora-u* '(I'll) have (you) eat.'	*kai-te mora-u* '(I'll) have (you) write.' *non-de mora-u* '(I'll) have (you) drink.'	*shi-te mora-u* '(I'll) have (you) do (it).' *ki-te mora-u* '(I'll) have (you) come.'
2. Humble favour	Gerund *itadak-u*		
	oki-te itadak-u '(I'll) have (you) get up (please).' *tabe-te itadak-u* '(I'll) have (you) eat (please).'	*kai-te itadak-u* '(I'll) have (you) write (please).' *non-de itadak-u* '(I'll) have (you) drink (please).'	*shi-te itadak-u* '(I'll) have (you) do (it) (please).' *ki-te itadak-u* '(I'll) have (you) come (please).'
3. Gentle request	Gerund *choodai*		
	oki-te choodai '(I'll) get (you) to get up (please).' *tabe-te choodai* '(I'll) get (you) to eat (please).'	*kai-te choodai* '(I'll) get (you) to write (please).' *non-de choodai* '(I'll) get (you) to drink (please).'	*shi-te choodai* '(I'll) get (you) to do (it) (please).' *ki-te choodai* '(I'll) get (you) to come (please).'

The form *choodai* (#3) is not an imperative form itself but rather a Sino-Japanese verbal noun meaning 'receiving'. Its use in this construction in its nominal form was probably initially prompted by its coincidentally similar ending to the auxiliary *kudasai* (grammaticalized from *kudasa-i* 'give.me(SHON)-IMP'; see §7.1.1). It is now thought of as an alternative to this auxiliary, with the same meaning ('give me (the favour of) doing'), but has a gentle tone and is used towards or amongst children.

7.2.2 *Strategies with the object honorific verb of request*

The most characteristic lexical item associated with giving commands is the verb *nega-u* 'to request, to implore' in its object honorific form:

(42) o-nega-i-shi-mas-u
     HON-request-INFIN-OHON.INFIN-AHON-NPAST
     (I) [humbly] request (you).

This expression appears in a wide variety of forms, including courteous, desiderative, potential question, etc.:

- o-nega-i-itash-i-mas-u (HON-request-INFIN-OHON(COURT)-INFIN-AHON-NPAST) '(I) [humbly] request (you) [courteously].'
- o-nega-i-dek-i-mas-u ka (HON-request-INFIN-be.able-INFIN-AHON-NPAST INTER) 'Can (I) [humbly] request (you)?'

7.2.3 *Different-subject desideratives*

The use of a desiderative as a command strategy is not as common as other forms in which the speaker is subject, and sounds somewhat self-centred.

(43) mat-te   hoshi-i
     wait-GERUND   desire-NPAST
     (I) want (you) to wait (for me).

8 Conclusion

This chapter has provided a brief glimpse into the forms and use of imperatives and commands in Japanese. Issuing commands in a social context that is characterized by constraints on who can command whom, and on how one maintains good relationships, good demeanour, and socially acceptable gender identity, clearly presents a challenge to effectively getting others to do what you want them to do. In such a context it is no surprise that there are numerous strategies to avoid using direct, imperative forms, and also evidence of the loss of the euphemistic qualities of several of these command strategies, as they gradually come to be reinterpreted as imperative forms themselves.

Acknowledgements

This chapter is the revision of a paper I presented at the 12th International Workshop on 'Commands', 28 September to 3 October 2015, at the Language and Culture Research Centre, James Cook University. I benefited greatly from feedback from other participants in the workshop, and most especially from Sasha Aikhenvald and Bob Dixon, to whom I am enormously indebted. I am also most grateful to my dear friends and colleagues who kindly assisted me with the Japanese data: Kazumi Ishii, Hiroko Kobayashi, Hiroko Komatsu, Hiroko Koto, and Harumi Minagawa.

Sources

Gendai Nihongo Kenkyuukai [Society for the Study of Modern Japanese]. 1999. *Josei no kotoba—shokubahen* [Female talk in the workplace]. Tokyo: Hitsuji.
Gendai Nihongo Kenkyuukai [Society for the Study of Modern Japanese]. 2002. *Dansee no kotoba—shokubahen* [Male talk in the workplace]. Tokyo: Hitsuji.

References

Jacobsen, Wesley, M. 1992. *The transitive structure of events in Japanese*. Tokyo: Kuroshio.
Martin, Samuel, E. 1975. *A reference grammar of Japanese*. New Haven: Yale University Press.
Mayuzumi, Shuichiro. 2014, June 30. 'Nihongo o kangaeru (sono go) "doita, doita", "katta, katta" wa, naze kakokei ka?' [Thoughts on Japanese (#5): Why the past form for "doita, doita" and "katta, katta"?] [Web log post], Retrieved 25/12/2015 from http://urgell.blog62. fc2.com/blog-entry-123.html?sp.
Miyazaki, Kazuhito. 2002. *Modariti* [Modality]. Tokyo: Kuroshio.
Morrow, Phillip R. 2015. 'Directives in Japanese: Evidence from signs', *World Englishes* 34: 78–87.
Saito, Junko. 2011. 'Managing confrontational situations: Japanese male superiors' inter- actional styles in directive discourse in the workplace', *Journal of Pragmatics* 43: 1689–1706.
Smith, Janet S. 1992. 'Women in charge: Politeness and directives in the speech of Japanese women', *Language in Society* 21: 59–82.
Takahashi, Hidemitsu. 2000. 'English imperatives and passives', pp. 239–58 of *Constructions in cognitive linguistics*, edited by Ad Foolen and Frederike van der Leek. Amsterdam: John Benjamins.
Takano, Shoji. 2005. 'Re-examining linguistic power: Strategic uses of directives by profes- sional Japanese women in positions of authority and leadership', *Journal of Pragmatics* 37: 633–66.
Yoshida, Kanehiko. 1971. *Gendaigo jodooshi no shiteki kenkyuu* [The historical study of Modern Japanese auxiliary verbs]. Tokyo: Meiji.

9

Linguistic expression of commands in Lao

N. J. ENFIELD

1 Preliminary information

1.1 Typological overview

Lao is an isolating/analytic language of the south-western Tai branch of Tai-Kadai (Enfield 2007). It is spoken by about 20 million people mostly in Laos, Thailand, and Cambodia. It is a tone language, with five lexical tones, indicated in this chapter by a numeral at the end of each word (see Enfield 2007 for conventions for transcription of Lao). The language has open classes of ideophones, nouns, verbs, and adjectives, plus closed classes of tense/aspect/modality markers, modifier classifiers and noun class markers, and phrase-final and sentence-final particles. The sentence-final particles are of particular importance in the expression of commands and similar speech acts, as is illustrated in this chapter. Systems of nominal classification mostly employ closed classes of classifiers (except in the case of numeral classifiers; that set is open). There is no inflectional morphology. Many verbs are flexible in terms of transitivity, often with ambitransitivity of the S=O type, and with multiple 'case frames' possible (Enfield 2007: 271–84). Grammatical relations tend to be signalled via constituent order (SV/AVO by default), though there is widespread zero anaphora, and movement licensed by information-structure considerations.

Clause types can be defined by semantic class of the sentence-final particle selected. The three classes are factive, interrogative, and imperative. To illustrate, we can begin with an unmarked declarative sentence:

(1) saam3   khon2   taaj3
     three   person   die
     Three people died.

Commands. First edition. Alexandra Y. Aikhenvald and R. M. W. Dixon (eds)
This chapter © N. J. Enfield 2017. First published 2017 by Oxford University Press

This can be converted into a question by adding a sentence-final particle, such as the unmarked polar question particle *bòò3*, the new inference polar question particle *vaa3*, or the independent presumption polar question particle *tii4*:

TABLE 1. Sentence-final particles in Lao (Enfield 2007: 43). These are placed at the end of the clause, after a clause-final juncture. They do not tend to combine with each other productively; several combinations are common but are idiomatic in meaning (i.e. the meanings of the combinations are not simply the combined meanings of the elements).

Interrogative	*bòò3*	Polar question, unmarked (QPLR)
	vaa3	Polar question, proposition newly inferred (QPLR.INFER)
	tii4	Polar question, proposition independently presumed (QPLR.PRESM)
	nòq1	Polar question, seeks agreement (QPLR.AGREE)
	kòq2	Content question, seeks information that is presupposed (Q.PRESUP)
	hùù2	Content question, emphatic, mild annoyance at not knowing (Q.EMPH)
	nòò4	Wondering, 'out-loud' question to oneself (Q.WNDR)
	buq2	Rhetorical question, speaker does not know (Q.UNKN)
Factive	*dêj2*	Factive, proposition is news to addr (FAC.NEWS)
	dêê4	Factive, gives info old in discourse but unknown to addr (FAC.FILLIN)
	juu1	Factive, weakens speaker's commitment to proposition (FAC.WEAK)
	dòòk5	Factive, resists addressee's current stance or presumption (FAC.RESIST)
	sam4	Factive, proposition unexpected or surprising in context (FAC.SURPR)
	naa3	Factive, makes explicit sth addressee should already know (FAC.EXPLIC)
	veej4	Factive, emphatic (FAC.EMPH)
	dee4	Factive, puts on record this was said (FAC.ONRCD)
	lèq1	Factive, confirms something already intended (FAC.PER)
Imperative	*mèè4*	Imperative, states addr is unimpeded (IMP.UNIMP)
	saa3	Imperative, suggests action to addr (IMP.SUGG)
	dèè1	Imperative, softens or plays down burden of request (IMP.SOFT)
	vaj2	Imperative, asks addr to hurry (IMP.RUSH)
	duu2	Imperative, pleading 'do it for me' (IMP.PLEAD)
Other	*dêê2*	Thematizes, asks 'What about X? (Q.THEME)
	qeej4	Vocative marker (VOC)
	kadaaj1	Afterthought marker (AFTH)
	baat5-niø	Thematizer (THZR)

(2) saam3   khon2   taaj3   bɔ̀ɔ3
    three   person   die   QPLR
    Is it the case that three people died?

(3) saam3   khon2   taaj3   tii4
    three   person   die   QPLR.PRESM
    Surely I'm correct in thinking that three people died?

(4) saam3   khon2   taaj3   vaa3
    three   person   die   QPLR.INFER
    Do I rightly infer that three people died?

A set of the most commonly used sentence-final particles is shown in Table 1.

1.2 Nature of sources

The data and analysis presented in this chapter are based on several sources of evidence gathered in regular fieldwork in Laos since 1990: participant observation, corroborative grammatical and lexical elicitation, and examples from a corpus of video-recorded informal home and village interaction. Many of the examples used here were identified in the course of a comparative project on request-type behaviour within the European Research Council Project 'Human Sociality and Systems of Language Use' (2010–14), in which a coding scheme was designed and used to investigate the elements of low-cost request-type sequences (i.e. minor impositions such as asking to pass salt, or to move an object out of the way) in everyday life (see Enfield 2014).

2 Expression of imperatives

2.1 Imperative as a sentence type

It is hard to mount a clear argument that imperatives are a special sentence type in Lao. Structurally, imperatives are formed like any other sentence type: a bare clause with a particle appended at the end. If there are distinctions, they have to do with the semantic category the particle comes from (see Table 1). Imperatives share their general characteristics—i.e. basic constituent order—with other sentence types, including interrogatives and declaratives.

Imperatives may be formed in Lao without any explicit marking, as in these examples:

(5) lom2 — bɔ̀ø   tɔ̀ɔng4   qaaj3
    talk   NEG   must   shy
    Talk—no need to be shy.

(6) qaw3   nang3   maa2   saj1   phii4
     take   hide   come   put   here
     Put the skin (of the fish) in here.

(7) paj3   qaw3   maa2
     go   grab   come
     Go and bring (them) here.

(8) pong3   long2   pong3   long2   pong3   long2
     set.down   descend   set.down   descend   set.down   descend
     Put (it) down, put (it) down, put (it) down.

If there is any specific use of intonation in commands it would appear to be in the
way the sentence-final particles are pronounced. As noted in Enfield (2007: 72–3),
sentence-final particles—unlike open-class words—are somewhat underspecified for
pitch and may vary in vocal delivery to capture pragmatic nuances.

2.2 Use of address in commands

Often, the addressee of a command is identified by the explicit use of their name, or
some other kind of person reference. It might be suggested that such use of a name in
initial position is in fact a way of marking commands:

(9) maa2   piing4   qiik5,   saaw3   nòòj4
     come   roast   more   girl   small
     Come and grill some more (of these), small girl.

(10) qaw3   nam4   juu1   naj2   lot1   còòt5   nan4,   nithaa3
     grab   water   be.at   inside   car   park   DEM.NONPROX   N
     Get some water from the car that's parked there, Nithaa.

(11) paj3   qaw3   sùa1   long2   maa2   puu3   haj5   nik1,   ñaaw2
     go   grab   mattress   descend   come   lay   give   N,   Ñ
     Go and get a mattress and lay it for Nick, Nyao.

In the above three examples, reference to addressee occurs at the end of the utterance.
In the following example the person reference is at the beginning:

(12) qòt2,   qaw3   taw3   maa2   haj5   kuu3
     Q   grab   pot   come   give   1SG.BARE
     Ot, get a/the pot for me.

There is a prosodic mark-off between the name and what follows (represented by a
comma), which distinguishes the command 'Ot, get the pot for me' from a declarative
sentence with Ot as the subject ('Ot got a/the pot for me'). Compare the following:

(13) qòt2   qaw3   taw3   maa2   haj5   kuu3
     Q   grab   pot   come   give   1SG.BARE
     Ot got a/the pot for me.

The vocative particle *qeej4* can be used with the name of the person intended to carry out the command. The particle is appended immediately after the name, as in the following:

(14) nithaa3,   jaa1   paj3   kaj4   laaj3,   nithaa3   qeej4
     N   NEG.IMP   go   near   very   N   VOC
     Nithaa, don't go close to him, O Nithaa.

The following examples show that simply calling out a person's name can function as a command, calling them to come to where the speaker is:

(15) qaaj4-dong3
     eB-D
     Dong! (Come here!)

(16) saang1   saang1
     tradesperson   tradesperson
     Tradesmen! Tradesmen! (Come here!)

There is no special marking of person distinctions in imperatives. This is because person distinctions are not grammatically marked in Lao, other than in pronouns. Pronouns tend not to be used in commands, but there are exceptions, as in the following two cases, with singular and plural second person pronouns, respectively:

(17) caw4   lòòng2   qaw3   paj3   hêt1   kin3   beng1   mèè4
     2SG.POL   try   take   go   make   eat   look   IMP.UNIMP
     You go ahead and take (them) and try cooking (them) to eat!

(18) suaj3   khaw5   mèè4   suu3
     toss   rice   IMP.UNIMP   2PL.BARE
     Prepare the rice you lot!

A possible explanation for the explicit use of pronouns in these examples lies in the fact that the pronoun system in Lao indicates distinctions in formality, respect, and social intimacy (Enfield 2007, 2015). The pronouns may seem redundant in commands such as (17) and (18), but in fact they add information above and beyond 'second person'. The choice of a 'polite' pronoun in (17) versus a 'bare' pronoun in (18) is arguably related to the speaker's framing of the request being made.

2.3 Interaction with verb serialization

Lao is a verb serializing language. The scope of an imperative is typically an entire serial verb. If a command consists of a series of actions, the marking for imperative appears just once, at the end. This is because the marker—a sentence-final particle— is by definition *sentence*-final. This is illustrated in the following examples (and many other examples throughout this chapter; examples (11) and (17), above, being especially rich serial constructions, each featuring six verbs):

(19) qaw3   kùa3   haj5   khòòj5   dèè1
      grab   salt   give   1SG.POL   IMP.SOFT
      Please give me the salt. (lit. grab salt give me)

(20) qaw3   maa2   haj5   khòòj5   nèè1
      grab   come   give   1SG.POL   IMP.SOFT
      Give (it) to me please. (lit. grab come give me)

(21) qaw3   makø-kiang4   maa2   haj5   hèèn5   nèè1
      grab   CT.fruit-orange come   give   chew.on IMP.SOFT
      Bring an orange for (her) to chew on. (lit. grab orange come give chew)

The following case, in which the particle appears between verbs rather than at the end, shows that the force of a command only applies to the material that precedes the particle (here, *kin3* 'eat'):

(22) kin3   mèè4   saw2   loot4   dêj2   naø
      eat   IMP.UNIMP   stop   NO.ADO   FAC.NEWS   TOP.PERIPH
      Go ahead and eat it, (then) your complaint will stop.

2.4 Khòò3 construction

Lao has a special verbal construction for making requests (for objects, services, or permission), involving the verb *khòò3* 'to ask for, to request'. This verb may else-where be used in simple declarative expressions such as *man2 khòò3 ngen2* [he ask. for money] 'He asked for money'. In requesting contexts, in which an unexpressed subject is understood to be first person, *khòò3* acts as a speech act verb meaning '(Please) may/can (I) have X'. (Note: This subjectless 'speech act' function of *khòò3* also occurs with the verbs *seen2* 'invite, (I) invite you to', *haam5* 'forbid, (I) forbid you to', and *khiaw5* 'hasten, (I) urge you to'.) In this function, *khòò3* is usually accompanied by the 'soft imperative' final particle *nèè1*:

(23) khòò3   ngen2   (nèè1)
      request   money   IMP.SOFT
      (Please) can I have some money.

The complement of *khòò3* may also be a verb. In these cases, the speaker is asking for permission to do the action predicated in the verb. Note that, as in the following example, the request for permission is often associated with a request to be given an object related to the requested action:

(24) qoo4   khanòòj5   khòò3   kin3   nèè1
      INTERJ   1SG.FORMAL   request   eat   IMP.SOFT
      Oh, can I eat (some) please. Or: Please (give me) some of that to eat.

The following example features both a nominal complement of *khòò3* and a further phrase that specifies the intended action in relation to the thing being requested:

(25) khòò3   makø-khaam3   som-som5   qan-nan4
      request   CT.fruit-tamarind   sour-REDUP   MC.INAN-DEM.NONPROX
      haj5   kin3   nèè1
      give   eat   IMP.SOFT
      Please can (I) have some of that sourish tamarind to eat.

2.5 *Use of interrogative marking in commands*

There are linguistic means of getting others to do things for you that do not involve direct encoding of command-like semantics. The following examples illustrate common indirect request strategies that use interrogative marking:

(26) miit4   juu1   saj3
      knife   be.at   where
      Where is (a/the) knife? (implies: Give me a/the knife.)

(27) miit4   juu1   lang3   caw4   bòò3
      knife   be.at   behind   2SG.POL   QPLR
      Is (the) knife behind you? (implies: Give me a/the knife.)

There are constraints, however, against the combination of imperative and interrogative force in a single clause. This is because imperative and interrogative force are marked by forms that occur as alternatives in the same grammatical slot (see Table 1). That said, it is possible to make complex constructions that combine imperative and interrogative force in two separate clausal elements. In the following example (based on example (6) above), a bare imperative has a 'tag question' type element appended:

(28) qaw3   nang3   maa2   saj1   phii4,   daj4   bòò3
      take   hide   come   put   here   can   QPLR
      Put the skin (of the fish) in here, can you?

This would be a way to slightly soften the force of the command, by ostensibly allowing that it might not be possible for the requestee to comply.

   If an explicit imperative particle is included in the main clause of (28), the addition of a 'tag question' is no longer grammatical:

(29) *qaw3   nang3   maa2   saj1   phii4   mèè4,   daj4   bòò3
     take   hide   come   put   here   IMP.UNIMP   can   QPLR
     (Put the skin (of the fish) in here, can you?)

Further, note that the use of an explicit imperative particle is not compatible with the use of aspectual-modal markers such as *siø* 'IRREALIS' as in (30) or *lèèw4* 'PERFECT' as in (31):

(30) (*siø)   qaw3   nang3   maa2   saj1   phii4   mèè4
     IRR   take   hide   come   put   here   IMP.UNIMP
     ((You will) put the skin (of the fish) in here!)

(31) qaw3   nang3   maa2   saj1   phii4   (*lèèw4)   mèè4
     take   hide   come   put   here   PER   IMP.UNIMP
     ((Have) put the skin (of the fish) in here!)

3 Negative imperatives

Negative imperative marking is not done with a final particle, but with a dedicated preverbal negative imperative marker, usually *jaa1* (which is not related to normal negation, though it occurs in the same syntactic slot as negation), but also sometimes *suu1*. The word *jaa1* may also occur as a stand-alone verb meaning 'desist' (used either declaratively or imperatively). Like positive imperatives, negative imperatives may also occur with a sentence-final imperative particle (as in example (32)), though one is not necessary. The negative imperative has a complement-like structure, in the sense that *jaa1* can be interpreted as a main verb which takes a clause as its complement. Like other complement structures in Lao, this is a kind of serial verb or multi-verb construction (see Enfield 2007: 427–54). The negative imperative is structurally distinct from the positive imperative due to the presence of the preverbal marker.

(32) jaa1   puk2   man2   dee4
     NEG.IMP   waken   3SG.BARE FAC.ONRCD
     Don't wake him/her up, y'hear!

(33) jaa1   cok2   khaw5   paj3
     NEG.IMP   put.hand.in   enter   go
     Don't put your hand in (there).

(34) nithaa3,   jaa1   paj3   kaj4   phen1
     N   NEG.IMP   go   near   3SG.POL
     Nithaa, don't go close to him.

In a unique and idiosyncratic interpretation, the verb *faaw4* 'hurry' has negative imperative force when completely unmarked (usually, but not obligatorily, repeated):

(35) faaw4 faaw4
hurry hurry
Don't rush! (= Slow down!)

Also note that the negated modal construction *bòø tòòng4* V 'no need to V' (illustrated in example (5) above) is a possible type of prohibitive. This is normally used with non-controlled verbs such as *qaaj3* 'be shy, ashamed, modest' or *jaan4* 'afraid'.

4 Semantic distinctions in commands

Different forms of command can be semantically distinguished from each other partly in terms of directness. Basic meaning differences can also be regarded as involving kinds or degrees of politeness, informality, or similar.

Commands tend only to occur with verbs that are controlled. If they are used with non-controlled verbs, they coerce a controlled reading. They tend not to occur with stative verbs. However, note the following with *qaaj3* 'shy, ashamed, modest':

(36) qaaj3 phen1 nèè1
shy 3SG.POL IMP.SOFT
Be modest/shy of him.

(37) lom2 — bòø tòòng4 qaaj3
talk NEG must shy
Talk—no need to be modest/shy.

The following sections illustrate some main distinctions in semantics of commands.

4.1 *Semantic distinctions in commands marked by sentence-final particles*

This section elaborates on semantic distinctions between the different sentence-final particles listed in Table 1 that can be used in forming commands (some parts of the following are from Enfield 2007).

mèè4—'Do it, go ahead, I don't know why you don't, nothing's stopping you' (imperative, states that addressee is unimpeded = IMP.UNIMP)

The particle *mèè4* is used in utterances which urge an addressee to carry out some action, where the speaker is conveying the idea that the addressee is unimpeded, that there is nothing stopping the addressee doing the action.

In an example, a mother is sitting with her youngest child, having just finished breast-feeding. An older woman is waiting for her to help with a mat-weaving task. The mother calls out to another of her children, who is asked to come and take care of the infant. The speaker's use of *mèè4* conveys the idea 'What are you waiting for?', but in this context it conveys impatience:

(38) maø   qaw3   nòòng4,   maa2   mèè4,
      DIR.ALL   grab   YG   come   IMP.UNIMP
      siø   ñèè1   saat5   haj5   mèø-paa4   niø   naa3
      IRR   insert mat   give   CT.MO-Pa.eZ TOP   FAC.EXPLIC

Come and take care of younger sibling, come on, what are you waiting for?
(I) am going to help this aunty do weaving, you must understand.

Another example is from a narrative tale about supreme beings in a heavenly kingdom and their exploits in the world of men. King Vetsuvan asks after his aide Kumphan, as he hasn't seen him report for duty. His assistants say they are afraid he has died, since he got into a fight with some humans (despite being urged not to). The king is not satisfied with this report and wants evidence. His command to go and find the body is marked with *mèè4*, which in this context conveys his impatience with his aides for not having already done this:

(39) man2   taaj3   juu1   saj3,   nam2-haa3   mèè4
      3SG.BARE   die   be.at   where   follow-seek   IMP.UNIMP

Where has he died? Go and find him, what are you waiting for?!

In a final example, a group of men are telling stories for the tape recorder. After one speaker has finished, another is asked to contribute a joke or an anecdote. He responds by saying that he doesn't think he can do it. Another urges him to speak, and by using *mèè4* conveys his disagreement with the man's claim that he is incapable—specifically, through its meaning 'there's nothing stopping you':

(40) vaw4   mèè4
      speak   IMP.UNIMP

Go ahead and speak, what are you waiting for?!

saa3—'Do it, it will be good if you do, I know you won't do it if you don't want to' (imperative, suggests course of action to addressee = IMP.SUGG)

The imperative particle *saa3* has a suggesting, non-imposing quality. By using *saa3* in a command, the speaker conveys the idea that it would be good if the addressee carried out the action, but that whether they do it is ultimately a matter of the addressee's own choice. The speaker can use *saa3* to either acknowledge or bring about a situation in which the addressee is treated as someone with authority over the course of action. *Saa3* provides a way to propose that the addressee do something, without being too imposing. The speaker claims less authority, making it explicit that it is up to the addressee whether they acquiesce.

In an example from a narrative, a head-butting contest is scheduled to take place, but the visiting team becomes terrified of the opposition. They go to their hosts and plead for more time. The use of *saa3* treats the addressee as the authority in making the decision:

(41) bòø   than2   nanø   lèèw4, mùù4   nii4, khòò3   qiik5
     NEG   on.time TOP.NONPROX   PER   day   DEM   request   more
     cak2   sòòng3   saam3   van2   saa3
     how.many   two   three   day   IMP.SUGG
     We're not ready today, (we) request another two or three days, please?

In another example, the hero Sinxay and his sidekick Sangthong are delayed on their travels by a giant snake which has transformed itself into a mountain range. They can't get past. Sangthong says to his master Sinxay:

(42) saa4   vêê2laa2, ñing2   man2   saa3,   ñing2   thim5   saa3
     slow   time   shoot   3.BARE IMP.SUGG   shoot   discard IMP.SUGG
     We're being held up, go ahead and shoot it, shoot it and get rid of it.

Sinxay is the leader of the expedition, and Sangthong's phrasing with *saa3* recognizes this by acknowledging that it is ultimately Sinxay's choice as to what course of action is taken.

    A final example is from a fable. A cow encounters a tiger, and asks the tiger to let her go home and feed her calf before allowing the tiger to eat her. The tiger agrees, but when the cow goes to her calf to explain this, the calf wants to let the tiger eat it instead, and spare the mother. The cow and calf end up both standing in front of the tiger, arguing about who should be eaten. Saying 'Eat me, not my calf', the cow's use of *saa3* conveys the idea that she would prefer this course of action, but it also shows respect to the tiger by acknowledging its freedom to decide:

(43) phañaa2-sùa3   qeej4, siø   kin3   khòòj5   kaø   kin3 saa3
     lord-tiger   VOC   IRR   eat   1SG.POL T.LNK eat   IMP.SUGG
     O tiger lord, (if) you are going to eat me, then please eat me (and not my calf).

dèè1—'Do it, please, it's not a big thing' (imperative, softens or plays down the burden of the request = IMP.SOFT)

The particle *dèè1* (with a variant *nèè1* which appears to have identical function and distribution) provides a polite way of asking someone to do some small favour for the speaker:

(44) peet5   patuu3   haj5   dèè1
     open   door   give   IMP.SOFT
     Please open the door.

In another example, a speaker is telling the tale of a man who is fighting another man who wants to take his wife. Both men fall to the ground, and their swords fly off and land at a distance. The husband calls out to his wife to fetch his sword for him:

(45) naang2 moo2laa2 qeej4, qaw3   ngaaw4 maø   haj5   qaaj4 dèè1
     miss   M   VOC   grab   sword   DIR.ALL   give   eB   IMP.SOFT
     O Miss Mola, take the sword and give it to me (i.e. older brother), please.

In another example, a man at the market sees sausages for the first time. He asks the sales lady whether there is a special way to prepare them, to which she replies, 'Yes indeed'. He responds:

(46) cot2   tamlaa3   haj5   khòòj5   dèè1
     write.down recipe   give   1SG.POL IMP.SOFT
     Write down the recipe for me please.

The use of *dèè1* with an imperative is a way of softening the imposition, as if to say 'it's not a big thing'. This meaning is related to other functions of *dèè1*. With assertions, *dèè1* can also attenuate the strength of a proposition, along the lines of 'a little', 'partly'. In this function, it occurs in the postverbal slot, before postverbal aspectual-modals. For example:

(47) jaak5   kham1   mùùt4   dèè1   lèèw4
     tend   evening dark   a.little PER
     It was already getting a little dark.

In another example, a speaker is talking about hippies from Western countries who lived in Vientiane just prior to the fall of the Royal Lao Government in 1975. He describes how these hippies were talking with him about the imminent takeover by a communist government. He remarks that these hippies could speak Lao a bit, conveying this notion of 'partly' or 'a little' by means of the particle *dèè1*:

(48) mii2   khon2 man2   vaw4   khuam2 laaw2 kaø   daj4   dèè1
     there.is person 3.BARE speak sense   Lao   T.LNK can   a.little
     Some people, they could speak Lao a little.

A complex construction which also relates to the idea of 'part, small amount' has the pattern X *dèè1*, Y *dèè1* (, Z *dèè1*), with the meaning 'Some X, some Y (, some Z)'. For example, a speaker describes conditions in a crowded holding cell, as detainees wait to be transported to a re-education facility:

(49) hòòng4-haj5 dèè1,   hiiw3   qahaan3 dèè1
     call-cry   in.part   hungry food   in.part
     Some were crying, some were hungry.

vaj2—'Hurry up and do it!' (imperative, asks the addressee to hurry = IMP.RUSH)

The particle *vaj2* is typically used with imperatives directed at children. As a verb, *vaj2* means 'fast'. In its sentence-final particle function, *vaj2* presupposes that the addressee will be compliant. It is therefore appropriate for familiar children, not for strangers. Here is an example:

(50) maa2   mian4   phaa2-khaw5   vaj2
     come   put.aside tray.table-rice IMP.RUSH
     Hurry up and come and clear away the dinner tray!

Here are two further examples, in which the speakers issue commands to children of around 12 years of age, who are being asked to help with simple but urgent chores in a shop and in the home:

(51) qii1-naa4, maa2 khaaj3 bat2 haj5 phen1 vaj2
     F.BARE-N come sell card give 3SG.POL IMP.RUSH
     Na, come here and sell them a phone card.

(52) nithaa3, qaw3 phaa2-khaw5 maa2 haj5 phòø-tuu4 vaj2
     N grab tray.table come give grandpa IMP.RUSH
     Nithaa, go and get a tray table for your grandfather.

duu2—'Please do it, for me?' (IMP.PLEAD)

The particle *duu2* conveys a kind of pleading tone to an imperative, as if the speaker is saying 'Do it, FOR ME'.

In an example, the speaker has been sitting and relaxing for some time with her grandchildren in one house while the children's younger sibling (also the speaker's grandchild) is asleep in their house just nearby. The grandmother is currently responsible for the child and asks if one of the siblings can go and check to see if the infant is awake and needs attention:

(53) paj3 ñaang1 beng1 nòòng4 duu2
     go walk look y.sib IMP.PLEAD
     Walk over and check on your younger sibling, could you?

In another example, the speaker is a shop owner. A customer has just asked for hot tea. The electric kettle needs to be switched on for hot water. The speaker asks her child (aged around 10 years) to plug the electric kettle in:

(54) siap5 faj2 haj5 man2 hòòn4 duu2 luuk4
     insert fire give 3SG.BARE hot IMP.PLEAD child
     Plug it (the kettle) in to make it hot, could you child?

4.2 Particles that are not semantically dedicated to signalling commands

Some forms that are often used in commands are not dedicated to imperative function. One is the 'factive, on-record' particle *dee4*:

(55) khan2 man2 tùùn1 laø qaw3 nòòng4 maa2 haj5 dee4
     if 3SG.BARE wake PER grab yG come give FAC.ONRCD
     If she is awake bring her to me, y'hear!

(56) maa2 dee4 maa2 dee4 long2 maa2 dee4
     come FAC.ONRCD come FAC.ONRCD descend come FAC.ONRCD
     Come here, come here, come down here, y'hear!

Elsewhere this particle can be used in assertions or instructions where the speaker wishes to put it on record that something has been said, to emphasize that what they are saying should be carefully noted.

A second one is *loot4*, a postverbal tense-aspect-mood marker that means 'right away, without hesitation or ado'. It normally only occurs with predicates of action. Here are some examples of *loot4* used in commands:

(57) mùng2   qaw3   paj3   loot4
      2SG.BARE   grab   go   NO.ADO
      You go ahead and take (them) right away! (Spoken by a man to a dog that is stealing the man's sausages.)

(58) pùak4   man2   fon3   saj1   kan3   loot4
      bark   3SG.B   grind   put   COLL   NO.ADO
      That's the bark of the medicine, just grind it in.

A third one is the verb *paj3* 'to go', which occurs in the sentence-final particle position in some commands (usually pronounced as [pah]; also commonly used all by itself with 'inclusive imperative' function to mean 'Let's go!'):

(59) qaw3   qoo3   paj3
      grab   bowl   go
      Go get a bowl.

(60) paj3   qaw3   khok1   maa2   tam3   paj3
      go   grab   mortar   come   pound   go
      Go get a mortar to do the pounding.

5 Social hierarchy and commands

In cases of commands that I examined from my corpus of conversation, I determined the relative social rank of the two people involved. This was done relative to local norms of hierarchy based mostly on age. Of over 200 cases examined, three-fifths were issued in a 'downward' direction, and only one-fifth issued in an 'upward' direction (with another fifth between people of roughly equal standing).

Asymmetry in sibling order is arguably the kernel of all social hierarchical relations in Lao-speaking society. It has many consequences (see Enfield 2015: 128–46):

- Kin terms: two siblings will necessarily use different kin terms for each other (the possibilities being *qùaj4* 'elder sister', *qaaj4* 'elder brother', *nòòng4* 'younger sibling').
- Pronouns: two siblings will necessarily use different pronouns for each other ('bare' downwards, 'polite' upwards).

- Titles: two siblings will necessarily use different titles when referring to each other ('nonrespect' title downwards, kin title upwards).
- Teknonymy: parent adopts name of first-born child, not younger siblings.
- Rights and duties: there is institutionalized delegation of chores among siblings in a downward direction only.
- Marriage rules: there are constraints in relations to sibling marriage, for example a younger sibling should not get married if an older sibling is still single; or, if A's elder brother wants to marry A's wife's sister, then the sister must be the *elder* sister of A's wife, irrespective of anyone's absolute age.
- Inheritance: last-born sibling tends to stay in parents' home permanently.

Broad-ranging consequences of age difference in sibling order lay a foundation in Lao society for careful attention to one's position in the social hierarchy. This is clearly observed in the domain of issuing commands. When commanding is done in an upward direction, this is often more explicitly marked. In the following case, an 'inferior' issues a command to a superior, featuring the use of an upward-looking kin title, polite second person and first person pronouns, and a 'softening' imperative particle:

(61) qaaj4-qòt2   caw4   qaw3 saat5 maa2 puu3 haj5 khòòj5   nèè1
     eB-Q   2SG.POL   grab mat   come lay give 1SG.POL   IMP.SOFT
     (Elder) Ot, you (polite) lay down a reed mat for me (polite) please.

Compare this case of a similar command issued in a downward direction, without any of those forms of marking:

(62) paj3   qaw3   maa2
     go   grab   come
     Go and bring (them) here.

Often, there is delegation of commands, whereby a commandee can immediately delegate a command to a lower-ranked person. In the following two examples, Person A issues a command to lower-ranked Person B, who then issues it directly to further lower-ranked Person C:

(63) a. sòòng3 phaa2   nan4   song1 khaw5 maa2 haa3 kan3
        two   tray.table   DEM.NONPROX   send enter come seek COLL
        Those two tray tables, bring them in here together. (A>B)

     b. paj3   qaw3   maa2
        go   grab   come
        Go and bring them here (B>C)

(64) a. tak2   paø-dèèk5   hêt1 viak4 lèèw4 laø cang1 paj3
        scoop CT.fish-jugged.fish   do   work PER   PER then go
        Scoop some jugged fish and do your work, and then go. (A>B siblings)

b. qee5   khiaw5   paj3   tak2   paødèèk5   paj3
   yeah   rush   go   scoop   CT.fish-jugged.fish   go
   Yeah, go and scoop some jugged fish. (B>C siblings)

6 Conclusion

Lao has a range of dedicated linguistic devices for formulating commands and related
speech acts, as well as a range of strategies for indirectly conveying the force of a
command. While these devices and strategies have been described separately in the
previous sections, they are often combined. This can be seen in many of the examples
already given. To conclude this chapter, we consider two further cases in which
multiple command strategies are combined in a single instance.

In a first example, the speaker is addressing a neighbour who is of a similar age to
the speaker's parents. The speaker has been eating dinner with her family, and the
available cooked rice has run out; she calls out to her neighbour to ask if they could
spare some rice. This example combines five distinct strategies listed above: (1) use of
the commandee's name; (2) vocative particle used with the name; (3) the requesting
verb *khòò3* 'ask.for' used as a complement-taking predicate; (4) the 'soft' imperative
particle *dèè1*; and (5) the 'on record' factive particle *dee4*:

(65)   mèè1-teng3   qeej4   khòò3   khaw5   maa2   kin3   dèè1   dee4
        mother-T   VOC   request   rice   come   eat   IMP.SOFT   FAC.ONRCD
        O Teng's Mum, can we have some rice to eat, our rice is finished.

In a second example, some visitors to a family home have been discussing herbal
medicines with their hosts. One of the visitors expresses interest in trying some of the
herbal medicine that the hosts have. It is a kind of bark that needs to be ground into
water using a stone. To do this, a bowl is needed. In this example, the speaker is
asking a family member to fetch the needed bowl. Four strategies are combined: (1)
use of an address term for the commandee; (2) bare form of the verb *qaw3* 'grab/get';
(3) the verb *paj3* 'go' as an imperative particle; and (4) the 'hurry up' imperative
particle *vaj2* (related to the adjective/verb *vaj2* 'fast'):

(66)   qiø-laa5   qaw3   qoo3   paj3   vaj2
        F.BARE-last.born   grab   bowl   go   IMP.RUSH
        Darling girl get a bowl.

These examples show that the functional domain of requests and commands is as
rich and complex as any other in language: multiple constructions and strategies can
be selected and combined, with the result that our expressive possibilities are
limitless.

Acknowledgements

I would like to thank Sasha Aikhenvald and Bob Dixon for comments on a draft of this chapter, and all participants in the 'Commands' workshop, Cairns, September 2015, for helpful comments and input. I gratefully acknowledge support from the European Research Council (through grant 240853 'Human Sociality and Systems of Language Use'), and the University of Sydney (through Bridging Grant ID 176605).

References

Enfield, N. J. 2007. *A grammar of Lao*. Berlin: Mouton de Gruyter.
Enfield, N. J. 2014. 'Human agency and the infrastructure for requests', pp. 35–50 of *Requesting in social interaction*, edited by Paul Drew and Elizabeth Couper-Kuhlen. Amsterdam: John Benjamins.
Enfield, N. J. 2015. *The utility of meaning: What words mean and why*. Oxford: Oxford University Press.

10

Imperatives and command strategies in Tayatuk (Morobe, PNG)

VALÉRIE GUÉRIN

1 The language

Tayatuk, known as Som (ISO code: smc), is one of the Papuan languages of the Morobe province in Papua New Guinea (PNG), shown in Figure 1. It is spoken in two villages, Gogiok and Torik, by about 500 people. Tayatuk is classified as an Uruwa language (along with Nungon, see Sarvasy, Chapter 11) in the Finisterre-Huon group (McElhanon 1973), although its inclusion in the Uruwa family may be blurred by sustained contact with the neighbouring Yopno family from which Tayatuk has heavily borrowed (Hooley and McElhanon 1970: 1074). Tayatuk has six vowels and 20 consonant phonemes. Graphemes which do not correspond to their IPA equivalents are presented in Table 1.

Morphologically, Tayatuk is head-marking, agglutinating with some fusion, and predominantly suffixing. Open word classes include nouns and adjectives. Closed classes include pronouns, deictics, adverbs, and verbs. Clauses are categorized as intransitive (with meteorological verbs such as *isî* 'daylight'; posture verbs such as *yit* 'stay, sit'; motion verbs such as *ku* 'go.level', which may take inherently locational nouns), ambitransitive (S=O ambitransitive verbs include *sa* 'cook, heat up'; S=A ambitransitive verbs include *pîta* 'get up, lift'), or transitive. As is common in many languages of PNG (Foley 1986: 128; Reesink 1987: 16), transitive verbs can be subdivided into three subclasses, depending on the form of the O argument: whether an NP; a prefix which marks the number of an inanimate O (e.g. *e* 'put, plant, write'); or a prefix which encodes the number and person of an animate O (such as *uk* 'hit, fight' or the ditransitive *nyi* 'tell'). Verbs can also be subcategorized based on the final segment of their root (whether a V or a C) and the morpho-phonological changes that apply to that root as a result of suffixation. Seven verb classes are identified in Tables 2 to 4. If all six vowel phonemes can appear in the coda of a verb root, in contrast, only two stops [t] and [p] and two nasals [m] and [n] occur in this position.

Commands. First edition. Alexandra Y. Aikhenvald and R. M. W. Dixon (eds)
This chapter © Valérie Guérin 2017. First published 2017 by Oxford University Press

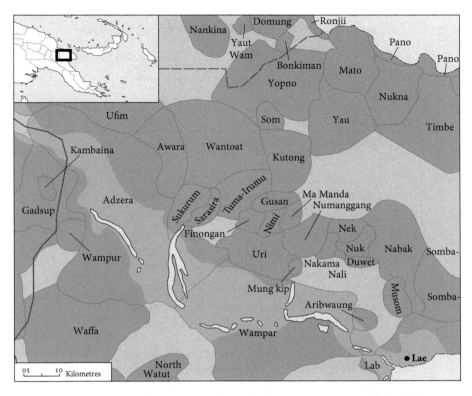

FIGURE 1. Geographical location of Tayatuk (Som). Map courtesy of SIL PNG

TABLE 1. **Grapheme/phoneme correspondence**

Phoneme	ə	ŋ	ɲ	dz	k^w	g^w	$ŋ^w$
Grapheme	î	ng	ny	z	kw	gw	ngw

TABLE 2. **Three classes of verbs whose roots end with a vowel**

	y-class	v-class	w-class
Root	di 'watch'	pa 'hold'	ya 'say/talk'
NF	di-ng	pa-ng	ya-ng
1sg:PRES	di-tat	pa-tat	ya-tat
1sg:PROX:FUT	di-yang-tat	pa-vang-tat	yu-wang-tat

TABLE 3. Two classes of verbs whose roots end with a stop

	t~w class	p~mang class
Root	pat 'sleep'	sap 'obstruct, tie'
NF	pak	sapmîng
1sg:PRES	pak-tat	sapmîng-tat
1sg:PROX:FUT	pu-wang-tat	sap-mang-tat

TABLE 4. Two classes of verbs whose roots end with a nasal

	m~v class	n~y class
Root	wam 'roll'	sîmîn 'fill up'
NF	wamîng	sîmîn
1sg:PRES	wa-vat	sîmîn-tat
1sg:PROX:FUT	wa-vang-tat	sîmî-yang-tat

The only nominal category marked on nouns is the genitive. At the clausal level, nouns relate to the head they are dependent on with case-marking postpositions indicating ablative, dative/goal, instrument, and location. The alignment is nominative-accusative, the pragmatically neutral constituent order is AOV/SV. The S, A, and O grammatical relations are expressed by NP ordering; cross-referencing of the number and person of S/A argument on the verb (and the O for a handful of verbs, as prefix); and differential (or optional) case marking. Subjects can be marked with the postposition *dî* when focused. Likewise, focused objects can be marked with *nîng* (singular) or *pîng* (plural), while other objects are unmarked. These phenomena are known as differential subject marking and differential object marking respectively. The postpositions *nîng* (singular) and *pîng* (plural) also mark instruments, while *dî* marks ablative.

Two major clause types can be identified: final (or main) clauses and non-final (or medial) clauses. The list of grammatical categories found on verbs in main clauses in non-imperative mood is detailed in Table 5. The structure of non-final verbs is detailed in Table 6.

Final verbs obligatorily inflect for reality status (unmarked realis) and minimally either for modality or for tense and person/number. In contrast, verbs of non-final clauses never inflect for modality and tense. Medial clauses track participant via switch reference. Non-final (NF) verbs can morphologically indicate whether their subject and the subject of the following verb are the same (SS) or different (DS). The

TABLE 5. **Morphological structure of final verbs in non-imperative mood**

Number (and person) of O argument	Stem	Reality		Modality	Aspect	Tense	Person and number of S/A argument	Evidential?
		Number	Status					

TABLE 6. **Morphological structure of non-final verbs**

Number (and person) of O argument of the marking clause	Stem	NF	SS	DS
		V-*ng* or final C mutation	Invariable suffix -*îk*	Person and number of the S/A argument of the marking clause

originality of Tayatuk is that DS inflection must attach to two dependency suffixes (NF and SS), although this 'stacking' is not unheard of (Roberts 1997: 137).

With these background notions in mind, we can now investigate commands in Tayatuk, starting with canonical imperatives in §2, non-canonical imperatives in §3, prohibitives in §4, and command strategies in §5. The data for this chapter are based on field notes, elicitations, and about 100 oral and written texts of various lengths and genres (personal histories, traditional stories, conversations) collected in Gogiok and Torik in 2014 and 2015.

2 Canonical imperatives

In Tayatuk, as in other Finisterre languages, such as Awara (Quigley 2002: 75), Ma Manda (Pennington 2014: 357), and Yopno (Slotta 2013: 5), canonical imperatives directed to a 2sg addressee consist of the bare stem of the verb, as shown in (1).

(1) gen-ga   du   ya!
    mouth-2sg:POSS some   say
    Say something!

It is also possible for the verb in Tayatuk to be followed by the imperative particle *te*, shown in (2).[1]

---

[1] Note in passing the presence of the diminutive which in many languages softens an imperative (Aikhenvald 2010: 204). Its function in Tayatuk remains to be investigated.

(2) gen-ga=yim   du   ya   te!
     mouth-2sg:POSS=DIM   some   say   2sg:IMP
     Say something!

The exact status of *te* is unclear. It can form a canonical imperative with all vowel-final verbs. With *t*-final verbs, *te* is used with the verb's non-final form (*pak te!* but **pat te!*). *Te* is not attested with other verb classes (**wam te!*). Instead, the imperative is expressed with the non-final form: *wamîng!* 'roll!'.

If the imperative is directed to two or more participants, the verb stem is followed by the suffixes *kon* '2du' or *kot* '2pl', as shown in (3) and (4) respectively. These imperative suffixes are used with all verb classes, irrespective of the quality of the stem-final segment.

(3) amdem   dî   uyeyi   duma   yi-n   ko
     woman   FOC   well   NEG   stay-3sg:IRR   TOP

     amînyi Seget   dî   ya-gu-t   'ku-kon!'
     again   church FOC   say-DIST:PAST-3sg:PAST   go-2du:IMP
     The wife not being well, the church council said again: 'you two go!'

(4) 'din   avît   p-apî-ng   mîk   arîng   gîn
     2pl   all   pl:O-bring.down-NF   ground   place   only

     pat-kot!'   ya-ng   ya-nyi-kang
     sleep-2pl:IMP   say-NF   3pl:O-tell-2/3pl:PRES
     'You all lie down on the ground!' they tell them.

Canonical imperative morphology is summarized in Table 7. If more than one verb appears in a command, the only verb cast in imperative is the last verb in the sequence, the other verbs being in non-final forms, as shown in (5).

(5) o-vîn   ya-nyi-gu-t   'na   tugi-ng
     go.up-3sg:IRR   3pl:O-tell-DIST:PAST-3sg   1sg   carry-NF

     a-ng   o-kon!'   ya-ng   ya-nyi-gu-t
     come-NF   go.up-2DU:IMP   say-NF   3pl:O-tell-DIST:PAST-3sg
     Going up, he told them: 'carry me up' he told them.

The examples adduced so far reveal that verb with any transitivity value can be cast in imperative. However, as mentioned in Aikhenvald (2010: 147–54, 188, 324), verbs

TABLE 7. Canonical imperative morphology

	2sg	2du	2pl
Stem	Ø / te / -NF	-kon	-kot

depicting action over which the speaker has no control (i.e. verbs of perception) usually do not appear in imperative form, or if they do, they acquire a slightly different meaning. This is the case of the verb *narî* 'non-visual sense' in Tayatuk. This verb does not have an imperative form **narî!* (intended meaning 'listen!'). Instead, it is common to hear someone shouting *gabîk!* 'hear!' (literally, the noun 'ear') at least three times to get the entire village's attention before delivering news. In school, on the other hand, the teacher often asks his class *narîkang?* 'do you all understand?', with the distinctive yes-no question intonation, to check for understanding, or *narîkang!* 'listen!' to ask the class to pay attention, instead of expected **narî-kot* (sense-2pl:IMP). The form *narîkang* (sense-2/3pl:PRES) is not an imperative but the present tense, whose literal meaning is 'you/they all listen/are listening' but pragmatically functions as a command. As far as we can tell, no other verb in present tense can act as a command. Additional command strategies are discussed in §5.

3 Non-canonical imperatives

Linguistic relatives of Tayatuk such as Awara and Nungon are reported to have a single homogenous imperative paradigm to express all person values. Tayatuk here stands apart: canonical and non-canonical imperatives are expressed with two different paradigms.[2] We saw in Table 7 that canonical imperatives form a paradigm of their own. To address first and third persons, a different paradigm—which is called here the irrealis paradigm, for lack of a better term—is recruited.[3] This paradigm, provided in Table 8, stands apart from other agreement paradigms (i.e. subject-agreement suffixes used with tense) in that it does not differentiate 3sg from 2/3du. That the irrealis paradigm in Table 8 can be used to express non-canonical imperatives is clearest when used with 1pl in interactions, as in (6).

TABLE 8. Irrealis agreement suffixes

	sg	du	pl
1	-w/v/ya	-r/da	-na
2	-w/v/yi	-w/v/yin	-w/v/yî
3		-w/v/yîn	

---

[2] Tayatuk is similar to the Keveng variety of Yopno, analysed by Reed (2000: 34) as lacking imperative forms for 1sg and 3.

[3] The irrealis paradigm in Tayatuk is formally related to the counterfactual and the DS paradigms. Similar facts hold in Nungon among other Finisterre languages, leading Sarvasy (2015: 480–2) to treat these paradigms as deriving from a proto tenseless form, matching the tense and modality of other verbs in context (in the spirit of Kiparsky's (2005) injunctive in Indo-European languages). See also England's (2013) treatment of tenseless *ma* in Mam, or Korowai's IMMEDIATE in de Vries, Chapter 12.

(6) 'gwaramĩk   a-ng   am-na'   ya-ng   yu-wĩn...
    carry.NF   come-NF   come.down-1pl:IRR say-NF   say-3sg:IRR
    'Let us carry (her) down' he said...

Example (6) sharply contrasts with the non-imperative use in (7): in a narration on past events, no one is summoned to do anything.[4]

(7) nin yik   sa-ng   eat:NF   emtan   tĩ
    1pl stay:NF   cook-NF   eat:NF   afternoon   GOAL

    am-da   Valerie   bĩn   pat-gu-mĩng
    come.down-1du:IRR   Valerie   COMIT   sleep-DIST:PAST-1pl
    We staying, cooking, eating, in the afternoon, we two came down (*let us two come down!), we slept along with Valerie.

Whether irrealis also expresses first singular and third person imperative is contentious at this stage. The cross-linguistic meaning of 1sg imperative 'implies suggestion, proposition or seeking permission' (Aikhenvald 2010: 73–5). In Tayatuk, none of these meanings are expressed by 1sg:IRR. The irrealis adds a sense of immediacy. It is the typical answer to a command, indicating immediate compliance, as in (8).

(8) A: nok   sa
        food   cook
        Cook!

    B: nok   su-wa
        food   cook-1sg:IRR
        Yes! (I'm just about to start cooking. Or: I have just started cooking)

It can refer to an immediate future, as in (9) with the temporal adverb *main* 'later'. The food was eaten in the following 15 minutes or so after the person uttered this sentence.

(9) main   na-va
    later   eat-1sg:IRR
    I'll eat later.

The closest we come to permission is in questions. It is very common to hear the 1sg:IRR form of the verb *nang* 'eat' with an interrogative intonation when presented with food, as reported in (10). The meaning of this question was conceivably to request permission but now it is just phatic, no answer is expected. The speaker is reaching for the food as s/he utters (10b).

---

[4] Note that 1pl:IRR in (6) is inclusive, whereas 1du:IRR excludes the interlocutor in (7).

(10) a. godeng   kut   nang!
        sweet.potato roasted eat
        Eat the roasted sweet potato!

     b. na-va?
        eat-1sg:IRR
        Shall I eat?

In a rhetorical question, 1sg:IRR expresses necessity or ability, as in (11) where the speaker reports on a time when he was lost at night in the bush.

(11) kîyi   uka   wesî-ng-îk-wîn   niyang a-va?
     already this.one dusk-NF-SS-3sg:DS how   do-1sg:IRR
     It being already dusk, what was I to do?

However, the fact that 1sg:IRR is found in interrogative speech acts also undermines the claim that it functions as an imperative.

A third person imperative has overtones of wish cross-linguistically (Aikhenvald 2010: 75). A similar meaning is not found in Tayatuk interactions. 3sg:IRR expresses an immediate future. In (12), the speaker does not wish for me to record the conversation, she does not indirectly command me to do so. She is simply stating a fact, she knows (like all parties involved in that episode) that I will record.[5]

(12) p-apî-ng-îk-wi   avît dî   yik-îk
     pl:O-get.down-NF-SS-2sg:DS all   FOC stay:NF-SS

     ya-ng-îk-wîna   main   p-a-vîn.
     talk-NF-SS-1pl:DS later   pl:O-get-3sg:IRR
     You bringing (them) down, we all sitting down talking, then (Valerie) will record (*may Valerie record).

4 Negative imperatives

Two grammatical features define negative imperatives. First, they contain the negative particle *ma* which is used elsewhere in the grammar to negate irrealis sentences (while *duma* negates realis sentences). Second, the verb must take the 2/3pl present tense agreement *kang*, regardless of the number of the subject. That is, in negative imperatives, all person and number distinctions are neutralized. Compare (13) clearly addressed to 2pl in the story and (14) which contains the 2sg pronoun.

(13) kasuk ma   a-kang!
     noise   NEG:IRR do-2/3pl:PRES
     Don't make any noise!

---

[5] It was suggested that the imperative could well apply to other verbs in the sentence. However, it is unlikely that the imperative would not have scope over the verb that hosts it.

(14) ga   wap   akena   ma   yi-kang!
     2sg   today here   NEG:IRR   stay-2/3pl:PRES
     Don't stay here today!

Negative imperatives differ from positive imperatives in the types of verbs that they can be formed with. As mentioned in §2, verbs of perception such as *narî* 'sense' do not appear in imperative mood, but they may appear in the prohibitive: *na tî ma narîkang* 'don't worry about me!'. Negative imperatives also differ from positive imperatives in that they do not need to address a specific person; they can be directed to a generic person. This was shown by a series of commands posted on a notice board in a classroom: *gen wetnyi ma yakang* 'do not use coarse language', *oben ma yikang* 'do not stay idle', do not play in class, do not steal, do not touch the teacher's material, etc. They were meant to be followed by anyone and everyone in class but no one in particular.

5 Commands strategies

Commands are pervasive in Tayatuk interactions, owing to the fact that they do not just order people to act, they also encourage them to do so. Canonical imperatives appear in speech formulae such as *emîng!* 'come in!' (literally 'come up') to invite the addressee to act, or *amîng!* 'welcome!' (literally 'come down') formed by analogy with Tok Pisin, to express gratitude. They describe actions that are about to take place anyway or have just started (as in §3; see also Aikhenvald 2010: 131). Someone who is rolling a cigarette and about to smoke will hear *kutuyukga piyi* 'smoke your tobacco!'. The pragmatic import of this imperative is to index the alignment and approval of the speaker. Prohibitives too have non-command meanings. The following was heard as the speaker was leaving for a three-hour hike and the sky was darkening, expressing his wish:

(15) kamok   ma   pî-kang!
     rain   NEG:IRR   come.down-2/3pl:PRES
     It can't rain! / May it not rain!

Conversely, not all commands take the form of an imperative. A bare noun can be understood as a directive. It is common during meals to hear someone say *tap!* 'salt!' as a request to be given salt. This sort of directive is generally immediately tended to. Adverbs too can have directive meanings. *Wayi* 'almost, yet' is used as a command to mean 'wait!'. In classrooms, the teachers often say *wop* 'quiet!' or *kasuk kasuk* 'noise!' which produces the opposite effect and requests silence. There is also one invariable lexeme in the language, namely *on!* which is uttered while giving something to someone and can be translated as 'here, take!'. *On* is likely a borrowing from Yopno *on* 'this, proximal'.

In the verbal domain, non-imperative forms may also assume imperative meanings. We mentioned in §2 the use of the present tense with perception verbs. The roles of near future and the dependent verb forms as command strategies are discussed in §5.1 and §5.2 respectively.

5.1 The near future

Imperatives are commonly used in phatic exchange with greeting-like overtones. When passing someone on the road, it is common to hear the minimal exchange reported in (16).

(16) a. tamîng   o-ta-t
          bush   go.up-sg:PRES-1sg
          I'm going up to the bush.

      b. uyep!   O   te!
          good   go.up   2sg:IMP
          OK! Go!

An alternative reply to (16a) would be (17), cast in the near future (composed of the potential and the present tense).

(17) uyep!   o-vang-ta-n!
      good   go.up-POT-sg:PRES-2sg
      OK! Go!

The near future can be used instead of the imperative in a few other contexts. It is co-opted to soften a command to a mild request. This request can be made even more non-imposing when framed as an 'ability question' (Aikhenvald 2010: 258). Example (18) was asked by a younger girl, who felt she did not want to impose on the addressee.

(18) nesin   uyep   na-m-ang-ta-n?
      betel   good   1o-give-POT-sg:PRES-2sg
      Would it be possible for you to pass me the betel nuts?

The near future is also used to express a distal command, for an action to be carried out far from the speaker (Aikhenvald 2010: 133–8). Thus, in Tayatuk, as in related languages (e.g. Ma Manda in Pennington 2014: 357–8), a distinction can be made between a near imperative (proximal in time and space), expressed by a bare verb root, and a remote imperative (distal in time and space) expressed by the near future. Consider example (19): the mother has sent her young daughter to pick up pepper vine some short distance away. The child has trouble finding the plant; the mother, who can see her, shouts, rather irritably:

(19) Arîgi!   Yuwo   rî   kewu   ku-ta-k   akaput
     DIST:up   MASC.NAME   FOC   road   go-sg:PRES-3sg   here.side

     tî   godeng   kuwak   ken   tî   di-yang-ta-n!
     GOAL   sweet.potato garden   LOC   GOAL   look-POT-sg:PRES-2sg

     Up there! Look for (it) in the sweet potatoes' garden, for (it) at the here-side of
     the road that Yuwo takes!

The form of the verb *di* 'look' is cast in near future, yet the mother is not asking her
daughter to perform the search in the near future but immediately. It is the distance
in space that is triggering the near future as a command strategy. Importantly,
the speaker is the deictic centre from which the distance is evaluated, not the addressee
(Aikhenvald 2010: 134). In the following example, the narrator recalls when he was
asked by the church council to go and work in a different village. Here, the near future
indicates a mild or polite command. There are obvious overtones of spatial distance,
since the speaker has to go to a different village. There are also obvious overtones of
temporal distance, simply because of the meaning of the near future (and because the
new assignment will not start right away).

(20) 'Tapen   k-wang-ta-n'   ya-ng   ya-gu-t.
     place.NAME   go-POT-sg:PRES-2sg   say-NF   say-DIST:PAST-3sg:PAST
     '(You will) go to Tapen' he said.

In interactions, whether the near future also indicates a distance in time is ambiguous
in (21).

(21) pî-ng   yu-wang-ta-n!
     come.down-NF   talk-POT-sg:PRES-2sg
     Come down narrate!

Here a wife is calling her husband to join her and tell a story (that I will record). She
uses the near future as her husband is physically far from her (and not visible).
Whether she used that form of the verb to also request for him to come later or not is
difficult to determine, especially since distance in time is a relative concept. The
husband came in the following hour or so.

5.2 Non-final verbs

The non-final form of a verb is used as a command strategy in two situations: to
make an entreaty and to give an order. Young children are taught to interact verbally
in an appropriate manner by being asked to repeat phrases their parents utter.
A parent would say (22) to entreat his/her child to say 'thank you' using a desubordinated clause (Evans 2007) with the non-final form of *ya* 'talk, say', although s/he
does not expect the child's compliance.

(22) 'wam   guyîk!'   ya-ng!
     liver   desire   say-NF
     Say(ing) 'thank you!'

Interestingly, desubordinated clauses with *yang* can also achieve the exact opposite effect: the sternest of commands (see Sarvasy, Chapter 11). At least under elicitations, the bare verb root imperative (*nam!* Give me!) is said to be less commanding than the dependent form of the verb. A third and even more authoritative variant was offered, reported in (23). It contains the dependent form of *m(î)* 'give' followed by a desubordinated clause with the non-final verb *ya* 'talk, say'.

(23) 'na-mî-ng!'   ya-ng
     1O-give-NF   say-NF
     Say(ing) 'give it to me!' (elicited)

Several factors distinguish the order from the entreaty. Different intonational contours and different contexts of utterance are expected. The entreaty in (22) is said as encouragement to a child (or any language learner, such as myself), the order in (23) is said when running out of patience. Also important are the final verb forms which would follow *yang* but are elided. The equivalent of (22) with a final verb would be (24). The final verb is bare, which is the less stern and most common imperative form. On the other hand, the completion of (23) would be (25).

(24) 'na-mî-ng!'   ya-ng   ya!
     1O-give-NF   say-NF   say
     Say 'give it to me!' (elicited)

(25) 'na-mî-ng'   ya-ng   ya-t!
     1O-give-NF   say-NF   say-1sg
     I said 'give it to me!' (elicited)

On Evans's (2007: 370–3) grammaticalization path, desubordinated clauses with *yang* are between stages 2 and 3: the main clause is elided, the interpretation 'is conventionalized to a subset of the grammatically tolerated possibilities' yet which clause can be restored is 'determined by process of conversational inference'.

5.3 Strategies and strength

Principles of iconicity are often solicited to explain differences in meanings between forms. For imperatives, 'the more polite the form, the longer and more morphologically complex it is' (Aikhenvald 2010: 33, 46). This principle is partially violated in Tayatuk. As seen in §5.2, the least and the most coercive commands have equal length, both using a desubordinated clause, as summarized in Table 9.

TABLE 9. **Command strategies and their strength**

(i)	*na-mî-ng* *ya-ng* *(ya)* 1O-give-NF say-NF say Say 'give me!'!			−coercive
(ii)	*na-m-ang-ta-n* 1O-give-POT-sg:PRES-2sg Could you please give me!			
(iii)	*na-m* 1O-give Give me!			
(iv)	*na-mî-ng* 1O-give-NF Give/giving me!			
(v)	*na-mî-ng* *ya-ng* *(ya-t)* 1O-give-NF say-NF say-1sg I said 'give me!'			+coercive

In terms of usage, we note that the most restricted form is (i). I have only witnessed it in one type of language learning situation (parents–children, consultant–linguist). The command strategy in (ii) having overtones of distance will be used to politely address any respected members of the community. In the context of a home, among friends, the imperative in (iii) is chosen. This seems to be the pragmatically neutral form. I have not witnessed (iv) and (v), the latter supposed to be the harshest of commands. Non-canonical imperatives and prohibitives do not display any variation in strength, as far as I can tell.

6 Concluding notes

Based on the evidence adduced so far, we can clearly identify imperatives and prohibitives as separate clause types in Tayatuk, as the grammatical properties they are associated with differ from the declarative and interrogative clause types. We mentioned the verb classes that can or cannot be cast in imperative, but the most obvious parameter that separates out imperatives from prohibitives and from other clause types lies in the verbal categories that their clauses require. Fewer distinctions are expressed in imperatives.

- **Morphological structure**: A well-formed declarative clause minimally requires either the verb stem with the irrealis (which always marks number) to form the potential, or the verb stem (with a zero realis marker) and an S/A agreement suffix to form the near past. Canonical imperatives do not submit to this requirement. A well-formed imperative can be expressed with a bare verb form. Prohibitives in that respect are marked like declaratives.

- **Tense, Aspect, and Modality**: At least five tenses, one aspect, and three modalities can be encoded on the verb in declarative mood, by a series of stacked suffixes, as shown in Table 2. Prohibitives seem cast in present tense. No other verbal categories can be marked. Canonical imperatives being bare verb stem do not mark any verbal categories; they are unspecified for the tense and modal systems found in declarative mood.
- **S/A number agreement**: Canonical imperatives and declaratives distinguish three numbers: sg, du, pl; while number is neutralized in prohibitives.
- **S/A person agreement**: The person agreement markers for canonical imperatives form a paradigm of their own, marking second person only. Prohibitives are expressed with an invariable suffix, person is neutralized. On the other hand, declaratives distinguish seven persons.

If morphology sets imperatives apart from other moods, the role of prosody remains to be established. A cursory look at PRAAT graphs reveal that the intonational contour of canonical imperatives (in Figure 2 elicited from an adult woman and Figure 3 extracted from a conversation between two elders) may start with a H(igh) pitch and ends on a L(ow), in a gradual fall.

(26) Yaim   sinîm   ango-ng   na-m!
     hurry   INTENS   take.up-NF 1O-give
     Bring and give it to me quickly! (elicited)

(27) nan   min-ga   bîn   man-nyi   ya!
     dad   mom-2sg:POSS COMIT   name-3sg:POSS   say
     Say your parents' name!

Likewise, prohibitives, in (28) from the same female speaker as (26), do not seem to stray too widely from the HL tune in Figure 4.

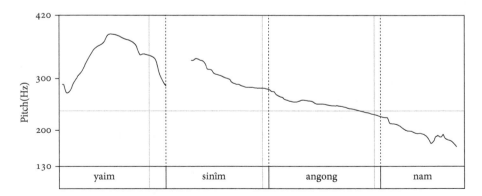

FIGURE 2. Intonational contour of the imperative in (26)

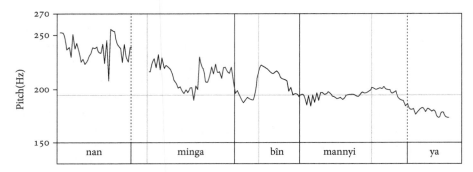

FIGURE 3. Intonational contour of the imperative in (27)

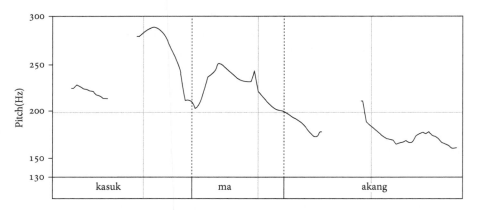

FIGURE 4. Intonational contour of the prohibitive in (28)

(28) kasuk   ma   a-kang!
     noise   NEG:IRR   do-2/3pl:PRES
     Don't make any noise!

Interestingly, imperatives and declaratives do not seem to differ qualitatively in their prosody. We may compare the above tunes to the ones in Figures 5 and 6 from the same speakers: the woman uttered the statement in (29) while conversing; the older male's example of a declarative utterance is provided in (30). The overall intonational contour of a declarative is HL too, as is common cross-linguistically (Himmelmann and Ladd 2008: 256; Hirst and Di Cristo 1998: 21).

(29) Naru-nyi   bu   rî   u-ng   ya-gu-t...
     child-3sg:POSS one   FOC   come-NF   say-DIST:PAST-3sg:PAST
     One of her children coming said...

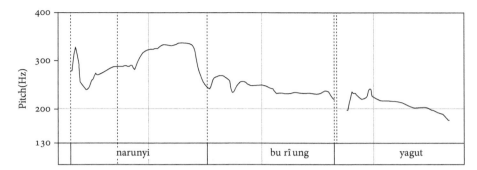

FIGURE 5. Intonational contour of the declarative in (29)

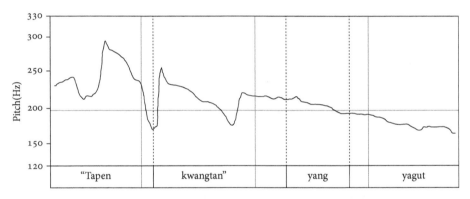

FIGURE 6. Intonational contour of the declarative in (30)

(30) 'Tapen   k-wang-ta-n'   ya-ng   ya-gu-t.
      place.NAME   go-POT-sg:PRES-2sg   say-NF   say-DIST:PAST-3sg:PAST
      'You will go to Tapen' he said.

In passing, we note that content questions, such as (31) from the same female speaker, also seem to have the same contour, from H to L (Figure 7). That different speech acts could have the same intonational contour is not unheard of (Hirst and Di Cristo 1998: 24–8). As Aikhenvald (2010: 90) mentions, intonation need not play a role in distinguishing clause types if the morphology already does the job.

(31) ga   mak   îsîk   gaken   ku–n?
      2sg   place daylight   where   go-2sg
      Where did you go this morning?

Prospects for further studies include: the restrictions on the occurrence of *te*; the exact pragmatic effect of the so-called irrealis paradigm used as non-canonical imperative; the negation of non-canonical imperatives (e.g. can the negated near

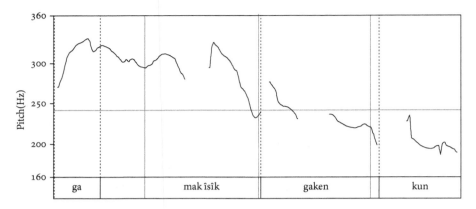

FIGURE 7. Intonational contour of the interrogative in (31)

future also express a distal prohibitive?); strategies other than imperatives to express non-canonical imperatives (e.g. can the near future be used to express non-canonical imperatives?). These questions require more data collection and are thus left for future studies.

Acknowledgements

I am indebted to the Tayatuk community for supporting my research, to Sasha and Bob for inviting me to the workshop, and for providing helpful comments to improve this chapter.

References

Aikhenvald, Alexandra Y. 2010. *Imperatives and commands.* Oxford: Oxford University Press.

England, Nora C. 2013. 'Marking aspect and mood and inferring time in Mam (Mayan)', *Proceedings of the thirty-third annual meeting of the Berkeley Linguistics Society* 33: 119–40.

Evans, Nicholas. 2007. 'Insubordination and its uses', pp. 366–431 of *Finiteness: Theoretical and empirical foundations,* edited by Irina Nikolaeva. Oxford: Oxford University Press.

Foley, William A. 1986. *The Papuan languages of New Guinea.* Cambridge: Cambridge University Press.

Himmelmann, Nikolaus P. and Ladd, D. Robert. 2008. 'Prosodic description: An introduction for fieldworkers', *Language Documentation & Conservation* 2: 244–74.

Hirst, Daniel and Di Cristo, Albert. 1998. 'A survey of intonation systems', pp. 1–44 of *Intonation systems: A survey of twenty languages,* edited by Daniel Hirst and Albert Di Cristo. Cambridge: Cambridge University Press.

Hooley, B. A. and McElhanon, Kenneth A. 1970. 'Languages of the Morobe district, New Guinea', pp. 1064–94 of *Pacific linguistics studies in honor of Arthur Capell,* edited by Don C. Laycock and Stephen A. Wurm. Pacific Linguistics C-13. Canberra: The Australian National University.

Kiparsky, Paul. 2005. 'The Vedic injunctive: Historical and synchronic implications', pp. 219–35 of *The yearbook of South Asian languages and linguistics*, edited by Rajendra Singh and Tanmoy Bhattacharya. Berlin: Mouton de Gruyter.

McElhanon, Kenneth. 1973. *Towards a typology of the Finisterre-Huon languages, New Guinea.* Pacific Linguistics B-22. Canberra: The Australian National University.

Pennington, Ryan. 2014. 'Non-spatial setting in Ma Manda', *STUF* 67: 327–64.

Quigley, Susan R. 2002. *The Awara verbal system.* Unpublished MA Thesis, Grand Forks: North Dakota.

Reed, Wes. 2000. *Yopno grammar essentials (revised to sketch level).* Ukarumpa: SIL.

Reesink, Ger P. 1987. *Structures and their functions in Usan.* Philadelphia: John Benjamins.

Roberts, John. 1997. 'Switch-Reference in Papua New Guinea: A preliminary survey', pp. 101–241 of *Papers in Papuan linguistics*, Vol. 3, edited by Andrew Pawley. Pacific Linguistics A-87. Canberra: The Australian National University.

Sarvasy, Hannah. 2015. 'The imperative split and the origin of switch-reference markers in Nungon', *Proceedings of the forty-first annual meeting of the Berkeley Linguistics Society* 41: 473–92.

Slotta, James. 2013. Coding the nonspatial setting in Yopno (Nian/Nokopo Dialect): Finite verb morphology and nonfinite verb constructions. Paper presented at the 'Non-spatial setting in Finisterre-Huon languages' special workshop of the Language and Culture Research Centre, James Cook University, Cairns, Australia, 8–9 October 2013.

11

Imperatives and commands in Nungon

HANNAH S. SARVASY

1 Introduction to Nungon

Nungon is a Papuan language spoken by about 1,000 people in the Uruwa River valley, Morobe Province, Papua New Guinea. Nungon is grouped in the tentative 'Finisterre' subgrouping within the Finisterre-Huon group of 60–80 Papuan languages (Claassen and McElhanon 1970). Finisterre-Huon languages are spoken on the slopes of the Finisterre Range and across the spine of the Huon Peninsula (McElhanon 1967, 1973).

Nungon forms the southern, higher-elevation half of a dialect continuum; the other half is referred to as Yau. (*Nungon* is the content question word 'what' in the southern dialects, and *yaö* is 'what' in the northern dialects—see McElhanon 1974 for similar use of 'what' as exemplar for dialect divisions in Kâte.) Each of the five villages where Nungon is spoken originally had its own dialect; four of these are still extant. Children still speak only Nungon as their first language.

Two SIL Bible translation teams were based in the Yau-speaking region from 1987 to 1997. Local Nungon and Yau elementary schools have taught SIL translator Urs Wegmann's practical Yau orthography for over 15 years now. This orthography is used here, except that the Nungon phonemic vowel length distinctions are here represented with double vowel symbols.

This chapter stems from my research on the Towet village dialect of Nungon since 2011. Examples are drawn from a 146,700-word corpus including 222 transcribed texts and my field notes, and from one additional transcript involving conversation between a child Nium, aged 2;10 (labelled C in these examples), and his mother (labelled M).

Commands. First edition. Alexandra Y. Aikhenvald and R. M. W. Dixon (eds)
This chapter © Hannah S. Sarvasy 2017. First published 2017 by Oxford University Press

1.1 Nungon grammatical overview

Nungon phonology is not unusual for Finisterre-Huon Papuan languages (McElhanon 1973). Only vowel phonemes are discussed here, since iconic vowel alteration may have played a role in the development of the Nungon Delayed Imperative form. There are six contrastive vowels—three back vowels, a low central vowel, and two front vowels—and phonemic vowel length. In Wegmann's practical orthography, the middle back vowel [o] is represented as <ö>, while the lower back vowel [ɔ] is represented as <o>. The middle back vowel /ö/ features lip protrusion, which gives it a lower second formant than the other two back vowels. The vowels are plotted by first and second formants in Figure 1.

Nungon is largely agglutinating, with some fusion. Constituent order is verb-final. Open classes include nouns, adjectives, and adverbs; verbs form a small class with likely fewer than 200 members, further divided into morphological subclasses (Sarvasy 2014a). Closed classes include a neutral and a contrastive/reflexive set of personal pronouns, and topographic demonstratives distinguishing three elevation levels and three distances.

Nungon has no grammatical gender. Two major number systems operate within Nungon grammar (Sarvasy 2015a). Only a closed subclass of 37 nouns may be formally marked for number, and then only when also marked as possessed by a singular possessor (Sarvasy 2017, 2015a).

Like many other Papuan languages of Papua New Guinea (Roberts 1997), Nungon features multi-predicate clause-chaining, in addition to single predicate serial-like 'tight multi-verb constructions' (Sarvasy 2014c). Clause chains are series of discrete clauses with minimally inflected verbal predicates, usually culminating in a clause with fully inflected verbal predicate (Sarvasy 2015b discusses 'non-canonical clause chains' that violate this). In the Papuan linguistic tradition, the minimally inflected non-terminal verb forms are called 'medial verbs', and the clauses in which

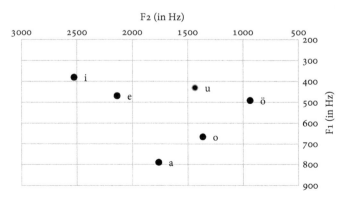

FIGURE 1. Nungon vowel formant chart

they serve as predicates 'medial clauses'; the fully inflected verb forms are 'final verbs', functioning in 'final clauses'. Clause chains are typically arranged tense-iconically (Farr 1999), with earlier events/actions/states mentioned earlier.

Nungon final verb forms inflect for subject (S/A) person and number, and tense or mood: all marked through suffixes to the verb root. A closed subclass of 15 verbs bear obligatory prefixes indicating person and number, or just number, of the verb's O argument (Sarvasy 2014a, 2017).

Nungon medial verb forms occur either unmarked or marked for subject person and number. If a medial verb lacks subject person and number marking, the subject argument of the unmarked medial verb is understood to be co-referential with that of the succeeding clause in a clause chain. If the medial verb bears subject person and number marking, this indicates a lack of precise co-reference between the subject arguments of the marked medial verb and the succeeding clause. This indexation of subject person/number only when precise inter-clausal co-reference is lacking is referred to as Different-Subject marking.

In Nungon, as in several other Finisterre languages (Sarvasy 2015c), two major formal sets of subject person/number suffixes can be identified. That is, there are two different forms that index 1sg subjects, two different forms for 2sg subjects, and so on. For Nungon, one set of suffixes applies for the five tenses, as well as the Future Irrealis and Delayed Imperative forms. The other set applies for the Immediate Imperative and Counterfactual final verb forms, and Different-Subject medial verb forms. These are shown in Table 1. Note that the formal distinction between Nungon second and third person is neutralized in dual and plural numbers (as in many Papuan languages; Foley 1986).

TABLE 1. **The formal divide between verbal S/A person/number suffixes (Sarvasy 2015c: 478)**

	follow tense or irrealis suffix			follow verb root directly	
	set 1a	set 1b: RF, IRR	set 1c: DEL IMP	set 2a: IMM IMP, CONTR	set 2b: DS
1sg	*-t*	*-t*	*-t*	*-wa/-e*	*-wa/-e*
2sg	*-rok*	*-rok*	*-rök*	*-i*	*-i*
3sg	*-k*	*-k*	*-k*	*-un*	*-un*
1du	*-mok*	*-n*	*-n*	*-ra*	*-ra*
2/3du	*-morok*	*-morok*	*-morök*	*-arun*	*-un*
1pl	*-mong*	*-n*	*-n*	*-na*	*-na*
2/3pl	*-ng*	*-ng*	*-ng*	*-arut*	*-u*

Nungon grammatical relations are marked with postpositions. Nungon has two negating elements: the negator *ma=* used with verbs and deverbal word forms, and the negative word *muuno* 'no, not' which occurs with all other word classes and may function as predicate in a verbless clause, and as negative response to a polar question.

(1) Awe,   morö   ma=t-i-ng.
     yet   large   NEG=do-NP-2/3pl
     They haven't yet grown large. [Referring to cucumbers on the vine]

(2) Maa-na   morö   muuno.
     speech-1sg-POSS   large   not
     My (recorded) speech is not long.

Positive-polarity final verbs distinguish five tenses—Remote Past (ancient times through yesterday), Near Past (yesterday through earlier today), Present (current moment, or gnomic present; also the past few hours, with present relevance), Near Future (later today, or general time), and Remote Future (tomorrow and beyond). Under negation, two tense distinctions are neutralized (per Aikhenvald and Dixon 1998): negated Near Past and Present tenses share a form, as do negated Near Future and Remote Future. Five aspects are marked, primarily through auxiliary constructions with the verbs *it-* 'exist' and *to-* 'do'.

Nungon clause types are differentiated both through intonation and formal marking (Sarvasy 2017). Commands—using both dedicated imperative forms and some imperative strategies—can involve greater pitch ranges than statements. Polar and echo questions usually feature a final pitch rise; polar questions may also be marked with the polar question marker *ha*, in which case there is no final pitch rise.

2 Imperatives overview

Nungon has two dedicated imperative forms. Immediate Imperatives (Table 2) carry urgency and expectation of immediate response, while Delayed Imperatives (Table 3) indicate compliance after some time and/or distance. Under negation, the tense distinction between Immediate and Delayed Imperatives is neutralized; there is a single Prohibitive form for all negative dedicated imperatives.

Nungon is permissive of imperative formation with verbs indicating states or uncontrollable actions; *omo-hi!* 'die!' and *dongko-hi!* 'rejoice!' are attested. Some intransitive change-of-state verbs are only attested in imperative form for non-canonical (Aikhenvald 2010: 3) imperatives. This reflects the improbability of ordering a person: 'burn (yourself)!'—the intransitive verb *di-* 'burn' does occur in 3sg imperative form, as a non-canonical imperative referring to wood: *di-hun* 'let it burn!'.

Because the 2/3 person distinction is neutralized in dual and plural numbers in verbal subject person/number suffixes, the canonical (Aikhenvald 2010: 3) second person imperatives necessarily share their form with non-canonical third person imperatives in dual and plural. This is one reason to consider canonical and non-canonical imperatives as belonging to a single paradigm. The immediate imperative is exemplified in (3).

(3) K-ep-pi!   Unga em=bon!
     sg.O-come-IMM.IMP.2sg   right now=RSTR
     Bring it! Right now!

The Delayed Imperative and Immediate Imperative both occur in the Nungon translation of the English song 'Rain, rain, go away' (taught in the elementary school), in example (4). Here and throughout the chapter, NPs comprising more than a single noun are in brackets.

(4) Bip, bip, gok   ongo-i!
     rain rain 2sg.PRO   go-IMM.IMP.2sg
     [Bongon   au]=dek   e-irök!
     day   other=LOC   come-DEL.IMP.2sg
     Rain, rain, you go (away)! Come another day!

Here, the rain's departure is directed to occur immediately using the Immediate Imperative form, while its return 'another day' is directed with the Delayed Imperative.

The Delayed Imperative forms are clearly formally related to the Remote Future tense, and the Future Irrealis form, as seen in Table 4.

TABLE 2. **The Nungon Immediate Imperative:** *hai-* 'cut'

	singular	dual	plural
1	*hai-wa*	*hai-ra*	*hai-na*
2	*hai-hi*	*hai-warun*	*hai-warut*
3	*hai-hun*		

TABLE 3. **The Nungon Delayed Imperative:** *hai-* 'cut'

	singular	dual	plural
1	*hai-wit*	*hai-rin*	*hai-nin*
2	*hai-wirök*	*hai-rimorök*	*hai-nung*
3	*hai-wik*		

TABLE 4. Nungon Delayed Imperative compared with Remote Future and Future Irrealis (Sarvasy 2015c: 485)

		singular	dual	plural
1	Del. Imp.	*haiw-i-t*	*hai-ri-n*	*hai-ni-n*
	Rem. Fut.	*haiw-i-t-ma*	*hai-ri-n-ma*	*hai-ni-n-ma*
	Fut. Irrealis	*haiw-i-t*	*hai-ri-n*	*hai-ni-n*
2	Del. Imp.	***haiw-i-rök***	***hai-ri-morök***	***hai-nu-ng***
	Rem. Fut.	*haiw-i-rok-ma*	*hai-ri-morok-ma*	*hai-ni-ng-ma*
	Fut. Irrealis	*haiw-i-rok*	*hai-ri-morok*	*hai-ni-ng*
3	Del. Imp.	*haiw-i-k*	***hai-ri-morök***	***hai-nu-ng***
	Rem. Fut.	*haiw-i-k-ma*	*hai-ri-morok-ma*	*hai-ni-ng-ma*
	Fut. Irrealis	*haiw-i-k*	*hai-ri-morok*	*hai-ni-ng*

TABLE 5. Raising and backing of vowels in final syllables in Nungon grammar

Phenomenon	Process		Description	Grammatical function
Call-At-Distance marking	/a/ in final syllable (closed or open)	→ /o/	rounding, backing, raising	Signals speaker's intention that speech carry over a long distance to addressee
Long-Duration expressive marking	/a/ in final open syllable of medial verbs	→ /o/	rounding, backing, raising	Indicates that action or state represented by medial verb continued over a long period of time
Postulated development of Delayed Imperative	/o/ in final syllable of Fut. Irrealis, most person/numbers	→ /ö/	raising, backing (by lip protrusion)	Would have indicated that action or state was intended to take place after a relatively long period of time or over distance in space
	/i/ in final syllable of Fut. Irrealis 2/3pl	→ /u/	rounding, backing	

The Delayed Imperative may have originated through iconic alteration (raising or backing) of the vowel of the final syllable of second person Future Irrealis forms. Such iconic final-syllable vowel alteration to indicate temporal duration or spatial distance is still productive elsewhere in Nungon grammar, as shown in Table 5.

The vowel alteration process resulting in distinct Delayed Imperative forms would have occurred first for the second person; as seen in Table 4, all first person forms used in Delayed Imperative contexts are identical to Future Irrealis forms. Because of the syncretism between second and third persons in dual and plural numbers, the altered vowels also apply to third person dual and plural forms. An example of a third

person plural Delayed Imperative is in (5). Here, a man instructs his nephew to bind
bundles of branches to be raised into a hunting platform in the forest canopy.

(5)   Hener-i-ya,   öö-ng   öö-ng   to-nung!
       tie.up-DS.2SG-MV   ascend-DEP   ascend-DEP   do-DEL.IMP.2/3pl
       You having tied (the bundles), let them be going up!

Here, the Delayed Imperative is used because the bundles are not yet ready to ascend
at the time of the speech act; the ascending is ordered to take place after the bundles
are prepared.

2.1 Imperative scope in clause chains

Medial verbs cannot be marked for imperative mood. An Immediate or Delayed
Imperative form may only occur at the end of a clause chain; all preceding medial
clauses are unmarked for imperative mood. Clause chains of which the final verbs are
dedicated imperatives may be understood to describe a series of related actions,
states, or events, all of which the speaker desires to come about.

A short such chain ending in an Immediate Imperative is in (6), a directive to the
child Nium from his mother.

(6)   M: Ngo-go   indongo-ng-a   ir-a,   hat   yo-i!
             this-ADEM   stand-DEP-MV   exist-MV   story   say-IMM.IMP.2sg
             Standing up like this, tell the story!

A longer chain ending in a Delayed Imperative is in (7). This is a quoted directive
from a grandfather to his two grandchildren.

(7)   Hon,   unga,   [haa   maa-no   Kungin Arang],
       2nsg.PRO   today   area   name-3sg.POSS   Kungin Arang
       Kungin Arang   öö-ng-a,   [naak   garet]   imor-a,
       Kungin Arang   ascend-DEP-MV   yam   stake   drive.in.ground-MV
       garet=dek   towi-ng-a,   hi-ng-a,   ep-di-morök!
       stake=LOC   arrange-DEP-MV   put-DEP-MV   come-IRR.du-DEL.IMP.2/3du
       You, today, the place called Kungin Arang; going up to Kungin Arang, planting
       yam stakes, arranging (the yam tendrils) on the stakes, setting them, come
       (home)!

The clause chains in examples (6) and (7) include no switch-reference marking, and
the imperatives in both are directed at second persons. The series of desired actions or
events described by the clause chain may, however, include actions by one or more
addressees that come tense-iconically early in the series. In this case, the addressee's
action is indicated by a medial verb unmarked for imperative mood; the clause chain's
dedicated imperative form may be first or third person. This can be seen in (8).

(8) Bip   n-et-ta-k.   Eep   hi-wi-ya,   oro-wa!
    rain   1sg.o-beat-PRES.sg-3sg   wood   put-DS.2sg-MV   bask-IMM.IMP.1sg
    Rain has hurt me. Put wood (on the fire), so I can bask (by the fire)!
    (lit. You putting wood, let me bask!)

Whether or not an action by the addressee is encoded with a dedicated imperative form depends on its place in the clause chain's sequence of actions. In (9), for instance, the 2sg and 1sg referents of (8) occur in the opposite order.

(9) Ga-ma-ya,   boo-hi!
    2sg.o-give.DS.1sg-MV   sew-IMM.IMP.2sg
    Let me give it to you so you can sew it! (lit. I giving (it) to you, sew (it)!)

A clause chain culminating in a dedicated imperative may include several switches in reference, from an addressee to the speaker or a third party and back again. The clause chain in (10) ends in a 2sg Immediate Imperative, but one of the medial verbs is also marked for 2sg.

(10) Um   woro-i-ya,   [biyum   opmou]
     bamboo.species   pull-DS.2sg-MV   tobacco   small

     na-ng-o   mot-dain-a,   ongo-i!
     eat-DEP-MVII   PERF-1du-MV   go-IMM.IMP.2sg
     Start a fire so we can consume a little tobacco, then go! (lit. You pulling *um* bamboo, we two smoking a little tobacco, go!)

As with isolated imperative clauses, the final imperative form in clause chains may inflect for any person/number combination. Example (11) ends in a 3sg Immediate Imperative.

(11) Mag-a=ha   mab-i-ya,   ep-pun.
     mother-2sg.POSS=BEN   call.to-DS.2sg-MV come-IMM.IMP.3sg
     Call your mother and let her come. (You calling for your mother, let her come!)

Here, the addressee's calling her mother and the mother's coming are related actions that are both desired by the speaker.

2.2 Imperatives and aspect

Nungon imperative forms only co-occur with two marked aspects: Continuous and Continuous Habitual (both marked through auxiliary constructions using the verb *it-* 'exist'; Sarvasy 2017). Three other marked aspects do not co-occur with imperative forms: Habitual, Inferred Imperfective (which combines non-firsthand evidential overtones with imperfective aspect), and Imminent.

Example (12) shows the Immediate Imperative with Continuous aspect:

(12) Nöng nöng   to-ng-a   it-ti!
     still   do-DEP-MV   exist-IMM.IMP.2sg
     Be being still!

Example (13) shows the Delayed Imperative with Continuous aspect:

(13) To-ng   ni-nde-ng-a   i-irök   y-u-ya,
      do-DEP   1nsg.O-show-DEP-MV   exist-DEL.IMP.2sg   say-DS.2/3pl-MV

      muuno,   ye-no-go-t.
      no   3nsg.O-tell-RP-1sg
      They having said, '(Stay here and) be teaching us!' I told them, 'No'.

2.3 Special imperative forms

Only two verbs have special forms of the Immediate Imperative, and these are both restricted to 2sg addressees. The verb *imo-* 'give', one of a closed class of verbs with obligatory object person/number prefixes, has a reduced special form for 'give (it to) me!' (Figure 2).

The verb *aa-* 'see, look at' also belongs to the closed class of verbs that bear O prefixes. When inflected for 2sg Immediate Imperative, reduced forms of the demonstratives *ngo* 'this, here' and *wo* 'that, there' may be prefixed to the null 3sg O prefix, as in (14).

(14) Ng-aa-hi!   W-aa-hi!
      this-3sg.O.see-IMM.IMP.2sg   that-3sg.O.see-IMM.IMP.2sg
      Look at this! Look at that!

The two forms in (14) exist alongside the full range of other O person/number combinations; Table 6 gives these forms.

Such demonstrative prefixation to *aa-* 'see' also occurs with 2sg subjects in Present tense questions that essentially function as directives. That is, the question *ng-aa-ha-rok* 'this-3sg.O.see-PRES.SG-2sg' 'Do you see this?' is generally used to direct the addressee's attention 'here' in the same way as the Immediate Imperative forms do.

standard form: 1sg O, 2sg A	reduced form: 1sg O, 2sg A
na-mo-hi!	*na-m!*
1sg.O-give-IMM.IMP.2sg	

FIGURE 2. Standard and reduced forms of 'give me!'

TABLE 6. 2sg Immediate Imperative *aa-* 'look at' with all O person/number combinations

	singular	non-singular
1	*n-aa-hi!*	*n-ii-hi!*
2	*g-aa-hi!*	*k-aa-hi!*
3	*aa-hi!*	*y-aa-hi!*

Demonstrative prefixation to *aa-* 'see' is unattested with other tenses or subject persons in questions, and also not found with 2du or 2pl Immediate Imperatives, or with the 2sg Delayed Imperative. Likewise, in statements, a form as in (15) is completely unattested.

(15) *W-aa-ha-k.
      that-see-PRES.sg-3sg
      He sees that.

The child Nium is able to use demonstrative prefixation with *aa-* 'see', and alternate between the full form *na-mo-hi* and reduced form *na-m*, as shown in (16). Here, he uses both for the benefit of his mother, who seems not to hear the reduced form clearly.

(16) C: K-oo-ng   na-m.
            sg.O-descend-DEP   1sg.O-give.IMM.IMP.2sg
            Take it down and give it to me.

      M: aa?
            Ah?

      C: K-oo-ng   na-mo-hi.
            sg.O-descend-DEP   1sg.O-give-IMM.IMP.2sg
            Take it down and give it to me.

2.4 Prohibitive

The Nungon Prohibitive follows a cross-linguistically attested pattern of the evolution of positive-polarity verbal forms into prohibitions (Aikhenvald 2010: 190). Negative commands are not formed with the verbal negator *ma=*; rather, the positive-polarity Future Irrealis form receives a final suffix *-a* for the Prohibitive. This *-a* may share an origin with the Attention suffix *-a*. Since the Future Irrealis form indicates possibility, this may be related to the grammaticalization pathway described by Pakendorf and Schalley (2007).

2.4.1 Source of the Prohibitive: the Attention suffix -a

The Attention suffix *-a* occurs as the final element on words of many different classes, always utterance-finally. It is attested with verbs inflected for all five tenses, and with members of other word classes. This suffix summons the addressee's special attention to positive, neutral, or negative events: 'be aware that X'. It contributes special vehemence, urgency, or import. An example of the Attention suffix with the Remote Past tense is in (17).

(17) Ma=möng-go-r-a!
      NEG=fall-RP-1sg-ATT
      I didn't fall!

In a text recorded in the Kotet village dialect of Nungon, one man is quoted as raising an alarm in the men's house on seeing two strangers approaching along a streambed:

(18) [Amna   yoi] [Titi akka]=gon   e-wa-moroc-a!
      man   two   Titi   bank=RSTR   come-PRES.nsg-2/3du-ATT
      Two men are coming just along the bank of the Titi!

2.4.2 The Nungon Prohibitive form: Future Irrealis with -a

The Nungon Prohibitive form comprises the positive-polarity Future Irrealis inflection plus final suffix -*a*. The Prohibitive suffix -*a* is in complementary distribution with the Attention suffix -*a*. That is, the positive-polarity Future Irrealis cannot be marked for Attention; if the positive Future Irrealis form bears a suffix -*a*, this can only be interpreted as Prohibitive. The Prohibitive -*a* never co-occurs with the Attention -*a*. Everywhere else the Attention -*a* occurs, Prohibitive interpretation is impossible. The Attention suffix may thus be the origin of the Prohibitive. A simple Prohibitive from Nium's mother to Nium is in (19).

(19) M: Usi-wi-rog-a,   oro!
          pull.out-IRR.sg-2sg-PROHIB   well
          Don't pull it out, now!

If the Future Irrealis is negated, the Prohibitive interpretation is no longer possible, and only an Attention interpretation is possible. Example (20) calls the addressee's attention to the fact that a man's family members are not trustworthy guardians of a gift left for him.

(20) Ma=i-mo-ni-ng-a!
      NEG=3sg.O-give-IRR.pl-2/3pl-ATT
      Be aware that they won't give it to him!

The Prohibitive 'let them not give it to him!' would take nearly the same form, but lack the negative proclitic.

2.5 Responses to commands

There is no standard response to a command. *Muuno* 'no' as a refusal in response to a command is attested in reported dialogues in narratives (see (13) and (22)), but rarely observed in conversation. It is likely that the direct refusal *muuno* is a face-threatening response. The positive response to a polar question, *öö* 'yes', is not a standard positive response to a command; in (33), this response shows that an imperative form actually serves in a question.

In the following narrative excerpt, a boy responds to his sister's directives with both the refusal *muuno* 'no' and a head-shake gesture. After his grandfather chastises him, the boy runs away from home. His sister follows him and pleads with him to return (imperative forms are in bold):

(21) Naat!   Nungon=ta   poto-ng-a   ep-pa-rok?
      different.sex.sibling what=BEN   desist-DEP-MV   come-PRES.sg-2sg
      'Brother! Why did you, abandoning (us), come?'

      E-i-ya,   **ongo-ra,**   i-no-go-k.
      come-DS.2sg-MV   go-IMM.IMP.1du   3sg.O-tell-RP-3sg
      'Come, let's go,' she told him.

      [Ura   nori]   **ep-pi**   ya-a-k.
      grandfather   1du.POSS   come-IMM.IMP.2sg   say-PRES-3sg
      'Our grandfather says: "Come!"'

      Ongo-ra,   bög-in.
      go-IMM.IMP.1du   house-LOC
      'Let's go, homeward.'

The brother is said to respond verbally and non-verbally, in (22).

(22) Y-un-a,   [naat-no   amna=ma]
      say-DS.3sg-MV   different.sex.sibling-3sg.POSS   man=SPEC
      kaag-o   aan   ngo-go   to-go-k.
      head-3sg.POSS   shake   this-ADEM   do-RP-3sg
      She having spoken, her sibling, the male one, shook his head like this.

      To-ng-a   m-un-a,   muuno,   yo-go-k.   Ma=ng-i-t.
      do-DEP-MV   PERF-3sg-MV   no   say-RP-3sg   NEG=go-IRR.sg-1sg
      Having done so, 'No,' he said, 'I won't go.'

2.6 Politeness and the dedicated imperative forms

The Delayed Imperative is politer than the Immediate Imperative. Certain expressions, such as leave-taking formulae, involve Delayed Imperative forms, especially for 2sg. When taking temporary leave of 2du and 2pl addressees, either Immediate Imperative or Delayed Imperative forms are acceptable (Sarvasy 2014c). But if a leave-taker is leaving the area for some time, only the Delayed Imperative forms are acceptable for all addressee numbers.

Another expression that typically uses the Delayed Imperative, either for politeness or because of an inherent delay, is that used for 'hear me out!' or 'understand (the following)!'. This is a complex predicate involving what may be an archaic word for 'ear', *orom*, plus the verb *hi-* 'put'. A younger man asked an elder to explain about traditional practices, ending with the directive in (23).

(23) Hat   y-i-ya,   orom   hi-na!
     story   say-DS.2sg-MV   ear   put-IMM.IMP.1pl
     Tell the story so that we can hear/understand/know it! (lit. You telling the story, let us hear/understand/know!)

The 1pl Immediate Imperative has clearly exclusive reference here. That is, the addressee already knows about the traditional practices, so he is excluded from the referents of 1pl. The older man responded:

(24) Orom   hi-wirök,   wo-ma-i.
     ear   put-DEL.IMP.2sg   that-SPEC-TOP
     Hear/understand/know (the following).

The Delayed Imperative form is used in such contexts either for politeness or because the understanding can only be gained after some delay—once the storytelling is complete.

In conversing with Nium, his mother sometimes follows one or more repetitions of the same verb in Immediate Imperative 2sg form with the 2sg Delayed Imperative form, despite the immediacy of the desired action. This seems to add extra encouragement, or endearment, and was sometimes accompanied by a smile. In (25), Nium's mother encourages Nium to pretend to cut something. Dedicated imperative forms are in bold.

(25) M: Ono=dek   **ongo-ra!**
          uphill.LDEM=LOC   go-IMM.IMP.1du
          Let's go up there!

     M: Indongo-ng-a,   eep   **maa-hi,**   urop.
          stand.up-DEP-MV   wood   cut-IMM.IMP.2sg   enough
          Stand up, cut wood, already.

     C: [Nandu=ma   au]   eep   **maa-wa.**
          something=SPEC   other   wood   cut-IMM.IMP.1sg
          Let me cut some wood or other.

     M: Karup! Yii   **ma-irök**   mama-na,   wo-rok.
          quick   vine cut-DEL.IMP.2sg   mama-1sg.POSS   that-SEMBL
          Quick! Cut the vine, my *mama*, that's it.

In (26), the child and his mother are playing with a homemade soccer ball.

(26) C: **Waga-wa.**
          pummel-IMM.IMP.1sg
          Let me kick (it).

      C: Nai-n,   k-e-i-ya.
          where-LOC   sg.O-come-DS.1sg-MV
          Where, bring it. (lit. you having brought it)

      M: **Waga-hi,**   oro.
          pummel-IMM.IMP.2sg   well
          Kick (it), all right.

      M: **Waga-hi.**
          pummel-IMM.IMP.2sg
          Kick (it).

      M: **Waga-irök.**
          pummel-DEL.IMP.2sg
          Do kick (it).

Conversely, the Immediate Imperative may be used with peremptory or abrasive overtones in a temporal context for which otherwise the Delayed Imperative would be more appropriate. Example (27) comes from a staged dialogue in which a mother rebukes her surly teenage son.

(27) Ongo-ng-a,   [[ketket   nug-a-i]   ittongo-ni-ng-ma],
      go-DEP-MV   boy   mate-2sg.POSS-pl   go.around-IRR.pl-2/3pl-REL

      y-a-i-ya,   ho-ng   ga-m-u-ya,
      3nsg.O-see-DS.2sg-MV   cook-DEP   2sg.O-give-DS.2/3pl-MV

      na-hi!
      eat-IMM.IMP.2sg
      Go on, find your friends who've gone around (aimlessly) so they cook for you, and eat! (lit. Going on, seeing your friends who will go around (aimlessly) so they cook for you, eat!)

Since the friends have not yet been located, it would seem to make sense for this to be framed as a Delayed Imperative. The mother's annoyance, however, seems to be better expressed through an Immediate Imperative.

2.7 Dedicated imperatives grammatical summary

The Immediate Imperative has the same person/number distinctions as declarative final verbs, while the Delayed Imperative has distinct forms only for 2sg, 2/3du, and 2/3pl. The two tense distinctions in imperative clauses with dedicated imperative forms are

TABLE 7. **Imperative forms compared with other final verb forms**

	Indicative final verbs	Imperatives
positive-polarity tenses	Five: Remote Past, Near Past, Present, Near Future, Remote Future	Two: Immediate, Delayed
tenses under negation	Three: Remote Past, Near Past/Present, Future	One: No distinction
marked aspects	Five: Habitual, Continuous, Continuous Habitual, Desiderative, Inferred Imperfective	Two: Continuous, Continuous Habitual
prefixation of demonstratives	no	With Imm. Imp. *aa-* 'look at'

TABLE 8. **Imperative clauses compared with other clause types**

	Declarative clauses	Imperative clauses	Interrogative clauses
Intonation	final fall	final fall, with greater pitch range in canonical imperatives	final fall: *ha*-marked polar and content questions; final rise: unmarked polar and echo questions
Standard response	none	physical compliance	polar, echo Qs: interjections; content Qs: contentful reply
Politeness distinctions	none	yes	if present, highly subtle
With Dubitative marking	epistemic doubt	softens command into suggestion	N/A

different from the five possible in declaratives—although, as with declaratives, there is neutralization of the formal tense distinction in imperatives under negation. Table 7 compares dedicated imperative forms with other final verb forms, while Table 8 compares clauses with dedicated imperative forms as predicates with other clause types.

3 Imperative forms in other clause types

Nungon imperative forms—both canonical and non-canonical—occur in questions and in statements, as well as in commands (Sarvasy 2017).

3.1 1sg Immediate Imperatives to ask permission, and in texts

It is common for 1sg Immediate Imperatives to be used to seek permission from an addressee. In this case, they are expressed with polar/echo question intonation. Figure 3 shows the intonational difference between the 1sg Immediate Imperative as a self-command and as a request for permission.

(28) Nogo   [ketket   torop]   yo-wa.
     1SG.PRO+FOC   boy   group   say-IMM.IMP.1sg
     Let me sing (the song) 'Youth Group'.

     Aap   yo-wa?
     song   say-IMM.IMP.1sg
     Shall I sing the song?

     Yo-wa,   urop!
     say-IMM.IMP.1sg   enough
     Let me sing it, already!

Similarly, Figure 4 shows a 1sg Immediate Imperative form used to ask permission.

(29) Honggir-e?
     grab-IMM.IMP.1sg
     Shall I grab it?

The 1sg imperative form of *yo-* 'say' also occurs in texts in self-corrections: 'let me say X', or 'let me first address Y'. This occurs in a monologue without feedback from listeners. In such instances, the form *yo-wa* tends to have similar pitch range to a statement, rather than a command, as seen in Figure 5.

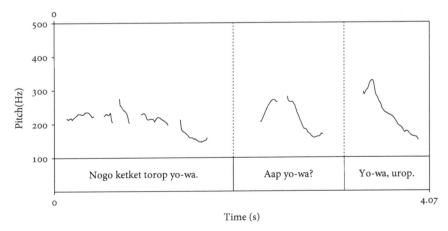

FIGURE 3. 1sg Immediate Imperative in question and self-command (Sarvasy 2017)

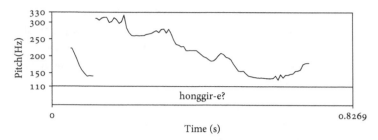

FIGURE 4. 1sg Immediate Imperative in question (Sarvasy 2017)

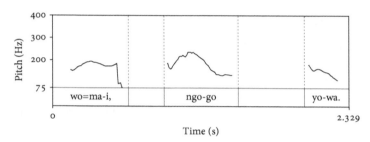

FIGURE 5. 1sg Immediate Imperative in text

(30) Wo-ma-i,   ngo-go   yo-wa.
      that-SPEC-TOP   this-ADEM   say-IMM.IMP.1sg
      That is, let me say it like this.

3.2 Imperatives in alternative questions

Two imperative forms may be conjoined as alternatives in alternative questions, as in (31).

(31) M: Ongo-ra   ha   wo   it-tun?
          go-IMM.IMP.1du   ALT   that   exist-IMM.IMP.3sg
          Shall we two go, or let it be?

In example (32), the second alternative may be interpreted as involving ellipsis of the imperative form.

(32) M: Opmou   mee=ho   wet   ho-ng   na-ra
          small   back=FOC   3sg.O.kill   cook-DEP   eat-IMM.IMP.1du

          ha   unga   em=bon?
          ALT   right.now=RSTR
          Shall we kill, cook, and eat it in a little while, or right now?

3.3 Imperatives in polar questions

A polar question in Nungon may be answered with the interjection *öö* 'yes', the negative word *muuno* 'no', or a statement confirming or denying the content of the question.

Dedicated imperative forms can occur in polar questions, measured both by intonation and by the response of the addressee. In (33), Nium interprets the 2sg imperative forms used by his mother as polar questions, judging by his responses.

(33) M: H-oo-ng   ga-ma-ya   y-aa-ng-a
         nsg.o-descend-DEP 2sg.o-give.DS.1sg-MV 3nsg.o-see-DEP-MV

         it-ti   hu?
         exist-IMM.IMP.2sg   DUB
         Shall you be looking at them, I having taken them down and given them
         to you? (lit. I having taken them down and given them to you, be looking
         at them, perhaps?)

     C: Öö
         Yes.

     M: Wo-ndo   hat   yo-ng-a   i-irök?
         there-LDEM story say-DEP-MV   exist-DEL.IMP.2sg
         Shall you be telling the story there?

     C: Öö
         Yes.

Note that the 2sg Immediate Imperative form occurs in combination with the Dubitative marker *hu*—another way to soften imperatives into questions.

3.4 The Conative form using imperatives

Imperatives occur in speech reports either as direct speech reports (as in (21)), or as part of the Conative construction (Sarvasy 2017), which facilitates expression of intentions as reported speech, a phenomenon that is common throughout the island of New Guinea and beyond (see Aikhenvald 2008: 391–2 for references).

The Conative construction involves a clause ending in a first person imperative form (Immediate or Delayed), followed by the medial form of *yo-* 'say', then the verb *to-* 'do'. In (34), a hunting dog and her puppies are described as desiring to bite a New Guinea eagle that had tried to prey on the puppies.

(34) Tung   wo   yi-i-na   yo-ng-a
     New.Guinea.eagle   that 3.o-bite-IMM.IMP.1pl say-DEP-MV

     to-ng=it-du-ng.
     do-DEP=exist-RP-2/3pl
     They kept trying to bite the New Guinea eagle. (lit. Saying, 'Let's bite the New
     Guinea eagle', they kept doing.)

3.5 Imperatives with discourse functions

As is common cross-linguistically (Aikhenvald 2010: 246–7), the Nungon command 'look here!' may function both literally and as a discourse marker, with cataphoric reference.

Literal use of *ng-aa-hi!* 'look at this!' may be seen in example (35), in which Nium's mother tries to direct Nium's gaze to an image in a book. The mother simultaneously points to the image and addresses the child with words.

(35) M: O   ngo   ngo   mama-na,   ng-aa-hi!
           as.for   this   this   mother-1sg.POSS   this-3sg.O.see-IMM.IMP.2sg
           What about this here, my *mama*, look at this!

Discourse-marking use is shown in example (36). Here, a Nungon speaker familiar with my speech idiosyncrasies begins to explain my question to another woman who had not understood. Here, *ng-aa-hi!* directs the addressee's attention to the speaker's subsequent utterances.

(36) Ngo-go=ha   ya-a-k,   ng-aa-hi . . .
      this-ADEM=BEN   say-PRES-3sg   this-3sg.O.see-IMM.IMP.2sg
      She's talking about this, look here . . .

4 Imperative strategies

Nungon has myriad imperative strategies (summarized in Table 9), of which the most frequent in the texts corpus is the use of medial verbs to command. 'Verbless directives' (Aikhenvald 2010: 280–1) also occur; see §4.1.

A. Dependent verbs are non-final verbs that lack the medial verb suffix *-a*. These cannot normally serve as predicate on their own, but occasionally function as strong, urgent, impersonal commands, as in (37).

(37) Ma=i-mo-ng!
      NEG=3sg.O-give-DEP
      Don't give (it) to him/her! (lit. Not giving to him/her!)

B. Like (A), **medial verbs that are not inflected for Different-Subject** have impersonal and stern connotations. (38) was a stern command from a mother to her 6-year-old son:

(38) Ma=to-ng-a!
      NEG=do-DEP-MV
      Don't do that! [lit. Not doing!]

C. Medial verbs that are marked for Different-Subject, on the other hand, have gentler overtones than (A) and (B). A mother instructed her children, who had accompanied her to a farm plot, to stay in one place while she worked. This lacked annoyance or peremptoriness.

(39) Hon   wo-ndo   i-i-ya.
     2nsg.PRO   there-LDEM   exist-DS.2/3pl-MV
     You stay there. (lit. you staying there.)

A medial verb serving as imperative strategy can be linked with a dedicated imperative form in an alternative question, just as two dedicated imperative forms can be linked (example (31)). One instance is in (40); Nium's mother asks a question with an imperative strategy and dedicated imperative as alternands.

(40) M: H-oo-ng   ga-ma-ya   ha
         nsg.O-descend-DEP   2sg.O-give.DS.1SG-MV   ALT

         wo   it-tun?
         that   exist-IMM.IMP.3sg
         Shall I take them down and give them to you, or let it be?

     M: Gogo   y-i-ya.
         2sg.PRO:FOC   say-DS.2sg-MV
         You decide. ['You saying (it).']

     C: H-oo-ng   na-mo-hi!
         nsg.O-descend-DEP   1sg.O-give-IMM.IMP.2sg
         Take them down and give them to me!

Here, Nium appropriately rephrases his mother's medial verb *ga-ma-ya* as an Immediate Imperative, showing understanding of the relationship between the strategy and the dedicated imperative.

D. A special **Iterative construction** (Sarvasy 2017) employs a repeated Dependent verb inflected to index its subject, followed by the Focus postposition. This generally indicates repeated or durative action. Especially with the verb *ongo* 'go', it may serve as an imperative strategy meaning: 'you go ahead and do X before me or others':

(41) Ong-i   ong-i=ho!
     go-DS.2sg   go-DS.2sg=FOC
     Go on ahead! (lit. you going ahead . . .)

E. Either of the two Nungon **future tenses** may be used as a stern command, as in (42), which a father reported he might say to his 4-year-old daughter as an order to eat:

(42) Na-wang-ka-rok.
     eat-PROB.sg-NF-2sg
     You will eat.

F. The force of social pressure may be applied to correct misbehaviour. I call this strategy the **Reasonable People** strategy (Sarvasy 2017). Acceptable behaviour is prescribed, framed in the Present Habitual with 2/3pl subject.

In well-known languages, addressing a command to a single addressee using the second person plural form or third person singular form makes the command more polite (Aikhenvald 2010: 219–21). In Nungon, these are combined in a single imperative strategy—not especially polite, however—that redresses aberrant behaviour by invoking social mores or established practices. 'They (reasonable people) do X', or 'they don't do X' reminds the addressee(s) of social expectations, implicitly directing them to comply.

In (43), Nium's mother asks him a question about a picture, but he is uncooperative. She uses the Reasonable People strategy to get Nium to provide the correct answer, and he understands this as a directive, complying.

(43) M: O   ngo   nungon-no,   ngo ...?
         as.for this   what-3sg.POSS   this
         And this is its what, this?

     C: Nandu=ma   au.
         something=SPEC   other
         Something else.

     M: Kaag-o   yo-ng=ir-a-ng!
         head-3sg.POSS   say-DEP=exist-PRES.nsg-2/3pl
         They say 'its head'!

     C: Kaag-o.
         head-3sg.POSS
         Its head.

G. Negated deverbal nominalization has impersonal overtones, like uninflected Dependent (A) and Medial verbs (B). It may have more general, less situation-bound, semantics: 'X is not done!'. Positive-polarity deverbal nominalizations as imperative strategies have not been observed.

(44) Wo-go   ma=to-k   to-k.
     that-ADEM   NEG=do-NOMZ   do-NOMZ
     That's not to be done.

H. Forbidding could be considered a 'delayed imperative strategy', since the aim is to proscribe behaviour at some point in the future. This is accomplished by Nungon speakers through the negative word *muuno* 'no, not' framed as reported speech of the person to whom the forbidding is attributed. Example (45) is from a dictated letter from a mother to her son at boarding school; here the dedicated Prohibitive is followed by the forbidding strategy.

TABLE 9. Imperative strategies summary (adapted from Sarvasy 2017: 463)

strategy	polarity	pragmatics	canonical/ non-canonical
A Dependent verb	both	impersonal, brusque	generally canonical
B Medial verb: uninflected	both	impersonal, brusque	generally canonical
C Medial verb: inflected	both	personal, gentle	both
D Iterative construction	positive	gentle	both
E future tense	both	stern	potentially both
F 'reasonable people' construction	both	pressure to conform to social mores	both
G deverbal nominalization	negative	impersonal dissuasion	both
H *muuno* 'no' in speech report	negative	forbidding	both

(45) Lae   ong-i-rog-a!   Non   muuno   ya-a-mok.
     Lae   go-IRR.sg-2sg-PROHIB   1nsg.PRO   no   say-PRES-1du
     Don't go to Lae! We forbid it. (lit. we say 'no.')

4.1 Verbless directives

Aikhenvald (2010: 280–1) discusses 'verbless directives': standardized commands that lack any verb. Nungon has at least three types of conventionalized verbless directives, largely observed among familiars. Some verbless directives may be understood to involve an ellipsed dedicated imperative. These include: *ööp!* 'quiet!' (*ööp it-ti!* 'be quiet!' is also used); Tok Pisin *wan!* 'fast!' and its Nungon counterpart *karup!* 'quick!' (with non-ellipsed counterpart *karup ep-pi!* 'come quickly!'); and *uwin!* 'far!' (*uwin ongo-i!* 'go far away!' also occurs). Other verbless directives, generally reactions to or comments on an in-progress action by the addressee, do not involve ellipsis of an imperative verb. These include: *urop!* 'enough!', implying 'stop!'; *uung-o!* 'taboo!', implying 'desist (from some taboo act)!'; and *moin-no!* 'bad!', implying 'put (some dirty item) down!'.

A third conventionalized nonverbal directive type utilizes the Benefactive form of the 1sg pronoun, *noga* '1sg.PRO:BEN', literally 'for me', often with final rising intonation and accompanied by an outstretched and upturned hand gesture. This is used to request food or some other item, usually at a time when the addressee is either eating or doling out such items. It has a familiar tone, and has been observed used by children or among adult close kin. Schieffelin (1985: 536) and Feld (1982: 79) describe similar begging use of *nelɔ* 'to/for me' in Kaluli.

In example (46), a mother recalled her adult son accosting her on a path. Since she was coming from the high forest, he assumed she was carrying pandanus nuts, which he requested using *noga*.

(46) Gemin   aa-wa-ya,   Edwut   Mak   noga
      Gemin   3sg.O.see-DS.1sg-MV   Edwut   mother   1sg.PRO:BEN
      soe   yo-go-k.
      pandanus   say-RP-3sg
      I having seen him at Gemin, Edwut said: 'Mother, pandanus nuts for me'.

The verb *imo-* 'give' includes prefixed indexation of the Recipient argument's person/number. The directive *na-mo-hi!* '1sg.O-give-IMM.IMP.2sg', 'give (it) to me!' (§2.3) may be used to request that the addressee give something to the speaker temporarily, or with the understanding that the item given is not a permanent gift. But when this verb co-occurs with a Recipient pronoun marked for Benefactive like *noga*, this usually indicates definitive transfer of ownership—'give it to me, for me to have/consume'. The verbless directive *noga* may thus be considered as shorthand for *noga na-mo-hi* '1sg.PRO:BEN 1sg.O-give-IMM.IMP.2sg'. Conceivably first person non-singular, second person, or third person Benefactive pronouns could also function as verbless directives, but these are not as conventionalized as the 1sg *noga*.

5 Origin of imperative forms

Sarvasy (2015c) examines the formal split between the Immediate and Delayed Imperative paradigms. As seen in Table 1, these paradigms are formally quite different. The formal alignment of the Immediate Imperative form with the Counterfactual and Different-Subject markers on medial verbs also holds for other Finisterre languages (Sarvasy 2014b, 2015c).

In §2, I suggested that the Nungon Delayed Imperative developed relatively late from a final-syllable vowel alteration to the Future Irrealis form, beginning with the second person and spreading through formal syncretism to the dual and plural third person.

A major difference between the two sets of subject suffixes in Table 1 is that Set 1 occur after a tense or irrealis suffix, while Set 2 follow the verb root directly. In Sarvasy (2015c), I propose that the Immediate Imperative, Counterfactual, and Different-Subject forms originated in a single, tense-less form which utilized the original Set 2 suffixes. This original form would have been similar to the reconstructed Indo-European Injunctive (Kiparsky 1968, 2005) in functioning in several unrelated contexts in which tense was unspecified: medial verbs in clause chains, counterfactual statements, and imperatives.

TABLE 10. **Nungon Immediate Imperative and Counterfactual forms of *to-* 'do'**

	singular		dual		plural	
	Imm.Imp	Contr.	Imm.Imp	Contr.	Imm.Imp	Contr.
1	*to-wa*	*to-em, to-wam*	*to-ra*	*to-ram*	*to-na*	*to-nam*
2	*to-i*	*to-im*	*ta-arun*	*ta-arun*	*ta-arut*	*ta-arut*
3	*to-un*	*to-un*				

The Nungon Counterfactual forms are closely related to the Immediate Imperative, as seen in Table 10. In fact, consonant-final Immediate Imperative forms are identical to Counterfactual forms, while vowel-final Immediate Imperative forms generally receive a final *-m* as the Counterfactual (the two 1sg Counterfactual forms are dialectal variants). Because the 3sg, 2/3du, and 2/3pl Counterfactual forms are formally identical to the 3sg, 2/3du, and 2/3pl Immediate Imperatives, context determines interpretation. In (47), for instance, the Counterfactual *g-er-arut* '2sg.O-kill-CONTR.2/3pl', 'they would have killed you', could serve as 3pl Immediate Imperative in another context: 'Let them kill you!'.

(47) Osuk=gon   hut=ta-i   gok   ngo-go   e-i-ya,
      first=RSTR   true=BEN-TOP   2sg.PRO   this-ADEM   come-DS.2sg-MV

      g-er-arut,   o   e-i-ya,   g-et-nam.
      2sg.O-kill-CONTR.2/3pl   ALT   come-DS.2sg-MV   2sg.O-kill-CONTR.1PL

      If you had actually come like this long ago, they would have killed you, or
      (if) you came, we would have killed you.

The *-m* added to vowel-final Immediate Imperative forms to yield the Counterfactual may have originally been related to the polyfunctional subordinator, relativizer, and specifier *=ma* (Sarvasy 2013). In any case, the formal similarity between the Nungon Immediate Imperative and Counterfactual is reminiscent of Russian use of the imperative form in conditionals (Aikhenvald 2010: 237 and sources there).

6 Acquisition of imperatives

In one 35-minute conversation between Nium, aged 2;10, and his mother, both Nium and his mother use dedicated imperative forms and imperative strategies. As seen in examples (6), (19), (25), (26), (31), (32), (33), (35), (40), and (43), Nium's mother uses Immediate Imperative, Delayed Imperative, and Prohibitive forms, as well as various imperative strategies (including unmarked and Different-Subject medial verbs functioning as commands, and the Reasonable People strategy). In the same session, as seen in (16), (25), (26), and (40), Nium uses the dedicated Immediate Imperative with 1sg, 1du, or 2sg subjects. He also correctly employs two imperative strategies—unmarked Dependent verbs and Different-Subject medial verbs. In this session, Nium does not use the Delayed Imperative or the Prohibitive. Further examination of Nungon children's speech will show whether the Delayed Imperative is indeed acquired later than the Immediate Imperative, as claimed for Kaluli (Schieffelin 1985: 543).

7 Dog commands

Nungon speakers have a long tradition of raising hunting dogs, and use special commands for dogs. A list is in Sarvasy (2017). These commands largely relate to hunting and tracking. Some commands are game-specific, using location or animal names in another Nungon dialect to instruct the dog how to search without alerting the game animal by calling its name.

Today key dog command terms are no longer transparently related to human speech. One command, *wuru!*, directs the dog to bark once from where it has game at bay, alerting the hunter to its location. Another series of commands employs a word *ori!* as the directive 'search!', usually followed by a location or type of game to search for. This *ori!* usually precedes location or game animal terms, as in (48), which is the standard command to search for an echidna.

(48) Ori   hor-o-n!   Ori!
      search.CANINE.IMP   root-3sg.POSS-LOC   search.CANINE.IMP
      Search on the ground! Search!

The constituent order of (48) and similar commands show that *ori!* may not have originated as a verb, since Nungon constituent order is generally verb-final. Related language Nukna has a same-elevation, far-distance topographic demonstrative *əring* (Taylor 2015: 53); it is possible that Nungon *ori!* was originally a demonstrative. The origins of *wuru!* and other dog command forms, however, are opaque.

References

Aikhenvald, Alexandra Y. 2008. 'Semi-direct speech: Manambu and beyond', *Language Sciences* 30: 283–422.

Aikhenvald, Alexandra Y. 2010. *Imperatives and commands.* Oxford: Oxford University Press.

Aikhenvald, Alexandra Y. and Dixon, R. M. W. 1998. 'Dependencies between grammatical systems', *Language* 74: 56–80.

Claassen, Oren R. and McElhanon, Kenneth A. 1970. 'Languages of the Finisterre Range—New Guinea', *Papers in New Guinea Linguistics* 11: 45–78.

Farr, Cynthia. 1999. *The interface between syntax and discourse in Korafe: A Papuan language of Papua New Guinea.* Canberra: Pacific Linguistics.

Feld, Steven. 1982. *Sound and sentiment: Birds, weeping and poetics in Kaluli expression.* Durham, NC: Duke University Press.

Foley, William. 1986. *The Papuan languages of New Guinea*. Cambridge: Cambridge University Press.

Kiparsky, Paul. 1968. 'Tense and mood in Indo-European syntax', *Foundations of Language* 4(1): 30–57.

Kiparsky, Paul. 2005. 'The Vedic injunctive: Historical and synchronic implications', pp. 219–35 of *The yearbook of South Asian languages 2005*, edited by Rajendra Singh and Tanmoy Bhattacharya. New Delhi: Sage Publications.

McElhanon, Kenneth. 1967. 'Preliminary observations on the Huon Peninsula languages', *Oceanic Linguistics* VI(1): 1–45.

McElhanon, Kenneth. 1973. *Towards a typology of the Finisterre-Huon languages*. Canberra: Pacific Linguistics.

McElhanon, Kenneth. 1974. 'The glottal stop in Kâte', *Kivung* 7: 16–22.

Pakendorf, Brigitte and Schalley, Ewa. 2007. 'From possibility to prohibition: A rare grammaticalization pathway', *Linguistic Typology* 11: 515–40.

Pilhofer, G. 1933. *Grammatik der Kâte-Sprache in Neuguinea*. Berlin: Verlag von Dietrich Reimer (Ernst Vohsen) A.-G.

Roberts, John R. 1997. 'Switch-reference in Papua New Guinea: A preliminary survey', pp. 101–241 of *Papers in Papuan linguistics* 3, edited by Andrew Pawley. Canberra: Pacific Linguistics.

Sarvasy, Hannah. 2013. 'The multifunctional *ma*'. Presented at the Workshop on Languages of Melanesia. Canberra: Australian National University.

Sarvasy, Hannah. 2014a. 'Non-spatial setting in Nungon', pp. 395–432 of *Non-spatial setting in Finisterre-Huon languages*, edited by Hannah Sarvasy. Special issue of *Language Typology and Universals: Sprachtypologie und Universalienforschung* 67(3).

Sarvasy, Hannah. 2014b. 'Four Finisterre languages: An introduction', pp. 275–95 of *Non-spatial setting in Finisterre-Huon languages*, edited by Hannah Sarvasy. Special issue of *Language Typology and Universals: Sprachtypologie und Universalienforschung* 67(3).

Sarvasy, Hannah. 2014c. 'A grammar of Nungon, a Papuan language of Morobe Province, Papua New Guinea'. PhD Dissertation, Cairns: James Cook University.

Sarvasy, Hannah. 2015a. 'Split number in Nungon'. Presented at Linguistic Society of America Meeting. Portland: Linguistic Society of America. Extended abstract available at: http://journals.linguisticsociety.org/proceedings/index.php/ExtendedAbs/article/view/2996

Sarvasy, Hannah. 2015b. 'Breaking the clause chains: Non-canonical medial clauses in Nungon', *Studies in Language* 39(3): 664–96.

Sarvasy, Hannah. 2015c. 'The imperative split and the origin of switch-reference marking in Nungon', in Anna E. Jurgensen, Hannah Sande, Spencer Lamoureux, Kenny Baclawski, and Alison Zerbe (eds). *Berkeley Linguistic Society 41 Proceedings* 473–92.

Sarvasy, Hannah. 2017. *A Grammar of Nungon: A Papuan Language of Northeast New Guinea*. Leiden: Brill.

Schieffelin, Bambi. 1985. 'The acquisition of Kaluli', pp. 525–93 of *The cross-linguistic study of language acquisition*, Vol. 1, *The data*, edited by Dan Slobin. Hillsdale: Lawrence Erlbaum Associates.

Taylor, Matthew. 2015. *Nukna grammar sketch*. Ukarumpa: Summer Institute of Linguistics.

Wegmann, Urs and Wegmann, Johanna. 1994. 'Yau anthropology background sketch'. MS Ukarumpa: Summer Institute of Linguistics.

The imperative paradigm
of Korowai, a Greater Awyu
language of West Papua

LOURENS DE VRIES

1 Introduction

Korowai is a Papuan language spoken by around 4,000 people in the rainforest
between the Eilanden and the Becking River of (Indonesian) West Papua. Korowai
belongs to the Becking-Dawi branch of the Greater Awyu family (de Vries, Wester,
and van den Heuvel 2012). It is a synthetic language with agglutinating morphology
and some fusion (van Enk and de Vries 1997). There are three open word classes,
verbs, nouns, and adjectives. Verb morphology is suffixing, with the exception of the
negative circumfix. Verbal suffixes express person and number of the subject, mood,
modality, negation, switch reference, temporality (sequence and simultaneity), tense,
and aspect. Nominal morphology is very simple compared to verbal morphology.
There are three major clause types in Korowai, all of them predicate final and with
nominative-accusative alignment: transitive, intransitive, and copula clauses.

This chapter describes forms and functions of Korowai imperatives. First, there is
an introduction to the Korowai verb system (§2). The imperative paradigm is the
topic of §3. The chapter ends with some concluding reflections on Korowai imperatives (§4). The Korowai data are from van Enk and de Vries (1997) unless indicated
otherwise. The unpublished Korowai language notes and extensive dictionary file of
Rupert Stasch were very helpful to complete and verify my description and analysis.

2 Introduction to the Korowai verb system

The Korowai verb system follows the pattern of all Greater Awyu languages (Wester
2014; de Vries, Wester, and van den Heuvel 2012): the realis–irrealis opposition is

Commands. First edition. Alexandra Y. Aikhenvald and R. M. W. Dixon (eds)
This chapter © Lourens de Vries 2017. First published 2017 by Oxford University Press

basic, there is systematic conflation of second and third person in singular and plural, and there are four basic verb types.

The first and most simple Korowai verb type are its medial same subject verbs (bare verb stem or stem plus same subject suffix *-nè*, for example *fu* and *bando-xe-nè* in (20c)). In addition, there are three types of independent verbs. The most simple type are zero-forms that consist of a verb stem followed by just one suffix slot, a person-number slot, e.g. *xa-fén* in (7). The term zero-forms is from Drabbe (1959: 127) who called them zero-forms because their broad 'injunctive' mood is expressed by zero (see §4 for injunctive mood). This mood paradigm occurs in all Greater Awyu languages, with different but related ranges of meanings. In Korowai, the zero-forms are an imperative paradigm (see §3). The second type of independent Korowai verbs have two suffix slots: a person-number and modality slot (realis and irrealis), e.g. *la-xe-lé* in (1). The third type of independent verbs have three slots: they add a tense suffix or aspect suffix to two-slot realis/irrealis verbs, e.g. *dépe-mémo-xa-lé* in (3).

There are two sets of person-number suffixes. The suffixes used in (1), the irrealis paradigm of *lai-* 'to come', occur with all independent verb forms, except the imperative paradigm that has its own specific set of person-number markers (see §3):

(1) sg   1   la-xe-lé
                      come-IRR-1sg

     non1   la-xé
                      come-IRR[-1sg]

     pl   1   la-xe-lè
                      come-IRR-1sg

     non1   la-xe-té
                      come-IRR-non1pl

Realis and irrealis verbs with two suffix slots may be expanded with either tense suffixes or aspect suffixes, creating independent verbs with three suffix slots. The same set of tense suffixes are attached to both realis and irrealis forms. When attached to realis forms, they are interpreted as past tense markers and when attached to irrealis forms, the suffixes have future tense readings. In other words, they express degrees of remoteness from utterance time irrespective of the time direction, e.g. *-mémo* means 'a moment ago/in a moment':

(2) i-méma-lé
     see-IMMED-1sg[REAL]
     I saw a moment ago.

(3) dépe-mémo-xa-lé
     smoke-IMMED-IRR-1sg
     I will smoke in just a moment.

Declarative mood is unmarked except for falling intonation towards the end of the utterance. Interrogative mood is characterized by a rising intonation towards the end and the optional presence of question clitics attached to the last word of the clause. There are two question clitics, =*xolo* and =*benè*:

(4) lu-mbo=benè?
     enter-DUR[non1sg:REAL]=Q
     Is he entering?

Out of context (4) may also mean 'Are you (sg)/is it/is she entering?'

3 Korowai imperatives

3.1 The meanings of the imperative paradigm

Korowai second person imperatives are an integral part of a single imperative paradigm (5) with first, second, and third person imperatives, just as in Mauwake, another Papuan language of New Guinea (Berghäll 2010: 32–3). The distinction between first person, second person, and third person forms, in singular and plural, makes the imperative paradigm of Korowai an extremely marked paradigm both in Korowai and more generally in the whole Greater Awyu family where all verb paradigms have just four forms, based on the speaker/non-speaker (first versus second/third person) and singular/plural oppositions.

The meaning of the Korowai imperative forms can best be glossed in English by 'Let X do Y or be Y' where X can be of all grammatical persons and X can be animate or inanimate, with or without agency. This abstract, generalized grammatical signal is used in a wide range of different directive speech acts: to command, to advise, to wish, to pray, in exhortations, and in the language used in rituals of magic. Body language, including facial expression, cultural context, and social relationship between speaker and addressee, is combined with the imperative grammatical signal to infer the nature and the force of the speech act intended by the speaker.

The imperative paradigm is not the only grammatical signal used by speakers and hearers to communicate and infer the directive intentions of the speaker. Other grammatical signals used in the pragmatic domain of directive speech acts are intonation, the grammatical person of the subject, a closed class of imperative adverbs, exclamative vowel clitics, and vocative forms of address. The term imperative is used in this chapter as a grammatical label for the Korowai imperative paradigm as a whole, not just for second person imperatives, a paradigm of verb forms with imperative, jussive, hortative, optative, and other contextual readings.

3.2 Imperative morphology

The imperative paradigm is formed by adding a person-number suffix to the verb stem. The paradigm is different from all other verb paradigms of Korowai. This is not just because the imperative paradigm distinguishes three grammatical persons where all other Korowai verb paradigms distinguish just two grammatical persons but also because the imperative paradigm has its own set of person-number suffixes (5) while all other verb paradigms in Korowai share another set (1). This is the imperative paradigm of *lu-* 'to enter':

(5) sg 1 lu-p
         2 lu-m
         3 lu-n
     pl 1 lo-f-un
         2 lo-m-un
         3 le-tin

3.3 Imperative adverbs

A closed set of mutually exclusive mood adverbs may occur in imperative clauses, and only in imperative clauses, with imperative verbs of all three persons. First, hortative *anè* that always precedes the imperative forms. It functions to strengthen the persuasive force (6)–(7). Second, the desiderative mood adverb *xolüp* (or shortened allomorphs: *xüp, xlüp* or *xup*) optionally follows the imperative verb (8) and (9).

(6) anè   lai-m
     IMP   come-IMP:2sg
     You must come!

(7) anè   xa-fén
     IMP   go-IMP:1pl
     Let us go!

(8) noxu   ima-fon   xüp
     we   see-IMP:1pl   DESID
     We wish to see! Let us see!

(9) xolo-xolo   aup   da-men   xup
     RECIP-RECIP   voice   listen-IMP:2pl   DESID
     You should/must listen to each other!
     (from Stasch's field notes)

The adverb *xüp* also occurs in idioms of strong refusal when the speaker makes very clear that he or she does not want to do something. The following example is from the field notes of Rupert Stasch, who describes the idiom as an oath-like formulaic expression that means 'I do not want to' used in negative contexts of frustration. This analysis is supported by Stasch's observation that the noun *wafol* 'worm' can be replaced by a number of other nouns with negative connotations (e.g. *laleo* 'after-death demon') or nouns referring to spiritual beings that are also used frequently as swear words (e.g. *xufom!*).

(10) wafol   xüp
      worm   DESID
      No way! (lit. worms would be good)

The third mood adverb is the prohibitive adverb *belén* (see §3.5 for negative imperatives):

(11) golo-m   belén=é
      be.afraid-IMP:2sg   NEG.IMP=EXCL
      Don't be afraid!
      (from Stasch's field notes)

Like the desiderative adverb *xüp*, the prohibitive adverb *belén* always occurs immediately after the verb. The desiderative *xüp* also occurs with negative imperative constructions that consist of a negated infinitive (see §3.5):

(12) dodu-n-da=xup
      split-INFIN-NEG=DESID
      don't split!
      (from Stasch's field notes)

3.4 *The imperative paradigm, tense and aspect*

Just like other independent verb paradigms, imperative verb forms can be expanded with the tense suffixes -*mémo* 'a moment removed from now' and -*lulo* 'a day removed from now' to create delayed imperatives, e.g. *dépemémom* 'smoke in a moment!' from *dépo-* 'to smoke'.

(13) sg   1   dépe-mémo-p
            2   dépe-mémo-m
            3   dépe-mémo-n
      pl   1   dépe-méma-f-on
            2   dépe-méma-m-on
            3   dépe-méma-tin

Korowai derives habitual-iterative verbs by reduplicating verb stems and adding the verb stem of *mo* 'to do'. Such derived habitual-iterative verbs also have imperative forms:

(14) sabu=ngga   xoxa   molo=xa   xoxa
      soap=CONN   thing   diving.glasses=CONN   thing

      fo-fo-ma-fon=o
      get-get-HAB-IMP:1pl=EXCL
      Let us get/We want to get things like soap and diving glasses regularly/ repeatedly!

3.5 Prohibitives

The opposition irrealis and imperative is neutralized under negation and the forms of (15) are used both as negative imperative and as negative irrealis forms. The negative circumfix *be-...-da* is used with all independent verb paradigms in Korowai:

(15) sg   1   be-dépo-pe-lé-da

              Non1   be-dépo-n-da

    pl   1   be-dépo-pe-lè-da

              Non1   be-dépa-tin-da

But Korowai also has dedicated negative imperative forms, all second person prohibitives. The first type of dedicated second person prohibitive verb form is derived from the irrealis negative paradigm (15) by deleting the negative prefix *be-*, making the imperative verb shorter, and by addition of the negative imperative adverb *belén*:

(16a)   dépo-n-da   belén

         smoke-IMP:2sg-NEG   NEG.IMP

         Do not smoke!

(16b)   dépa-tin-da   belén

         smoke-IMP:2pl-NEG   NEG.IMP

         Do not smoke!

The second way to create prohibitive verb forms is by deriving infinitives and modifying them by the negative imperative adverb.

(17)   dépo-n   belén

       smoke-INFIN   NEG.IMP

       Do not smoke!

(18)   dépo-ŋga   belén

       smoke-INFIN.CONN   NEG.IMP

       Do not smoke!

The negative infinitive also occurs without *belén* to signal strong and forceful prohibitive intentions (*noxu ülmexo-ngga-da* in (19b)). Example (19a, b) is part of a story published by van Enk and de Vries (1997: 186–205) that tells how Korowai people reacted to the first Dutch missionary worker who tried to contact them in 1979:

(19a)   anè   xe-nè   ülmexo-fon   de-té

       IMP   go-ss   shoot-IMP:1pl   say-non1pl[REAL]

(19b) sé   mbolo-mbolop   lefu-lon   de-té
       next   grandfather-grandfather   some-FOC   say-non1pl[REAL]

       él   noxu   ülmexo-ngga-da
       well   we   shoot-INFIN.CONN-NEG

       noxu   wola-lelo-xai   de-nè   de-té
       1pl   world-be[non1sg]-IRR   say-SS   say-non1pl[REAL]

Let us shoot them, they said, but the elders said 'Well, we must not shoot them, lest our world ends'.

3.6 Scope of imperative forms, clause chaining and switch reference

In clause chaining, clauses with dependent verbs are under the scope of the imperative verb of the final clause. For example the medial verb *bando-xe-nè* in (20a) receives an imperative reading under the scope of the imperative verb in the final clause. The following examples are taken from a text that contains a (reported) prayer-like call that is directed at the ancestors after a pig sacrifice (van Enk and de Vries 1997: 159–62):

(20a) wof-e=xa   mbolow=è   ge-mba-mbam-pexo
       there-TR=CONN   ancestor=VOC   your-child-child-COMIT

       if-e=xa   bando-xe-nè   lé-m=é
       this-TR=CONN   bring-go-SS   eat-IMP:2sg=EXCL

Oh forefather over there, with your children, you should take this and eat it!

(20b) lé-m=daxu   noxup   dél=o   füon=o
       eat-IMP:2sg=SS   1pl   bird=COORD   marsupial.species=COORD

       gol=o   fédo-m=do   le-fén=è
       pig=COORD   give-IMP:2sg=DS   eat-IMP:1pl=EXCL

Eat and give birds and marsupials and pigs for us to eat!

(20c) damol   fo   fe-nè   fu
       back   get[SS]   get-SS   put[SS]

       woto=fexa   mbolo=fexo   ge-mambüm=pexo
       sacred.place=one   grandfather=COORD   your-children=COORD

       ge-yano=fexo   ge-ni-xül=fexo   if-e=xa
       your-people=COORD   your-wife-pl=COORD   here-TR=CONN

       bando-xe-nè   le-mén=é
       bring-go-SS   eat-IMP:2pl=EXCL

And having presented the back (part of the sacrificial pig) (they say), 'hey, you forefather of that certain sacred place, with your children, your people, and your wives, you should take this and eat it!'

(20d) le-mén=daxu   [noxu   lép-telo-xai=xa]   noxu
       eat-2pl:IMP=SS   we   ill-be[non1sg]-IRR=CONN   1pl

       mano-pa-mon=do   xi-telo-fon=è
       good-CAUS-2pl:IMP=DS   healthy-be-1pl:IMP=EXCL
       You must eat it and if we fall ill, cure us and let us be healthy.

The whole prayer is in imperative mood, with first and second person imperative verbs. Tail-head linkages (de Vries 2005) link the final imperative clause of chain (20a) to (20b), and (20c) to (20d). The subordinate clause *noxu lép-telo-xai* in (20d) is a peripheral argument of the clause *manopamon*. Therefore it is not under the scope of the imperative mood of the clause chain. The embedded clause does not contain an imperative verb but an irrealis verb. The clause can be glossed as 'given that we fall ill'/'if we fall ill'.

Notice that (20d) also shows that first person plural forms of the imperative paradigm can be used in contexts where the addressee is excluded: you (ancestors) must help us and we (your descendants) must be healthy (*xitelofon*) (cf. Nungon, Hannah Sarvasy, Chapter 11). But the first person plural inclusive reading is the more usual one.

3.7 Relationships between irrealis modality and imperative mood

The close synchronic relationship between the imperative and irrealis in Korowai is shown by the fact that the negative forms of the irrealis paradigm also function as prohibitive forms, i.e. the opposition irrealis versus imperative is neutralized in the negative forms (15). It is not uncommon for irrealis forms to be used in polite directive speech acts in Papuan languages (Roberts 1990). The use of Korowai negative irrealis forms as negative imperatives fits this pattern. Second, by shortening the second person forms of the negative irrealis paradigm and adding an imperative negative adverb, dedicated prohibitive forms are derived from the negative irrealis (16a, b).

Diachronically, irrealis paradigms and imperative paradigms are also closely linked within the Greater Awyu family. In the Awyu-Dumut branch there is, just like in the Becking-Dawi branch (Korowai, Tsaukambo), an irrealis paradigm but whereas in the Becking-Dawi branch there is both an irrealis paradigm and an imperative paradigm, the languages of the Awyu-Dumut branch have just an irrealis paradigm that is used in all contexts of unactualized events, including directive contexts (hortative, jussive). Only for second person subjects there is a dedicated imperative paradigm in the Awyu-Dumut branch, formally distinct from the irrealis paradigm, with an imperative prefix and (often) suppletive imperative stems.

This will be illustrated with data from Yonggom Wambon. Yonggom Wambon, like other Awyu-Dumut languages, has suppletive imperative stems. It derives imperative stems by prefixing an element *na-* or *n-* and suffixing *-n* to a primary or secondary stem (Drabbe 1959: 130; de Vries, Wester, and van den Heuvel 2012: 287). An alternative way is to add the imperative stem *nok* of the auxiliary verb *mo* 'to do' to a (secondary) verb stem. By adding a plural suffix *-nin,* plural imperatives are formed. There are many irregularities in the formation of imperative forms. Some examples:

(21)   *Verb stems*   *Imperative sg   Imperative pl*
       mba-, mbage- 'to sit'   na-mbon   na-mbon-in
                                  mbage-nok
       en- ande- 'to eat'   n-an   n-an-in
                                  ande-nok

Prohibitives are formed by adding the prohibitive suffix-*tit* to a secondary verb stem. The plural suffixes *-na* and *-an* surround *-tit* to pluralize the prohibitive (Drabbe 1959: 141). Notice that the systematic conflation of second and third person, a defining characteristic of the Greater Awyu family, absent in the neighbouring Asmat, Marind, and Ok families, occurs also in these Yonggom Wambon negative imperatives. Some examples of prohibitive forms:

(22)   jo-tit
       call-PROHIB
       you (sg) must not call/let him/her not call!
       (Yonggom Wambon, Drabbe 1959: 141)

(23)   jo-na-tir-an
       call-pl-PROHIB-pl
       you (pl)/they must not call, do not call/do not let them call
       (Yonggom Wambon, Drabbe 1959: 141)

Irrealis forms of Yonggom Wambon are zero-forms, formally unmarked for TAM and used for events or actions that have not (yet) been actualized. Interestingly, the irrealis forms may also have directive mood meanings (adhortative, optative, desiderative, jussive). Consider this irrealis paradigm of Yonggom Wambon, Drabbe 1959: 128–9):

(24)   irrealis of *majo* 'to come down'
       1sg   majo-p
                come.down-1sg[IRR]

       non-1sg majo-n
                come.down-non1sg[IRR]

       1pl   majo-p-an
                come.down-1-pl[IRR]

       non-1pl majo-n-an
                come.down-non1-pl[IRR]

Example (25) shows three irrealis verbs expressing directive mood with first and second person subjects:

(25) Mbage-p   ka-n   werepmo-j-ip
      sit-1sg[IRR]   go-non1sg[IRR]   be.healthy-TR-1sg[IRR]
      Let me stay until I am recovered! (lit. Let me stay and let it (the illness) go away and I want to be healthy/let me be healthy/I must be healthy)
      (Yonggom Wambon, Drabbe 1959: 135)

There is not only functional overlap between Awyu-Dumut irrealis and Becking-Dawi imperative paradigms (both may be used in directive contexts with first and third person subjects) but the two paradigms are also cognate. Compare the Korowai imperative paradigm (5) with the Yonggom Wambon irrealis paradigm (24). Notice that the Yonggom Wambon irrealis has the normal paradigm with four forms based on the first person versus non-first person opposition that we find in all Greater Awyu languages, except in Becking-Dawi imperative paradigms (Korowai, Tsau-kambo). Korowai imperative *lu-p* (1sg) corresponds to Yonggom Wambon *majo-p* (1sg), the 1pl forms are also cognate (in both languages intervocalic /p/ becomes a voiced continuant in morpheme sequencing). Finally, the non-1sg Korowai *lu-n* and Yonggom Wambon *majo-n* correspond. Crucially, both paradigms are zero-forms, only marked for person-number. But the grammatical place of the zero-forms is overlapping but different in both branches: it is a dedicated imperative paradigm in Korowai and an irrealis paradigm in Yonggom Wambon (that includes imperative readings with first and third person subjects; second person imperatives have their own distinct paradigm).

What may have happened in the Awyu-Dumut branch (exemplified by Yonggom Wambon) is that from the original zero-form paradigm, inherited from proto Greater Awyu (three persons, two numbers), the second person zero-forms were dropped after the formation of separate, dedicated imperative second person forms. This resulted in a zero-form paradigm with four forms that conforms to the Greater Awyu standard of speaker versus non-speaker.

Kombai (de Vries 1993), the eastern Awyu-Dumut neighbour of Korowai, also dropped second person forms of the proto Greater Awyu zero-paradigm, but in addition Kombai dropped the third person zero-forms. Kombai uses non-1 future forms to express imperative meanings with third person subjects. This means that Kombai has just first person zero-forms left. The same is true for Digul Wambon, where de Vries and de Vries-Wiersma (1992: 31) only found first person zero-forms in texts. In other words, we see the inherited zero-form paradigm in reduced forms in the Awyu-Dumut branch. The other branch (exemplified by Korowai) retained the complete zero-form paradigm of proto Greater Awyu. The reason that only first person imperative forms survived in Kombai and Digul Wambon is their very high frequency. The high frequency of first person zero-forms is caused by the fact that quotative framing of emotion, thoughts, intention requires first person zero-forms in all Greater Awyu languages (26).

(26)   Yarimo   xo   fera-f-e-ne
       garden   go.ss   see-1sg:IMP-CONN-QUOT.sg
       He wants to go and see his garden. (lit. He says 'Let me go and see the garden.')
       (Kombai, de Vries 1993)

3.8 Limits of imperatives

Given the right context, any Korowai verb seems to be able to have imperative forms. In my corpus of Korowai texts, I found examples of imperatives with both volitional and non-volitional verbs where the subject has no control over the action of the verb, and with both inanimate, low-agency subjects and high-agency human subjects. The examples of imperatives with non-volitional verbs and low-agency subjects are from the *Gom* song (van Enk and de Vries 1997: 220). Both the young boys and the sago palms of various species are the subjects of the second person imperative forms of the intransitive and non-volitional verb *melu* 'to grow':

(27a) xofél   gabüm-gun   mbolop   gabüm-gun
       boy   knee-group   grandfather   knee-group

       xofé   manop   pelu-m=é=o
       boy   good   grow-2sg:IMP=EXCL=EXCL
       Knee-dancing boys' group, knee-dancing older people's group, boy, grow well!

(27b) xaxül   melu-m=o   lahial   melu-m=o
       xaxül.sago   grow-2sg:IMP=EXCL   lahial.sago   grow-2sg:IMP=EXCL

       lé   melu-m=o   amo   melu-m=o
       kind.of.sago.tree grow-2sg:IMP=EXCL   amo.sago   grow-2sg:IMP=EXCL
       Xaxül sago, grow! *Lahial* sago, grow! *Lé* sago, grow! *Amo* sago, grow!

(27c) xofé   manop   pelu-m=é=o
       boy   good   grow-2sg:IMP=EXCL=EXCL
       Boy, grow well.

3.9 Imperative verbs, politeness, and egalitarian cultural practices

The anthropologist Stasch (2014: 87) writes that 'Korowai are intensely egalitarian in their political ethos. For example, they historically lacked any named roles of political leadership, and in the present as in the past they are quick to rebuke any person who tries to tell others what to do.' But Stasch (2014: 87) also makes clear that 'the absence of stable roles of political authority is not the same as absence of social subordination as such. On the contrary, Korowai have a clear idea of the possibility of subordination in social life. They often marvel approvingly at it when it occurs, as a realization of values of relatedness and coordination.'

Both elements, of egalitarianism and subordination tied to specific relational dyads and cultural contexts, shape the way that Korowai speakers perform directive speech acts. In most contexts, it is completely acceptable to use just short imperative forms, including second person forms, without any negative politeness strategies (in the sense of Brown and Levinson 1987: 129–211) to reduce the imposition on the addressee. On the contrary, it is precisely the absence of such strategies that signals solidarity, harmony, trust, and cooperation (cf. Karawari, Borut Telban, Chapter 13).

The following example shows such a short direct command in a cooperative context, where Korowai speakers work together to give visitors the idea that they meet 'stone age' people who never saw 'white people'. The Korowai dialogue has been filmed and occurs in a French documentary film with the title *Path to the Stone Age* (Stasch 2014: 83). The French cameraman asks some Korowai men through a Korowai interpreter whether they have ever seen white men. The Korowai interpreter is subtitled as saying, 'Have you ever seen white men?' but Stasch (2014: 83) reports what the Korowai interpreter is really saying during that film fragment: 'Say "No, none". Say "None at all". Say "I have not seen white-skinned people, this is the first time".' The Korowai interpreter in the film starts to 'translate' the question whether the interviewee has ever seen white people by giving the Korowai interviewee a short command:

(28) Mafem   di-m.
     no   say-2sg:IMP
     Say 'no'!

Such short commands, without any redressive action in the domain of politeness, are very frequent. They are not seen or meant as rude. On the contrary, the absence of (elaborate) redressive politeness makes (28) a command that in the egalitarian Korowai context conforms to norms of pleasant behaviour and expresses smooth cooperation between speaker and addressee when they work together with a shared goal, in this case to adjust their answers to the 'primitivist' expectations and hopes of visitors who want to meet Korowai people in their pure, uncontacted state (Stasch 2014).

But egalitarian ideologies and practices do not imply that there are no relations or situations with elements of subordination and seniority, e.g. mother–child, husband–wife, ancestor–descendant (Stasch 2014: 83). Giving commands to outgroup members, especially foreigners, also demands tact and often requires that the speaker makes clear that he does not want to force the foreign addressee in any way to do something that they do not desire to do. The speaker will adjust the linguistic form of the imperative speech act in such contexts to the situation or the relationship between speaker and addressee, for example by using a polite or honorific term of address before performing the imperative speech act, by adding imperative adverb *xup* DESID that may have the force of 'please' in English, by adding long exclamative vowels and pronouncing these with a pleading tone, by using a polite, kind, and cooperative intonation contour in the speech act as a whole, and by body language and facial expression.

Korowai and Kombai use the noun *yale* (Kombai, de Vries 1987: 114) and *yalé(n)* (Korowai) with the basic meaning 'old man' as an honorific form to address a respected male person who has some form of seniority with respect to the speaker. They also add these nouns as an honorific seniority clitic to nouns referring to persons, especially personal names (e.g. *Xolənelə se=ale* 'honoured Kornelis', from Stasch's notebook). Van Enk and de Vries (1997: 145) describe the Korowai *lebaxop* as the female honorific counterpart of *yalé(n)* (29).

Subjects are often left implicit in imperative clauses. In this respect, they are not different from other clause types because the general tendency in Korowai is to prefer clauses with just a verb, or a verb with at most one nominal that conveys new or important information. Whereas overt subject phrases tend to be avoided to keep the syntax of the clause simple, extra-clausal themes that precede a clause, but are not syntactically part of the clause, occur very frequently (de Vries 2006). Second person addressees may be expressed by a vocative phrase in this theme slot. The form of address in the theme slot has a major impact on the level of politeness of imperative speech acts with second person subjects:

(29) Lebaxop,   gup   lai-m=do   noxup
      old.lady   you   come-2sg:IMP=DS   1pl

      ima-fon   xüp
      see-1pl:IMP DESID
      Madam, you must come and let us see you!

The honorific form of address in (29) is respectful. The use of the desiderative imperative adverb in combination with this form of address turns (29) into a polite invitation. The vocative phrase preceding the imperative clause, the desiderative adverb, and the pronominal subjects in the clauses make the imperative sentence longer and that also softens the intrusion on the autonomy of the addressee.

The vocative phrase is often pronounced in a relatively loud voice, with exclamative and vocative vowels cliticizing to the form of address (30). Exclamative interjections may precede the imperative utterance (30). The longer the exclamative or vocative vowel lasts, the more forceful the imperative speech act will be.

(30) hey   n-até=o
     EXCL   my-father=VOC

     golo-m   belén=é
     be.afraid-2sg.IMP   NEG.IMP=EXCL

     nu   kolufo-yanof=é
     I   Korowai-person=EXCL

     Hey, my father, do not be afraid! I am a Korowai person.

Example (30) is taken from the *Xenil-xenil* narrative (van Enk and de Vries 1997: 189). The situation in the story is tense because total strangers meet. The kinship term is used by the speaker as a polite form of address, adding that he is a (normal) Korowai person, not to be feared. Kinship terms or terms of friendship (friend, mate) are the preferred choice for the vocative slot. Kinship terms are dyadic terms evoking the duties and obligations, levels of distance or closeness, associated with the dyad.

4 Summary and discussion

Typologically, Korowai imperatives stand out in a number of interesting ways. The distinction canonical imperatives (second person) versus non-canonical imperatives (first and third person) is not made in the Korowai imperative paradigm. Second, imperative clauses are used in tail–head linkage. Finally, first person plural imperatives of Korowai are used not only in addressee-inclusive contexts but also in addressee-exclusive contexts. The imperative paradigm not only expresses the same distinctions as the other independent verb paradigms but it makes more distinctions than the others, viz. in grammatical person. The imperative clearly is not the impoverished little sister of the declarative in Korowai. The role of the imperative forms in grammar and language use is very prominent because imperative verb forms are not just used for a broad range of directive speech acts but also in quotative framing in the domains of thought, emotion, cognition, and perception. This makes forms of the imperative paradigm very frequent, as in many other Papuan languages (de Vries 1990, 2006).

Irrealis and imperative paradigms are closely related in the Greater Awyu family, both synchronically and diachronically, and Korowai is no exception. This is because they are zero-forms. The zero-paradigm, formally unmarked except for person-number, has the same set of person-number suffixes in the whole family (Wester 2014: 91). The zero-paradigm brings together irrealis, optative, imperative, hortative, and desiderative meanings in different permutations in the two branches. In the Awyu-Dumut branch the zero-paradigm is used for both non-directive and directive speech acts in utterances with irrealis, optative, hortative, and jussive readings. In addition, there is a dedicated canonical imperative paradigm with only second person forms in the Awyu-Dumut branch. However, in the other branch, at least in Korowai, the zero-paradigm is exclusively imperative, in three grammatical persons, and in contrast with an irrealis paradigm.

The Greater Awyu zero-paradigm is formally and functionally reminiscent of the injunctive paradigm of Proto-Indo-European, formally unmarked for tense and mood (Progovac 2015: 40; Kiparsky 1968). Progovac (2015: 40) points out how Indo-Europeanists like Kuryłowicz (1964: 21) and Gonda (1956: 36–7) describe the injunctive paradigm as the only mood in earliest Proto-Indo-European, moreover a mood that expressed a wide range of meanings in the domain of unactualized events including irrealis, optative, and imperative. The type and range of directive speech acts that can be performed by the injunctive forms (I want X, I want you to do X, let us do X, I wish Y to happen) are basic, in many ways more basic than declarative speech acts, certainly in first language acquisition and perhaps also in the evolution of language, according to Progovac (2015: 170) who sees the imperative as the 'paradigm case of an unmarked mood form'.

References

Berghäll, Liisa. 2010. *Mauwake reference grammar*. University of Helsinki, Faculty of Arts.

Brown, Penelope and Levinson, Stephen C. 1987. *Politeness: Some universals in language usage*. Cambridge University Press.

Drabbe, P. 1959. *Kaeti en Wambon: Twee Awju-dialecten*. The Hague: Nijhoff.

van Enk, Gerrit J. and de Vries, Lourens. 1997. *The Korowai of Irian Jaya: Their language in its cultural context*. Oxford: Oxford University Press.

Gonda, J. 1956. *The character of the Indo-European moods (with special regard to Greek and Sanskrit)*. Weisbaden: Harrassowitz.

Kiparsky, Paul. 1968. 'Tense and mood in Indo-European syntax', *Foundations of Language* 4(1): 30–57.

Kuryłowicz, J. 1964. *The inflectional categories of Indo-European*. Heidelberg: Carl Winter Universitätsverlag.

Progovac, L. 2015. *Evolutionary syntax*. Oxford: Oxford University Press.

Roberts, John R. 1990. 'Modality in Amele and other Papuan languages' *Journal of Linguistics* 26(2): 363–401.

Stasch, Rupert. 2014. 'Powers of incomprehension: Linguistic otherness, translators, and political structure in New Guinea tourism encounters', HAU: *Journal of Ethnographic Theory* 4(2): 73–94.

de Vries, L. 1987. 'Kombai kinship terminology', *Irian, Bulletin of Irian Jaya* 15: 105–18.

de Vries, L. 1990. 'Some remarks on direct quotation in Kombai', pp. 291–309 of *Unity in diversity*, edited by Harm Pinkster and Inge Genee. Dordrecht: Foris.

de Vries, L. 1993. *Forms and functions in Kombai, an Awyu language of Irian Jaya*. Canberra: Australian National University Press.

de Vries, L. 2005. 'Towards a typology of tail-head linkage in Papuan languages' *Studies in Language* 29(2): 363–84.

de Vries, L. 2006. 'Areal pragmatics of New Guinea: Thematization, distribution and recapitulative linkage in Papuan languages', *Journal of Pragmatics* 38: 811–28.

de Vries, L. 2012. 'Some notes on the Tsaukambo language of West Papua', *Language and Linguistics in Melanesia*, Special Issue 2012, 165–93.

de Vries, L. and de Vries-Wiersma, R. 1992. *An outline of the morphology of Wambon of the Irian Jaya Upper-Digul area*. Royal Institute of Linguistics and Anthropology. Leiden: KITLV Press.

de Vries, L., Wester, R., and van den Heuvel, W. 2012. 'The Greater Awyu language family of West Papua', *Language and Linguistics in Melanesia*, Special Issue 2012: 269–312.

Wester, R. 2014. *A linguistic history of Awyu-Dumut: Morphological study and reconstruction of a Papuan language family*. PhD Dissertation, Vrije Universiteit Amsterdam.

13

Commands as a form of intimacy among the Karawari of Papua New Guinea

BORUT TELBAN

1 Introduction

Over three thousand Karawari-speaking people live in nine villages and numerous camps in the swampy region of upper Karawari River, upper Kanggramai Creek and lower Konmei Creek of the East Sepik Province, Papua New Guinea. There are four dialectal groups embracing the following villages: (a) Konmei, Manjamai, Kundiman (two separate villages); (b) Meikerobi, Kaiwaria, Kungriambun; (c) Masandenai; and (d) Ambonwari. Beside other terms of reference (see Telban 1998: 15, 2014a: 260) Ambonwari also call those from the group (a) *yakwaym* (*yokoim*), which in Ambonwari is a homonym of both a hen and a small plant (Telban n.d.), and those from the group (b) *yaringgi* '(people from) sago forests', identifying them with their environment.[1] Following my visit to all Karawari-speaking villages, and discussing this issue with the people, it became clear that dialect of the group (b) and their mythical past are the closest to those in Ambonwari. However, the people from all the villages mentioned see themselves nowadays

---

[1] My anthropological research in Ambonwari, which is with over 750 people the largest Karawari-speaking village, has spanned more than 25 years. The ethnographic and linguistic data, collected since my initial fieldwork between 1990 and 1992, have been supplemented by over a hundred hours of videotaped spontaneous interactions recorded by Daniela Vávrová during our joint research in 2005, 2007, 2008, and 2011. Many short video clips were also made by children and youngsters, when they were given cameras to record in the absence of adults. Additional hours of different kinds of myths, stories, and songs were audiotaped. Both video and audio recordings were transcribed and translated into Tok Pisin already in the field, and provided a good material for subsequent discussions. The assistance of local elementary teacher Julius Sungulmari was invaluable.

Commands. First edition. Alexandra Y. Aikhenvald and R. M. W. Dixon (eds)
This chapter © Borut Telban 2017. First published 2017 by Oxford University Press

as being Karawari people who speak Karawari language, while dialectical differences are well recognized.[2]

Karawari villages, or clusters of villages, are not homogenous units but heterogenous compounds, with ancestors of individual clans coming from different directions often speaking different tongues (see the maps in Telban 1998: 72–3; see also Telban 2008, 2014b; Foley 2016). This knowledge, together with the names of each clan's ancestors, men's houses, and spirit-things, is preserved in their myths of origin, legends, and songs. Some individuals and groups were adopted (a named individual is as a rule equated with a whole group, be it lineage or clan, and vice versa; see Telban 1998: 152–5), while others broke up and formed their own settlements. These adoptions and separations are remembered and recalled mainly at the times of ritual and disputes between lineages, clans, and villages. All this and more is important for local politics and people's perception of their belonging to a specific land, men's house, spirit-being, lineage and clan, and their relationships to others. All of them have names, which are used as terms of reference, and to all of which a specificity of language is attached.

Being one of the languages of the Lower Sepik Family, Karawari shows notable similarities with closely related Yimas language (Foley 1991) although the two languages are not mutually intelligible. The distinguishing characteristic of the Lower Sepik Family (belonging to a large group of New Guinean languages known as Papuan or non-Austronesian) is that all six languages of this family (Murik, Kopar, Angoram, Chambri, Yimas, and Karawari) are morphologically agglutinative, employing a large number of prefixes and suffixes (Foley 1986). Like neighbouring Yimas (Foley 1986: 218; 1991), Karawari is a four-vowel system (/a/, /i/, /i/, /u/) and has two major word classes: nouns (eight major noun classes) and verbs (the most morphologically complex class). The latter are divided into intransitive, transitive, and ditransitive verbs. Prefixes mark modality, person, and number of both the subject and object of the verb and the class of the co-referential noun. Suffixes on verbs express tense, aspect, and mood. There are seven distinct tenses, with only one of them used for the future. When speaking about an event which happened or will happen in the evening or at night, another suffix *-kia* is used preceding suffix marking tense. Verbal reduplication and serial verb constructions are common. Reduplication

---

[2] In the web-based publication *Ethnologue: Languages of the world*, published by SIL International, and the *Ethnologue language family index*, Karawari is classified under Ramu-Lower Sepik Family, subgroup Lower Sepik, and is divided into two languages: Yimas and Tabriak, where the latter has the alternative name Karawari. In Ambonwari the term *tabriak* is used neither for the language nor for its speakers. *Tabriak* is used only in Konmei, Kundiman, and Manjamai for 'talk' while in Ambonwari (where, when speaking with the villagers previously mentioned, *tabriak* is pronounced as *sapriak*) people use *mariawk* (*mariak*, *mariok*) instead. This, however, neither makes them two separate languages nor justifies the use of Tabriak as a cover term for all Karawari-speaking people and their language.

refers to pluractionality, while serial verb constructions describe a series of interconnected subevents.

2 The use of commands in Ambonwari

The Ambonwari regularly use commands, especially the short ones, and feel good doing so. Being used as directives, demands, requests, instructions, exhortations, advice, and even greetings, they actually generate and reflect close relationships and intimacy between people. Moreover, being frequently heard in conversation between parents and children they are a means for the inculcation of village morality, values, and norms of behaviour (Rumsey n.d., 2003).[3] This, however, is only their functional aspect, which is not necessarily always part of a conscious attempt to socialize the children into desired adults. There is also a more immanent 'interactive role that language plays in mediating and negotiating social relations' (Schieffelin 1986: 167).

Commands are pervasive in daily interactions between people. High frequency of commands has also been observed by Aikhenvald in another Sepik society, the Manambu (2008: 278). While for a culturally insensitive foreigner these often abrupt and quite loud speech acts may be disconcerting (see Chapter 1), for the Ambonwari it is just the opposite. For such an egalitarian kinship-based society, commands are actually a common way of daily communication reflecting the closeness of living together and directness of expressions clearly showing people's desires and intentions (see Rumsey 2003). Parents often complain about their children that *mbu wara mariawk andiri* 'they (children) do not listen to talk', that they do not obey what they are told or asked to do. Like among other egalitarian societies in Papua New Guinea 'it is difficult to compel anyone to do something that he or she does not wish to do' (Schieffelin 1986: 168).

By providing a context in which different imperative forms are used, one can learn what kind of directives are preferred by children, which norms and values are especially likely to be targeted, and what kind of situations exhibit the use of specific directives among the adults. To request something, for example, although not in excess and all the time, is good. To be or act as being self-sufficient, that is, not demanding anything, is not good. Such an individual would be seen as a stingy

---

[3] In his comparison of Japanese, Catalan, Spanish, and Ku Waru, Rumsey (2003) focuses mainly on socialization and interaction between infants and others. In all four languages he finds that the first verbal inflections learned by most infants are those of imperative mood without the use of pronouns. He (2003: 177) cites Schieffelin who says that among the Kaluli of Papua New Guinea talking to young children consists mainly of 'imperatives, negative imperatives and rhetorical questions' (1990: 93). Rumsey concludes that 'children master the imperative before the personal pronouns' (2003: 169). He expands Benveniste's (1971) argument from the linguistic category of person being instrumental in constitution of a subject to 'another set of linguistic categories—those of mood or modality—through which expressions of desire are indexically grounded even in the absence of explicit reference to the subject to whom it is to be attributed: the speaker' (Rumsey 2003: 170).

person who rejects relationships and pertaining expectations. Commands correspond to the intrinsic verbal component of sharing, exchange, and cooperation, on
which people's lives and society as a whole depend. Moreover, if or when somebody
did not use them, or tried to express his or her wishes in a more 'polite' way, people
would soon become suspicious, thinking that such a person is insincere and hides his
or her intentions.

Daily commands among the Ambonwari are often reflection of play, friendship,
kindness, benevolence, and affection. Moreover, they help people not to trouble
themselves with paralysing anxiety and embarrassment (or even shame) in front of
the eyes of other people, which are two extremely powerful emotional conditions
recognized as such all over Papua New Guinea (Telban 2004). Commands help
people to get a necessary confidence and not to stutter because of these emotional
states. Commands are often reflections of people's wishes, desires, worries, irritations, or annoyances, which have to be immediately dealt with in order not to
produce *sukunang* (long-lasting feeling of being offended) or *mambara* (short-lasting
feeling of being offended), two forms of powerful resentment, among their kin
(Telban 1993). On the other hand, adults learn to suppress their desires; if not,
they are perceived as greedy (*karisikin* 'strong, hard, stingy'), something that is
socially unacceptable. When used for faithfulness to a partner or bravery in fights,
'strong' can also have a positive connotation.

3 Short non-verbal commands

A command is often expressed with a variety of short directives. They can be uttered
in high volume and falling intonation explicitly requesting a specific action from
the addressee or in a rather gentle way telling the other what is expected from them.
Non-verbal single word commands do not change according to number and sex
of the addressee. Thus, for example, when distributing food, one can hear a child
saying *Ama, ama!* 'I, I!' or *Amangok!* 'Me too!' using a personal pronoun as a form of
command, i.e. 'Give it to me!' A child may also employ the first person plural pronoun
Apia! 'We!' with the same intention. This is a culturally specific and widespread
practice of using the first person plural pronoun in situations when a person wants
something only for himself or herself (see examples (7), (18)). The mother will
usually reply with another command: *Mi nggok!* 'You wait!', *Nggok!* 'Later! Not yet!
Wait!' or *Nggoka!* 'Wait!' In the last case, the command is intensified with the
final suffix *–a*. Many other short non-verbal imperatives, especially adverbs, can be
additionally marked with this suffix which has the same form as the elative. These
expressions, with characteristic falling tone and high voice, are used as a response
to a child who impatiently and repeatedly asks for food. A mother can get irritated
with her children, saying *Mba!* 'Enough! Stop it!' and intensifying her request with
repetition: *Mba! Mba! Mba!*

Adverbs are often used in commands: *Auraur!* 'Quickly! Hurry up!', *Wasanarin!* 'Slowly! Do it slowly/gently/carefully!', the latter intensified in reduplication form *Wasawasanarin!* 'Very slowly! Do it very slowly/gently/carefully!' Adverbs of place such as *Saman!* 'Here!', 'Come here!', 'Bring it here!', *Wasayn!* 'Come closer! Get near!', and *Kwandayn!* 'Far away!' with the meaning 'Get out of the way! Stay away from me!' are also frequently heard.

A single noun can also be used as an imperative. Thus, when one shouts *Kamin!* 'Flies!' they demand that the addressee, who sits next to the plates of food, chase flies away or cover the plates with banana leaf, a dry flower sheath of a palm, or another plate. *Paminginma!* 'Horsefly!' and *Yanggun!* 'Mosquito!' are exclamations urging the addressee to kill them. A short question can also express a command, usually a non-verbal negative command. Thus *Mi waria!?* 'What (are) you (doing)?' or 'What (do) you (want)?' is actually a command meaning 'Stop (doing) it!', 'Stop asking (for something I do not have)!' The interrogative with a specific high volume and in this case with sharp rising intonation on the last syllable can be used without a personal pronoun either in singular *Wara!?* 'What!?' or plural *Waria!?* 'What!?' with the same meaning. The most usual answer to these commanding questions is *kaya* 'no, not, nothing' in the sense of 'I am not doing anything' or 'I do not want anything'.

To protect their coconut and betel nut palms, for example, the Ambonwari use visual prohibitives in the form of leaves tied around the trunk (Vávrová 2014: 186–7). Prohibition in terms of going to the places of spirits, calling of particular names, or seeing things in the men's house is expressed with a gentle *Pasi!* 'Don't!' with additional meanings of 'never mind', 'it doesn't matter', or 'don't bother'. It is the most common among short non-verbal negative commands, often used as aversive in association with children. For example, when a small child was approaching the men's house his older sibling warned him:

(1) nggun   pasi!
     there   do.not
     Do not (go) there!

When a teacher wanted to stop children making too much noise he requested:

(2) wurumin-darin   pasi!
     play-DESID   do.not
     Do not play!

4 Canonical verbal imperatives marked with the suffix *-ra* or *-nda*

This imperative mood is made of a verb inflected with the suffix *-ra* or *-nda* (when the verb stem ends on a nasal m, n, or ng). These endings do not change according to gender and number of addressee. In tens of short clips recorded by Ambonwari children on video camera (Vávrová 2014), short verbal and non-verbal commands pop up all the time. The imperatives with -*ra* and -*nda* suffixes are by far the most often heard and are the first to be learned by Ambonwari children.

4.1 Short verbal commands

Ambonwari often use short positive imperatives without pronouns. If we take, for example, greetings and farewells, which belong to the most common daily practices, they follow the following pattern. A person asks:

(3) mi   sanggwan-a?
     2sg   where-INTER
     Where (are) you (going)?

The question is answered by either *pambin* 'upriver, upstream, east' or *masir* 'downriver, downstream, west'. Then the one who has greeted a person with the initiating question will use imperative form with a falling intonation saying either:

(4) ma-kura-p-ra!
     upriver-go-DIR-IMP
     Go (upriver, away from the speaker)!

or:

(5) kur-ia-ra!
     go-DIR-IMP
     Go (downriver, away from the speaker)!

The person will leave saying:

(6) sa-ra!
     stay-IMP
     Stay!

In the case that a person is leaving in a canoe, they will be told: *Mawambra!* 'Go (paddle upriver, away from the speaker)!' or *Apasipra!* 'Go (paddle downriver, away from the speaker)!' In this kind of short communication the verbs marked with imperative suffix, when uttered with gentle falling intonation, have non-command meanings of 'you can go, don't worry about me, I'll stay' and 'you can stay, don't worry about me, I can go alone'. This short exchange of words leaves one person behind at a particular place and sends another person off without feeling bad about not accompanying a person going to do some work or leaving someone behind and not taking him or her with them (for a similar use among the Manambu, see Aikhenvald 2010: 242–3).

Besides greetings and farewells one can hear the following abrupt request on a daily basis:

(7) yaki   a-nja   anga-ra!
     tobacco   POT-1plA   give-IMP
     Give me (lit. us) tobacco!

In this clause, the pronominal prefix *anja* in *anja angara* 'you give (it) to us', or *anjangara* when shortened, is a potential used in mild requests (see examples (18) and (19) and §7.2). It is most often taken as 'you (sg) to me'. In daily requests *yaki* 'tobacco' is often replaced with *payn* 'betel nut', *kamyang* 'betel pepper', *as* 'lime', or *imbrim* 'leaf (paper for rolling cigarettes)'. These items are part of the most common and widespread daily practices, when small gifts are constantly changing hands. Such requests could and probably should be seen as an independent form of greeting.

Many other short canonical verbal commands take the form of an abrupt order: *Apasra!* 'Go/come out (of the house)!', *Waminda!* 'Go/come into (the house)!', *Mariawkusira!* 'Talk!', *Aminda!* 'Eat!', *Kwasara!* 'Get up!', *Iminda!* 'Stand!', *Aynginda!* 'Jump in (canoe)!' Probably the most heard command in Ambonwari is the interjection *Apra!* 'Come!' with additional meanings of 'Give (it, them) to me!' or 'Let me see (it, them)!'

All the imperatives mentioned remain the same for second person singular, dual, or plural addressee. Like other Karawari imperatives they cannot have tense distinctions. Certain aspectual distinctions (example (8)), however, are common (for a similar case in Mauwake, see Berghäll 2010: 285). A series of short commands following one another as independent clauses occurs frequently. When a girl was restless in a canoe, relentlessly hanging over the prow, her mother said:

(8) mi   sa-nda-ra!   ma-sa-nda-pia-ra!
     2sg   sit-CONT-IMP   upriver-sit-CONT-DIR-IMP
     You sit (still)! Come down (towards me) and sit (still)!

4.2 Some contextual uses of commands

The imperative mood is used as much as declarative and, with the exception of elementary school where two teachers regularly use questions, more than the interrogative one. Statements can be heard one after another, often repeated either word by word or in the manner of parallelism, whenever people observe a certain action or thing or listen to talk or noise in the rainforest. Commands, especially the short ones, are also heard all the time in daily communication.

When Bapra Kumbranggawnja was explaining to her older brother Jack Amun where they would process sago the next day and how to find them she did not use the future tense but the imperative form:

(9) Jack   mi   arin   ma-wamb-ra
     Jack   2sg   tomorrow   upriver-paddle.upriver-IMP
     yaring-gina   Ambanwurin! kupa   wupuning-gina   ma
     sago.forest-OBL   Ambanwurin   big   grassland-OBL   upriver
     akisa-ra!
     land-IMP
     Jack, tomorrow you paddle upriver (away from the speaker) to Ambanwurin sago forest! Land at the big grassland upriver!

Commands can follow one another as separate or repeated clauses, where the verbs in each of them are marked with imperative suffix (see examples (8), (15), (27), (28)). Serial verb constructions are rarely inflected for imperative, but when they are the imperative marker comes at the end of the final verb. If a series of actions appear in a command, the verbs denoting the preceding actions get sequential suffix -*mbin* while only the last one is marked for imperative (see examples (29), (38)). Another possibility is when two clauses are separated by *sayn* 'and then, thus, therefore'. Then the verbs in both clauses are marked for imperative. In the following example the women wanted to make lots of sago pudding but did not have a sufficiently big dish to make it. One of them said to the other:

(10) kupan ma-kama-ra sayn saman ma-pay-pia-ra!
      big upriver-find-IMP and.then here upriver-carry-DIR-IMP
      Find a big one up (the village) and then bring (it) down here!

Causative constructions express 'the idea that the actor brings about a change of state in some object, often through coercing or otherwise persuading some secondary actor to perform it' (Foley 1986: 153). In Karawari, when the coercion is verbal (and not physical), this can be expressed by a transitive verb *yay-* 'talk' inflected by imperative or desiderative suffix on the main verb of action (see Telban 2014a: 267–8).

(11) ama pi-ka ya-r-a bini wapa-ra!
      1sg O-3sgA say-IMMED.PAST-3sg so climb-IMP
      I have told him: 'Climb!' (I made him climb)

Direct speech reports are common in myths, legends, and other narratives dealing with past events. Negative imperatives display the following pattern (see also example (33)):

(12) min pi-nga ya-r bini mi yam-in wara
      3sg O-1sgA say-IMMED.PAST so 2sg house-OBL not
      sa-r-imbi-a!
      stay-IMP-POT-NEG
      He has told me: 'Do not stay in the house!'

4.3 Imperative forms of transitive verbs

In transitive verbs the verb is first marked with the imperative suffix followed by a suffix marking a transitive object. These verb-final suffixes differ according to class and number of the noun (see Table 1).

(13) krinjing-ind-ing! (simindaning)
      split-IMP-Vsg (rattan.Vsg)
      Split it (rattan)!

When Julius was teaching about the environment in the elementary school, he ordered the children:

TABLE 1. Verbal suffixes taken by transitive verbs depending on class and number of the direct object

CLASS	SG	DL	PL
I	-*ar*	-*inggri*	-*mas* -*i* (CHILD)
II	-*ma*	-*inggri*	-*inga*
III	-*ar*		-*ia*
IV	-*a*		-*i*
V	-*ing*	-*inggri*	-*inggi*
VI	-*im*	-*imbri*	-*ia*
VII	-*i*		-*i*
VIII	-*ma*	-*mindi* (PAUCAL)	-*inggi*

(14) ipa   minda   yuwan   mina-ki-ok   wi
      3pl   this   tree   its-VIIsg-too   name.VIIsg
      ma-sari-nja-r-i!
      upriver-call.name-CONT-IMP-VIIsg
      You (pl) call the name of this tree too!

Negative command is expressed by negative particle *wara* 'not' and additional verb-final negative suffix -*a*:

(15) wanya   wara   apana-r-ing-a!   pasi!
      knife   not   throw.at-IMP-Vsg-NEG   do.not
      pa-mbay-sipas-ra!
      REDUP-carry-come.down-IMP
      Do not throw the knife (on the floor)! Do not (do it)! Carry (it) down (from the house)!

In the last example, in which three independent commands follow each other, a woman tells her daughter not to throw the knife on *andingjaming* 'floor of the house' (nominal class and number of transitive object determine the suffix -*ing* on the verb) but to bring it outside.

4.4 *Intensifying a command*

Aikhenvald writes: 'The degree of an imperative's strength can vary from a strict order implying unquestionable authority and compliance to a soft and mild command bordering on suggestion' (2010: 203). While all of this is achievable with intonation and volume of voice, there are also specific forms when increased illocutionary force is formally marked. When urgency is required the adverb *auraur* 'fast, quickly, hurry up' can be added to all commands. When standing alone, it becomes a short non-verbal command in itself.

(i) A command can be strengthened with a special word *karka* 'must' placed before the verb (see §7.1 for the imperative prefix *ka-* when command is directed towards the third person). This form of command is perceived as being very strong, and is usually addressed to children:

(16) mi   wasanarin   karka   sa-ra!
     3sg   quietly   must   sit-IMP
     You must sit quietly!

Karka can neither stay alone, without a verb marked with imperative suffix, nor be used with the short non-verbal commands discussed earlier. A further intensifying of command can be achieved by either repetition (*karka karka*) or by placing the adverb *pan* 'very, truly' before *karka*:

(17) mi   pan   karka   am-inda!
     2sg   very   must   eat-IMP
     You really must eat!

Karka is used also in commands with transitive verbs:

(18) mi   a-nja   karka   anga-r-ing   yawng!
     2sg   POT-1plA   must   give-IMP-Vsg   egg.Vsg
     You must give me egg!

A negative command cannot be expressed with *karka*. Prohibitive is realized with *wara* 'not' and the verb being marked with additional negation suffix -*a*:

(19) mi   wara   a-nja   anga-r-ing-ga   yawng!
     2sg   not   POT-1plA   give-IMP-Vsg-NEG   egg.Vsg
     Do not give me egg!

(ii) When a command is meant to be executed fast or immediately, the action verb is followed in a serial verb construction by *kura-* 'move, walk, walkabout'. This way of intensifying the requirement is possible only in canonical commands.

(20) ma   ya-kura-ra!
     upriver   get-move-IMP
     (Go and) get (it) immediately from upriver!

(iii) The strength of command can be intensified also with a verbal prefix *way-*. This prefix cannot be repeated in the way that *karka* can.[4] The prefix *way-* indicates that

---

[4] *Way-* is also a verb meaning 'burn, cook something in fire' or 'grow up, become fat' or 'float'. It can be reduplicated forming a serial verb construction as in *way-way-anga-n* (REDUP-cook.in.fire-give-PRES) 'cook in fire and give'.

the action has to be executed quickly or immediately. The command can be add-itionally strengthened by using *karka* 'must', *pan* 'very', or both.

(21) ipa   pan   way-wapa-ra!
      2pl   very   INTENS-come.up-IMP
      You (pl) come up very quickly!

5 Verbal imperatives/hortatives marked with the suffix *-n*

In another form of command the verb is marked with the suffix *-n* (verb-final position), which can be, depending on the ending on the verb stem, realized as *-in* or *-un*. Contrary to the imperative marked with suffix *-ra* or *-nda* where the addressee is near the speaker, this imperative mood is used when two people are at some spatial distance, and the speaker wants the addressee to come closer and do something.

(22) kupa   sipa-n!
      2du   bathe-IMP
      You two (come to) bathe!

When discussing short verbal commands, *mi aminda!* 'you eat!' is a command when food is near the addressee. On the other hand *mi amin!* 'you (come to) eat!' or *mi yakin amin!* 'you (come to) eat it!' (see below for transitive verbs) are markings used when a person calls someone to come (e.g. into the house) and eat. The imperative suffix *-n* on verbs (*am-in* '(come to) eat') is the same as the oblique suffix on nouns (e.g. *yam-in* 'to/in the house'), with the same directional meaning of coming or going to some place.

The imperative, when a verb is marked with suffix *-n*, overlaps with the hortative form. It is therefore used also for the first person dual and plural, when a practice is agreed between two parties and they are co-performers. Similarly to Yimas (Foley 1991: 273), this hortative mood expresses a strong wish in terms of wanting to do something together or true exhortation (e.g. 'let us do something!'). In other words, if for the second person regardless of number the verbal suffix *-n* means 'you (come to) do it!', for the first person dual and plural it means 'let us (go to) do it!'. When there is a meeting or fight somewhere in the village and people want to go there and hear from the participants what is going on, they say:

(23) apia   andi-n!
      1pl   hear-IMP
      Let us (go to) hear!

5.1 Transitive verbs

In transitive verbs when the addressee is second person singular the pronominal prefix additionally marks the imperative mood. The first part of this prefix changes according to the nominal class and number of the transitive object while the second part, marked with imperative -*kin*, remains unchanged:

(24) mi   i-kin   mamanggay-n   inja   kay!
      2sg   VIIsgO-IMP   paddle-IMP   this.VIIsg   canoe.VIIsg
      You (come to) paddle this canoe!

(25) Sanggra   yakus   ya-kin   aw-un!
      Sanggra   string.bag   IIIsgO-IMP   get-IMP
      Sanggrmari, (come to) get the string bag!

A ditransitive verb gets additional marking for the third person (-*a* for singular and -*mbin* for dual and plural):

(26) Maya   yandia   kanggining   ya-kin-a   sipanga-n-a!
      Maya   these   something.IIIpl   IIIplO-IMP-downriver   wash-IMP-3sgA
      Maya (come to) wash his/her things!

Ambonwari use commands also in Christian prayers and songs sung in the local vernacular (e.g. *Maria konggong mi anja singgaminda!* 'Mary, show us/me the (right) path!') and when talking to spirits as in the following example.

In August 2011 a newborn baby suddenly got sick. At the same time some men found a dead python with a cloth, in which the baby's placenta had been buried, in its mouth. It was the area of important spirits of the land (see Telban and Vávrová 2010). Late in the afternoon the big men went to talk to them. A stick 'decorated' with betel nuts, shells, and money was thrust into the ground as an offering to the spirits. After a man called the names of several spirits of the land, he directed his talk towards Ibrismari, who lives in a nearby creek and is beside the 'spirit of the village', the main spirit of Ambonwari.

(27) mi   ap-ra!   mi   mariawk   ya-kin   su-n!
      2sg   come-IMP   2sg   talk.IIIsg   IIIsgO-IMP   talk-IMP
      You come! You (come to) tell your story!

Then the men decided to call the 'big' spirit of the village too and offer all of them a stick to which betel nuts and money were attached:

(28) mi   imingga   binan   makuria-ra!   mi-ok
      2sg   village   its.IVsg   come.downriver-IMP   2sg-too
      mi   apas-ra!
      2sg   come.out-IMP
      You (the spirit) of the village, come downriver (towards us)! You too come out (from the ground)!
      ipa   sakrim   pi-nan   aw-un!
      2pl   stick   VIsgO-2plA   get-IMP
      You (pl) (come to) get the stick!

If there is a series of actions following one another in a single sentence, only the verb in the last clause gets marked for imperative. When a girl was looking into the lenses of a camera, she saw *anggindarkwi* 'reflections, images' of water in them. She called to her brother:

(29) wasayn   kambasa-mbɨn   i-kɨn   sanggwa-n!
      near   stand-SEQ   IVplO-IMP   look-IMP
      (Come to) stand closer and see them!

When command is directed towards second person dual or plural, as was the case in example (28) above, the second part of the pronominal prefix in transitive verbs is not marked with imperative *-kɨn-* any more. The whole prefix, which is made of two parts, follows ordinary inflection for transitive object O and transitive subject A. The verb-final imperative suffix *-n* stays the same.

(30) ipa   kɨ-nan   am-ɨn   mambayng-gi!
      3pl   VplO-2plA   eat-IMP   banana-Vpl
      You (pl) (come to) eat bananas!

Negative form is expressed with negative particle *wara* 'not' and verb in future tense:

(31) mi   wara   i-n   amɨng-ɨr   sipi
      2sg   not   VIIsgO-2sgA   eat-FUT   sago.pancake.VIIsg
      You will not (be allowed/able to) eat sago pancake.

6 Potential form used in mild commands

There is another form of a second person imperative, when the verb marked for imperative gets the additional potential suffix *-mbi*. While discussing this kind of expression with the villagers, they explained that the addressee had in the past already thought or talked about doing something. Although being aware of his or her intention, however, it is not known if the action will actually be carried out. There is a possibility or ability. The commander actually wishes that the addressee will finally execute the action, and demands from him or her to do it.

(32) mi   simɨ-nd-ɨmbi!
      2sg   talk-IMP-POT
      You should talk! (You thought about it and now you should talk!)

Prohibitive (see also example (12)) is made with negative particle *wara* 'not', potential suffix *-mbi*, and verb-final negative suffix *-a*. Such a prohibitive is perceived as a kind of advice, instruction, or tentative obligation:

(33) Sten   wasayn   wara   sa-nda-r-ɨmbi-a!
      Stan   near   not   sit-CONT-IMP-POT-NEG
      Do not sit so close to Stan!

7 A note on non-canonical commands

First and third person imperatives have a special form and overlap in terms of the verbal morphological marker *-mba*. However, there is a difference in the pronominal prefix. As there is no space to enter into the complexity of transitive and especially ditransitive verbs, I will address only the most general characteristics of the verbs inflected for 'jussive' and 'hortative' mood.

7.1 Third person imperatives

In a request, directive, or instruction oriented towards the third person, the first part of the pronominal prefix is imperative *ka-* while the second part changes according to nominal class and number of a transitive subject (see Table 2). At the same time the verb is marked with the imperative suffix *-mba*.

(34) mi   mi-nya-ki   ka-i   sa-mba!
      2sg   2sg-POSS-VIIsg   IMP-VIIsgA   stay-IMP
      Let your (thing) stay!

(35) mɨn   ka-n   yay-mba!
      3sg   IMP-IsgA   cry-IMP
      Let him cry (he must cry)!

To change imperative into declarative, the verb-final suffix becomes *-m*: *mɨn ka-n-yay-m* 'let him cry'. Negative third person imperative is achieved with negative particle *wara* 'not' and verb-final negative suffix *-nga*:

TABLE 2. Prefixes used for non-canonical obligatory action (with additional inflections for location in brackets: the first for upriver and the second for downriver)

	Classes I and II	Class III	Class IV	Class V
SG	*ka-n(-ma,-a)*	*ka-n(-ma,-a)*	*ka(-ma,-ka)*	*ka-nggi(-ma,-ka)*
DU	*ka-nggri(-ma,-ka)*			*ka-nggri(-ma,-ka)*
PL	*ka-mbu(-ma,-ka)*	*ka-ia(-ma,-ka)*	*ka-i(-ma,-ka)*	*ka-nggi(-ma,-ka)*
CHILDREN PL	*ka-i(-ma,-ka)*			
	Class VI	Class VII	Class VIII	
SG	*ka-mbi(-ma,-ka)*	*ka-i(-ma,-ka)*	*ka-n(-ma,-a)*	
DU	*ka-mbri(-ma,-)*		*ka-nggri(-ma,-ka)*	
PL	*ka-ia(-ma,-)*	*ka-i(-ma,-ka)*	*ka-nggi(-ma,-ka)*	

(36) nggri   wara   ka-nggri-ipunggia-mba-nga!
     2du   not   IMP-IduA-jump-IMP-NEG
     Don't let them (du) jump (they should not jump)!

7.2 First person imperatives

Combination of imperative mood and potential modality is used for the first person imperative (optative), when the speaker is involved in a speech act saying that they want to and should do something. The verb is marked with imperative suffix *-mba*. The potential prefix *and-* is realized for different numbers as follows: *andika* (1sg), *angga* (1du), or *anja* (1pl) (e.g. *apia anja siamba* 'let us sing and dance'). In the following example the imperative inflection in the first sentence is followed by the 'hortative' inflection in the second. During a dispute between a man and two other members of the same clan, he said to them:

(37) kupa   kupa-na   kay   ka-ra!   ama   ama-na   kay
     2du   2du-OBL   way   live/be/stay-IMP   1sg   1sg-OBL   way
     and-ika   kay-mba!
     POT-1sg   live/be/stay-IMP
     You two live (your life) your way! Let me live (it) my way!

A series of actions is marked in the same way as in example (29):

(38) nggoka!   ama   and-ika   pay-mbin   kwasa-mba!
     wait   1sg   POT-1sg   sleep-SEQ   get.up-IMP
     Wait! Let me sleep first and then get up!

Negative imperative for the first person is, like the one for the third person, achieved with negative particle *wara* 'not' and verb-final negative suffix *-nga*:

(39) ama   wara   and-ika   kwasa-mba-nga!
     1sg   not   POT-1sg   get.up-IMP-NEG
     I don't want to get up!

8 Conclusion

Short verbal and non-verbal commands are heard all the time in Ambonwari. They are part of both language socialization and intimate relationships between people and between people and other beings. In a society where honorific registers towards socially superior addressees do not exist, the same forms of imperatives are used towards children, senior men and women, spirits, or God. The general characteristic of imperatives is falling intonation and the higher volume of voice. When rising intonation is used, mainly at times of irritation and annoyance, there is a specific high pitch on the last syllable. Canonical imperatives may be differentiated into three groups: those marked with *-ra* or *-nda* ('do it!'), those marked with *-n* ('come to do

it!'), and those marked with potential *-mbi* ('should do it!'). Non-canonical imperatives directed toward the first person can be marked either with *-n* ('let's go to do it')
or with *-mba* and potential prefix *and-* ('let's do it', 'should do it'). Imperatives
directed toward the third person are marked with *-mba* and imperative prefix *ka-*
('let them do it'). Negative imperatives—the simplest being with addition of *pasi!*
'don't!'—have fewer forms than positive imperatives, which is common in many
languages (see Chapter 1). While a negative particle *wara* 'not' is used in negative
constructions of both declarative and imperative clauses, it is the morphological
markings on verbs which make a distinction together with a specific intonation and
volume of voice.

Imperatives and prohibitives are an indispensable part of Ambonwari social linguistics and sociology of life generally. Commands are a necessary part of close relationships between the people, sometimes spilling over into playfulness and joyfulness.
This does not mean that people do not get annoyed and irritated with each other. To
the contrary, they do. These annoyances, irritations, and recurrent desires prompt
people, more so in relation to children, to raise their voice and repeat their requests,
even using physical force. A command or prohibitive thus becomes a combination of
illocutionary force of directive speech act and physically directive action. All this,
however, depends on kin and other social relations, into which strategies of communication, including those pertaining to commands, are embedded.

References

Aikhenvald, Alexandra Y. 2008. *The Manambu language of East Sepik, Papua New Guinea.*
Oxford: Oxford University Press.
Aikhenvald, Alexandra Y. 2010. *Imperatives and commands.* Oxford: Oxford University Press.
Benveniste, Émile. 1971. *Problems in general linguistics.* Coral Gables: University of Miami
Press.
Berghäll, Liisa. 2010. Mauwake reference grammar. PhD Dissertation, University of Helsinki,
Faculty of Arts.
Foley, William A. 1986. *The Papuan languages of New Guinea.* Cambridge: Cambridge
University Press.
Foley, William A. 1991. *The Yimas language of New Guinea.* Stanford: Stanford University
Press.
Foley, William A. 2016. 'The languages of the Sepik-Ramu Basin and environs', pp. 197–432 of
The languages and linguistics of the New Guinea area: A comprehensive guide, edited by Bill
Palmer. Berlin: Mouton de Gruyter.
Rumsey, Alan. 2003. 'Language, desire, and the ontogenesis of intersubjectivity', *Language &*
Communication 23: 169–87.
Rumsey, Alan. n.d. Language, affect and the inculcation of social norms in the New Guinea
highlands and beyond. Manuscript.

Schieffelin, Bambi B. 1986. 'Teasing and shaming in Kaluli children's interactions', pp. 165–81 of *Language socialization across cultures*, edited by Bambi B. Schieffelin and Elinor Ochs. Cambridge: Cambridge University Press.

Schieffelin, Bambi B. 1990. *The give and take of everyday life: Language socialisation of Kaluli children*. Cambridge: Cambridge University Press.

Telban, Borut. 1993. 'Having heart: On caring and resentment in Ambonwari, Papua New Guinea', *Bulletin of the Slovene Ethnographic Museum* 3(54): 158–77.

Telban, Borut. 1998. *Dancing through time: A Sepik cosmology*. Oxford: Clarendon Press.

Telban, Borut. 2004. 'Fear, shame and the power of the gaze in Ambonwari, Papua New Guinea', *Anthropological Notebooks* 10(1): 5–25.

Telban, Borut. 2008. 'The poetics of the crocodile: Changing cultural perspectives in Ambonwari', *Oceania* 78(2): 217–35.

Telban, Borut. 2014a. 'Saying, seeing and knowing among the Karawari of Papua New Guinea', pp. 260–77 of *The grammar of knowledge: A cross-linguistic typology*, edited by Alexandra Y. Aikhenvald and R. M. W. Dixon. Oxford: Oxford University Press.

Telban, Borut. 2014b. 'The poetics of the flute: Fading imagery in a Sepik society' *Folklore* 125(1): 92–112.

Telban, Borut. n.d. The ethnographer's dictionary of Ambonwari's Karawari. Manuscript.

Telban, Borut and Vávrová, Daniela. 2010. 'Places and spirits in a Sepik society', *The Asia Pacific Journal of Anthropology* 11(1): 17–33.

Vávrová, Daniela. 2014. 'Skin has eyes and ears': Audio-visual ethnography in a Sepik Society. PhD Thesis, James Cook University.

14

Commands in Wolaitta

AZEB AMHA

1 Introduction

Wolaitta (also written as Wolayta) is spoken in south-west Ethiopia, in the Zonal administration that is known by the same name. Wolaitta is the largest Omotic language with about 1.7 million native speakers, as indicated in the 2007 national Population and Housing Census. Since 1994, the language is used as the medium of instruction in primary and secondary schools and in vocational colleges, local administration, and court sessions. A local radio station transmits programmes using Wolaitta and Amharic alternatively; the latter is one of the official languages of the Federal State.

In his classification of Omotic languages, Fleming (1976: 47) places Wolaitta as part of the North Ometo group of Omotic. Omotic itself is a member of the Afroasiatic phylum. The linguistic neighbours of Wolaitta are the Cushitic languages Alaba, Hadiyya, and Kambata in the north, the closely related North Ometo languages Dawro in the west, Gofa (of Kuch'a variety) and Gamo in the south, Ganjule, Gatsame (Omotic), and Bayso (Cushitic) in the south-east. Its eastern boundary is the Bilate river, separating it from Sidama (Cushitic).

Wolaitta is a synthetic language exhibiting both agglutinating and fusional properties. Open word classes include nouns, verbs, adjectives, and ideophones. Pronouns, demonstratives, and numerals each constitute a closed word class. A small set of adverbs are lexical: *haʔʔí* 'now', *wónta* 'earlier', *háa* 'here', and *yáa* 'there' whereas adjective plus locative *-n* or ideophones are widely used for the expression of adverbial notions, e.g. *lóddan* 'slowly' < *lódda* 'slow' + *-n*.

Morphological categories that are marked on nouns include definiteness, number, gender, and case. The last three are also distinguished in pronouns. Two gender distinctions are made: masculine (M) and feminine (F) that are marked in nouns and in third person singular pronouns and verbs. Similarly a two-way number distinction is made: singular unmarked and plural morphologically marked by *-t* (on most

Commands. First edition. Alexandra Y. Aikhenvald and R. M. W. Dixon (eds)
This chapter © Azeb Amha 2017. First published 2017 by Oxford University Press

nouns) and -*nt* (on some relational nouns, e.g. *miʃʃontá* 'sisters' versus *miʃʃó* 'sister'). Several core and peripheral cases, including nominative, accusative, genitive, dative, ablative, and locative, are morphologically distinguished. These nominal categories are strongly interdependent: for example, the value for definiteness determines whether accusative case is zero-marked/unmarked or overt. Overt case affixes in turn have morphological variants depending on the gender of the noun: for example, accusative case marker on masculine nouns is -*á* whereas on feminine nouns it is -*ó*. Some case markers show syncretism between masculine singular and plural nouns: so, the accusative marker is -*á* for masculine singular as well as plural nouns whereas the genitive case has distinct forms for feminine, masculine, and plural: *naʔée keettáa* 'the girl's house', *naʔáa keettáa* 'the boy's house', *naatú keettáa* 'the children's house'. In glossing the syncretized nominative and accusative cases, I use the labels that correspond to the singular forms.

Verbs are morphologically marked for subject-agreement; object agreement is not marked. Tense (past, present, future), aspect (perfective, imperfective), mood (declarative, interrogative, imperative), and negative or positive polarity are distinguished (see Appendix). Adjectives share morphological properties with both nouns and verbs but they can still be established as a distinct class on syntactic (and semantic) grounds. Productive verb-derivation processes including causative, passive, intensive/iterative/distributive are used. Several verb-to-noun and noun-to-noun or noun-to-adjective derivations exist (e.g. 'agentive' *zalʔánʧa* 'trader' from *zalʔé* 'trade', and '(abstract) noun' *hiyyesátetta* 'poorness' from *hiyyeésa* 'poor'). However, noun-to-verb derivations are restricted to inchoatives, e.g. *kawó* 'king' and *kawotiísi* 'he became king'.

Constituent order in intransitive clauses is SV and AOV in transitive ones. Generally phrasal modifiers precede the head and the language uses suffixes only. Grammatical relations are marked on nouns by case affixes. Case marking is differential. Definite and indefinite S/A-nouns are designated by distinct nominative case markers. O is morphologically marked by the accusative case only when the noun is definite. S is obligatorily co-indexed on the verb. Object is not marked on the verb at all.

In texts clause chains are common. These are a series of dependent clauses followed by a final independent clause headed by a fully inflected verb. Clause chains involving anterior and simultaneous converbs morphologically indicate whether or not the subject of subsequent clauses is the same or different.

The data used in the present contribution are mainly from narratives and conversations which I recorded during various field trips. Transcripts from overheard spontaneous speech as well as some extracts from books published in the Wolaitta language (school textbooks and collections of stories) are also included. Occasionally, I used my own native speaker intuitions to illustrate some grammatical features.

2 Sentence-type distinction

In Wolaitta, declarative or indicative, interrogative and imperative/optative moods are distinguished. The values for these morphological categories are marked by affixes that also indicate person, number, and gender of the subject (PNG), tense (present, future, or past), and polarity (positive or negative) values. The order of morphological slots and a few of the exponents of PNG, tense or mood can be recognized but it is impossible to consistently isolate morpheme boundaries in the various paradigms without assuming a number of zero-affixes, double-marking or without making recourse to historical accounts. For this reason I do not analyse the morphemes following matrix verbs in the first line of examples, but rather separate the glosses with a period (.) in the second line of translation.

2.1 Declarative

Affirmative and negative declarative clauses are morphologically distinguished from affirmative and negative interrogative ones. In example (1), the affixes on the verb *ʔoottádasa* 'you did' contrast with that on *gaásu* 'she said' only in the value of person: second versus third person. *ʔoottádasa* 'you did' and *yábeíkka* 'you did not come' in (2) have the same value for PNG, tense and mood but they contrast in polarity: i.e. affirmative/positive versus negative polarity.

(1) číi   lóʔʔo   ʔoott-ádasa   g-aásu
     no,   good   do-2SG.PAST.AFF.DEC   say-3SGF.PAST.AFF.DEC
     She said, 'No, you did well/the right thing'.

(2) ʔammant-íya   lágg-íya-ra
     feel.confident-IMPERV.SU.REL   friend-DEF.M.ACC-COMIT
     y-ábeíkka
     come-2SG.PAST.NEG.DEC
     You did not come with a reliable friend.

The main verbs in examples (3a) and (3b) respectively illustrate the inflection of the verb for third person past tense affirmative and negative declarative.

(3a) soh-úwa   ʃamm-ídí   duússa
     place-DEF.M.ACC   buy-SS.ANT.CONVB₂   living.ACC
     doómm-íisi
     start-3SGM.PAST.AFF.DEC
     Having bought a house he started living (there).

(3b) mátʃʃó   ʔekk-íbeénna
     wife.ACC   take-3SGM.PAST.NEG.DEC
     He is not married.

See Appendix for the inflection of the verb for the remaining person, number, and gender values in the affirmative declarative mood.

2.2 *Polar interrogative*

Polar interrogative clauses have distinct inflection for person, number, and gender of the subject, tense, and polarity. Compare the second person singular subject, past tense, affirmative interrogative verb *ʔúyádíi* 'did you drink?' in (4a) with the negative interrogative verb *demmábeíkkíí* 'didn't you find?' in (4b).

(4a) tukké   ʔúy-ádíi
      coffee.ACC   drink-2SG.PAST.AFF.INTER
      Did you drink coffee?

(4b) néná   maadd-íya   ʔasá   demm-ábeíkkíí
      2SG.ACC   help-IMPERV.SU.REL   person.ACC   find-2SG.PAST.NEG.INTER
      Didn't you find someone who would help you?

The highlighted verbs in example (5) illustrate the second person singular affirmative and negative question forms; they differ from the main interrogative verbs in (4) in their value for tense. The sentence in (5) can be interpreted as a threat, a follow-up for unheeded command.

(5) haʔʔí   miízz-iyo   háa   kess-áy
     now   cow-DEF.F.ACC   here   take.out-2SG.PRES.AFF.INTER
     kess-íkkí
     take.out-2SG.PRES.NEG.INTER
     Now, would you take out the cow immediately or not?
     (lit. Now, do you take out the cow or don't you take it out to here?)

Fully inflected main verbs illustrated in (1)–(5) above may be affixed with discourse-functional or attitudinal morphemes, e.g. *-yye* in (6).

(6) háa   gel-ídá   dóʔa   ʔubbáa-ppe   né
     here   enter-PERV.SU.REL   w.animal.ACC   all.ACC-ABL   2SG.SU
     goob-áy-yye
     be.strong-2SG.PRES.AFF.INTER-DM
     Are you stronger than all the wild animals that have entered here?
     (*Wolaitta Tales*, p. 75)

Without the addition of *-yye*, the verb form *goobáy* 'are you strong?' in (6) forms a complete grammatical utterance, which would be interpreted as a simple information question. The addition of *-yye* results in a dubitative meaning to the sentence: 'you seem to think that you are strongest but that does not seem to be the case'.

3 Imperative

The imperative in Wolaitta forms an independent mood category contrasting with the declarative and interrogative that we introduced in §§2.1 and 2.2 respectively. It is used in commands, wishes, blessings, curses, and leave-taking. In the present section we examine the structure of this clause type in detail, by dividing it into three sections along person distinction. First we briefly evaluate earlier studies on Wolaitta imperatives, showing analytic and terminological differences (§3.1). In §§3.2–3.6, we present alternative analyses and interpretation where relevant. In §3.7 verbal morphological categories of imperatives are summarized and compared with those of other main clauses. In §4 we discuss the use of imperative clauses, concluding the chapter with general remarks in §5.

3.1 Previous studies

Previous studies agree that there is a third mood type that is morphologically distinct from the declarative and interrogative. However, the studies have differences in the labels used, in the morphological forms that are included or excluded as part of the construction, and in the meanings attributed to some of the morphemes within the construction type. For example, Adams (1983: 123–5) divides clause types which he identified as 'command variants' into two: imperative (second and third person) and requestive (first person). In Table 1 we present the complete inflectional possibilities of *b-* 'go' to illustrate morphological differences along the person distinction Adams established. Lamberti and Sottile (1997: 162) also have a single 'jussive/imperative' paradigm with first, second, and third person forms but

TABLE 1. The morphology of Wolaitta affirmative imperatives following Adams (1983)

	'Command variant'	
	Imperative	Requestive
	2nd and 3rd person only	1st person only
1sg	——	b-óo 'Let me go!/may I go?'
1pl	——	b-iinóo 'Let us go!/may we go?'
2sg	b-á 'go!' (sg)	
2pl	b-iité 'go!' (pl)	
3sgF	b-ú 'let her go!'	
3sgM	b-ó 'let him go!'	
3pl	b-óná 'let them go!'	

the morphological forms they present for first persons are different from those shown in Table 1: e.g. *tá/nu ʔoottaná* 'let me/us work!'. However, as most other authors agree, *-aná* marks the future tense affirmative declarative/indicative, not the imperative. Hirut Woldemariam (1999: 68–70) uses 'imperative mood' to refer to verbs which take the same affixes as the second person forms in Table 1 and she uses 'jussive' to refer to those corresponding to the third person forms. Wakasa (2008: 786–95), on the other hand, labels the second and third person verb forms illustrated in Table 1 as 'optative'. Following the suggestion in Chapter 1, I decided to use here a single label (imperative) for second and third person forms rather than using 'imperative' versus 'jussive' or 'optative' on the basis of the person of the subject.

The studies mentioned above treat the first person forms differently. Adams (1983) notes the affixes in the first person command resemble question forms prosodically (vowel length and rising intonation), hence his label 'requestive'. Wakasa (2008: 786) explicitly states that his 'optative' construction, which 'roughly corresponds to the "imperative" and the "jussive" in Semitic linguistics', lacks first person forms. Hirut Woldemariam also excludes the first person forms in her discussion of the imperative/jussive. It is correct that the first person imperative forms share some formal and functional properties with question forms. However, they also exhibit morphological and semantic properties which distinguish them from other first person question forms and somehow relate them to the imperative mood (cf. §3.4).

Finally, existing studies also differ in identification of subtypes of commands. Hirut Woldemariam (1999: 70) reports a 'polite imperative' for the second person singular: *pittarki* 'please sweep!'; whereas Wakasa (2008: 800–2) and Adams (1983: 215) analyse similar constructions as 'interrogative' and 'hypothetical-desiderative aspect'. See §3.6 for discussion on this.

3.2 Second person imperatives

Positive command directed to a single addressee is formed by suffixing *-á* to the verb stem (7a). The second person singular marker in affirmative declarative and interrogative clauses is formally distinct. Thus *-á* in (7a) indicates both mood and the person and number of the addressee. Tense is not marked in imperative clauses but aspect can be indicated, as illustrated for the completive in example (7b).

(7a) wot't'-á   ne   miʧʧ-íyo   tooh-úwa
      run-2SG.AFF.IMP   2SG.GEM   sister-DEF.F.ACC   bundle-DEF.M.ACC
      maadd-á
      help-2SG.AFF.IMP
      Hurry! Help your sister with carrying the bundle!

(7b) ʔasá-y   y-eennán   keettáa
     person-DEF.M.NOM   come-FUT.NEG.CNV   house.DEF.M.ACC
     pítt-árg-á
     sweep-COMPL-2SG.AFF.IMP
     Clean up the house before people come!

When command is directed to more than one person the plural imperative marker
-*ité* is affixed to the verb stem, as in (8), which is an instruction in a textbook exercise
directed to pupils in general.

(8) goʔétt-ído   mat'aáfa-t-a   malaat-ité
     benefit.from-PERV.OBJ.REL   book-PL-PL/DEF.M.ACC   indicate-2PL.IMP
     Indicate the books which you used as references.

All lexical verbs can be inflected for affirmative singular and plural imperative using
the morphemes -*á* and -*ité*, including existential and secondary 'BE or copula' verbs
such as *han-* and *deʔ-* in (9).

(9a) neé-ssi   loʔʔaá-ga   han-á
     2SG.GEN-DAT   be.good-IMPERV.REL-M.NOMZ.ACC   BE/happen-2SG.IMP
     Do /be what you like! (i.e. it is your business)

(9b) lóʔʔo   deʔ-ité
     good   exist-2PL.IMP
     Stay well! Goodbye!

The (final) vowel of the imperative can be articulated extra-long to express warning
after initial command or advice, e.g. *ʔaggáaaa* 'stop!' (implying: 'it would not be good
for you if you do not stop'). Also, it is common to lengthen the final vowel of the
imperative morpheme in a call, announcement, or command addressed to a general
public or to dispersed and undetermined audience, e.g. *sibseba kíyiteeeee* 'get out for
the public meeting!'.

3.3 *Third person imperatives*

The third person imperative is marked by -*ó* (M.sg), -*ú* (F.sg), and -*óna* (M/F PL). It
is used in indirect commands in which the speaker and the participant(s) that carry
out the action are not in a direct or face-to-face communication situation. The
utterance in (10) is a command a lady who was away from home on a family visit
gives to her family members back home through a messenger.

(10) miiʃʃá-y   nuúnnu   máta-n   **deʔ-ó**   ʔí-ppe
     money-DEF.M.NOM   Nuunnu   near-LOC   exist-3SGM.IMP   3SGF.GEN-ABL
     ʔekk-á   ʔekk-á   ʔabb-íya
     take-Sh.ANT.CONVB₁   take-Sh.ANT.CONVB₁   ʔabbe-DEF.F.NOM

naa-t-ú-ssí	giyáa	**zal?-ú**
child-PL-GEN-DAT	market.DEF.M.ACC	trade-3SGF.IMP

Let the money be kept by Nuunnu; taking (part of the money) from her (i.e. Nuunnu) as needed, let Abbe do shopping for the children!

Example (11) illustrates the third person plural imperative form. It is a translation from the Creation Story of a command/wish God made giving privilege to humans over other animals.

(11)	biittá	bólla	wot't'-í	k'aat't'-íya	meréta
	earth/soil	body	run-Sh.ANT.CONVB₂	move-IMPERF.SU.REL	creature

?ubbá	haar-óna[1]
all	own-3PL.IMP

Let them own every creature on earth!

In the expression of blessings or wishes, either the second or third person imperative form can be used: for example, *diʃʃá* 'Be big, be successful!' or *néná t'oossí diʃʃó* 'May God make you successful!'. Note that *diʃʃ-* is an active intransitive verb whereas *diʃʃ-* is its transitive/causative counterpart. In the former the addressee is (experiencer) subject while in the latter s/he is the affected object (*néná* 'you.OBJ') and *t'oossá* 'God' is the agent, marked for the nominative case. In both cases the addressee is the participant directly affected by the outcome of the event rather than realizing it him/herself.

3.4 First person requestive, optative or imperative?

As mentioned in §3.1, the first person singular and plural verbal forms with *-óo* and *-óníi* are understood as questions, correctly labelled 'requestive' in Adams (1983). Unlike other polar interrogative forms in the language (cf. §2.2 and Appendix), this verbal form is typically used in request for permission, as in (12).

(12)	tá	?íntenaa-ra	bóo
	1SG.Sh.SU	2PL.OBJ-COMIT	go.1SG.REQSTV

May I go with you?

The requestive can also be used in an information question (13a) and it typically generates a response in the imperative (13b).

(13a)	yoot-ékkéti	?au-gáa	bírš-óo
	tell-2SG.POL/2PL.PRES.NEG.INTER	which-M.NOMZ.ACC	untie-1SG.REQSTV

Sir/madam, wouldn't you tell me? Which one may I untie?

---

[1] *wot't'- k'aat't'-* [run- move-] is an idiomatic expression of 'everything', 'things in total'.

(13b) k'eera-nn-ó   bírʃ-a
       small-F.NOMZ-DEF.F.ACC   untie-2SG.IMP
       Untie the smaller one!

A positive verbal response to a canonical second person singular imperative (14a) involves the phatic interjection or particle ʔeró 'OK, all right' expressing agreement or obedience (14b). In contrast, a positive reply to the requestive (15a) by default involves ʔéé 'yes' (15b), further confirming that clauses with -óo and -ónii are not commands, as translations in earlier studies ('let me...!') suggest.

(14a) má   eat!

(14b) ʔeró maaná   All right, OK, I will eat.

(15a) móo   May I eat?

(15b) ʔéé má   Yes, eat!

It would not be ungrammatical in (15b) if a reply to the requestive is ʔeró má 'All right, OK, eat!' but in this case the utterance is not a direct reaction to the original request (15a), but a positive reply countering the speaker's intended response, i.e. s/he is inclined to reply in the negative ʧíi moóppa 'No, don't eat!' but changes his/her mind and gives a positive response ʔeró má 'All right, OK, eat!'.

Unlike the distribution sketched above about the use of ʔeró 'all right, OK' versus ʔéé 'yes' in commands versus requestives, the same particle, ʧíi 'no', is used both in a negative response to a command and in the requestive:

(16a) má   eat!

(16b) ʧíi miíkke   No, I won't eat!

(17a) móo   May I eat?

(17b) ʧíi moóppa   No, don't eat!

The example in (18) illustrates the use of the first person plural requestive.

(18)   [Siblings to their eldest sister]:
       ʔaawá-y   minj-oó-gáa-ppe   ʔekk-inóo
       father-DEF.M.NOM   save.OBJ.REL-M.NOMZ.ACC-ABL   take-1PL.REQSTV
       May we take (some grain) from that father has put away?

The response to the requestive in (18) is a negative imperative/prohibitive in (19):

(19)   ʧíi   he-gáa   boʧʧʃ-ópp-íte
       no   DIST-M.NOMZ.ACC   touch-IMP.NEG-2PL.IMP
       No, don't take any of that, do not touch it!

Wolaitta does not make morphological distinction of inclusive and exclusive reference in the first person plural. When the context is not known, it is difficult to tell whether a requestive such as that in (18) is a permissive question or a suggestion for an activity involving the addressee. The reply in (19) indicates that the addressee is not included among the referents of the first person plural form *-inóo* in (18). If the response was *ɟíí boʧʧókko* 'No, we will not touch/take it!' (first person negative declarative), then the request in (18) can be interpreted as including the addressee, a suggestion for a collective action rather than a request for permission.

To conclude the present section, the first person verbal forms with *-óo* and *-ónii* are question forms (cf. Wakasa 2008, Adams 1983). So why do we deal with them in the discussion of the imperative? First, because requestives typically generate responses in the imperative unlike the other first person interrogative clauses. Second, and more important, because they are negated in the same way as canonical imperatives, as will be shown in the discussion in the next section. Negation of other interrogative clauses is totally different from negation of the requestives (cf. Appendix).

3.5 *Negative imperatives or prohibitives*

The negative imperative is marked by *-ópp/-úpp* affixed to the verb stem. It is obligatorily followed by the person and mood marking morphemes discussed in §§3.2–3.4.

(20a)   ta   miiʃʃáa   boʧʧ-ópp-á
        1SG.GEN   goods.DEF.M.ACC   touch-IMP.NEG-2SG.IMP
        Do not touch/use my stuff!

(20b)   símí   táná   beʔ-iíddí   ʔotoró
        DM   1SG.OBJ   see-SS.SIMUL.CONVB₂   arrogance.ACC
        ʔotorétt-ópp-íte
        be.arrogant-IMP.NEG-2PL.IMP
        Seeing what has happened to me (you should behave different): do not be arrogant.

Other than affixing *-ópp/-úpp* the clausal structure of the imperative is kept intact and the same person, number, and gender distinctions are made. This suggests that we are dealing with the negative counterpart of the imperative rather than a separate 'prohibitive' mood. The various person, number, and gender forms of the negative imperative are given in (21).

(21)   2sg   ʔekk-ópp-a   Do not take! (2sg)
       2pl   ʔekk-ópp-íte   Do not take! (2pl)
       3sgM   ʔekk-ópp-ó   Let him not take! or Do not let him take!
       3sgF   ʔekk-úpp-ú   Let her not take!
       3pl   ʔekk-ópp-óná   Let them not take!
       1sg   ʔekk-ópp-óo   You would rather that I do not take?/Shouldn't I take?
       1pl   ʔekk-ópp-ónii   You would rather that we do not take? Shouldn't we take?

The first person forms *ʔekkóppóo* and *ʔekkóppónii* in (21) show the same segmental and inflectional pattern as the second and third person negative imperative verbs. However, as their translations above indicate, the first person forms are questions and they are not commands (see §3.4 for first person requestives). In these forms, whether or not the event in question (e.g. *ʔekk* 'take' in (21)) takes place is mainly dependent on the wish or judgement of the addressee rather than that of the speaker. That the first person form is different in the expression of the imperative mood is further confirmed in the so-called 'polite imperative', to which we turn in the next section.

3.6 Polite imperatives

Polite, honorific, or respect form is expressed by using second and third person plural pronouns and/or verbs, in the imperative as well as in declarative and interrogative clauses. The speaker's choice in using the polite form is influenced by age, social status (such as marriage, having children), position (holding public office), and/or occupation (e.g. teacher–student relation irrespective of age and/or social status). The use of polite forms implies not only social but emotional distance or familiarity between speech participants. Perhaps for this reason, children rarely address or refer to their parents using the honorific/polite form. Also, it is common to change from polite address and reference to common/direct address and reference when familiarity increases.

The utterance in (22) is addressed to a single individual but both the dative pronoun and the imperative verb are in the plural.

(22) ʔinté-ssi   túma   táná   maar-íté
      2PL.OBJ-DAT   true   1SG.OBJ   forgive-2PL/POL.IMP
      You are right, forgive me!

In a joking remark to a young girl about the way she helped in the kitchen (23), the speaker used the third person plural imperative verb (*beʔóna*) with the corresponding polite form *ne ʔaayéntí* 'your mother' designating the subject of the imperative verb (implying that the mother would reproach or punish the girl if she found out).

(23) miiʃʃá   koror-iss-aása   ne
      goods.ACC   IDEO-CAUS-2SG.PRES.AFF.DEC   2SG.GEN
      ʔaayéntí   ha-gáa   beʔ-óna
      mother.KIN.PL/POL.PL.NOM   his-M.NOMZ.ACC   see-3PL.IMP
      You are making noise and not handling the utensils well. Let your mother see this!

Wolaitta also has a special construction that is interpreted as polite imperative in Adams (1983: 282) and Hirut Woldemariam (1999: 70). Adams (1983: 282) provides the following example to illustrate the polite imperative.[2]

(24a) ʔissi   biraa   ʔimmarkkii
      one   *birr*   please, will you not give?
      'Please give me one *birr*.' (to a single addressee)

If the request is made to plural addressees, or if the speaker wished to express politeness to the addressee, the form of the verb would be as in (24b):

(24b) ʔissi   biraa   ʔimmerketii
      one   *birr*   please, will you (pl) not give?
      Please give me one *birr*.

Third and first person have verbal inflectional forms which pattern in a similar way morphologically as the second person singular -*árkii* and second person plural -*érketi*. These are: -*árkínaa* (1sg), -*órkónii* (1pl), -*árkee* (3fsg), -*eérénne* (3msg), and -*órkónaa* (3pl). However, the latter are interpreted differently, e.g. *ʔekk-árkínaa* 'If I had taken, I wish I had taken'. Adams (1983: 215) analyses the second person forms as 'polite imperative' and the first and third person forms as part of the 'hypothetical-desiderative aspect'. Wakasa (2008: 800–2) on the other hand argues that these are 'interrogative' constructions because there is systematic segmental correspondence between the morphemes listed above and verbal inflectional affixes in the present tense negative interrogative paradigm. For reasons of space this issue cannot be further discussed here but it merits close examination.

It seems that the meaning of the morphemes -*árkii* and -*érketi* is so far not properly understood. We claim that the function of these morphemes is not expressing politeness towards the addressee. Rather they are used to mark the utterance as a 'plea' or 'appeal' (see Chapter 9 on Lao for a particle with comparable meaning). The meaning of politeness in some utterances containing these morphemes perhaps derives from the implicit social hierarchy that may exist between a speech participant who pleads or seeks empathy and the addressee who is in a position to grant it. There are three indications that expression of politeness is not the basic meaning of -*árkii* (sg) and -*érketi* (pl). One of these is the use of the plural form -*érketi* to address a single individual to express politeness or respect, as in (25b).

(25a) guúttáa   maadd-árkii
      little. ACC   help-2SG.PLEAD.IMP
      Please help (me) a little!
      (only to a single addressee, with no honorific meaning)

---

[2] Transcription and glossing as in the original: without tone-accent marking. *Birr* is the name of the Ethiopian currency.

(25b) guúttáa   maadd-érketi
little.ACC   help-2PL.PLEAD.IMP
Please help (me) a little!
(to a single addressee with honorific meaning or to plural addressees)

Second, speakers use the verb *wooss-* 'beg' when quoting or referring to utterances that contain the morphemes *-árkii* and *-érketi*, as in (26), indicating that the construction with these two morphemes is used in an appeal for empathy rather than expressing politeness.

(26)   [monkey to three men travelling with honey pots on their heads]:
hái   ta   godaa-t-óo   táná   tookk-ídí
INTERJ 1SG.POS chief-PL-VOC 1SG.ACC   carry-SS.ANT.CONVB$_2$
ha   wóraa   **pint-érkéti**   yáa-g-aádá
this forest.ACC make.cross-2PL.PLEAD.IMP   that-say-SS.ANT.CONVB$_1$
wooss-aásu
beg-3SGM.PAST.AFF.DEC
She *begged* them saying 'My lords, *please carry me and help me cross* this forest'.

Third, *-árkii* and *-érketi* can be used when addressing someone who otherwise does not fit in the social norms of address using the polite form, as in (27).

(27)   [Mother to daughter]:
Astu tukk-íya   ʔess-árkíi
Astu coffee-DEF.M.ACC   make.coffee-2SG.PLEAD.IMP
Astu, please make coffee (for me)!
(Astu = endearment form of the proper name *Aster*, borrowed from Amharic)

Example (27) is interesting because it illustrates that more friendly terms of addresses, e.g. *Astu* in (27), *ta godaatóo* 'my lords' in (26), are used with verbs inflected with *-árkii* and *-érketi*. In contrast, starting a command by addressing someone with his/her full name preceded by a vocative pronoun indicates that the speaker is angry, annoyed, or is not interested in being nice to the addressee (28). The morphemes *-árkii* and *-érketi* do not fit with such type of vocative constructions.

(28a) bíí   Asteér   ʔellé   tukk-íya
2SGF.VOC Aster.VOC   quick   coffee-DEF.M.ACC
bógg-á
do.sth.with.haste-2SG.IMP
Aster! hurry and make coffee!

(28b) laa   naá-t-óó   ʔellé   méh-íya   sóo
      2sgM/PL.VOC   child-PL-PL.VOC   quick   cattle-DEF.M.ACC home
      zaar-ité
      guide-2PL.IMP
      Children! hurry and guide the cattle home!

A hostile or unfriendly command or order is addressed by purposely leaving out the addressee's proper name, and instead using a nominalized form of the demonstratives *ha* (proximal) and *he* (distal), as illustrated in (29). Directed to a stranger whose name the speaker does not know, the forms *hegóo* 'you there (M)', *hannée* 'you here (F)' are less harsh, but in this case, too, more appropriate address forms would be *taiʃaú* 'my brother!', *ta naʔeé* 'my daughter', and similar others.

(29) ha-g-óo,   kiʧʧ-á   ha
     PROX.DEM-M.NOMZ-M/PL.VOC   remove.one.self-2SG.IMP   PROX.DEM
     heéraá-ppe
     area-ABL
     You here (M), go away from this area!

3.7 Grammatical categories of imperatives

The verb in an imperative clause makes the same number of distinctions of nominal categories as verbs in declarative and interrogative clauses make: i.e. person, number, and gender of the subject are distinguished in the imperative. Negation is marked in declarative, interrogative, as well as imperative verbs but the level of distinction and the morphemes used are different. While the imperative has a single negative marker -*ópp/-úpp*, declarative interrogative clauses each have distinct negation markers that co-vary with the person, number, and gender of the subject. The main difference between the imperative and the other two sentence types is that the imperative is not

TABLE 2. **Grammatical categories of imperatives compared to declarative and interrogative**

	Person	Number	Gender	Negation	Tense
Level of morphological distinctions	Same 1st, 2nd and 3rd person	Same two-way sg–pl distinction	Same only in 3rd person sg	Different IMP only one NEG form	Different Not distinguished in imperatives
Form of morphemes marking the category	Different	(Partly) similar -t	Different	Different	
Meaning	Same	Same	Same	±Different Denial vs. prohibition	

marked for tense at all. In Table 2, we show whether or not the marking of grammatical categories is the same or different in declarative and interrogative clauses.

4 On the use and meanings of imperatives

As illustrated in the previous sections, the imperative in Wolaitta is used to express command/order, wishes, blessings, curses, and leave-taking. Imperatives are also used to advise, discipline, and scold. In a story about a widower who moved to his eldest son's home, the narrator tells how the old man inadvertently spoilt his relationship with his daughter-in-law and grandchildren when he tried to be a useful member of the family by taking on the duty of disciplining the children. The speaker first stated the following three sentences (separated by //): *naatá ?issíba ?issíba zorées* 'He advises the children on certain things' // *?issíba ?issíba hank'éttées* 'He scolds them on others' // *seerées* 'He disciplines them'//. Then the speaker illustrated what the old man said to advise, scold, or verbally discipline the children (30). All of the sentences quoted are in the imperative:

(30a) maatáa   poó?oó-ra   buútʃ'tʃ'-ídí   y-iité
       grass.DEF.M.ACC light.INST   mouw-S.ANT.CONVB₂ come-2PL.IMP
       Get grass before dark!

(30b) der-íyá-n   kaa?-ópp-íte
       open.field-DEF.M.ACC-LOC play-IMP.NEG-2PL.IMP
       Do not play in the fields!

(30c) ?əə   miízzáa   ?asá   kátá-n
       Ehh   COW.DEF.M.ACC person.GEN grain-LOC
       gel-iss-ídí   heémm-ópp-íte
       enter-CAUS-S.ANT.CONVB₂ herd-IMP.NEG.2PL.IMP
       Ehh, don't get cattle in someone's fields!

Imperatives or bare verb stems may be used in directives to domestic animals, to disperse them or to lead them to certain directions or positions. In such usage the singular imperative morpheme is employed, irrespective of the number of domestic animals 'addressed'. Interjections are also used for this purpose. In Table 3 we illustrate four directive expressions that can be addressed to oxen and cows. These are extracts from Azeb Amha (2013: 227–8), where summonses, dispersal, and other directives to domesticated animals in Zargulla, Maale, and Wolaitta are compared.

    Ferguson (1977: 69–76) lists eighteen grammatical features that are widely attested in the 'Ethiopian language area'. One of these involves the existence of an irregular verb for the imperative of 'to come': either a totally different stem (suppletive stem) or a verb with an exceptional formation is attested. The following examples are from

TABLE 3. Directives to domesticated animals

	Domestic animal addressed: oxen /cows			
Form of address	*ʔaatt-á*	*waah-á*	*hirk-á* *yuušš-á*	*t'ók' t'ok'*
'Meaning' of directive	'Start/continue movement!'	'Stop movement!'	'Enter barn!'	'Move up!'
Does form have lexical meaning in communication with humans?	Yes. *ʔaatt-* 'let pass'	No lexical meaning	*hirk-* has no lex. meaning. *yuušš-* 'turn (tr.)'	± Yes, *t'ók'k'a* 'upper' *t'ók'k'u g-* 'move up'

Hayward (1979: 246), in which a historical-comparative examination of the forms, especially of Cushitic languages, is made (see also Banti 2005).

Amharic (Ethio-Semitic):	mät't'a	'He came'
	na	'Come!'
Eastern Oromo (Cushitic):	in-ɗufe	'He came'
	kottu	'Come!'
Burji (Cushitic):	inaa intaani	'He came'
	aam	'Come!'
Dasenech (Cushitic)	he-yimi	'He came'
	kari	'Come!'

In Wolaitta too, the imperative *haáya* 'Come!' is different from the corresponding declarative *yiísi* 'he came'. However, *haáya* 'Come!' may be considered exceptional only in so far as it incorporates the directional adverb (*háa* 'here'). The same is observed in the imperative of *b-* 'go': *yaába* 'go away!'. Other motion verbs do not fuse with the adverb in a similar way. As Aikhenvald (2010: 321–3) documents cross-linguistically, use of suppletive or irregular imperative forms of motion verbs is widely attested.

5 Concluding remarks

Morphological and syntactic properties that distinguish the imperative mood from the declarative and interrogative are discussed. The three moods have in common overt marking of verbal morphological categories such as person, number, gender aspect, and negation, which are overtly marked on the imperative verb. Tense, however, is not marked in the imperative. As might be predicted, second person imperative has a wide range of possibilities morphologically, such as a special morphology for 'plead', whereas third and first person imperative (in that order) have increasing restrictions and limitations in interpretation, conforming to cross-linguistic typological tendency. Particularly the first person forms marked by *-óo* and *-ónii* share morphological properties with canonical imperatives (e.g. negation by *-ó/úpp*) but they are interpreted as interrogative.

Appendix: Verb inflection in Wolaitta

Affirmative declarative

Present		Past	
ʔekk-aísi	'I take'	ʔekk-aási	'I took'
ʔekk-aása	'You take'	ʔekk-ádasa	'You took'
ʔekk-eési	'He takes'	ʔekk-iísi	'He took'
ʔekk-aúsu	'She takes'	ʔekk-aásu	'She took'
ʔekk-oósi	'We take'	ʔekk-ída	'We took'
ʔekk-eéta	'You (pl) take'	ʔekk-ídeta	'You (pl) took'
ʔekk-oósona	'They take'	ʔekk-ídosona	'They took'

Affirmative interrogative

Present		Past		Future	
ʔekk-aíná	'Do I take?'	ʔekk-ádína	'Did I take'	ʔekk-anée	'Will I take?'
ʔekk-áy	'Do you take?'	ʔekk-ádí	'Did you take?'	ʔekk-uúte	'Will you take?'
ʔekk-ií	'Does he take?'	ʔekk-ídé	'Did he take?'	ʔekk-anée	'Will he take?'
ʔekk-áy	'Does she take?'	ʔekk-ádé	'Did she take?'	ʔekk-anée	'Will she take?'
ʔekk-íyó	'Do we take?'	ʔekk-ídó	'Did we take?'	ʔekk-anée	'Will we take?'
ʔekk-eétí	'Do you (pl) take?'	ʔekk-ídétí	'Did you take?'	ʔekk-uúteti	'Will you take?'
ʔekk-íyóná	'Do they take?'	ʔekk-ídóna	'Did they take?'	ʔekk-anée	'Will they take?'

Negative declarative

Present/Future		Past	
ʔekk-íkke	'I don't/won't take'	ʔekk-ábeíkke	'I did not take'
ʔekk-ákká	'You don't/won't take'	ʔekk-ábaákká	'You did not take'
ʔekk-énná	'He doesn't/won't take'	ʔekk-íbeénná	'He did not take'
ʔekk-úkkú	'She doesn't/won't take'	ʔekk-ábeíkkú	'She did not take'
ʔekk-ókko	'We don't/won't take'	ʔekk-íboókko	'We did not take'
ʔekk-ékkétá	'You (pl) don't/won't take'	ʔekk-íbeékkétá	'You (pl) did not take'
ʔekk-ókkóna	'They don't/won't take'	ʔekk-íboókkóná	'They did not take'

Negative interrogative

Present/Future			Past	
ʔekk-íkkíná	'Don't/won't I take?'		ʔekk-ábeíkkína	'Didn't I take?'
ʔekk-íkkíi	'Don't/won't you take?'		ʔekk-ábeíkkí	'Didn't you take?'
ʔekk-énnée	'Doesn't/won't he take?'		ʔekk-íbeénné	'Didn't he take?'
ʔekk-ékkée	'Doesn't/won't she take?'		ʔekk-ábeékké	'Didn't she take?'
ʔekk-ókkóo	'Don't/won't we take?'		ʔekk-íboókkó	'Didn't we take?'
ʔekk-ékkétíi	'Don't/won't you (pl) take?'		ʔekk-íbeékkétí	'Didn't you (pl) take?'
ʔekk-ókkónáa	'Don't/won't they take?'		ʔekk-íboókkóná	'Didn't they take?'

Acknowledgements

I would like to thank Professor Alexandra Y. Aikhenvald for helpful comments on an earlier version of the chapter. Thanks to participants of the International Workshop on Commands, Cairns Institute /CASE, James Cook University, 28 September to 3 October 2015, for feedback on the earlier version presented. I am grateful to Professors R. M. W. Dixon and A. Aikhenvald for their invitation and kind hospitality.

References

Adams, Bruce A. 1983. A Tagmemic analysis of the Wolaitta language. PhD Thesis, SOAS, London University.

Aikhenvald, Alexandra Y. 2010. *Imperatives and commands*. Oxford: Oxford University Press.

Azeb Amha. 2013. 'Directives to humans and to domestic animals—the imperative and some interjections in Zargulla', pp. 211–29 of *Proceedings of the 5th International Conference on Cushitic and Omotic Languages, Paris, 16–18 April 2008*, edited by Marie-Claude Simeone-Senelle and Martine Vanhove. Cologne: Köppe.

Banti, Giorgio. 2005. 'Comparative notes on the Cushitic imperative', pp. 55–91 of *Studia semitica et semitohamitica: Festschrift für Rainer M. Voigt anläßlich seines 60. Geburtstages am 17. Januar 2004*, edited by Bogdan Burtea, Josef Tropper, and Helen Younansardaroud. Münster: Ugarit-Verlag.

Ferguson, C. A. 1976. 'The Ethiopian language area', pp. 63–76 of *Language in Ethiopia*, edited by M. L. Bender, J. D. Bowen, R. L. Cooper, and C. A. Ferguson. London: SOAS.

Fleming, Harold. 1976. 'Omotic overview', pp. 298–323 of *The non-Semitic languages of Ethiopia*, edited by M. L. Bender. Michigan: Michigan State University.

Hayward, R. J. 1979. 'Some inferences from an irregular imperative form in Saho', *Israel Oriental Studies* 9: 245–57.

Hirut Woldemariam. 1999. Linguistic description of the Wolayitta language. Manuscript.

Lambert, Marcello and Sottile, Roberto. 1997. *The Wolaytta language*. Studia Linguarum Africae Orientalis, 6. Cologne: Köppe.

Wakasa, Motomichi. 2008. *A descriptive study of modern Wolaytta language*. PhD Thesis, University of Tokyo.

15

Veiled commands: anthropological perspectives on directives

ROSITA HENRY

1 A question of command

As commands are the 'real-world' counterparts of 'imperatives', they are as interesting a topic for social or cultural anthropologists as for linguists. In this chapter I consider some anthropological approaches to commands by focusing on the politics of command performances, or the way that commands are actually given and received. I explore how culturally specific strategies for authority, politeness, and diplomacy might be encoded in the ways people deliver directives to others. I focus on public speeches in the Western Highlands of Papua New Guinea (PNG) and especially strategies related to egalitarian values and concepts of autonomy and power.

What particularly interests me about commands is the many ways that they can be veiled in different cultural contexts. Many years ago, following a robbery at our family home, I adopted as a guard dog a Rottweiler that had been abandoned by his previous owners. Nervous to have such a large, untrained dog around my young children, I invited a retired police-dog handler to come to the house to advise me on how to train him. While the dog handler was present, my son, who was about 5 years old at the time, started kicking his football around the kitchen, so I called out to him something like:

'Rurik! Would you mind not kicking the ball in the house?'

Or perhaps it was:

'Could you please stop kicking the ball in the house?'

Rurik, however, ignored me and kept kicking. At this point the dog handler told me that a child was much like a dog and that I should have given Rurik a short, direct order like, 'Stop kicking!' The way I had expressed it, according to the dog handler, I had given my son a choice; and he had chosen not to obey.

Commands. First edition. Alexandra Y. Aikhenvald and R. M. W. Dixon (eds)
This chapter © Rosita Henry 2017. First published 2017 by Oxford University Press

Although I continued to be polite to the dog handler until he left, I was not at all impressed with him for presuming to lecture me about how I should talk to my child. After all, my son was not a dog, I thought, and children needed to learn the language of human diplomacy to get on in life!

From infancy, among the first things that children learn from their parents or other carers are directives, including imperatives such as 'No! Stop! Ta (give it to me)!'. They also learn to reflect on and evaluate such directives. As Duranti (2015: 202) notes,

> over time, in being directed, children are not only oriented to attend to objects or to perform certain actions on them, they are also exposed to various ways of reflecting on their own experience of such objects and more generally on their life experiences. This in turn entails an ability to move from the 'natural attitude' of the here-and-now to the 'theoretical attitude' of evaluating the type of ongoing activity or the type of person that such an activity entails or invokes. In some cases, the 'theoretical attitude' appears in situations in which children challenge or resist a particular request that is being made from them.

Children also learn the linguistic strategies that are used in their particular cultural contexts to soften or disguise direct orders.

In English and many other languages, directives are often veiled as questions. Unlike the dog handler's claim, being given a directive in the form of a question does not necessarily mean that the addressee is actually made to feel they have a *choice* in the matter. It may be that veiling the command as a question strategically *obliges* the addressee to accept the command and to comply.

As Enfield (2013: 92) argues, the 'fundamentally dialogic nature of speech acts' means that it is not merely the intention of a speaker that defines a command. Thus, in the study of any type of speech act one must consider the listener(s) as much as the speaker and, importantly, the nature of the relationship(s) between them. In addition, one must also consider the wider social situation and especially who else (apart from the speaker and the addressee) might be present at the time of the interaction. In the case of the interaction in my kitchen, had the dog handler not been present, I might have chosen to phrase my command to my son quite differently and might even have included an expletive: 'Stop kicking that bloody ball!'

2 Directives in an intersubjective world

Directives, which include commands, are one of five types of speech act identified by the philosopher John Searle (1994: 21[1969]) on the basis of the intentional state or individual cognition of the speaker, rather than on social relations (Enfield 2013: 90). The other types are assertives, commissives, expressives, and declarations. As Enfield (2013: 89) points out, these speech acts are not mutually exclusive. Thus, for example, as several other contributors to this volume have shown, assertives can also serve as directives.

Searle (1976) also introduced the concept of 'direction of fit' to distinguish between these types of speech act. Directives, he argues, have a *world-to-word* direction of fit. In other words, a person giving a directive is trying to make the world change according to the words that are uttered. My command 'Silence!' upon entering a classroom, for example, causes something to happen in the world by directing the students to be quiet. In contrast, if the students were already quietly working and I said, 'there is silence in the room', I would be describing an already existing state of affairs, a *word-to-world* direction of fit.

Searle draws on Austin's (1975) division of speech acts into locutionary, illocutionary, and perlocutionary acts, where an illocutionary act is an action that speakers perform in saying something (such as a directive), and a perlocutionary act is speech that generates an effect of some kind. By saying 'Silence!', I am prohibiting the students talking (an illocutionary act) and, by means of uttering this command, I may cause them to respond in one way or another (a perlocutionary act); they might stop talking, but they might also become resentful, ignore me, or be annoyed that I should presume to silence them, and so on. As James Slotta (2015: 517) puts it in his paper focusing on the 'agentive role of listeners' and perlocutionary effects among Yopno people in Papua New Guinea: 'The perlocutionary facet of speech acts concerns speech as an activity that gives rise to consequences', whether they be intentional or not. This raises what I think is the most interesting question for an anthropologist, that is, the *relationship* between illocutionary force and perlocutionary effect. Between an illocutionary act and a perlocutionary act it is necessary for there to be yet another kind of act—an act of interpretation, where listeners adopt a theoretical attitude and reflect upon the action of a speaker, and where in turn a speaker might try to predict how a listener might receive words and respond (even ignoring or refusing to do what a speaker commands constitutes a response). Thus, to fully understand a directive and its perlocutionary effects requires close attention to cultural context and to the social relationships of the people involved in the communicative exchange. It requires 'a relationship-thinking framework that highlights the distribution of social agency…and the interpersonal relationships that form the fabric of human social life' (Enfield 2013: 218).

Searle's speech act theory became increasingly influential during the latter part of the twentieth century and has been the focus of much critical attention in more recent years, not only within philosophy but also other scholarly disciplines, including literary and legal studies, psychology, and anthropology (Green 2015). A key issue of debate has been the importance of context (Fetzer and Oishi 2011), as for example expressed in the concept of 'the speech situation', or 'the situated speech act' (Mey 2001, 2011; Oishi 2006, 2011). Another matter that has been strongly debated is the notion of 'uptake', particularly in relation to gendered 'illocutionary silencing' when, for example, the refusal of a sexual advance is not taken up by the addressee. At issue is the role of the hearer in the constitution of a speech act. Some scholars have argued that an illocutionary act, such as the command 'Don't touch me!', is a relational phenomenon that requires both the speaker's words and uptake of them by the hearer (Hornsby and Langton 1998), whereas others argue that 'uptake is not in general required for illocution' (Bird 2002: 1). The question is the role of extralinguistic factors, such as gender and power relations, in how natural language works (Grünberg 2011: 173).

Alessandro Duranti (2015) provides a detailed account of Searle's speech act theory and some of the issues that anthropologists have had with it. These include, 'the notion of the autonomous self that seemed to be implied by the model' and 'the treatment of linguistic communication as caused by mental states'. According to Duranti (2015: 19), 'Searle's perspective was criticized for not acknowledging the ambiguous, dialogical, intertextual quality of human discourse and, more generally, the ubiquitous indexical value of language as a situated and situating human activity that might not be controlled or controllable by the individual.'

The anthropologist who perhaps most famously critiqued Searle's speech act theory in relation to commands was Michelle Rosaldo (1982). Focusing on the extensive use of overt directives in daily life among the Ilongot in the Philippines, Rosaldo (1982: 216) argued that speech act theory concentrates too much on the speaker's intentions or on 'actor-based prerogatives and wants', and not enough on the social relationships that are 'affirmed and challenged' as an ongoing part of everyday life. According to Rosaldo (1982: 209), for the Ilongot, undisguised direct commands are not rude or harsh, but 'the exemplary act of speech', 'the very stuff of language', and this is because they use commands to articulate and display kinship bonds (see also Telban, Chapter 13). Rosaldo notes that while Ilongot distinguish between various kinds of directives and have different names for them, which she translates as commands, prohibitions, orders/warnings, requests, appeals, and so on, these are not distinguishable in terms of grammar nor are there any ways to differentiate 'soft' or 'polite' from hard command forms (as in the use of interrogatives in English). Instead, according to Rosaldo (1982: 223), the Ilongot classification system relates to the cooperative activities evoked by these different directive utterances. Thus, the most significant thing about directives, which Rosaldo argues was missed by Searle, is that they are in essence *social acts*. They are not just grounded in an individual's intentions but demand *uptake*.

Searle partly moderated his views in his later writings by introducing the notion of 'collective intentionality' (Searle 1990). However, as Duranti (2015: 209) argues, drawing on the phenomenological notion of intersubjectivity, the distinction that Searle proposed between individual and collective intentions is 'both theoretically and empirically problematic' as 'the world of the individual is always a social world'. Thus, a phenomenologically informed anthropological approach to commands, or any other kind of speech act for that matter, would start with the assumption that we 'are always in a world of others' and are *aware* of others (Duranti 2015: 232).

Speech acts have been conventionally examined by linguists in terms of one-to-one speech. Discussion and examples of speech acts tend to refer to 'THE speaker and THE hearer, and questions of intention and inference are always formulated in terms of only these two presences' (Pratt 1986: 61). Yet, speech situations often involve 'multiple participants, with multiple intentions to one another' (Pratt 1986: 61). Even when the exchange is seemingly just between two people, there are frequently others around, whose presence might influence a speech act (as in the example above where I tempered my command to my son due to the presence of a stranger in my home, the dog handler). Thus, to fully understand the nature of commands requires attention also to social situations in which a speechmaker is addressing a wider audience, or perhaps the intended specific addressee/s is within the presence or earshot of others, such as in the Western Highlands of PNG examples, which are now discussed.

3 Speech acts in the Western Highlands, Papua New Guinea

The group of people among whom I have conducted most of my research in the Western Highlands of PNG identify as members of the Penambi tribe. They have no particular name for their language, but simply refer to it as *bo ung* (lit. seedling talk) or *tok ples* in Tok Pisin. The language is classified as Papuan, of East New Guinea Highlands Stock and of the Chimbu-Wahgi family. Penambi *tok ples* belongs to a sociocultural and linguistic continuum that includes Melpa in the Hagen area, which has been extensively documented by Marilyn Strathern and Andrew Strathern, and Ku Waru in the Nebilyer Valley, which has been the focus of research by Alan Rumsey and Francesca Merlan. I draw on and acknowledge here the foundational work of these scholars.

As anyone who has ever been to the PNG Highlands will have observed, and as many researchers have noted, one of the most noticeable features of social life among Highlanders is not only the apparent fondness people have for talk, but also for talking about talk. Merlan and Rumsey (1991: 222–3), for example, note the 'striking volume of talk which characterises proceedings at public events in the Hagen/ Nebilyer area' and observe that talk 'is not indigenously considered mere verbiage, but a form of social action which, in some contexts at least, is perceived as the most salient and socially-valued form of *doing*, efficacious action'.

Speeches characterize proceedings at all public events, especially events such as funerals, compensation payments, brideprice exchanges, and at times of dispute or conflict, when leaders may stand up to urge men to fight or to dampen their passion and anger, depending on the situation. High value is given to oratorical skills, not only the confidence to speak in front of a crowd, but also the ability to talk with a certain rhythmic fluency so as to be able to *make oneself heard*, to capture the close attention of those present. I have observed on many occasions a crowd fall into almost complete silence during the speech of a particularly good orator, while other speakers were not able to gain much of a hearing and could barely be heard.

There is a performative style that lends efficacy to a speech. This style is called *el ung* (*el ik* in Melpa). *Ung* is the word for speech or language, and *el* is the word for fight. Merlan and Rumsey (1991: 98–9) describe this kind of oratorical style as being different from everyday language in terms of pitch contour. Also characteristic is that each line of a prosodic unit 'terminates with an abrupt fall to an overlong [a::] or [o::]', which does not make any lexico-grammatical contribution to the line. Merlan and Rumsey refer to this as the 'line terminating *el ung* marker'.

In addition to these distinctive prosodic features, there are also typical para-linguistic features that mark this style of oratory. The speaker strides back and forth in a straight line, pacing his steps in rhythm with his words. It is always a man. Although I have witnessed women speaking in public, I have never seen a woman use this style of speech and performance. Public speaking is a gendered social activity that is generally the preserve of men. This is the case, in spite of, or perhaps all the more reinforced by, the few women who are exceptions to the rule. Below is a case in point:

I am a woman but I am standing up in front of a lot of people here at the sing sing ground. I do it because my husband's dead. I am a widow and I have never seen widows doing the things I am doing now, but I have the strength to stand up and talk because my brothers…are here and I have the strength to talk because I have contributed much and I have even brought in a pig…I am making this speech because I have sympathy for the family and I have brought cash and a pig and I want to give it to my sister Rita. I am sorry that I will not give it to any of you brothers in the village but I will give it to my sister Rita. That's why I am making this small speech…

It is important to note that during her speech, this woman repeated several times that she was a widow. Given the politics of gender among Highland peoples, it is unlikely that she would have stood up and given a speech if her husband was still alive. Women generally sit on the sidelines at formal ceremonial gift exchanges. It is men who are the orators on the ceremonial ground and it is they who control the proceedings and decide who gets to speak and who does not. When a man speaks he usually speaks as a member of a segmentary group, and sometimes even as if he embodies his whole group by using what Merlan and Rumsey (1991) and Rumsey (2000) refer to as the 'segmentary person'. That is, a man will use the first person singular in reference to his whole lineage, clan, or tribe and when referring to a different group he will use the second person and third person singular (Henry 2013). For example, a man might say 'I killed him' meaning not that he killed anyone himself but that his segmentary group as a whole was culpable. Speech situations, in which a speaker talks for or through other people, or as a part of a collective whole, present a fascinating challenge for linguistic philosophers, as indicated by Pratt

(1986: 62) in her critique of the tendency among speech act theorists to analyse speech acts in terms of 'strikingly monolithic...lone pairs of speakers and hearers'. Pratt (1986: 67) takes Searlean speech act theorists to task for not taking into account 'affective relations, power relations and the question of shared goals', noting that 'some people get to do more talking than others, some are supposed to do more listening, and not everybody's words are worth the same'. Certainly, in the Western Highlands men get to do more talking than women in public contexts, women are expected to do more listening, and the words of some men appear to be worth more than others.

Significantly, the woman quoted above, while she acknowledged her clan identity, did not speak as if she embodied her whole clan, and when she gave the cash and the pig, she gave it not for general redistribution among her patriline (her brothers), but to a specific individual, another woman with whom she had an existing long-term exchange relationship. Rena Lederman (1984: 102) makes a distinction between group transactions and network transactions and argues that in Mendi in the Southern Highlands of PNG 'the male/female distinction can come at times to stand for this group/network distinction'. It could be argued that a similar formula holds for the Hagen area, but in this case the woman took the opportunity to appropriate the space of male group transactions in order to pursue network transactions in which she was normally engaged outside of the formal context of the ceremonial ground. Thus, to understand the total social situation of any speech act, one must not only understand how power relations operate in the particular context, but also the different strategies that are available for circumventing or challenging these relations.

4 Veiled words materialized

The high value that people of the Western Highlands place on the interpretation and understanding of talk is evidenced by the rich system of metalinguistic expressions that are used to characterize the art of speech and ways of talking (see Merlan and Rumsey 1991: 347–9). For example, throughout the Hagen area there is a special style of figurative speech called *ung eke* (Ku Waru) or *ik ek* (Melpa), literally meaning 'bent talk', which Andrew Strathern (1975) refers to as 'veiled speech'. In Tok Pisin this style of speech is translated as either *parable tok* or *tok bokis*. Highlanders say that one has to have a special talent to be able to speak in this way. While people recognize *ung eke* as a style when they hear it spoken, especially in the context of *el ung* speeches, they may not understand the full import of the actual tropes used by a speaker. Ambiguity leaves room for alternative interpretations.

While it is a style of speech that only men are thought to have a talent for, my friend Maggie Wilson, whose father Patrick Leahy was among the first white men in the Highlands, was exceptional in this regard. Maggie was the first women to ever stand for election in the Hagen area. During her election campaign in 1982, an orator at the rally said, 'You can give your vote to your own kind or else to the cross breed between the white pig and the wild cassowary.' At first Maggie did not understand what he meant but then it clicked that he was referring to her. She insisted on speaking and 'used his *parable tok* back at him', saying, 'Even those crossed animals are feeding from you and speaking your language. Are they not therefore one of you?' According to Maggie, people loved her speech and one old man even came up to her and put his *omak* around her neck.[1] This was a significant gesture of respect as the neckpiece is usually only worn by male leaders or 'big-men' who have conducted *moka* ceremonies involving the large-scale public exchange of pigs and other valuables.

After public events, people usually go home and talk about the talk, dissecting it in terms of its illocutionary force and perlocutionary effects and trying to come to some interpretation or understanding about what might have been meant by the various speakers and their actions. They do this in spite of the fact that they claim that it is impossible to really know what is in another person's mind. Although they espouse what Robins and Rumsey (2008: 417) have dubbed 'the opacity of other minds' doctrine, Penambi people actually spend a great deal of time trying to work out other people's intentions. One way that they believe it is possible to do so is through observing the condition of people's skin and the health of their bodies (O'Hanlon 1989; Strathern 1979; Rumsey 2008; Henry 2012). Unlike talk, which is thought to hide people's 'true' feelings and intentions, 'exterior signs, such as bodily states, physical comportment, adornment (or lack of it), are thought to reveal the inner states of both individuals and groups' (O'Hanlon 1989: 21).

Another way that Penambi and other Western Highlanders try to figure out what might be hidden behind, or in, words is through a consideration of the gifts that sometimes accompany them. A key way that talk is remembered and understood is through being tied to something material. After a public event, people will often recount what was said at the event by enumerating the gifts that were given. Thus, the intangible is thought to be discoverable in the tangible.

An example of how words are interpreted in terms of their materialization as things can be found in an interview I recorded in English the day after a brideprice exchange I attended. A kinsman of the bride told me that the intermarrying groups had been 'enemies in the old days' but that at the brideprice ceremony a kinsman of the groom had given a significant speech in *tok ples* (Melpa) about 'a curse that he wanted to break':

---

[1] An *omak* consists of a panel made of thin sticks of bamboo made to hang down a man's chest. It was added to during a man's lifetime, each additional bamboo stick marking another successful *moka* or large ceremonial exchange event, signifying his growing status as a leader.

You know, my age group are young but the older guys knew what he was talking about. He gave out 300 kina and one pig to break that curse…[The bride] has only two girls and they believe that if they break that curse the next child will be a boy…so they have broken that curse and given out the 300 kina and the pig which was smart and a good idea.

The speech by the groom's kinsman at the brideprice exchange had included recitation of the history of a particular tribal war that had occurred in the 1920s, during which the bride's great-grandmother was killed. The pig and money given at the brideprice ceremony materialized the acknowledgement of a past wrong committed against the bride's side. The story of this tribal war and the death of the old woman is an important narrative in the Penambi oral history of dispersal and resettlement of their tribal territory. Public recognition by the groom's kin on their ceremonial ground of the *truth value* of the Penambi narrative was appreciated and will be remembered as 'a smart and good idea' because the acknowledgement was given material form through the presentation of a pig and some kina. The gift enabled the indirect admission of segmentary group responsibility for the death of the old woman, through its displacement into things. As Annette Weiner (1984: 174) puts it:

With objects, unlike 'hard words', the danger in exposure for both parties is displaced. Objects represent the societal constraints in the regeneration of social relations. The constraints are the tensions between autonomy and domination. These tensions give to objects the power of displacement.

Thus, the perlocutionary effect of the speech about the breaking of the 'curse' was not realized as a consequence of the words alone, but also the gifts that were given. To understand any speech act, including a command, requires attention not only to what is said but also to what remains unsaid but acknowledged via other means, including gestures, gifts, pregnant silences, and so on. We live in an intersubjective world where human intentionality is not just a matter of the mental states of individuals, but is also expressed in 'embodied actions and dispositions' as well as 'cultural artefacts, cultural categories and, culturally organised activities' (Duranti 2008: 491).

5 Your wish is (not) my command

Most speeches that are given in public contexts in the Western Highlands consist of long recitations of histories of relations of alliance and enmity between segmentary groups. However, such speeches are also used to variously command, direct, or persuade people to action (usually only certain groups and/or individuals among those present). Yet, saying something does not easily make it so in this cultural context and even strong leaders, well recognized for their oratorical skills, are not always able to convince people to attend to their words. Merlan and Rumsey's (1991) transcript of Ku Waru speeches at a compensation payment event in 1983 provides some good examples:

(1) Ya   pilyikimil-i   -o
     here listen-PRES PROG-2/3pl   -el ung marker
     Listen here!

(2) Ung pilyik   takan molung-ko
     talk listen-2/3pl quiet be-PERV-ko
     Listen and be quiet!!! (strong command form, lit. You have been quiet)

Directives can also be conveyed in Ku Waru in a roundabout way via a question. As discussed, English speakers sometimes couch commands in the form of questions (as I did when commanding my son not to kick the ball). It has been argued that this strategy tends to be favoured by women and signals their relative powerlessness (Lakoff 1994), but this is not necessarily the case. Use of this strategy suggests subtle skills of diplomacy, where the speaker attempts to soften a command to achieve a desired outcome through solidarity and the creation of rapport.

However, among Ku Waru speakers, rather than representing a gentle or polite form, commands couched as questions may instead be used to express what we might call sarcasm, as in, for example, the question *Kung mabola kalung-i*? 'Have you put on pig grease?', recorded by Merlan and Rumsey (1991: 247). Traditionally Ku Waru speakers would rub themselves with pig grease before public events as a form of self-decoration. According to Merlan and Rumsey (1991: 112), in the context of trying to get the crowd's attention and where the answer to this rhetorical question is obviously no, the question was a way of directing those being addressed that they 'are not qualified to speak' and so should just sit down and be quiet. Putting a directive in the form of a sarcastic question is also possible in English, as in 'Are you deaf?' to mean 'Listen!'

The many exhortations to be quiet and listen during speeches in the Highlands reveal that people have to be convinced to take notice and challenge any assumption that those who issue commands must occupy secure roles of authority and power. A speech requires oratorical and performative skill to capture attentive listeners and the collaboration of at least some of the participants is crucial to its success.

Fundamentally, speech acts are activities that are jointly, or communally, accomplished. Therefore, understanding the relationship between a command and its consequence/s requires an understanding of the total social situation and, in particular, cultural concepts regarding perlocutions. As Slotta (2015: 544) writes of the Yopno:

A would-be leader's word is nobody's command; the success of efforts to direct community members is understood to be contingent on the way directions are 'handled' by their recipients. Speakers frame their contributions with an eye toward their addressees' uptake, submitting their speech to the receptive activity of others. While some may have the verbal skill to reliably stir their addressees to act, their influence remains precarious—they exercise verbal power at the pleasure of the communicative recipient.

The 'agentive role' of listeners is similarly considered significant in communication among peoples of the Western Highlands and great attention is paid to the perlocutionary effects, both negative and positive, that talk might have.

6 Conclusion: veiled commands, egalitarian values, and language materiality

The way directives are given and received in the Hagen area is related to political values of autonomy and equivalence but also to *tensions* between these values and other values, such as relatedness (group identity) and dependence, as well as new forms of inequality of race, class, and gender. As I have discussed, one means by which people avoid or rectify the use of words that cause conflict, and mediate the tensions between obligations that arise from being in relationship with others and individual autonomy, is through the exchange of things (pigs, cash, and so on). Thus it is important to take into account the linguistic and the material within the same analytic framework. Shankar and Cavanaugh (2012) offer the term 'language materiality' to characterize what they identify as an emerging field of enquiry within anthropology that brings together the linguistic, which is usually seen as immaterial, and the material which is usually considered 'concrete and non-discursive' (p. 346), to understand 'how words and objects work together' (p. 358).

Andrew Strathern (1975) argues that Hagen people use indirect, allusive speech in a range of situations to express matters that if spoken about directly or openly might provoke violence. According to Strathern, using veiled (indirect) speech enables a person to air contentious issues while at the same time preserving social relations and maintaining social control. Veiled speech is politically significant in terms of values of autonomy and equality because it enables 'a certain flexibility of response' from the people addressed (Lederman 1984: 88). However, the use of indirect speech is not universally associated with egalitarian values. Indirect speech also facilitates authoritarian relationships in some cultural contexts (Bloch 1975) and can do so even in the Western Highlands. The fact that a directive is veiled as a question for example, or that figurative speech is used, may be a stronger way of demanding a response from a communicative recipient than a direct command, depending on the social situation.

A great diversity of command strategies can be found cross-linguistically, as evidenced in Aikhenvald (Chapter 1) and by the other contributors to this volume. The authors provide rich comparative material for consideration by linguistic philosophers. No doubt speech act theory will continue to generate productive debates on the metaphysics of speech acts; how illocutionary acts such as commands are situated in context, indeed the very definition of context (Mey 2011: 178; Pratt 1986: 63); the relationship between illocutionary and perlocutionary acts; intersubjectivity and the nature of 'uptake' of commands; 'language as action' (Marcondes de Souza Filho 1985); the distinction between a speech act as an ideal type and speech action as a concrete 'natural' event (Grünberg 2011: 176); and the relationship between speech action, power relations, politics, and diplomacy (Mey 2011: 176–7; Green 2015). Examination of the material in this volume indicates that while there may be correlations between certain command strategies and the political contours of social life, these are not necessarily universal. Does this mean we should give up comparative projects in favour of particularism, or are there some generalizations to be made about the apparently widely recurring tendency for people to veil their commands, whatever linguistic strategies they might use?

Pointing out the presence of ethnographic exceptions is a favourite form of anti-universalist argument in anthropology. Yet, as Bloch (1975: S27) writes, 'we cannot ignore the fact that so many people, in different cultures all around the world, are saying similar things again and again. Such recurrences are a challenge that anthropology should not dodge by finding occasional counter examples.' As Bloch (1975) argues, it is possible to study recurrences across different contexts and to generalize without necessarily universalizing. While it may be impossible to say that veiled commands are universally linked to an egalitarian ethos, perhaps one could generalize that in any context veiling is related to concepts of personhood, relatedness, autonomy, and responsibility, and to the human awareness that the world we inhabit is always a social world, a world of intentional others full of hopes, desires, and fears, and the capacity not only for honesty and sincerity but also for deception and trickery.

Acknowledgements

I wish to express my gratitude to Alexandra Aikhenvald and R. M. W. Dixon for inviting me to participate in their workshop on 'Commands' held at the Language and Culture Research Centre, James Cook University, and for the wonderful opportunity to engage in discussion and reflection on directive speech acts with an inspirational international group of linguists and anthropologists. I especially thank Professors Aikhenvald and Dixon for their unfailing encouragement and invaluable advice on how to improve the paper that I presented at the workshop for this publication.

References

Austin, J. L. 1975. *How to do things with words*. Oxford: Clarendon Press.
Bird, Alexander. 2002. 'Illocutionary silencing', *Pacific Philosophical Quarterly* 83: 1–15.
Bloch, Maurice. 1975. 'Introduction', pp. 1–28 in *Political language and oratory in traditional society*, edited by Maurice Bloch. London, New York and San Francisco: Academic Press.

Duranti, Alessandro. 2008. 'Further reflections on reading other minds', *Anthropological Quarterly* 81(2): 483–94.

Duranti, Alessandro. 2015. *The anthropology of intentions: Language in a world of others.* Cambridge: Cambridge University Press.

Enfield, N. J. 2013. *Relationship thinking: Agency, enchrony, and human sociality.* Oxford: Oxford University Press.

Fetzer, Anita, and Oishi, Etsuko. 2011. Editors of *Context and contexts: Parts meet whole?* Amsterdam, NLD: John Benjamins Publishing Company.

Green, Mitchell. 2015. 'Speech acts', *The Stanford Encyclopedia of Philosophy*, edited by Edward N. Zalta. http://plato.stanford.edu/archives/sum2015/entries/speech-acts/

Grünberg, Angela. 2011. 'Saying and doing: Speech actions, speech acts and related events', *European Journal of Philosophy* 22(2): 173–99.

Henry, Rosita. 2012. 'Gifts of grief: Performative ethnography and the revelatory potential of emotion', *Qualitative Research* 12(5): 528–39.

Henry, Rosita. 2013. 'Being and belonging: exchange, value, and land ownership in the Western Highlands of Papua New Guinea', pp. 274–90 of *Possession and ownership*, edited by Alexandra Aikhenvald and R. M. W. Dixon. Oxford: Oxford University Press.

Hornsby, J. and Langton, R. 1998. 'Free speech and illocution', *Legal Theory* 4: 21–37.

Lakoff, Robin. 1994. 'Language and women's place', pp. 280–91 of *The women and language debate: A sourcebook*, edited by Camille Roman, Suzanne Juhasz, and Christine Miller. New Brunswick, NJ: Rutgers University Press.

Lederman, Rena. 1984. 'Who speaks here? Formality and politics of gender in Mendi, Highland Papua New Guinea', pp. 85–107 of *Dangerous words: Language and politics in the Pacific*, edited by Donald Brenneis and Fred R. Myers. Prospect Heights, IL: Waveland Press.

Marcondes de Souza Filho, Danilo. 1985. *Language and action: A reassessment of speech act theory.* Amsterdam, NLD: John Benjamins Publishing Company.

Merlan, Francesca and Rumsey, Alan. 1991. *Ku Waru: Language and segmentary politics in the Western Nebilyer Valley, Papua New Guinea.* Cambridge: Cambridge University Press.

Mey, Jacob L. 2001. *Pragmatics: An introduction.* Oxford: Blackwell. 2nd edition.

Mey, Jacob L. 2011. 'Speech acts in context', pp. 171–80 of *Context and contexts: Parts meet whole?*, edited by Anita Fetzer and Etsuko Oishi. Amsterdam, NLD: John Benjamins Publishing Company.

O'Hanlon, M. 1989. *Reading the skin: Adornment, display and society among the Wahgi.* London: The Trustees of the British Museum.

Oishi, Etsuko. 2006. 'Austin's speech act theory and the speech situation', *Esercizi Filosofici* 1: 1–14. http://www.univ.trieste.it/~eserfilo/art106/oishi106.pdf

Oishi, Etsuko. 2011. 'How are speech acts situated in context?', pp. 181–204 of *Context and contexts: Parts meet whole?*, edited by Anita Fetzer and Etsuko Oishi. Amsterdam, NLD: John Benjamins Publishing Company.

Pratt, Mary Louise. 1986. 'Ideology and speech-act theory', *Poetics Today* 7: 59–72.

Robbins, Joel and Rumsey, Alan. 2008. 'Introduction: Cultural and linguistic anthropology and the opacity of other minds', *Anthropological Quarterly* 81(2): 407–20.

Rosaldo, Michelle Z. 1982. 'The things we do with words: Ilongot speech acts and speech act theory in philosophy', *Language in Society* 11(2): 203–37.

Rumsey, Alan. 2000. 'Agency, personhood and the "I" of discourse in the Pacific and beyond', *The Journal of the Royal Anthropological Institute* 6(1): 101–15.

Rumsey Alan. 2008. 'Confession, anger and cross-cultural articulation in Papua New Guinea', *Anthropological Quarterly* 81(2): 455–72.

Searle, J. R. 1976. 'The classification of illocutionary acts', *Language in Society* 5(1): 1–23.

Searle, J. R. 1990. 'Collective intentions and actions', pp. 401–15 of *Intentions in communication,* edited by Philip R. Cophen, Jerry Morgan, and Martha Pollack. Cambridge, MA: MIT Press.

Searle, J. R. 1994 [1969]. *Speech acts: An essay in the philosophy of language.* Cambridge: Cambridge University Press.

Shankar, Shalini and Cavanaugh, Jillian R. 2012. 'Language and materiality in global capitalism', *Annual Review of Anthropology* 41: 355–69.

Slotta, James. 2015. 'The perlocutionary is political: Listening as self-determination in a Papua New Guinean polity', *Language in Society* 44: 525–52.

Strathern, Andrew. 1975. 'Veiled speech in Mount Hagen', pp. 185–203 of *Political language and oratory in traditional society,* edited by Maurice Bloch. London, New York, and San Francisco: Academic Press.

Strathern, Andrew. 1979. 'The self in self-decoration', *Oceania* 49: 241–57.

Weiner, Annette. 1984. 'From words to objects to magic: "Hard words" and the boundaries of social interaction', pp. 161–91 of *Dangerous words: Language and politics in the Pacific,* edited by Donald Brenneis and Fred R. Myers. Prospect Heights, IL: Waveland Press.

Index of authors

Index of languages, peoples, language families and areas

Index of subjects

restrictions on imperatives 4, 20–2, 47, 55,
    78, 91–3, 159, 221, 299, *see also* stative
    verb, uncontrolled action
resultative 185

same subject 8, 22, 27, 48, 76, 251, *see also*
    switch reference
scope of imperative 22, 76, 88, 149, 194, 211,
    230, 256–7
secondhand evidential, *see* reported
    evidential
self-quote 29, *see also* quote
semantics of imperative, *see* meanings of
    imperative
serial verb construction 19, 22, 88, 138, 142,
    149, 194, 196, 225, 268, 273, 275
social hierarchy 1–3, 17–18, 27, 30, 36, 38,
    83, 171–3, 178, 182, 202–4
softening a command 15, 18, 23, 26–7, 30,
    39, 302
    in Aguaruna 64, 78–9
    in Ashaninka Satipo 64, 78–9
    in Japanese 173–4, 185
    in Korowai 262
    in Lao 190, 199–200, 203
    in Nungon 238, 241
    in Tayatuk 209, 215
    in Zenzontepec Chatino 114
speech act 264, 290–4, 311, *see also* mood
speech formula, *see* conversational formula
stative verb 20–1, 33, 94, 197, *see also*
    uncontrolled action
strategy, imperative, *see* imperative strategy
strength of command, *see* force of command
strengthening a command 29, 39, 57,
    162, 253, 275–6, *see also* softening
    a command
subject honorific 170, 175, 178, 182
subjunctive 8–9, 152–3, 160
suppletion 8, 12, 92, 120, 148, 153, 173–4,
    178, 257, 297–8
switch reference 48, 63, 74, 208–9, 230, 250,
    256, *see also* different subject, same
    subject
synthetic language 148, 169, 250, 307

tag question 23, 26, 49, 67, 195, *see also*
    interrogative as command strategy,
    interrogative clause type
tense 2, 9, 11–13, 14, 19, 26, *see also* delayed
    imperative, distance in time, future
    imperative
    in Aguaruna 62–70
    in Ashaninka Satipo 85, 94
    in Dyirbal 130, 136, 141
    in Japanese 170
    in Karawari 267, 272, 278
    in Korowai 250–1, 254, 263–4
    in Lao 189, 202
    in Northern Paiute 149, 154, 161–2, 165
    in Nungon 226–33, 237–8, 243–6
    in Quechua 48, 51–5, 59
    in Tayatuk 208–15, 219
    in Wolaitta 284–8, 294–8
    in Zenzontepec Chatino 110
tenseless form 32, 149
third person imperative 7, 9, 70, 91, 94,
    161, 181, 213, 228, 252, 279, 289–90,
    see also non-canonical imperative
tone 2–3, 26, 106–11, 114, 117, 124, 184,
    187–9, 201, 245, 262, 269, 294
topic 49, 76, 86, 98, 108–10, 120, 152, 164,
    169, 171, 181, 250

uncontrolled action 20–1, 49, 94, 117, 211,
    227, 260, 304, *see also* stative verb

valency-changing derivations, *see* antipassive,
    applicative, causative, passive
validator 49, 52–3, *see also* evidential
verb classes, *see also* restrictions on imperatives
verb of motion 28, 57, 88–92, 94, 114, 206, 298
verb of perception 20–1, 211, 214, 215, 232, 263
verb of posture 28, 149, 152, 206
verb of speech 28, 81
vocative 30–1, 58, 81–2, 102, 114, 190, 193,
    204, 252, 262–3, 295
volition 20–1, 115, 176–80, 260

warning 10, 38, 94–5, 98, 129, 133, 143, 159,
    179–80, 289, 304, *see also* apprehensive